23.15

MUIRHEAD LIBRARY OF PHILOSOPHY

An admirable statement of the aims of the Library of Philosophy was provided by the first editor, the late Professor J. H. Muirhead, in his description of the original programme printed in Erdmann's *History of Philosophy* under the date 1890. This was slightly modified in subsequent volumes to take the form of the following statement:

'"The Muirhead Library of Philosophy was designed as a contribution to the History of Modern Philosophy under the heads: first of Different Schools of Thought—Sensationalist, Realist, Idealist, Intuitivist; secondly of different Subjects—Psychology, Ethics, Political Philosophy, Theology. While much had been done in England in tracing the course of evolution in nature, history, economics, morals and religion, little had been done in tracing the development of thought on these subjects. Yet "the evolution of opinion is part of the whole evolution".

'By the co-operation of different writers in carrying out this plan it was hoped that a thoroughness and completeness of treatment, otherwise unattainable, might be secured. It was believed also that from writers mainly British and American fuller consideration of English Philosophy than it had hitherto received might be looked for. In the earlier series of books containing, among others, Bosanquet's *History of Aesthetic*, Pfleiderer's *Rational Theology since Kant*, Albee's *History of English Utilitarianism*, Bonar's *Philosophy and Political Economy*, Brett's *History of Psychology*, Ritchie's *Natural Rights*, these objects were to a large extent effected.

'In the meantime original work of a high order was being produced both in England and America by such writers as Bradley, Stout, Bertrand Russell, Baldwin, Urban, Montague, and others, and a new interest in foreign works, German, French and Italian, which had either become classical or were attracting public attention, had developed. The scope of the Library thus became extended into something more international, and it is entering on the fifth decade of its existence in the hope that it may contribute to that mutual understanding between countries which is so pressing a need of the present time.'

The need which Professor Muirhead stressed is no less pressing today, and few will deny that philosophy has much to do with enabling us to meet it, although no one, least of all Muirhead himself, would regard that as the sole, or even the main, object of philosophy. As Professor Muirhead continues to lend the distinction of his name to the Library of Philosophy it seemed not inappropriate to allow him to recall us to these aims in his own words. The emphasis on the history of thought also seemed to me very timely; and the number of important works promised for the Library in the very near future augur well for the continued fulfilment, in this and other ways, of the expectations of the original editor.

H. D. LEWIS

MUIRHEAD LIBRARY OF PHILOSOPHY

General Editor: H. D. Lewis

Professor of History and Philosophy of Religion in the University of London

𝕸𝖚𝖎𝖗𝖍𝖊𝖆𝖉 𝕷𝖎𝖇𝖗𝖆𝖗𝖞 𝖔𝖋 𝕻𝖍𝖎𝖑𝖔𝖘𝖔𝖕𝖍𝖞

EDITED BY H. D. LEWIS

REASON AND GOODNESS

by the same author

THE NATURE OF THOUGHT

REASON AND ANALYSIS

REASON AND GOODNESS

BY

BRAND BLANSHARD

Sterling Professor of Philosophy
Yale University

Based on
Gifford Lectures at the University of St Andrews
Noble Lectures at Harvard University

LONDON: GEORGE ALLEN & UNWIN LTD

FIRST PUBLISHED IN 1961
SECOND (CORRECTED) IMPRESSION 1966

PRINTED IN GREAT BRITAIN
BY PHOTOLITHOGRAPHY
UNWIN BROTHERS LIMITED
WOKING AND LONDON
(L 4689)

To

THOMAS MALCOLM KNOX

Principal of the University of St Andrews

PREFACE

This book is the second in a series of three, which discuss successively the position of reason in the theory of knowledge, in ethics, and in theology. Each is concerned with the vindication of reason against recent philosophical attacks. The first volume, *Reason and Analysis*, is based in part on the Carus Lectures presented to the American Philosophical Association in 1959. The second, *Reason and Goodness*, and the third, *Reason and Belief*, which is yet to appear, are based on the Gifford Lectures delivered at St Andrews in 1952 and 1953. The last two volumes are also based in part on the William Belden Noble Lectures delivered at Harvard University in 1948 and incorporated with the Gifford series by kind permission of the Harvard Board of Preachers. Each of the three books is designed to stand by itself, but if a reader of the present volume finds himself impatient because some point of importance has been too cavalierly dealt with, he may perhaps find a fuller treatment of it in the earlier and epistemological volume.

In the ten months during which my wife and I were resident in St Andrews, we received more hospitality and kindness than I can record or properly acknowledge. I owe a special debt to Professor Edgar P. Dickie, chairman of the Gifford Committee at St Andrews, who presided with heroic patience over the long series of lectures and gave me much wise counsel and encouragement. One of my happiest recollections of those months is of the many Sunday evenings of good talk at Craigard, The Scores, St Andrews, then the residence of Professor and Mrs T. M. Knox. Since then the Knoxes have moved across the road into the massive house of the Principal of the University; but on revisiting them in St Andrews in 1959, we found ourselves instantly enfolded again in the atmosphere we had remembered, of high talk and untiring friendliness. The dedication of this volume is a small token of an enduring gratitude.

Although the appearance of the book has been unduly delayed, it would have been delayed still longer but for the generosity of the American Council of Learned Societies, which gave me one of its munificent senior awards in 1958. Yale capped this by granting me leave, and I went promptly off to my favourite outpost for research, the British Museum library, for a year of reading and happy scribbling. Though I have said many critical things about recent developments in British philosophy, my debt to British philosophers will be obvious throughout. If special mention were to be made, it should be of Professor G. E. Moore, who, to my great good fortune, was my guest in America for six months during the last war, and of Dr A. C. Ewing, with whom I have found over the years a fortifying community of views. The editor of the Muirhead Library of Philosophy, Professor H. D. Lewis, has subjected my pages to kindly but searching criticism, which has freed them from some mistakes I should have been sorry to make. And the largest of all my debts is to my wife.

BRAND BLANSHARD

ACKNOWLEDGMENTS

Citations have been made from A. J. Ayer's *Philosophical Essays* and Edward Westermarck's *Origin and Development of the Moral Ideas* by permission of the Macmillan Co. of London; from C. D. Broad's *Five Types of Ethical Theory* by permission of Routledge and Kegan Paul; from Paul Edwards' *Logic of Moral Discourse* by permission of the Free Press of Glencoe, Ill.; from A. C. Ewing's *The Definition of Good* by permission of the Macmillan Co. of New York; from R. M. Hare's *The Language of Morals* and W. D. Ross's *The Right and the Good* by permission of the Clarendon Press, Oxford; from R. B. Perry's *General Theory of Value* by permission of the Harvard University Press; from Perry's *Thought and Character of William James* by permission of Mr Bernard B. Perry; from B. Russell's *History of Western Philosophy* by permission of Simon & Schuster; from P. A. Schilpp's *The Philosophy of John Dewey* by permission of the Tudor Publishing Company; from C. L. Stevenson's *Ethics and Language* by permission of the Yale University Press; from H. Rashdall's *Is Conscience an Emotion?* by permission of Houghton Mifflin & Co. I acknowledge the courtesy of these publishers with thanks.

ANALYTICAL TABLE OF CONTENTS

CHAPTER IV

THE DIALECTIC OF REASON AND FEELING IN BRITISH ETHICS

CHAPTER V

SUBJECTIVISM

CHAPTER VI

DEONTOLOGY

CHAPTER IX

THE LINGUISTIC RETREAT FROM EMOTIVISM

CHAPTER X

THREE THEORIES OF GOODNESS

CHAPTER XI

HUMAN NATURE AND GOODNESS

CHAPTER XII

'GOOD', 'RIGHT', 'OUGHT', 'BAD'

CHAPTER XIII

THOUGHT AND DESIRE

CHAPTER XIV

REASON AND POLITICS

CHAPTER XV

THE RATIONAL TEMPER

CHAPTER I

THE TENSION BETWEEN REASON AND FEELING IN WESTERN ETHICS

1. The main question of our time in ethics is whether moral judgment expresses knowledge or feeling. When we say that happiness or understanding is something worth pursuing for its own sake, are we expressing a belief that is, or may be, true, or are we giving voice to the satisfaction we take in these things? When we say that cruelty is wrong, are we making an assertion, or are we giving utterance to a dislike, an entreaty, or a command? Or are we, perhaps, doing both?

The issue bristles with difficulties, as we shall see. But it is of vast importance, theoretic and practical. It is important in theory because upon its outcome depends the place we assign to value both in knowledge and in the world. Traditionally, three kinds of knowledge have been recognized: knowledge of fact, as in 'this rose is red'; knowledge of necessity, as in '$2 + 3 = 5$'; and knowledge of value, as in 'Gandhi was a good man'. This last class of judgments is very wide, for it is not confined to moral matters; judgments of value may express our sense of what is beautiful or ugly, comic or tragic, appropriate or rude, indeed in any way desirable or undesirable. The question currently raised is whether any of these judgments expresses insight or apprehension at all. If they do, what sort of attributes are these of goodness or beauty or rudeness? They seem to be neither sensible qualities nor relations, and even those philosophers who believe there are such attributes are perplexed and divided about them. On the other hand, if value judgments do not express insights or truths, much that has passed as philosophy will have to be dismissed as meaningless. Ethics and aesthetics as traditionally pursued must be abandoned, since the attempt to find what sort of acts are right or what sort of things are beautiful will now be recognized as misguided. A kind of ethics may remain, but it will be either meta-ethics, that is, an inquiry into the use of ethical words, or else a branch of anthropology, a description of how people in fact do feel and behave in certain types of situation. And the notion that values exist in the world apart from such attitudes or responses will have no meaning.

2. The issue, we suggested, is of practical as well as theoretical importance. When the view that moral judgments were expressions of feeling was proposed by Westermarck in 1906 and in a more extreme form by Ayer in 1936, many moralists responded not only with dissent, but with outright moral condemnation. They urged that the acceptance of such a view would have disastrous moral consequences. I do not think that the behaviour of converts to it gives much occasion for alarm; and certainly the analysis of moral judgment in a way that the facts seem to require is no ground for condemning anyone, even if the consequences are unfortunate. It is the philosopher's business to follow the argument where it leads, not to trim or pad his conclusions to suit our desires, or even our moral needs.

On the other hand, to say that the issue is without practical importance seems to me untrue, if only because an emotivist ethic would, by its own avowal, cut the nerve of connection between rightness and reasonableness. Most moralists in the past, and probably most plain men, have conceived of the right as also the reasonable. They have felt that if it was their duty to refrain from pilfering their neighbour's purse, there was a rational ground for doing so. They have admired reasonableness in other people; they did not like to be called unreasonable themselves. Their pride in being reasonable was thus an ally, and sometimes a powerful one, of their sense of justice and decency. If moral judgments say nothing and are incapable of rational refutation or support, as many noncognitivists have held, this alliance rests upon an illusion, and is bound with increasing enlightenment to be broken. It is unlikely that this parting of company will be without psychological effect. For a man to realize that he can no longer say with truth that one action is better than another, or that there is any rational ground for avoiding the infliction of pain, does, I think, weaken the felt claim upon him of moral obligation, and not through some confusion on his part, but on the contrary through his coming to see that what he took to be an important ground of right conduct is in fact an illusory ground. I repeat that this gives no reason for dismissing a subjectivist analysis. Facts are facts, and morality may be less broadly based than we thought. But it does make clear that the great issue of our day in ethical theory is more than one of theory. For the issue inevitably leads to the further question, Why should I be moral? If there is no *reason* for being so, is there any obligation to be so? That is an intensely practical question.

In spite of the practical importance of the theoretical issue, the layman who turns to the specialists for light upon it is likely to come away puzzled. He finds much technical discussion of cognitive versus emotive meaning, of the possibility of a logic of imperatives, of the correct analysis of value sentences as opposed to empirical and logical sentences, and of the almost inexhaustible shades of meaning in the word 'good'. To anyone 'hot for certainties' about what to do with a day or a life, or how to go about it to decide, such discussions are likely to seem trivial. Some of them certainly are. Some of them, on the contrary, conceal under the currently fashionable dress of linguistic analysis a genuinely penetrating insight, and if the layman could supply the context necessary for their understanding, he would no doubt concede their importance. What he needs to see is the bearing of these apparently verbal discussions on questions more obviously important. The question whether the meaning of the word 'good' should be described as emotive or cognitive does not strike him as world-shaking. What he needs to see is the bearing of these apparently verbal discussions on questions more obviously important. How is this to be shown? The most straightforward way would be to argue the matter out before him, developing each position into its logical ramifications. In the end nothing short of this will serve.

3. But there is another and perhaps easier way to begin, namely to see the steps by which the question reached its present form. The issue whether good is a predicate, discussed in the professional journals between cognitivist and non-cognitivist philosophers seems almost as remote and technical as a problem in nuclear physics. As a matter of fact, it has sprung up inevitably from the tension between the two main strands of western ethical thought. It is only the most recent form of an issue that has been brewing in the western mind for two thousand years, the issue of the relative places of reason and feeling in the good life. Not that this larger question is the same as the technical question now debated. The older and larger question is, What are the roles of intelligence and of the non-rational parts of our nature in achieving the good life? The newer and more technical question is, What are the roles of intelligence and of the non-rational parts of our nature in moral judgment itself? Though the questions are different, the first inevitably leads to the second. If reason is to guide conduct, it must be able to judge or appraise it. But centuries of debate and experiment passed before the issue reached its present sharp definition. And it has reached such definition nowhere but in the west. The present issue is far more than a wrangle between academic hair-splitters. It is the culmination of a tension, millenniums old, between major trends in western ethics.

Our ethics has two principal sources, Greece and Palestine. For the leading teachers of the Greeks, what was all-important to the good life was a certain kind of understanding, and if this was gained, practice in accordance with it followed automatically. For Christianity, what was essential was rather an attitude of the 'heart', a disposition of feeling and will, and if this were present, we could be sure that all other important things would be added to it. Thus the conflict of emphasis that was to trouble the intervening centuries was already implicitly present in the teaching of the two moral pioneers of the race, Socrates and Christ. Let us look at this conflict in its original form.

4. Greek thought about the good life was planted with remarkable firmness on the facts of human nature. Long before it had the evidence to prove the evolutionary speculations of Anaximander, it divined the affinity between human and animal life, and recognized that, in a sense not easy to define, yet plainly true, the kingdom of animate nature was a realm of purpose. Every organism grew; growth was everywhere under the constraint of a pattern which the organism to all appearances was striving to realize; indeed the very question '*what* is this?', if asked of any growing thing, was naturally answered by reference to what it was becoming. What was an acorn, or the sapling that grew from it? It was that which, if allowed to take its natural course, would become an oak. What was the difference between a gosling and a cygnet? They looked very much alike, but there was a fundamental difference between them; one was an undeveloped goose, and the other an undeveloped swan. What was a baby, a child, or a stripling? There was only one natural answer: it was an undeveloped man. If you were to conceive what any animate thing was essentially (Plato extended this way of thinking even to the inanimate), you must conceive it in terms of the end which it was striving to embody. The Greek would have said, as William James said long afterwards, that 'the meaning of essence is teleological'.

But what do we mean when we speak of a 'striving' on the part of the cygnet to become the swan or of the acorn to become an oak? We must admit that we know only dimly; we are interpreting other natures by analogy with our own; and while we do this confidently enough in dealing with other persons, our meaning and our confidence dwindle as the analogy becomes more remote. That seeking or striving is present in forms of life lower than our own seems unquestionable, but what really goes on in the bee that constructs a honeycomb or in a bird that builds its nest we do not know. The reason is that, with us, striving has become so much an affair of consciousness in which we are aware of our ends and choose our means to them deliberately that we can hardly conceive a process of striving that is not so directed. The bee and the bird cannot work from an ideal blueprint as an architect does; we can. Yet it is easy to overrate our advance. Even in ourselves the process of seeking has come only vaguely and brokenly to consciousness. Cunningly calculating as we are, compared to bird or bee or ape, we still hardly know where we are going, and life remains for the most part a stumbling along by trial and error. The young man who chooses a vocation, a political party, and a life-partner, is making momentous decisions, and knows it; yet in making them he is so much at the mercy of inclination that, as he looks back at them later, he often feels that they were made in a state of sleepwalking and that heaven must have been taking care of one so unable to take care of himself. Even with our lesser enterprises the story is the same. A man starts somewhat idly making a garden, gets engrossed in it, and finds his pride and his plans extending themselves till the back yard is transformed. A novelist sits down to tell his tale and presently finds it running away with him; the characters will not stay put; the design alters as it unfolds; and he is himself astonished at what comes out. Life for all of us, in short, is an adventure in self-discovery. We do not know at the beginning what we want, what would really satisfy us, and the sad fact is that many of us never learn.

5. Here was where Socrates started. His mission was to wake men up to this curious fact that they did not know what they wanted and to make clear to them that until they discovered it, their lives would be largely waste motion. He was a stone-cutter himself, and he liked to make his points from those who worked with their hands, because within their own limits, these people had an especially clear idea of what they wanted to achieve. If one asked a smith who was hammering away at his anvil what he was trying to do, his answer would be clear and definite; he was making a sword, and the best one he could. This definiteness of aim gave his work confidence, economy, and pleasure. But it was Socrates' awkward business to show to the smith and to everyone else the shortness of their vision by repeating the question 'Why?' Why should the smith make swords at all? Answer: To equip the army. But why should the army want swords? Answer: To fight better. But why should we want a fighting army? To keep our state in being against those who would destroy it. But why keep the state in being? Because it guarantees our freedom. But why should we insist on freedom? Because then we can pursue un-hampered the goods we want. But what precisely are these goods? Sooner or later, everyone wavered and broke under this insistent questioning, as no doubt most of us would to-day. We should have to admit that we are in a great hurry and bustle to go—well, where?

Now the secret of the good life for Socrates and his two successors, who were, fortunately, more given to the use of the stylus, lay in discovering by self-examination the implicit aim of our efforts, and from that time forth guiding them deliberately. The nature of this aim was more clearly seen by these successors than by Socrates him-self. Plato and Aristotle were in remarkable agreement about it. They held, somewhat in the manner of the dynamic psychologists of our own day, that a man is a bundle of impulses and emotions—of hunger, thirst, and sex, for example, of combativeness and self-assertion—that each of these has its own special satisfaction, that in different men the 'drives' are differently combined, and that each of us should make it his business to find out what his own combination was and to live in such a way that their satisfactions could be united in the richest and most harmonious whole. All this is very modern and almost trite. But in one important respect, Plato and Aristotle were far behind, or far ahead, of current theories; they were both what present-day psychologists would call intellectualists. They not only distinguished among human impulses a separate impulse toward knowledge, as is done by many writers of our day; they argued that the realization of this impulse was the prime condition of realizing the others. Conceding that the several satisfactions of hunger, sex, and combat were matters of sense and feeling, they pointed out that the relations between these, which must be grasped and maintained if the good life were to be achieved, were not themselves apprehended by sense or feeling, but by intellect or reason. For Plato, as for Kant, sense without conception was blind. The architectural design of the good life could be drawn by intelligence only. To be conscientious was to be scrupulously reasonable.

How did reason work in conduct? In the ordinary case, very much as conscience is now supposed to work in ourselves. Conscience, said Leslie Stephen, is the concentrated experience of the race. It makes us wiser than we know, because it is the deposit of parental example, of the instruction of teachers, and of the pressure of society, themselves in turn the product of centuries of experimentation. Conscience is thus the voice of our own hitherto accepted ideal, recording its yes or no to a proposed line of conduct. It does not in general argue; it simply affixes its seal or enters its protest. Its vast authority Socrates recognized in the respect he gave to his 'monitor'. Many, Quakers and others, have taken such 'inward light' as infallible. Here Socrates would have drawn back. Granting that it is the best guidance we have at the moment, we must admit that it is sometimes irrational guidance. It has been known to pass without demur a man's edging up in a queue, and also his indignant protest when this is done by someone else. Conscience, Socrates thought, must be educated by reflective criticism into clearness and coherence; otherwise the ideals in terms of which we must pass judgment on the actual will themselves be confused. Life is a series of crises in which we are daily and hourly prompted in different directions, and here reason must be arbiter. In Plato's image of the soul as charioteer, driving abreast the black horse of appetite and the white horse of passion, it is reason that gives us the intimation when either is beginning to run wild. In Aristotle's picture of the good life as one of judicial balance, without excess or defect, it is again reason, operating not by rule, but by that sense of the fitness of things which produces a work of art, that determines the pattern of conduct.

6. Once one has entered on this process of appraising particular satisfactions by their part in a larger whole, it is not easy to stop. How much time, for example, should one devote to physical exercise? That depends on how it fits in and contributes to the life that your particular powers appoint for you. But then that life is itself a fragment only; it is a life lived in a community, and it must be chosen and judged by the way it, in turn, fits into the communal life. And you cannot say what is the good life for this community without noting that it is, again, part of a nation whose welfare plainly depends on whether its component groups take an interest in it and play their part in it—economic, political, and military. But then the nation, as we now see more clearly than the Greeks did, is only a part of a world community, and above all nations is humanity. Mankind is a single whole, knit together with increasing closeness. A new policy adopted by Russia or the United States will affect the amount of rice that a South Indian has for his dinner; it will decide whether Giovanni in Genoa can marry Tina or must go off instead into the army. For the Greek the statesman was a higher authority on the end of life than the private moralist, for his view was more comprehensive.

Was the world statesman, then, to be the highest authority of all? Socrates would have been ready to stop there. Plato took a higher flight and carried Aristotle most of the way after him. Is even the whole of humanity a self-sufficing unit? Is it not itself a part of nature? And may we not suppose 'that there is a wider, though still purposive, order that embraces not only human experience but the whole of nature in one system, and that the end of our own life is to be truly seen only as a fragment of this over-all design? With whatever justification, this was what Plato thought. He thought that if we appealed from the statesman to the philosopher, we should learn that the world itself was an intelligible system, in which everything had its appointed part. Nothing short of this vast design, which he called 'the form of the good' would give us the ultimate measure of any community, any life, or any act. Practical wisdom was good enough for short-range decisions. The trouble was that few if any decisions proved in fact to be of the short-range kind. In every act we are, or may be, determining a vast future. And the final estimate of the act could only be made, Plato thought, by a sweep of vision so imperial as to embrace 'all time and all existence'.

7. In the view of many, this conviction of the Greek thinkers, that speculative reason was the supreme court in the realm of values, has seemed to be intellectualism gone wild. Even if we grant them, these persons will object, that such comprehensive knowledge is the test of goodness, it can surely not be held that by itself it will make a man good. To see the good is not to do it. For that, something quite different is required, namely the will to do it. Our records are full of intelligent people who, for all their clear heads, have gone wrong; *video meliora proboque, deteriora sequor;* what I would I do not, and what I would not, that I do; is not this everyone's experience? Indeed a bad man is all the more formidably bad for his intelligence, as Iago notoriously was. Happily too, there are dull men in plenty who are the salt of the earth. If Kingsley was not inspired, he was at least not muddled in advising, 'Be good, sweet maid, and let who will be clever'.

Socrates and Plato would have insisted that he was muddled. If cleverness meant intelligence, even a sweet maid could hardly afford to be without it. 'By all means let her be virtuous', Socrates would have said, and then he would have added his inevitable and confident comment, 'but of course by virtue I *mean* knowledge'. By this he could not have meant anything so absurd as that unreflecting habits of respecting oneself and others are worthless; indeed Aristotle made such habits themselves the condition of the insight that disclosed their value; it is the man bred as a gentleman, he held, who had the most sensitive perception of what that particular ideal required. Nor was it meant that the mere abstract knowledge that temperance is better than indulgence would impose the needed restraint upon the toper with money in his pocket and his foot on the brass rail. But Socrates would have insisted, as James did later, that the control of the will is, far more than we commonly realize, a matter of the control of attention. *Is* it the case that the toper, in ordering the further bottle, chooses the worse in full view of the better? Or is it rather that he turns his back on the better because he has already allowed it to slip out of his mind?

If it is insisted that he knows perfectly well, and at the very moment of his indulgence, that he is making a beast of himself, the shade of the Greek questioner, if it were still about, would ask, 'What do you mean by "perfectly well"?' If you mean the sort of pale and general knowledge that would produce a verbal assent that he was acting grossly, you are no doubt right, but that is not the knowledge I am talking about. I am saying that if he held vividly in mind the particular consequences of this act—the hang-over of the morning after, the self-disgust of being beaten again, the step down into deeper hopeless-ness, perhaps the tongue-lashing from a Xanthippe at home, and all the rest of it—if he saw these consequences steadily for what they were, and likewise the alternative and decent course for what it was, the day of his toperdom would be ended. No one ever, while seeing with full clearness and vividness what is good, deliberately embraces evil. The secret of right doing, therefore, is knowledge, firmly held in mind. If we violate that knowledge, it is because, under the influence of desire, we have allowed ourselves to be deceived. Nothing, of course, is easier. Even the most vicious course of action has something to be said for it, and if one wants very much to do it, one can make it look excusable by confining oneself to its attractions. Thus wrongdoing everywhere is due either to ignorance or to self-delusion. That this doctrine, opposed as it is to our common way of thinking, is no mere foible of the schools is suggested by the fact that it has convinced such modern moralists as Bentham and T. H. Green. Probably Sidgwick's conclusion on the issue is the soundest one, namely, that though the deliberate doing of what we clearly see to be wrong does occur, it occurs surprisingly seldom, and that, when it does, it is usually by way of a sin of omission rather than of commission; i.e. we fail to do what we see we ought to do rather than do what we see we should not.[1]

8. To critics whose morals have a closer linkage with religion, the Greek conception of goodness may seem intolerably cold and calculating, as carefully wrought, but also as dead, as a Greek statue. In an ethics that makes so much of balance and sanity, there would seem to be no place for much that western minds have come to admire— for St Francis let us say, or for the unreckoning self-sacrifice of love; and it is sometimes said that when confronted by major ills like destitution, disease, or death, this morality is bankrupt, that to face these things more is necessary than an ethics of reasonableness, even when it is touched with the mystical exaltation into which the thought of Plato and the schools that followed him so often issued. Whether a rationalist morality will really serve our needs we must consider in due time, but let us note in passing that such criticisms as this last are less than just. So far was Greek rationalism from being merely a shower of dialectical fireworks that it was the practical code of some of the noblest characters on record. After all, it produced Socrates, Epictetus, and Marcus Aurelius, who dealt with the ills of life and death as few men ever have.

That it did have signal defects is true. Neither the communal organization proposed in the *Republic* nor the ideal of personal character proposed in the completest of Greek handbooks, the

[1] See the essay 'Unreasonable Action' in his *Practical Ethics*.

Nicomachean Ethics, will stand a critical scrutiny. It must be admitted, again, that in the great mass of ethical discussion in these books there is curiously little in the way of definite and solid result regarding the proper method of ethics. Socrates' struggle to define the virtues seldom achieved a result satisfactory even to himself; Plato never got clear about the 'form of the good' or showed how it could be usefully employed in practice; Aristotle's classification of virtues is illogical and incomplete; his analysis of 'well-being' is not carried through; his famous general rule of conduct, 'nothing in excess', is almost scandalously vague. Indeed Greek ethics generally, under close inspection, is inchoate and fragmentary. But it is fragmentary in the sense that the Parthenon is a fragment. There appears among its rough stones and its cracked and pitted columns an imposing design for the good life. And the great point about it is that reason is the architect of this design. We cannot use the term narrowly or precisely, because the Greek writers themselves did not use it so. But it is clear that, in their view, only that man could be really good who possessed a cultivated intelligence and directed his life to an end reflectively arrived at and firmly held before him, an end which was to be given complete ascendancy over his feelings, desires, and impulses.

9. When we turn to the other major source of western ethics, we are almost at the opposite pole. The emphasis of the Christian ethics is not on reason but on love; and love, if not merely a feeling, is at least an attitude in which feeling plays an essential part. Goodness for Jesus lay among the inner springs of conduct. It manifested itself, of course, in action, but what gave it its quality and value was the attitude of the 'heart'. Wherever he started in his discussions, he seems always to have come back to this as the crucial point. In the people around him, the fountain of moral authority was the Mosaic law embodied in the Pentateuch, a law which, as interpreted by the Pharisees, prescribed the rules of good living in detail. Jesus knew these laws and respected them, but insisted that conformity to them was hollow unless it sprang from the right inward source, and that violation of them was innocent if it did. He said of the ceremonial alms-giving of the Pharisees what he would have said of the ostentatious largesse of Aristotle's 'great-souled man', that the widow's mite meant far more, because of the spirit in which it was given. If keeping the Sabbath meant inhumanity to an ox, it was better to break the rule than to be unkind even to an animal. This emphasis on the inner state, instead of relaxing the demands made of morality, intensified and extended them enormously. It was no longer enough that one should refrain from injuring one's brother, for one must now avoid the very anger that would make one want to injure him; one was to avoid not only adultery but lustful desire. Nor was the new disposition to be limited to those of one's own family, nation, or race. Plato had complimented the Athenians on having felt toward the Persians 'a pure and heartfelt hatred of the foreign nature' that went beyond that of any of the other Greeks. The love enjoined by Jesus was to be shown alike to Jew and Gentile, man and woman, bond and free; we were to love even our enemies and continue to be forgiving, no matter how long they went on provoking and persecuting. When asked for a summary of his teaching, Jesus offered it in two commandments, both of which were demands for love: love God and love man. Since he wrote nothing and his sayings were reported only in fragmentary fashion along with much that was plainly hearsay, there is a great deal in the existing record of him that is obscure and of doubtful genuineness, but 'the most certain thing about the teaching of Jesus is that He did teach this doctrine of universal love.'[1]

10. What did he mean by love? There are those who would deny that in using the term he was referring to a feeling. Love, they say, is something that he enjoined or commanded, and he would have commanded only what is within the control of our wills. The feeling of love is not thus within the control of our wills, and he could not, therefore, have required it of us. To meet this difficulty, Dean Rashdall suggested that 'the love towards all men which the Christian rule and rational morality demand is primarily a direction of the will', and 'will is a name for the dominant desire which has passed into action'. Further, 'What I imagine the Christian and rational precept of love towards mankind as such to prescribe is that the ultimate laws of human conduct should be determined by the principle that every man should be treated as an end in himself according to his intrinsic value.'[2] This seems to impart too much of both will and reason into the original Christian spirit. Certainly the good will of Jesus was not the good will of Kant, a settled respect for the rational rule of duty; that would have been far too cold. J. R. Seeley

[1] H. Rashdall, *Conscience and Christ*, 108.
[2] *Ibid.*, 192, 193

would seem to be more nearly right about it: what Christ held to be all in all was 'spontaneous warmth, free and generous devotion'; 'as we commonly behave rightly to anyone to whom we feel affection or sympathy, Christ considered that he who could feel sympathy for all would behave rightly to all', indeed that 'no heart is pure that is not passionate; no virtue is safe that is not enthusiastic'.[1] He thought that men were naturally trustful and affectionate towards each other, and that the secret of human goodness and happiness lay in removing the shell of indifference, suspicion and fear which, in virtue of occasional rebuffs, each man had built around him, and in returning to that joyful, childlike, and trusting affection of which he was himself an example. So far as is known, there was nothing erotic about this affection. In the love of mankind and even in the love of God as described by some later Christian writers, particularly mystics, expressions do creep in which suggest that this love is a sublimation, or scarcely even that, of a feeling markedly romantic and sensuous. It is the more noteworthy in the light of this that the New Testament never uses the word ἔρως, and generally employs instead the word ἀγάπη which was relatively free from sensuous associations.[2] The core of Christian love was an eager, joyful affection, kindliness, and trust, which was capable of being directed upon many different objects, and took a varying complexion as these objects changed—of pity when given to the sick or poor, of forgiveness when given to wrongdoers, of reverence and gratitude when given to God.

If anyone objects that the Christian stress was not merely on feeling and disposition, and that goodness involved also a consideration of others' welfare—the healing of the sick, the feeding of the hungry, and the clothing of the destitute—we of course agree. Genuine love for another does not go with indifference to his misery. Nevertheless, there are two striking facts about Jesus' treatment of what would be commonly called the good consequences of conduct. The first is the relatively small amount of attention he gave them. He insisted that if men sought first the inward kingdom and achieved it, the outward kingdom would take care of itself. Those who have attempted to make of Christianity a social gospel, while presumably nearer right than such exegetes as Kierkegaard, who would make the Christian callously indifferent to ordinary human needs, have had no little difficulty in fitting into their picture the unconcern

[1] *Ecce Homo*, 5th ed., 191, 186, 9
[2] cf. J. Moffatt, *Love in the New Testament*, 38 ff.

of Jesus about the morrow, his apparent approval, in the parable, of the employer's distribution of wages, his teaching that poverty is a better soil for goodness than wealth, and his indifference to politics. What he was primarily interested in was the springs of conduct rather than any changes of circumstance in which it might issue. Secondly, if our own chief good is a loving temper, it must also be the good of others, and the best service we can render them is to encourage them too to cultivate that better part which is not, like the tangible goods we might give them, liable to be taken away. Jesus developed no special technique for disseminating this temper of spirit. He was confident that if he approached men with transparent liking and trust, love would be its own interpreter, and they would repay him in kind; malignance could not hold out against a firm affection; 'fear wist not to evade as love wist to pursue'; the enemy would cease to be an enemy when he realized that he was fighting nothing but an invincible good will. Jesus committed himself to carrying through in practice this amazing adventure in universal affection, and kept his confidence in it till near the end, when, for a moment at least—a moment not easy to bear, even in retrospect—he thought his trust had been flung back in his face by both God and man.

11. We are of course not concerned here with developing the Christian ethic as a whole, any more than we were with the Greek ethic. Any adequate account of it would have to show how the love of men was bound up in the thought of the founder with the love of God, how morals were blended with, and inseparable from, religion. We cannot go into these matters, important as they are. What we want to point out is the extraordinary antithesis between the Greek and Christian ideas of goodness, and the resulting tension in the history of western thought between the ethics of reason and the ethics of feeling and attitude. The Greek gentleman, as Aristotle painted him, was a man who, with a high native intelligence, carefully cultivated, ordered his life deliberately and in detail with reference to an end defined by reason, and would have regarded the suggestion that he direct himself by the promptings of love, poured out alike upon man and woman, citizen, barbarian, and slave, as fantastic sentimentality. The early Christian was a man who thought that the one thing needful was to feel towards men as brothers and towards God as Father; about 'the wisdom of this world'—the scientific knowledge, dialectical acuteness, and philosophic sweep of Aristotle, for example —he knew and cared nothing. So far as we know, the Greek and Hebrew conceptions of life were worked out in complete independence of each other. Aristotle might have heard, but apparently never did, of those Hebrew prophets in whom many of Jesus' attitudes were foreshadowed; and there are no traces in Jesus' teaching of the slightest influence from the great succession of Greek thinkers. This is the more striking because in the Palestine of his day, the Greek language must have flowed freely round him, and he was not averse, like many of his countrymen, to contacts with foreigners. There is a curious incongruity, however, in the very thought of Jesus in conversation with a man like Aristotle. One can only suppose that the calculating and distinguishing ethical method of the Greek rationalist would have been scarcely less repellent to him than the Greek moral ideal.

12. The history of western ethics has been largely an attempt to define precisely the part played in good conduct by the Greek and Christian components and bring them into some sort of harmony. It is obvious that the intelligence which can view an action in the light of its consequences is in some sense important in recognizing and doing the right act. It is equally obvious than an act which has precisely the same consequences as another may be morally inferior to it if done from hatred rather than love, and therefore that the beginning of an act as well as its end, the inward state as well as the outward result, is morally important. If we were asked which was the more important, we should hardly care to answer. We value each enormously, though in different ways. Indeed they are the foundations of the two main types of goodness that we recognize. Among the heroes of the modern world are many men whose inner life was probably somewhat commonplace, but who are nevertheless placed on high pedestals by reason of the intelligence and power with which they 'organized victory' and refashioned the political order, men like Cromwell, Washington, Franklin Roosevelt, perhaps Lenin. On the other hand, an idolatry equally strong has been given to the heroes of the other moral tradition, who, regardless of their outward accomplishment, are safe in mens' affections for what they were, men like St Francis, John Woolman, and Gandhi. Each of us has elements of both these human types in his own nature; indeed all moral conduct seems to be the product at once of feeling and of more or less intelligent design. And the questions pressed themselves on moral analysts: are both these components essential in conduct that is morally admirable, and if so what is it that each contributes?

To begin with, are both of them really essential? This has not always been admitted. Fortunately the matter has been put to something like an empirical test. History has provided a large-scale laboratory in which astonishingly radical experiments have been tried; whole lives have been lived, and lived by great men with remarkable courage and consistency, on the theory that one or other of the two components could be dispensed with. In the next chapter we shall describe an experiment in the surrender to reason, to the almost total exclusion of feeling; in the chapter following an experiment in the surrender to feeling, to the almost total exclusion of reason. The outcome of these experiments should be illuminating.

CHAPTER II

STOICISM AND THE SUPREMACY OF REASON

1. Stoicism is the most remarkable experiment on record in the surrender of life to reason at the expense of feeling and desire. It was not a wholly new conception of the good life; like so much else in western thought, it had its root in the teachings of the three great Greeks. The stress of the great three was on the connection of goodness with intelligence, which they conceived as the highest of human faculties. According to Aristotle, what was distinctive in man was not his bodily processes of sensation, feeling, and impulse, for these he shared with the animals, still less such processes as growth and reproduction, for these he shared with all living things. It was rather his reason, taken as the power to grasp concepts and their connections. The ability to live and move in this region was what made the human mind human. Plato had taught that the real world was a framework of these concepts, intelligibly connected, and Socrates had taught that if we achieved rational knowledge, virtue automatically followed. The Stoics put these teachings together. The maxim of the good life, they held, was to follow nature, which meant: (1) to follow the guidance of that which was distinctive and essential in our own nature, namely, reason; (2) to conform to that which was likewise essential in outward nature, namely, its intelligible law, conceived as expressing a divine reason to which our own might respond.

The tendency of a view that exalted thought so highly was to make men try to live not only in accordance with their reason but *in* it, and to find their good in abstract contemplation. Marcus Aurelius went so far as to say that a man's self is identical with his reason. So far as he can retreat into this reason and live there, he will be beyond the reach of the ills that flesh is heir to. In a sense, he cannot avoid going outside himself, for his thought must have objects to deal with, but such objects will not be the particular things and successions that present themselves to the senses, but the changeless concepts and laws of which these are the appearances; like the mathematician, the philosopher will use particular figures only as aids to the universal. In living on this level, he will be participating in the nature of God himself. 'What is the nature of God?' asks the other saint of Stoicism, Epictetus, and answers, 'It is intelligence, knowledge, right reason.'[1] The wise man will thus be in the world but not of it. 'Material things cannot touch the soul at all, nor have any access to it. . . . The soul is bent or moved by itself alone, and remodels all things that present themselves from without in accordance with whatever judgment it adopts within.'[2]

2. Now when we 'remodel things' in this way by reflective judgment, what do we see? We see that whatever happens around us, whatever happens to us, is governed by intelligible law, and therefore had to occur exactly as it did. This is just as true of the actions of persons as it is of the flow of rivers and the falling of the rain. When a man insults you, when a lover jilts you, when a supposed friend betrays you, you can always see in the light of the circumstances that what happened was inevitable. If you are angry or depressed about it, that is because you were taken by surprise, because you did not know enough to foresee the inevitable and adjust yourself to it. Emotion, at least of the violent and disturbing kind, is always due to this lack of vision. Hence, as our understanding grows, our emotions die away. If we suppose that someone who has offended us has done so out of wanton malignance, we shall probably be furious with him. When we realize that he was only acting in accordance with such lights as he had, and, given these imperfect lights, was bound to act so, we shall say, 'There, but by the grace of God go I', and think no more about it. 'Whenever someone offends you, consider straightway how he has erred in his conceptions of good and evil. When you see where his error lies, you will pity him, and be neither surprised nor angry . . . Your duty then is to forgive.'[3]

Thus to understand all is to forgive all. Indeed, in Stoic thought, it is to go very much farther. It is to eradicate from our experience all fear, grief, and even desire. We can see on reflection that we feel these things because our reason has been invaded from below. Our

---

[1] *Discourses*, Bk. II, Ch. 8
[2] Marcus Aurelius, *Meditations*, V, 19
[3] *Ibid.*, VII, 26

animal nature is full of restless impulses and desires, and these seep up into our thought and delude us into taking their ends as really good or bad. We can see on reflection that they are neither the one nor the other, that to the man who lives in his understanding, they are beneath notice. They are particulars, and he lives in the universal; they are bound up with the body, and since his real riches are in his mind, his heart will be where his treasure is. It will therefore be genuinely indifferent to him whether his food is appetizing or his clothes in style, even whether his house burns down or his friends desert him, whether he is a slave like Epictetus, or lord of the civilized world like Marcus Aurelius. The ups and downs of fortune cannot touch him where he really lives, which is in the eternal world of unchanging ideas and relations. To desert this world and go off in search of particular and sensual satisfactions is a sort of treason to one's own nature.

It may be replied that some of these ills are not due to any perverted chasing after false gods, but are imposed by nature itself; if one's house burns down, that is surely an infliction from without, but none the less bad because it is nature's work. In his dissent from this view, the Stoic showed an element of faith that has often reappeared in rationalist philosophies. He believed that what satisfied the reason must in the end satisfy the demands of the moral sense; a world which is rational through and through will also, and therefore, be good; hence, whether we can see the justification of our house's burning or not, we can rest assured that, being necessary in both the causal and logical senses, it is necessary also to the moral order of the world. To think otherwise would be for a Stoic a species of impiety. In Marcus Aurelius this mood of faith and resignation found a lyric religious expression: 'I am in tune with all that is of thy harmony, O Nature. For me nothing is too early and nothing is too late that comes in thy good time. All is fruit to me, O Nature, that thy seasons bring. From thee are all things, thou comprehendest all, and all returns to thee. The poet says "O dear City of Cecrops!" Shall I not say, "Dear City of God"!'[1]

3. A cynic might remark that this high line about fear, anger, and loss was all very well if one sat in an emperor's seat and could make good from a bottomless treasury the deficiencies of one's theory. But not everyone is so happily placed, and not all evils are so obliging

[1] Marcus Aurelius, *Meditations*, IV, 23

as to vanish before this somewhat airy exorcism. What about pain? Let anyone try to prove to himself in this fashion that the pain of a broken leg is unreal and see how far he gets. These criticisms were not unknown to the Stoics. Indeed they received in the life of Epictetus a more striking answer than could be provided by any sort of dialectic. Epictetus was at the opposite end of the social ladder from the emperor, and, as a slave, he was in a better position to put their joint theories to a convincing test. If tradition is to be trusted, he came through the test impressively. He was a cripple, and there is a well-known story that when a brutal master once began to twist his leg by way of a savage joke, Epictetus warned him, without anger, that if he went on, he would break the leg, and when he did break it, bore the pain with what we should call stoicism and without resentment. Cicero, who was much influenced by the Stoics, reports that when Pompey went on a visit to the Stoic teacher, Posidonius, he found him ill and in great pain, and expressed his disappointment that he was not able to hear the discourse he had expected. 'But you *are* able', said Posidonius, and proceeded with his discourse on the nature of the good. When the paroxysm of pain returned, he paused only long enough to say, 'It is no use, pain! No matter how you attack me, I will never admit that you are an evil.'[1] It is small wonder that among a people so given as the Romans were to admiration for stern self-command, the ethics of such teachers, with its call to a passionless wisdom beyond the reach of circumstance, should have been for some two centuries the successful rival of Christianity.

4. Our own interest in it is as the most notable of all experiments in a morality, and indeed a religion, of pure reason, with feeling virtually excluded. Was the experiment a success? Certainly it achieved a surprising measure of what it set out to do, and it did so because it laid hold of a very important principle, namely that emotion can be indirectly controlled by means of its object. Some object or other an emotion must normally have, and since that object is largely an intellectual construction, it can be modified by thought. Take fear, for example. If you are afraid, there must be, in fact or in idea, something that you are afraid of—a dog, lightning, drunken men, the failure of your business. Suppose it is a dog. Then the fear is due to some belief about the dog, such as that he is likely to attack you when you are passing his gate. He may be as friendly as a kitten, but

[1] Tusculan Disputations, II, 61

not knowing his ways, you are free to clothe him in surmises which in turn give rise to fear. As soon as these are replaced by definite knowledge that he is in fact unaggressive and friendly, the object that aroused your fear is transformed into something neutral. This principle that feeling can be induced, removed, or modified, through the intellectual reconstruction of its object, provides the main channel for the influence of thought on feeling. Its understanding is indispensable if we are to gain any sort of insight into the religious and moral experience of peoples culturally remote from us. For example, the practice of killing parents when they reach the borders of old age seems like appalling heartlessness till one learns the intellectual situation in which it is done, which is perhaps that these killers conceive the parents as retaining through eternity the powers they take with them from this world; when seen in the light of such a belief, actions that seemed like heartless cruelty may take on the aspect of devotion. The way to understand the practice or to alter it is to change the conception that has produced it.

5. The Stoics grasped this principle and applied it with remarkable results. They saw that the most common and lasting of men's emotions are the negative ones of fear, dislike, envy, anger, and worry; they saw that with the possible exception of love, these emotions were more intense than the positive ones, just as our capacity for pain is greater than our capacity for pleasure; they were convinced, therefore, that emotion tended, on the whole, to make life miserable; and they discovered that it could be largely controlled by the discipline of thought.

This discipline did not take the easy form adopted by some optimists of simply averting one's eyes from the evils of the world and fixing them elsewhere, nor the fanatical form of denying that such things as pain and death occurred, nor yet the purely conjectural form of holding that these things were punishments for past sins or means of educating us for an unknown future. Their line was an intellectual one. They held that what makes us angry or worried was always a partial aspect or appearance, that as we set this appearance in its context of causes and effects, and ultimately in the context of the universe as a whole, its character was transmuted for us into something to which anger and worry were no longer appropriate responses. We have seen how effective this may be in the case of anger. William James, who was an indeterminist, once suggested that it would be a good practical rule to believe that we ourselves had free will and that everyone else was determined; such determinism regarding others he thought an excellent recipe for charity, as no doubt it is. Nor can it be denied that Marcus Aurelius's practice of trying to see things in larger perspective is a good working specific for worries and petty egoisms. Bertrand Russell tells us that there was a period in his life when having to make a public speech always plunged him into a misery of apprehension. He found that an effective way of curing this was to ask himself precisely what difference it would make a hundred years hence whether his speech was a failure or a success. In the light of the obvious answer, he could face the ordeal with calm. Emerson has described how, rushing out in a passion one night from some meeting or other, he looked up at the stars and seemed to catch a quiet rebuke from them, 'Why so hot, little man?' That is in the mood of Aurelius.

6. Thought can do much, then, to control and reduce emotion. But we can only concede that the rationalism which sought by means of it to blot emotion out altogether proved in the end a failure, a failure both in practice and in theory. There are some things that continue to be repellent and fearful, no matter how fully we understand them and how much their context is widened. Understanding can reconcile us to them in the sense that it can prepare us for them, and prevent their taking us by surprise, but not in the other sense of making them really acceptable to us. One reads, for example, how the devoted and kindly Mary Lamb went insane and killed her mother with a knife; is one's horror dissipated when one gathers from a psychiatrist's account that such a result was inevitable? A changed perspective may reduce a major tragedy to a minor one, but the tragic element does not simply vanish. Even in the neutralizing perspective of a century, the failure of a speech is still a failure and not a success.

Death is a crucial test case here, as the Stoics recognized. Unfortunately, not all the consolations of philosophy and religion can make death acceptable to most men. To some, indeed, they seem to have done so. Santayana wrote in old age, 'Think what an incubus life would be if death were not destined to cancel it, as far as any fact can be cancelled. That is the very image of hell.'[1] In others reflection has induced a comparative neutrality; Charles Kingsley said that he looked forward to the day of his death with profound

[1] *The Middle Span*, 105

curiosity. But probably most thoughtful men would agree with W. H. Hudson: 'When I hear people say they have not found the world and life so agreeable or interesting as to be in love with it, or that they look with equanimity to its end, I am apt to think they have never been properly alive nor seen with clear vision the world they think so meanly of, or anything in it—not a blade of grass.'[1] And the brave and honest T. H. Huxley wrote, 'I find my dislike to the thought of extinction increasing as I get older and nearer the goal. It flashes across me at all sorts of times with a sort of horror that in 1900 I shall probably know no more of what is going on than I did in 1800. I had sooner be in hell a good deal—at any rate in one of the upper circles, where the climate and company are not too trying.'[2] Against death as a mere transition the dialectics of Epicurus, borrowed by the Stoics, were fortifying enough; in a sense it is not an experience at all, for 'when we are present, death is not, and when it is present, we are not'. But death as the blotting out, once and for all, of one's joy, achievement, and hope, is something to which no Stoic or other dialectic has ever succeeded in reconciling the normal lover of life.

7. In this attempt to deal with the ills of the world by understanding them there is a further difficulty which has always given trouble to those who have tried to retain optimism along with a thoroughgoing rationalism. If evil things lose their evil when placed in a broad explanatory context, are not good things bound to lose their goodness when treated in the same way? We say that fear will be dissipated when, by reflection on its object, we come to see that it contains nothing really fearful. Must we not also say that love will be dissipated when by reflection we come to see that in its object there is nothing really lovable? How can we introduce this sort of alchemy into the world and put any limit to its dissolving effects? Why should we suppose that the argument is applicable only to the bad things that we want to see transformed and not also to the precious things that we would keep just as they are? The argument, if valid at all, lets loose a sort of tidal wave whose final work, as Spinoza saw, is not to turn apparent evil into good, but to engulf all good and evil in a limitless grey sea. The tendency of such reasoning to get out of hand is a notorious danger to theologians who wish to use the argument from design. They have often maintained, for example, that the

---

[1] *Far Away and Long Ago*, 331
[2] L. Huxley, *Life and Letters of T. H. Huxley*, II, 351–2

good in the world requires the belief in a good Designer. When it is pointed out that the evil in the world is hardly consistent with that conclusion, the reply is made that if we saw this evil in perspective it would not be evil at all. The next step, however, is to realize that if this line of reflection is extended, it will show that 'good' is not really good. But the argument started from the premise that we observe around us many things that really are good, and with the retraction of that premise, there is nothing to argue about.

8. Most persons who have reasoned in this way seem to have convinced themselves that what is good will somehow resist the dissolving process they have applied to evil. It is one of the merits of the Stoics to have tried, at least, to avoid such incoherence and to carry their case consistently through. In doing so they frankly admitted that goods which the normal man prized most of all had no attraction for them. 'If you love an earthen jar, say, "It is an earthen jar that I love",' writes Epictetus, 'for when it is broken, you will not be disturbed.' Sensible enough, we say. But then he continues, 'if you kiss your little child or your wife, say that it is a human being whom you are kissing, for when either of them dies, you will not be disturbed'.[1] Here we feel the touch of icy fingers. Most of us find something admirable in a self-control so stern that it can regard pleasure and pain alike as indifferent; but we hang back if one goes on, as the Stoics did, to draw the logical consequence that pity and sympathy with others' suffering are signs of weakness. 'When you see a person weeping in sorrow', says Epictetus, ' . . . so far as words go, do not be unwilling to show him sympathy, and even if it happens so, to lament with him. But take care that you do not lament internally also.'[2] Such coldness seems scarcely human. With heroic consistency the Stoics carried their indifference through to the point where life itself seemed a thing of small value, to be cast aside like a worn coat when the owner wearied of it; Zeno, Cleanthes, Seneca, Cato, all took their own lives, not in desperation, but calmly and deliberately; 'the cabin smokes—so I take leave of it. Why make ado?'[3] Here the logic that sought to dignify life has managed instead to cheapen it. Assume that whatever nature sends is necessary, that whatever is necessary is reasonable, and that whatever is reasonable is good, and you have in

---

[1] *Encheiridion*, III
[2] *Ibid.*, 16
[3] Marcus Aurelius, *Med.*, V, 29

your hands a proof that life and death are both good, as are pleasure and pain, health and disease. But this is absurd. For if all these things are to be called good alike, the line between good and bad has ceased to exist, and goodness has lost all distinguishing marks. In short, where everything is good, nothing is.

9. Unfortunately, the psychology of this extreme rationalism is as defective as its logic. Suppose that, recognizing the disturbing influence of emotion, one institutes a campaign against it which eradicates it completely. What will be the result? One will have triumphantly got rid of fear, hatred, jealousy, melancholy, worry, and grief, and may return—so it may be thought—to the placid enjoyments which form for most of us 'the C major of this life'. But we must play the game fairly. Enjoyment is itself a feeling or emotion, and if our experiment is to be decisive, that must vanish with the rest. Very well, we abolish it too. Would such a general ban be disastrous? It would not seem so at first sight. An enormous range of experience would apparently be left us—the whole range of science, the whole of history, the dispassionate contemplation of the philosopher, and such part—not great, perhaps—of the life of action as could be carried on by knowledge and will without feeling. Much of our social life we should have, indeed, to forgo; and we should have to do without art, since such experiences as poetry, music, and the enjoyment of painting would be closed to a mind incapable of feeling. It would be pointless, for example, for a person who could not be moved by either grief or 'verbal magic' to read *Lycidas*, for the poem in its very essence is an expression of feeling, and to anyone incapable of responding in kind, the poem would not strictly be a poem. Similarly of all other genuine art.

But then a suspicion arises. Would *anything* have value for us if we were incapable of feeling about it? We have suggested that for a feelingless man the realm of knowledge would in theory still be open. But would it? The people who sit over their microscopes for hours daily, watching the performance of paramoecia, are fascinated by what they see; whatever it may be to us, the behaviour of unicellular organisms is for them interesting and even exciting. But suppose they had absolutely no feeling about it, one way or the other, would they ever be moved to study it, or attach any value to knowledge of it? Probably not. Someone tells us that the knowledge of trigonometry is valuable. We ask him why he thinks so. He tells us that he finds such knowledge satisfying in itself. We ask him whether that means that he takes satisfaction in it, in the sense that he enjoys it and finds it interesting. Yes, he says, that does seem to be what he means. Well then, we ask, would the knowledge of trigonometry have this value for anyone who did not feel that way about it? No, he answers, perhaps not. Still, he goes on, even for such persons it still has value in another sense; though it may not have value in itself, it may have value as a means; it is indispensable for example, to engineers in the building of bridges. The value of mathematics, then, turns on the value of such things as bridges; very well, do *they* have value? Of course they have, we are told; people make use of them constantly to get to their offices and their golf. The value of the bridge, then, turns on the value of the activities it makes possible; do *these* have value? It is needless to go on; we can see where we are going to come out. All instrumental goods are valued in the end because they are means to what is valued in itself, such as comfort and the respect of one's fellows, or, on a smaller scale, the experience of playing a difficult hole in par. Regarding these, we must ask again the question we asked about knowledge in itself. Suppose that in point of feeling, a man were absolutely indifferent to what others thought or felt about him; would their respect be good for him, or have any sort of value? It is hard, surely, to say anything but no. Of course, this lack on his part would not prevent others, who did find satisfaction or enjoyment in such things, from talking about their value. But to the man himself who found no satisfaction or enjoyment whatever in them, they would be salt that had no savour.

10. Such feelinglessness would wreck the moral life. Where no prospective experience is more attractive than any other, and the results of every action are equally indifferent, why should one seek or avoid any of them, or prefer one to another? If the question presented itself, Shall I read Shaw this evening or listen to a broadcast of Schubert, a man would be practically, though not theoretically, in the position of Buridan's ass, which, placed at exactly equal distances from two equally appetizing bales of hay, starved to death. The only difference would be that in this case the alternatives, instead of being alike in attractiveness, would be alike in having no attraction whatever. It might be said that though one took no interest oneself in music, one could still recognize that others did, and if one believed this to be true, it would provide a sufficient motive for trying to give them the experience, indeed one might have a clear, though purely intellectual, recognition that one *ought* so to try, and this of itself might move one's will. But we must remember that such a person could have no conception of what being interested in anything meant, nor, therefore, what the point would be in trying to satisfy that interest; and further, that doing his duty would itself have no more attraction for him than doing nothing. To say that a man ought to do something when he can take no satisfaction in duty or in achieving anything that dutifulness might bring, is to ask what is practically superhuman.

11. The point has been laboured enough. But the importance of feeling, if any of the goods of life are to be realized, has been so strikingly shown in the autobiography of a famous writer that we must make at least a passing reference to it. John Stuart Mill, as is well known, was trained by his father from babyhood to be a philosopher. From the age of three, when he began the study of Greek, he lived in his intellect; and his achievements in this realm during his tender years would be past belief if they were not so well attested. But these achievements were bought at a price. He explains that the normal growth of his feelings was not only stunted by his being cut off from the play and companionship in which most boys find their interest, but also by his analytic habits themselves. One's coming to find value in something is, at least very commonly, a casual matter of association; whether a boy likes dancing or stamp-collections or novels, or on the contrary hates them, is likely to depend on whether his early exposure to them has given him associations of delight or the reverse. But if, before habits of enjoying such objects can firmly fix themselves, critical reflection is brought to bear upon them, questioning whether enjoyment would be well-placed, and breaking the object up after the manner of mental analysis, the normal habits of unreflective delight never grow up; they are withered before they can take root. Mill wrote that when he reached the age of twenty,

'it occurred to me to put the question directly to myself: "Suppose that all your objects in life were realized; that all the changes in institutions and opinions which you are looking forward to could be completely effected at this very instant: would this be a great joy and happiness to you?" And an irrepressible self-consciousness distinctly answered, "No!" At this my heart sank within me: the whole foundation on which my life was constructed fell down. All my happiness was to have been found in the pursuit of this end. The end had ceased to charm, and how could there ever again be any interest in the means? I seemed to have nothing left to live for. . . . I was thus, as I said to myself, left stranded at the commencement of my voyage, with a well-equipped ship and a rudder, but no sail; without any real desire for the ends which I had been so carefully fitted out to work for: no delight in virtue, or the general good, but also just as little in anything else. . . . I frequently asked myself, if I could, or if I was bound to go on living, when life must be passed in this manner.'[1]

Fortunately, Mill did decide to go on living. After some months of this bleak existence, suddenly and to his surprise he found himself moved to tears in the course of reading a French memoir. The emotionally starved young analyst was delighted and relieved to find that he could be moved by anything. 'From this moment my burden grew lighter. The oppression of the thought that all feeling was dead within me was gone. I was no longer hopeless: I was not a stick or a stone.' With the help of Wordsworth, whose writing managed to bathe familiar things with gentle feeling, 'I gradually found that the ordinary incidents of life could give me some pleasure; that I could again find enjoyment, not intense, but sufficient for cheerfulness, in sunshine and sky, in books, in conversation, in public affairs'.[2]

What is proved by these cases of emotional starvation? Not, I think, that the value of things is reducible to, or simply consists in, the feelings we have about them. This view is now widely held, and must be considered later. But such cases do show this, that our experience of value is normally bound up with our feelings, and that in their absence we are value-blind. A man may increase his knowledge and develop his intellect without limit, but if he is unable to feel, the world will hold for him no goodness and no attraction.

[1] *Autobiography*, 133–4, 139, 140
[2] *Ibid.*, 141. Some rather similar cases, described under Ribot's name of anhedonia, are given by James in *The Varieties of Religious Experience*, 145 ff.

CHAPTER III

ST FRANCIS AND THE SUPREMACY
OF FEELING

1. In considering the places of reason and feeling in morals, we have found it useful to begin by applying Mill's method of difference. Take feeling away and leave reason—what do you get? The Stoics tried the experiment, to our lasting instruction and benefit. Of course, the experiment was not perfect. Reason and feeling are so pervasive of experience that we perhaps never have a state of mind in which both are not present in some degree. Though the Stoics tried to make reason dominant to the exclusion of feeling, not even Aurelius or Epictetus achieved the ideal of the 'passionless sage'; at least the gentler emotions of the tranquil life had to be admitted. Still, imperfect experiments may be highly enlightening, and certainly this one was.

Has history given us any case of the converse experiment, in which what we may call the Greek element in morals has been, so far as possible, pushed out, and the guidance of life surrendered to feeling? Something very like it was tried by the Greeks themselves in the morals of Aristippus of Cyrene, who taught that the art of life lay not in ordering conduct on a large and rational plan, but in squeezing from each successive moment its fullest yield of pleasure. A somewhat similar gospel, urging that true success lay in burning with 'a hard gem-like flame' of aesthetic delight, was current in Victorian times and ascribed, with varying justice, to Baudelaire, Swinburne, Whistler, Pater, and Wilde. It would be not uninstructive to consider this gospel. But if one is to study the rule of life by feeling, it is best to take it at its strongest, and this is hardly to be found among such apostles of self-indulgence as the Cyrenaics or a somewhat sickly crop of Victorian *fleurs du mal*. The passion for pleasure, even for aesthetic pleasure, is not a very convincing candidate for the governorship of life. If one wants an example whose appeal comes home to nearly everyone, it would be better to turn to a man who is often regarded as the most lovable being in human annals, an Italian named Giovanni Bernardone, who lived his strange and short life in the twelfth century. He is better known to history as St Francis of Assisi.

2. St Francis was a poet who produced only one poem of importance, but that a lyrical masterpiece, namely his life. He was that exceptional sort of Christian who took the summing up of the law and the prophets in 'love God and love man' in all seriousness, and sought to make his life an embodiment of it down to the last detail. Fortunately, he had a temperament that found the command congenial. From the beginning he was gay, carefree, and affectionate, though there was nothing in his early years that would suggest his extraordinary destiny. The son of a well-to-do Italian merchant, he spent his youth much as one would expect, partly in learning the business, partly in being a popular young man about town. He was regarded as one of the leaders of the younger and gayer set, the more readily as he was sociably inclined, fashionably dressed, given to merry-making, and, to the paternal distress, a prodigal free with his father's money. Though he was something of a dreamer, his dreams were of the standard variety and seem to have played generally around his own brilliant future as a chivalrous and dashing man-at-arms.

In his early twenties a profound change came over him, no one knows quite how or why. Setting out to join a military expedition, he fell ill and had to come home; and, as he recovered, he spent more and more of his time in solitary reveries and in wandering through the fields and woods beyond the Assisi walls. His parents and friends did not know what to make of him. What was really going on in him, and continued for some two years, was a struggle between incompatible ways of life. On the one hand he could be, if he wished, a successful and prosperous man of the world; on the other, his imagination was more and more dominated by a wholly different sort of adventure, the wild adventure of assuming that the gospels were true. If they were, it really did not matter whether one had any material goods or not; such needs as one had would be taken care of by the great lord of creation to whom all things were possible, who felt for his creatures the concern of a father for his children, and whose chief desire for them was that they should love both him and their fellows. These things were either true or not. If they were not, the life that contented most men, and had been marked out also for Francis, namely the pursuit of security through place and money, was an altogether sensible choice. If they were true, it was an absurd and impossible choice. Francis took the second view.

3. With his adoption of it there came an enormous relief and release. He had always been rather like a carefree and affectionate child, and the mandate of the gospel, instead of laying on him an intolerable cross, seemed like a summons to be himself. His father having disinherited him, he gave away what little he still owned and delightedly became a beggar. He wanted to own nothing at all, not a house, or a bed, or even a loaf of bread. His business was to go about spreading the good news of the love of God and inviting men to turn from their worried preoccupation with getting on, and live as if this were true. He did not denounce people and threaten them. He had no ecclesiastical position to awe them with; he was not a theologian; he was not even a priest. He was a little man in the cheapest of brown tunics, with a rope for a belt, who wanted to tell people that if they woke up, as he had done, to what a wonderful world it was, they too could be as happy as he. And of his deep, irrepressible happiness there could be no doubt. He would sing French songs as he trudged along the highways; he was called the *jongleur de Dieu*, the *joculator Dei*, God's clown and minstrel; it is told that his followers, when they went to church, would occasionally break out in peals of laughter for the sheer joy of living in such a world, and have to be put out by the sextons.

It would of course be a great mistake to take the happiness of St Francis as the mere exuberance of animal spirits. Such happiness is still bound to 'brother ass', the body, and is liable to suffer if that faithful but lowly beast is ill fed or uncared for; and the joy of Francis was of the twice-born kind that is never far from tears of compassion for those who are still in this slavery. He had made his escape from it, and seemed genuinely beyond concern for himself. But most men plainly had not, and for them his sympathy was inexhaustible. Since he was quite fearless, and worldly position meant nothing to him, he was always acting in unpredictable ways that seemed, after the event, to have an inspired propriety. If he saw a leper whose limbs were rotting away, he was as likely as not, instead of avoiding him, to rush up to him, put his arms around him and kiss him in a pure transport of pity. Being distressed by the conflict and misery of the first crusade,

he set out with a few companions to stop it all by telling the Moham-
medans how lovable they too were, and how much they missed by
killing Christians instead of treating them as brothers. He sailed to
Egypt where the Crusaders were besieging Damietta, made his way
through the enemy lines, secured an interview with the Saracen
emperor Saladin, and preached to him also his one simple sermon.
Saladin received him courteously, but seems to have continued in
his opinion that Mohammed, rather than this strange apparition in
brown, was the true prophet of Allah. What would have been the
course of history, one wonders, if this meeting with Francis had ended
as such meetings usually did?

4. The affection of Francis was not limited to those of his own kind.
It ran over in all directions. He could hardly have learned his pity
and respect for the animal world from either pagan or Christian
sources; it was a new note of his own, so striking to his contemporaries that they wove endless legends around it. It seems to be more
than mere legend, however, that he had a special delight in birds,
was sure that they understood him, and at times gravely preached
to them and remonstrated with them. There are pleasing tales of
how they reciprocated his fondness, how, for example, when he was
preaching at Olviano, the swallows, by way of greeting him, 'so
filled the air with their chirping that he could not make himself
heard. "It is my turn to speak", he said to them; "little sister swallows,
hearken to the word of God, keep silent and be very quiet until I
have finished".'[1] No doubt they hid their heads under their wings.
In *The Little Flowers of St Francis*, it is recorded how, when he was
in the city of Agobio, he learned of 'a very great wolf, terrible and
fierce, the which not only devoured animals but also men and women,
so that all the citizens stood in great fear', and the men who left the
city carried arms to protect themselves. Francis had his own method
of dealing with the beast. He went out alone and unarmed to the
wolf's lair and called to it in his gentle voice, 'Come hither, friar
wolf'. It came out and eyed him suspiciously. Then he went on to
explain to it that he knew how hungry it was, but that it was acting
very wrongly nevertheless. He would see to it that the citizens no
longer hounded it, but undertook to feed it regularly if it would agree
to treat them in the like friendly way. The wolf gave him its paw in
abashed contrition, trotted along after him like a pet dog into the

[1] Sabatier, *Life of St Francis*, 177, following Thomas of Celaro.

city, and because the citizens kept Francis' pledge to it, became a pet of theirs too.[1]

Sheer childish mediaeval myth? In detail, no doubt, but not in substance. The exquisite tenderness of the man toward all living things that had reached the dignity of pain penetrates through the legends that surround him like a beam of pure light. This certainly was no invention. And since he was a poet, his sympathy did not stop even with the lowlier living things. His *Canticle of the Sun* suggests that if nature is in truth the creation of God, then everything testifies of his goodness.

'Praised be my Lord God with all his creatures, and especially our brother the sun, who brings us the day and who brings us the light; fair is he and shines with a very great splendour: O Lord, he signifies to us thee! Praised be my Lord for our sister the moon, and for the stars, the which he has set clear and lovely in heaven. Praised be my Lord for our brother the wind,'[2]

and 'our sister water', 'our brother fire', and 'our mother the earth'. All these things he took as not only beautiful but, in mystical fashion, as somehow well disposed toward those who felt delight in them. When he was ill and nearly blind, a heavy-handed surgeon of the day decided that one of his eyes should be cauterized, the method being to heat an iron rod white hot in a flame and then apply it to the eyeball. When Francis saw the preparations, he gave a respectful little speech to the flame: 'Brother fire, you are beautiful above all creatures; be favourable to me in this hour; you know how much I have always loved you; be thou courteous today.' Legend reports, one hopes correctly, that he escaped the pain.

5. I have suggested that the life of Francis may be regarded as an experiment in the guidance of life by feeling. It may be objected that in fact he regulated his life by the New Testament. In a sense no doubt he did. But what he borrowed left room for much that was his own. He could hardly have borrowed from Christ a code of living, for Christ had no such code to lend. What he took was an example which he interpreted as teaching that one should act in each case as one's own love suggested, whatever prudence or reason or custom

---

[1] *The Little Flowers of St Francis*, Heywood's trans., Ch. 21.
[2] *Canticle of the Sun*, Matthew Arnold's trans.

might say to the contrary. From that point on, Francis' life had the originality of his own unique quality of love.

Of course he did not wholly exclude calculation and principle; no one can possibly do that. But there is perhaps no man in history of comparable influence whose reliance on the intellect was so small. It must be frankly said that intellectually he was always something of a child. His range of knowledge was very narrow. He was a rank above St Joan of Arc, in that he was able to read; but he read little, and when he tried to write, he formed his letters with some difficulty. Though he lived in the country of Horace, Virgil, and Cicero, 'nothing of the antique, no distinct bit of classical inheritance, appears in him.[1]' 'He had no distinctly intellectual interests. . . . Hence he was averse to studies which had nothing to do with man's closer walk with God and love of fellow. "My brothers who are led by the curiosity of knowledge will find their hands empty in the day of tribulation . . . for such a time will come when they will throw their good-for-nothing books into holes and corners."'[2] 'Suppose that you had subtility and learning enough to know all things, that you were acquainted with all languages, the courses of the stars, and all the rest, what is there in that to be proud of? A single demon knows more on these subjects than all the men in this world put together.'[3] A young disciple begged him on one occasion for permission to own, and take with him on his journeys, just one book, a Psalter. Francis gave the permission, but a little later felt he had done wrong, and with sorrowful apology withdrew the permission.

6. Are we not told, it may be asked, that Francis spent much time in meditation? We are indeed. But meditation is not thought, if that means the analysis of ideas or the sort of critical reflection which proceeds by the laborious shaping of hypotheses until they fit the facts. For thought in that sense Francis had neither competence nor taste, nor does he seem to have considered it important. Even his theology was of the simplest—a few leading ideas of which he had no doubt, since those prime producers of doubt, science and philosophy, held no temptations for him. The world was a neat, small world, bounded by the creation and the second coming, and made as a testing place for man, who was surrounded by angels and demons, and might be

[1] H. O. Taylor, *The Mediaeval Mind*, I, 417
[2] *Ibid.*, I, 428, 9, quoting the *Speculum Perfectionis*.
[3] *Admonitio*, 5, trans. by Sabatier, *op. cit.*, 281.

addressed, as Francis thought he was from time to time, by the Creator himself. When such transcendent counsel was available, the labour of thought was hardly necessary.

Even if, in difficult cases, the prompting of love was not quite clear, Francis was still reluctant to appeal to the cold court of the mind. When his followers had reached the number of three, one of whom was a rich man, he was perplexed as to the programme the little society should adopt, and his way of settling the matter was to kneel before an altar with a copy of the gospels in his hand, and accept as divine direction the passage on which his eye first fell. When he sailed for Egypt with the Crusaders, so many friars wanted to accompany him that the ship's captain refused to take them all, and Francis was compelled to make a choice. His method was characteristic:

'he led all his friends to the port and explained to them his perplexities. "The people of the boat", he told them, "refuse to take us all, and I have not the courage to make choice among you; you might think that I do not love you all alike; let us then try to learn the will of God." And he called a child who was playing close by, and the little one, charmed to take the part of Providence put upon him, pointed out with his fingers the eleven friars who were to set sail.'[1]

Whatever one may say of this method of solving problems, it is economical of reflective effort. But the need of supplementing it by an organizing intelligence seems to have been implicitly admitted by Francis when, early in the history of his order, he resigned from its headship, declaring himself incompetent for the post.

7. What are we to say of this experiment in the exaltation of feeling over reason as the guide of life? I do not understand how anyone could read about Francis, let alone how anyone could meet him, without falling into some measure of captivity to him. It is as if some tender and exquisite idyll had come alive, or as if there had strayed into the quarrelsome and bloody twelfth century some wanderer from the childhood of the world when men could still live with each other like brothers and sisters. But our concern is not with an idyll, however touching or beautiful, but with an immensely important experiment in morality.

[1] Sabatier, *op. cit.*, 227

An interpreter of Francis who had much of his hero's childlike power of living in a freer world beyond the senses, Gilbert Chesterton, has said that St Francis, 'however wild and romantic his gyrations might appear to many, always hung on to reason by one invisible and indestructible hair'.[1] This is an interesting comment because one would expect that if a man guided his life as much by feeling and as little by reason as Francis did, he would soon stumble into self-contradiction with himself. And with all respect to Chesterton, I am afraid this is what we do find.

In Francis' budget of love, all was earmarked for others and none for self.

'Love took up the harp of life, and smote on all the chords with might,
Smote the chord of Self, that, trembling, pass'd in music out of sight.'

For himself he would claim nothing. If bread was distributed, he would take the blackest and hardest bit; if there were not enough blankets to go round, he must be the person to do without one; if there were not beds enough, he would sleep on the ground; he must not have a tunic of his own if a beggar was in sight who was clothed in sorrier rags. As for goodness, he was a gross sinner from whom God might justly avert his face. 'Through all his plunging and restless days ran the refrain: I have not suffered enough; I have not sacrificed enough; I am not yet worthy of the shadow of the crown of thorns.'[2]

8. Disarming and humbling as this attitude is, it has its difficulties. It begins to break down when more than one man adopts it. A insists that B shall have the last blanket; B insists that A shall have it. How is such a duel of generosities to be settled? It cannot be settled by love alone, for neither man's love can be given precedence over the other's. Only as love goes beyond itself into justice is there any ground for a decision. If A is old and B young, if B is ill and A well, there is some reason why the blanket should go to one rather than to the other. But a contest in pure affection must end either in a stalemate or in a victory of the strongest, and while a victory for the strongest impulse of self-effacement is the least imminent of dangers, it would, after all, be as irrational a victory as that of self-assertion. We do not think that a man is right because, being stronger than

[1] *St Francis of Assisi*, 180
[2] *Ibid.*, 142

another, he actually prevails. Neither can we say that a man is right merely because his love is stronger than another's and thus prevails. He will probably be more admirable, and will certainly be more unusual than his competitors, but he may be both these things without being right.

President Butler of Columbia once complained that it was so much harder to be right than to be clever; unhappily, it is also harder to be right than to be loving. The mother who, out of love for her children, offers herself as a living sacrifice for them, is not necessarily taking the right course. The daughter who, out of love for her parents, gives up the chance of a life of her own may be acting nobly, but may also be giving what they have no right to ask, and what she holds herself too cheap in giving. However rare it may be to need an application of brakes to love, and however difficult it may be to fix the point at which justice should apply them, it is plain that there is such a point, which love itself cannot determine. A community of men like St Francis, each committed to giving himself for others, would be a very much more amiable society than Hobbes's 'state of nature', but its members would be afflicted with the same sort of helplessness in deciding their chivalrous rivalries so long as they had love only as their arbiter.

9. Compare, again, Francis' attitude toward his own sins and toward those of others. He conceived of himself as living in a great family, in which God was father and all men brothers. The father set an example for his children by being infinitely tender and solicitous about them; he was concerned about every hair on their heads; he had enjoined them to be perfect even as he was; they were to forgive seventy times seven, that is, without limit. If anyone ever achieved this infinity of charity, it was Francis. And yet when it came to his own sin, he professed to find it so black that God would be serving him right by turning his face from him altogether. His sin was mountainous and monstrous; there was no health in him; with all his love and service for others, he was worse than worthless; once, when he exceeded his small allowance of food, he had himself publicly flogged in penance. Men as a rule are so self-righteous that they stand open-mouthed before such conduct. The man who can achieve it must be, they think, some extraordinary kind of saint.

So Francis undoubtedly was. But one wonders whether the grace of humility is to be purchased only at the price of inaccurate and incoherent belief. Francis was not really a blacker soul than other men. Rare and winning trait that it is for a man to think himself the worst of sinners, if he is in fact kindly, brave, and dutiful, is there not something amiss with a rule of humility that would require him to see himself as he is not? Virtue built on untruth, even if amiable untruth, is a precarious kind of virtue. And if Francis was right that the divine goodness could consistently turn its back on such as he, then in his humility he had conceived a dogma which involved in ruin the whole structure of his religion and morals. By the only standard we know, Francis was a good man; if not, who ever was? A God who would regard it as just to condemn such a man to perdition would not be good in our sense at all, nor could human beings become good by being like him. If the most devoted service of which man is capable is still to be set down as sin, as some modern theologians go on repeating, the effect is not to exalt our notion of God, but to make it unintelligible, not to stimulate us to higher exertion, but to confuse our morals hopelessly. We are being made to call good in God what would be wickedness in ourselves. We are told to love men infinitely while being told that they are infinite scoundrels, ourselves included —though we are left to infer that we shall be somewhat less contemptible if we think ourselves the worst of them, even if the belief is false. This confused way of looking at things is natural enough to a sensitive and anxious mind that craves affection and approval, and feels that it may gain the love of God if it can appease his anger by self-abasement and protestations of guilt. But its spring is in emotion, not thought. At any rate, it is incoherent, and what is incoherent cannot be true.

10. Consider, again, Francis' attitude toward material goods and the needs of the body. In his love of others, he was prompted to give away everything he owned. In his enthusiasm for life on the highest level, he treated 'brother ass', the body, with contempt. Both policies recoiled upon him, the first logically, the second practically also. If he were remonstrated with for giving away money and clothes as fast as he got them, he would no doubt say that these things were of little or no value, that spiritual goods alone were of importance. But if materials things are of small importance, then in giving them to others, what he was giving was unimportant, and charity itself, by so much, lost its value.

His difficulty over the body was far graver. The man who lives so much in the spirit as to disdain the claims of the body is always defeated, and the more exclusive his devotion, the earlier defeat overtakes him. To be sure, Francis survived under his own uncompromising regime a surprising time. He reached the age of forty-four, dying after a long and lingering illness in extreme exhaustion and emaciation. The illness was precipitated by his going to an island and giving himself over to spiritual ecstasy, alone and without food, for forty days. He once made the discovery that his body rebelled when fed with cakes cooked in oil, so in a period of Lent he ate cakes cooked in lard, which his body could accept. For this compromise with the flesh he was deeply repentant, however, and thereafter he ignored its preference. He seems to have lived by deliberate choice in a state of bodily filth, since frequent washing showed too great a concern for the body.

Such spirituality is tragic folly. That there is something touching and noble about it, as about nearly everything Francis did, is true; but, once again, at bottom it is incoherent. If the body is really so useless an appendage as this to the spirit, if its primal needs are at warfare with those of the higher life, it would seem the most sensible course to shuffle off the mortal coil at once and altogether, and pass to the realm where one no longer needs, as Yeats would say, to drag around a dying animal. On the other hand, if the spirit has its root in the body, as it obviously does, then to treat it as Francis did is to cut at the root those very flowers of the spirit which he so much valued. Zeal not according to knowledge has often led to something like spiritual as well as physical suicide. It is true that within the very considerable limits in which the mind can work on the body, Francis did remarkable things. If faith will not move mountains, there are at least men who can draw more fully than others on those mysterious powers of influencing body through mind which are now so imperfectly understood, and he seems to have been one of them; there are well attested parallels to the tradition of his stigmata, and it is quite possible that it is true. What he did not succeed in showing is that the spiritual life, if lived intensely enough, can afford to ignore the conditions under which nature has appointed that it must be lived.

11. When love ignores these conditions, it is likely to be self-crippling. Sympathy it can supply in plenty. Sometimes this is all that is needed and, when it is, true Franciscans come into their own.

But what men commonly want and need is not so much sympathy as opportunity, a soil in which their particular variety of weed or flower can flourish. Their need is for health, tools, laboratories, books, leisure, a room of their own, and countless other things whose configuration is alike in no two cases. One who loves another will be more likely, no doubt, to sympathize with these needs and wishes, and try to fulfil them; indeed without a special concern for others, it is only too probable that one would never think of their needs at all. Hence the spirit of a John Woolman or an Elizabeth Fry or a Dick Sheppard is a valuable yeast in any community, which it would be absurd and wrong to dispraise. Nevertheless, much of the humanitarian work of the world has been done by persons who had no particular affection for the people they served. They have been persons who, like John Howard, saw an injustice they thought should be righted, and proceeded to right it, or, like Walter Reed, saw that a disease must be eradicated and proceeded to apply their scientific resources to its mastery.

Even when personal or Christian affection is present in the highest intensity, it must be somehow implemented; what must implement it is intelligence and knowledge; and if love is jealous of knowledge, as it was in the mind of St Francis, it may cut its own throat. So far as I know, the only time when Francis was quite uncharitable was when he cursed with a terrible malediction one of his disciples named Pietro Staccia, and even refused to withdraw the curse when he was told that Staccia was about to die. The chief offence of this man appears to have been that he organized the disciples in Bologna into a sort of college where learning was pursued—a radical perversion of his leader's aims.[1] Love that is so superior to knowledge may be a public danger. Francis presumably approved the mediaeval practice, when an epidemic was raging, of calling the people together for a joint renewal of their devotion and thus providing, in solicitous ignorance, for the spread of the disease. Being practically a man of one book, which seemed to him sufficient for men's needs, he held a view in which science was subordinate to religious imagination, and disbelief in the products of this imagination was sin, a view which, if it had prevailed, would have made the modern intellectual world impossible. He thought to improve the community by encouraging large numbers of the best men and women to forgo family life and give themselves over to a consecrated sterility, and his conception of

[1] Sabatier, *Life*, 280

solving the problem of poverty seems scarcely to have gone beyond that impulsive kindness that would take off its last garment and give it to a beggar, regardless alike of the deserts of the beggar and of the tendency of such charity to produce more beggars. Such considerations do not destroy the idyllic beauty of his life. But they prepare one for the sad comment on his practical achievement that has been made by Lord Russell: 'The net result of St Francis's life was to create yet one more wealthy and corrupt order, to strengthen the hierarchy, and to facilitate the persecution of all who excelled in moral earnestness or freedom of thought. In view of his aims and his character, it is impossible to imagine any more bitterly ironical outcome.'[1]

12. It is only too clear that love cannot of itself supply the means, often complicated and technical, required to put it into effect. Unfortunately, it cannot supply the ends either. What exactly is the loving man to help others attain? Love cannot of itself supply the answer. If one says that love itself is above all things to be desired, it is not love that passes that verdict; there is plainly some other agency in us which, standing outside our love and hate, our pleasure and pain, passes comparative judgments on them; the love of love supplies no adequate estimate of its object, any more than the hate of hate or the scorn of scorn. That this is true may be seen from the fact that love often singles out and squanders itself upon objects that are clearly unworthy. It may lavish itself upon a lap-dog, or upon the most worthless of men. When it is showered on everyone with the catholic impartiality of Francis, it tends to blur the moral differences between its objects; a democracy of feeling that goes out with approximately equal solicitude to turtle-doves, criminals, and saints, can justify itself only by falling back on mystical doctrines about equality in the sight of God which conceal, but cannot obliterate, its conflict with general convictions. Love, as McTaggart pointed out, is curiously and sometimes gratefully unselective in the character of its object. The love of a mother for a son may be unaffected by a jury's verdict that he is a traitor and murderer. If Hitler aroused much hatred, he aroused also a great deal of devoted and self-immolating love. The moral of such examples is plain enough. Love contains in itself no principle of selection. Unless guided by an insight other than its own, it showers itself alike on the just and on the unjust, and is

[1] *History of Western Philosophy*, 472

capable of a passionate devotion to personal and communal ideals
that reflection can only condemn.

13. Let us take our bearings. We began by noting that western
ethics is drawn from two main sources, Greek and Christian. In these
two sources the emphasis was placed heavily, though not exclusively,
on different components in the moral life. The Greek moralists placed
the stress on reason; Christianity placed it on the attitude of 'the
heart'. They cannot both be right, and the tension between them has
run through the entire moral history of the west. For a period in the
early Roman empire, the Greek influence became dominant and led
to an experiment in which a great school of moralists tried to surrender their lives to the control of reason alone, and to exclude influence of feeling. The experiment broke down both in theory and
in practice. Then for many centuries Greek thought was superseded
by Christian, which achieved a dominance in the thirteenth century
that it has never held before or since. At the peak of its power another
historic experiment was made, this time in following the dictates of
feeling, to the virtual exclusion of reflective reason. Impressive as the
venture was, we could only say that if regarded, not as a lyric, but
as a design for living, it also broke down tragically in incoherence
and maladjustment to the world.

The conclusion suggested by these experiments is that the attempt
to live the life of reason or the life of feeling exclusively can end only
in disaster. The offices of both are indispensable. Nature may spread
before us the richest possible banquet of good things, but if we can
look at them only with the eye of reason, we shall 'care for none of
these things'; they will be all alike insipid. There would be no
'knowledge of good and evil' in a world of mere knowers, for where
there is no impulse or feeling, no aversion or desire, good and evil
would be unrecognizable. Even the pursuit of knowledge would be
motiveless. A motive is a desire, and a desire involves a want, and a
want is not an exercise in cognition. To a pure intellect nothing
would seem of more value than anything else.

But we should be in a similar position if we were mere creatures
of impulse or emotion. To find an act right or wrong, to find value
in friendship, religion, or art, to care in any degree for knowledge,
requires the use of powers that go far beyond any form of feeling.
And a life that directs itself by feeling, even of the most exalted kind,
will be a ship without a rudder. It will all too probably end in ship-

wreck, and, because sailing without lights, involve others too in the wreck. The achievement of good is a joint product of our power to think and our power to feel.

CHAPTER IV

THE DIALECTIC OF REASON AND FEELING
IN BRITISH ETHICS

1. For the achievement of a good life, indeed for the achievement
of anything good, thought and feeling are both necessary. The exclusion of either makes the other sterile. So much we have seen. But
what does each contribute?

Unfortunately this is too large a question for us. Thought and
feeling contribute so subtly and variously to the achievement of
every form of good that no full account of their interplay is practicable.
If we are to deal with the issue at all, we must narrow it sharply.
Happily we may do so while keeping before us that form of the issue
which is of principal interest to the moralist of cur time. Though the
functions of reason and feeling in the good life generally are beyond
our compass, we may quite well discuss with profit their functions in
moral judgment. This question, though smaller than the other, is
still of crucial importance. Upon its outcome depends the solution of
many of the issues most eagerly canvassed in our day—whether, and
in what sense, there are objective moral standards, whether right is
relative or not to one's own taste or opinion, or to that of a particular
culture, whether moral disagreements are matters of belief or of
feeling, whether moral convictions can be made out by rational argument. Indeed, a more fruitful ethical question could scarcely be
raised.

Let us get it clearly before us without delay. When we decide that
a certain action is right, or our duty, what is it that does the deciding?
Our reason? Our feeling? Or both? Or perhaps something different
from either?

The answer of common sense would probably be 'Both'. Judgments on moral questions seem to stand about midway between
purely rational judgments on the one hand and pure expressions of
taste or feeling on the other. When we say that Richard's killing of

the princes in the Tower was wrong, we are expressing something of a different kind from what we are in 'a circle has a larger area than any polygon inscribed in it', and this difference is not simply one of subject-matter. In a judgment that murder has been committed, our feelings are engaged; we are not performing an ethical classification merely; we are expressing revulsion toward the act; while in the judgment about the circle, nothing of the kind need be involved. On the other hand, it seems equally clear that when we call the killing wrong we are expressing more than taste or feeling. Our remark is not like the sigh of boredom with which one might contemplate a gallery of non-objective paintings, or a swearing at someone in anger. We are not merely ejaculating or exclaiming; we mean to say something true, something that many would think as self-evidently true as what we said about the circle. On the surface, at least, a moral judgment is the expression *both* of an insight into truth *and* of an attitude or feeling.

But which is it primarily? When we say an action is right or wrong, do we mean to assert something as true, and then find on later inspection that our assertion was accompanied by feeling, or do we mean to express attraction or repulsion, though in a form of words deceptively like a statement? Among contemporary philosophers each of these views is firmly held. Professor Paton writes: 'It is just as certain that deliberate cruelty is wrong, as it is that grass is green or that two and two make four. Cruelty cannot be consistently willed by men who are trying to live coherent lives in the service of a coherent society.'[1] Here a moral judgment is regarded as an assertion of which we may demand truth and coherence. Rudolf Carnap takes an opposite view. Of the statement, 'killing is evil', he holds that 'it is merely the expression of a certain wish'; 'this statement is not verifiable and has no theoretical sense, and the same thing is true of all other value statements'; 'a value statement is nothing else than a command in misleading grammatical form'.[2] It is obvious that both these views cannot be true.

2. The issue, though so acute at present, is one to which much thought has been devoted by acute minds in the past. We shall do well at first to follow their lead. In considering the larger conflict between reason and feeling in western morals, we have seen that history

[1] *The Good Will*, 371
[2] *Philosophy and Logical Syntax*, 24–5

has provided some very illuminating experiments. In considering more narrowly the place of these two functions in ethical judgment, we shall again find it helpful to give some attention to history. We shall find, indeed, that in modern thought there has been a more or less steady advance, in which the suggestions of one school have been corrected and supplemented by the suggestions of another, so that the issue as it now comes to us has been greatly clarified and sharpened. Here again, for simplicity's sake, we shall narrow the field. The problem before us has been of particular and persisting interest to the succession of British moralists. Not only have all of them been concerned with it in one way or another; they have generally argued with their immediate predecessors in mind, so that their thought displays an instructive dialectic which brings the problem in the end to our own doorstep. I shall try to follow the main steps of this dialectic. But my concern is logical mainly, not historical, so I shall not feel bound at all points to cling to the historical order; what I shall try to show is how a series of able thinkers have successively closed blind alleys for us, and narrowed the problem to its present form.

3. If we by-pass the large figure of Hobbes, whose thought, however impressive, is not much to our present point, the first British thinkers to give themselves to our problem were thoroughgoing intellectualists. Some of them, notably Cudworth and More, took their cues from Plato. One of them, Samuel Clarke, a careful student of Newton, approached ethics from the side of mathematics and offered a case for the rational character of moral judgment that is so simple, clear, and modern in its sound, as to impress even a critical reader of the present day. He stated this case in the Boyle Lectures for 1705, which he delivered in St Paul's Cathedral. We may remark in passing that after the lectures had appeared in print, Clarke received a series of criticisms from an anonymous correspondent in Gloucester, criticisms so cogently argued that in a later edition Clarke published them together with his replies. It turned out that the weighty critic was a twenty-one-year-old student in an academy at Tewkesbury, who had induced a confederate to put Clarke off the scent by posting his letters in Gloucester. The later history of these young rogues is a lesson on the tragic fate of deceivers. The writer of the letters grew up to be Bishop Butler, his confederate to be Archbishop Secker of Canterbury. It was characteristic of Clarke's chivalrous spirit that, not many years later, he got his young critic appointed to the Rolls Chapel where Butler preached his classic *Sermons on Human Nature*.

Clarke's contention is that there is the closest kind of analogy between the fitness we find in right conduct and the necessity we find in mathematics. We see in a particular case, by the help of pins or apples, that two and two make four, or that a whole is not equal to its part. By implicitly comparing cases, we come to see that the special natures of apples and pins are irrelevant, that the relation is the same whatever the material, and that the whole *as such* is greater than the part. Our mind works in the same way in morals. A boy 'borrows' without permission a companion's ball; someone, to his indignation, serves him in the same way and then he begins to see that principles are involved, that the act, as such, of taking other people's property without their leave is wrong, and that treating other people as one would object to being treated oneself is in the nature of the case unreasonable—or wrong; they mean the same thing.

> 'He that refuses to deal with all men equitably, and with every man as he desires they should deal with him, is guilty of the same unreasonableness and contradiction in one case as he that in another case should affirm one number or quantity to be equal to another, and yet that other at the same time not to be equal to the first.'[1]

According to Clarke, then, when we call a particular act right or wrong, we are implicitly asserting a rule which, when abstracted and put nakedly before us, is self-evident. If I owe another man a duty this is not in virtue of *everything* in my nature, or everything in his, or of all the relations between us; that is why it is so easy to go off on a false scent in judging conduct, and why the reflective moralist has an advantage over the plain man. If I have the choice between telling someone the truth and telling him a falsehood, and, as far as consequences are concerned, cannot see that either course is better than the other, I should still tell him the truth, by reason of what he is and what I am, and the relations that hold between us. I am a being capable of speech who knows something he does not; he is a being who is interested in knowing what I know; an intelligent man would see as plainly that when two such natures were brought into touch, one should supply truth to the other, as that when a pentagon is in-

[1] Clarke, *A Discourse Concerning the Unchangeable Obligations of Natural Religion*, 1st ed., 65

scribed in a circle it must have the smaller area. In both cases the relation is a necessary one, prescribed by the natures of the terms. This necessity in the moral case Clarke describes as 'fitness'. His use of this term reminds us strongly of its use by the deontologists of our own day:

> 'that there is a fitness or suitableness of certain circumstances to certain persons, and an unsuitableness of others, founded in the nature of things and the qualifications of persons, antecedent to all positive appointment whatsoever; also that from the different relations of different persons one to another, there necessarily arises a fitness or unfitness of certain manners of behaviour of some persons toward others, is as manifest as that the proportions which flow from the essences of different mathematical figures have different congruities and incongruities between themselves. . . .'[1]

To the question, then, whether the judgment of right, in its main intention, is an expression of reason, of feeling, or of both, Clarke's answer is unequivocal: it is purely an expression of reason. To see that an act is right is to see that in view of the natures of the persons involved and the character of the circumstances, the act is fitting. Such insight is not only cognition, it is rational cognition, because it involves a grasp of the logically self-evident; it is as intellectual as anything in Euclid.

4. Now that there is much in our moral judgments which answers more or less closely to this description seems to me true. (1) In our judgment that a gratuitous falsehood is wrong there is surely something very like self-evidence. Such a judgment is not like 'this rose is yellow', where, for all we can see, the flower might just as well have some other colour, for the wrongness of lying seems to arise out of the character of lying as such. It does not always arise out of ill effects that we can foresee, since even if there is nothing to choose between the foreseeable consequences of lying and telling the truth, we should still find something morally unfitting in wanton deception. Nor does the judgment seem like a deduction from anything else. If someone were to challenge us and say that in these circumstances lying was a perfectly right and proper course, we should suspect that he was being cleverly perverse, and if he proved serious and persisted, we should probably be puzzled how to proceed. The case, as Clarke

[1] Clarke, *A Discourse Concerning the Unchangeable Obligations of Natural Religion,* 1st ed., 47

would remind us, is like that of two and two making four; if someone challenges that, you feel little hope of finding anything clearer or more certain that you can offer as evidence for it.

(2) We feel called upon to make our moral judgments consistent with each other, just as we do our geometrical judgments. When David was exulting over his success in stealing Bathsheba from Uriah, Nathan told him the story of the rich man who stole a poor man's ewe lamb; and when David swore that the man should die for it, Nathan pointed his prophetic finger and said 'Thou art the man'. Though David's moral sense was not of the acutest, even he could see that if what the rich man had done to the poor man was wrong, what he himself had done to Uriah could hardly be right, for to say so would be in principle to contradict himself. In short, judgments of rightness would seem to be expressions of reason not only when taken individually but also when taken jointly, in the sense that in making them we bow to the obligation that they should fit consistently together.

(3) They seem to be like mathematical judgments, again, in claiming to be impersonal and objective. We should think it absurd if a man who differed from another as to the sum of a column of figures suggested that on these matters tastes might differ, that we must not be intolerant, and that each of us had a right to his own opinion. Regarding a picture by Matisse, we may resign ourselves to such diversity, though even here we should do so rather reluctantly. But this is certainly not our attitude on moral issues, in spite of all that some uncritical anthropologists have done to encourage us in it. When a popular leader appears who argues that the 'big lie' is justifiable if he can get it widely enough accepted, or that breach of treaties is right if there is profit in it for the breaker, we do not regard this as an interesting and legitimate novelty in moral taste; we hold that a man has no right to such a taste; and we think that the man who allows his ambitions and desires to determine his position on such issues shows the same lack of integrity as the scientist who cooks his results to his own advantage. One can no more make such things right by feeling or calling or thinking them right than one can make the column of figures come out according to desire by becoming emotional about it. Against writers like Hobbes, who had held that right and duty were conventions merely, which did not exist in 'the state of nature', that conduct first began to be right or wrong only when men made an agreement to obey the law, Clarke's case was

crushing. He had only to point out that unless obligation were already recognized before the agreement was made, the very agreement that was supposed to bring it into being would have had no force. The claims that morality make upon us, like those of logic and mathematics, may help to explain our habits of thinking, but they are plainly more than habits of thinking themselves. A habit we can change. We can no more make the gratuitous infliction of pain upon another right than we can square the circle.

5. Such considerations as these make the rationalist reading of moral judgment highly plausible. Yet Clarke's argument proved so unpersuasive that within his own lifetime a reaction set in toward the extreme opposite of his view. The idea that a judgment of right is really the same sort of thing as a judgment in mathematics failed to convince the majority of moralists, and has continued to fail. Why?

(1) For one thing, because the concepts used in moral judgment have nothing like the *definiteness* to be found in mathematics. Mathematical concepts—notions of two and four and equality, of straight line, circle, and triangle—are as sharp and clear as human notions can possibly be, and as they are exchanged from mind to mind, we can be sure, for all practical purposes, that they remain absolutely the same. But who could say that in judging 'I ought not to deceive another gratuitously', the concepts of the two natures, in virtue of which the duty follows, has anything like this precision? Clarke tries to secure this precision for his concepts by making them abstractions and saying that just as the geometer uses, not the concrete figure before him, but the abstract and perfect circle which it stands for, so when we think about moral cases, we are not thinking about Jones and Brown, but about the rational-human-being-as-such displayed in each. But let anyone try to conceive precisely what the humanity is in Brown in virtue of which Jones should tell him the truth, and then compare the result with his concept of a circle, and the contrast will be painfully clear. And where the terms related are vague, the relations that unite them will, as a rule, be correspondingly vague. The precise necessities of geometry would vanish if the lines were not perfectly straight and the circles only moderately circular. Yet this is the sort of unsatisfactory material with which our moral judgments must commonly deal. We are not dealing with abstractions, but with *persons*, whose differences count. A man would fail grotes-

quely in his duty if he treated his wife as if she were the Platonic idea of a wife, his friends as if they were types out of La Bruyère, and his community as if it were the eternal essence of all communities, laid up in heaven. That is just not the way in which a morally sensitive person thinks. Hence the rationalist of this type is confronted with a dilemma. So far as he achieves definiteness by skimming the pure cream of abstraction from his terms, the grounds for his ascription of rightness disappear and his thought becomes ethically empty. On the other hand, so far as he preserves those individual differences which are all-important in actual judgment, the mathematical analogy melts away.

6. (2) Again, mathematics is timeless; it considers consequents, but never consequences. Most moral judgments, on the contrary, are passed on temporal acts that have trains of temporal consequences. Such consequences or the pre-vision of them, totally irrelevant in any mathematical context, are of the first importance for judging rightness and wrongness. At first glance it is plausible, as we have seen, to say that if lying is wrong, and self-evidently wrong, it is purely in virtue of men being rational beings. But see where this leads. If the connection is a necessary one, then between such beings lying must be wrong everywhere and always. And we cannot really accept that. It implies, for example, that the theatre manager was doing wrong when, knowing that the theatre, with many children present, was on fire, he announced to the audience in regretful tones that the leading lady had been taken ill and the performance would have to be adjourned, thereby averting panic and perhaps saving many lives. One cannot disregard consequences without breaking disastrously with our actual moral thinking.

Clarke never succeeded in reconciling their importance with his quasi-mathematical ethics. He did point out that many of our duties would remain duties, even though there was nothing to choose between the foreseeable consequences of doing them and not doing them. This was indeed significant, but it was not enough. Putting it on a merely individual basis, suppose a man sees that by doing his duty, he will involve himself in certain ruin or death; does that leave the duty unaffected? Clarke's answer to this showed the strain he was under; indeed it abandons his main position. He admitted that 'men never will generally, and indeed it is not very reasonably to be expected that they should, part with all the comforts of life, and even life itself, without expectation of any future recompense'.[1] But this is to set up two different kinds of reasonableness, one of which lies in doing the duty prescribed by abstract reason, and the other in ordering one's action with reference to the consequences. Plainly these two might conflict. And Clarke had nothing left, no convenient super-reasonableness, to arbitrate between them.

The best he could do was to suggest that if a man did his duty at great cost to himself, he would not, after all, be the loser in the end, since God would see to it in the next life that his sacrifice was duly rewarded. Unfortunately even this retreat was not logically open. For when asked on what ground he believed that God *was* thus just and benevolent, he gave an answer that made the appeal to this later reward untenable. The ground, he said, was that since the principles of right conduct, like those of mathematics, were self-evident and necessary, they must be God's principles also. But this was to argue that only because it was an absolute duty to *disregard* consequences did we have any ground for believing that we might reasonably take them into account; reason was still giving two incompatible verdicts. Besides, if God himself was committed to the first kind of reasonableness, why should he regard with favour, and generously reward, conduct that could only be justified by the other kind of reasonableness? Clarke's position thus collapsed. He saw that the appeal to consequences must be allowed; but could find no way of allowing it that did not involve him in incoherence.

7. (3) But perhaps the most obvious objection to this sort of rationalism, and the one that in fact prevailed against it, is that it gives no place to feeling in moral approval. Men remain obstinately convinced that in such approval feeling does have a part, though precisely what, they are not clear. They would be ready to agree that in mathematical judgments it plays no part at all. There is no reason to suppose that a man bereft of the power of feeling would have trouble in understanding what another man was saying as he ran through the multiplication table, since nothing but intellect is involved here. But suppose he heard what people commonly say as they read their newspapers. They read about a captain who sticks to his ship when it is in danger of foundering and does his best to save it, and they use such words as 'courageous', 'noble', 'devoted', in describing his conduct. Or they read of the use by certain govern-

[1] *Op. cit.,* 119

ments of drugs, sleeplessness, and torture, to extract from prisoners the sort of confession they desire, and describe such proceedings as 'base', 'wicked', and 'dastardly'. Would a man incapable of emotion catch what they meant? If the conduct of the captain or the torturers consisted merely of their bodily movements, he could no doubt follow such conduct with his mind's eye as clearly as anyone else. But what would he make of their nobility or their dastardliness? Are these emotionally neutral, like three-sidedness and circularity? Surely not. Feeling seems to have penetrated their very essence. And a man incapable of any glow of admiration or sympathy, or any warmth of moral indignation, who viewed the human scene as if it were nothing but a set of elaborate intersections of circles and triangles, would remain blind to what moral judgments are about.

8. In the second stage of the dialectic, the intellectualism of Clarke, Cudworth, and More was abandoned for an opposite extreme. Shaftesbury and Hutcheson thought the true analogue of moral judgment was to be found not in mathematics but in aesthetics, not in the judgment of necessity but in that of beauty. Both were men of keen artistic sensitiveness. Both were students of Aristotle, and for Aristotle goodness and beauty of character were indistinguishable; he used the compound word καλοκἀγαθός to suggest their convergence. The two philosophers, again, were inclined to restrict their thinking about ethics to a single one of the provinces, that of virtue and vice, that is, the state of one's dispositions or habitual affections, and this is the part of ethics—as opposed, for example, to the theory of merit, punishment, or obligation—to which the analogy of beauty most readily applies. Finally, they fixed their attention on that part of the moral act where the analogy is most plausible. No one would say that there need be anything beautiful in the outward embodiment of goodness, in Sidney's act, for instance, of passing the cup to the wounded soldier; the beauty lay within, just as the moral ugliness of Iago lay within, and as the beauty of character as a whole lies in the harmony and proportion of the affections.

What is it, then, that we are attributing to an act when we call it right, or to a character when we call it good? Is it simply beauty? Shaftesbury and Hutcheson often write as if it were. But that is not what they really mean. Goodness is not beauty, though it is the same sort of attribute and arouses in us similar feelings. Can it be defined? Hutcheson, the more exact and careful of the two, says that 'an action is formally good when it flowed from good affection in a just proportion'. This is not very helpful, since we are moved to ask at once what is then meant by 'good' when thus used of an affection, and what is meant by a 'just' proportion. It is useless to look to these writers for sharp answers to such questions, and probably if they had been pressed, they would have replied, like many writers of the present day, that ultimate moral qualities are beyond analysis or definition, though not for that reason either unreal or unclear. One cannot define 'relation' or 'time' or 'space' or 'red' or 'sweet', but most people do not find these notions obscure. Similarly we know perfectly well, these writers would say, what we mean by calling conduct good, even though the notion resists analysis into anything simpler. We are referring to a quality belonging not to outward behaviour, and not to the consequences of that behaviour, but to the attitude of will and feeling that it springs from; 'we have a distinct perception of beauty of excellence in the kind affections of rational agents'.[1]

9. What faculty or process is it by which this quality is grasped? Plainly not reason or intelligence. Intellectual gifts are useful in scheming for the future, but to reduce the perception of goodness or badness, as Clarke very nearly did, to the grasp of logical necessity seemed to these philosophers absurd. Men of fine moral perceptions have often been helpless infants in logic and mathematics. What is needed is something more akin to sympathy, though it is not precisely that either, but rather something rendered possible by sympathy. Here again our best key lies in the perception of beauty. What are we doing when we appreciate music? We are hearing sounds, of course, but the beauty of the music does not consist of the sounds, nor even the arrangements of the sounds; it is a quality that belongs to this arrangement, incapable itself of being heard, and yet as indubitably there as the sounds themselves. Since our experience of it is not active, as in thinking, but passive as in seeing or hearing, we may well call it a process of sense; but since it is not a sensing of any material thing or any strictly sensuous content, we may well distinguish it from our other senses as 'the aesthetic sense'.

Now the perception of goodness is closely parallel to this. The goodness of a man's conduct is not a characteristic like movement that can be actually seen in his behaviour; it is not his affection for others, nor even, if we speak exactly, the harmony or balance of his

[1] Hutcheson, *Enquiry into the Original of Our Ideas of Beauty and Virtue*, 118

affections, though the two writers sometimes say such things. It is a non-sensuous quality attaching to his affections. And what better name can be found for our response to it than 'the moral sense'? Like the sense of beauty, this moral sense is so imbued with feeling that our authors find no harm in describing it as itself a kind of feeling. To perceive the goodness of an action is to approve it; to approve it 'is to feel approbation for it or to appreciate it; and appreciation is emotion. The pendulum thus swung in a generation from the extreme rationalism of Clarke to its opposite pole in Shaftesbury and Hutcheson. What was approved in conduct was no longer a fitness apprehended by reason, but a quality belonging to the agent's feelings, a quality whose presence we could discern only with the aid of sympathy, and whose apprehension was itself essentially a matter of feeling. The seat of moral judgment had abruptly shifted from head to heart.

10. The next step in the dialectic was taken by a philosopher of greater stature than any of these men, David Hume. Hume is sometimes thought of as an arch-destroyer. And for those whose allegiance is to reason in ethics and metaphysics, the description is no doubt justified. Certainly in ethics he is much nearer to Hutcheson than to the rationalist Clarke. Still, he departed widely from both, while partly accepting both; if our dialectic were Hegelian, Hume would represent a synthesis of which Clarke and Hutcheson were thesis and antithesis. And since his position is a highly sophisticated one which is still thought by many philosophers to be in all essentials sound, it will be well to look rather closely at the roles that he assigned to reason and feeling in moral approval.

Hume held as firmly as Shaftesbury and Hutcheson did that the rightness of conduct could not be perceived or established by reason. In writing on ethics, both in the *Treatise* and in the *Inquiry*, he makes it his first concern to show this, and he offers a variety of arguments for it. None of these, singly or taken together, seem to me conclusive. But Hume's authority has carried so much weight that we shall do well to examine at least those of them that he regarded as most decisive.

11. (1) First, to say that the rightness of action is perceived by reason, he argues, is equivalent to saying that an insight of reason can move us to act, but since it is clear that no such insight *can* move us to act, the perception of rightness cannot be a rational one. This must be expanded a little. Suppose I see that I ought to do a certain act, say keep a promise, and suppose this 'seeing' is a rational process. Then, says Hume, we are asked to believe that this purely rational perception of duty can serve as a motive for doing my duty. If this were not true, if we could never say that we did something *because* we saw we ought to do it, then rational conduct, in the sense of conduct ordered by reason, becomes impossible; and it is for the rational ordering of life that rationalist writers on morals are pleading. Very well, is it the case that knowing something to be our duty does at times make us do it? No, Hume answers, never. By thinking about keeping our promise, we may see that keeping it is bound up with much that we want—the confidence and goodwill, for example, of the man to whom we have made it, but that which moves us to action is never anything that thinking reveals to us; it is the chance existence in us of *desires* for what thinking may disclose. If we felt no desire for the confidence of others, or anything else that is bound up with keeping promises, knowledge, even if omniscient, would not produce the faintest flicker of action; 'reason of itself is utterly impotent in this particular'.[1] Since, then, the rationalist view of how duty is perceived entails that this perception should be able to move the will, and this implication is false, that which entails it must also be false, and the rationalist view must be rejected.

In spite of the stress Hume placed on it, this argument is quite unconvincing. (a) The entailment on which it turns is no necessary part of the rationalist case, and could hardly have been thought so except by confusing different meanings of 'approval'. If, in considering whether to keep a promise, I approve the proposal, that may mean, and often did mean indiscriminately among earlier writers on ethics, either (i) the recognition that the act would be right, (ii) the feeling of an 'approving' emotion toward it, (iii) the desire to do it, or (iv) the actual election of it in practice. Now there is no reason why a rationalist should not hold that (i), the recognition of the act as right, is quite distinct from the others, and indeed may be present while any or all of the others are absent. It is perfectly possible to say that my recognition of an act as the right one is a purely intellectual affair, but that I shall not go on to do it unless moved by something else, such as a feeling, desire, or resolution. What the rationalist is maintaining is that the discernment or recognition itself is the work of reason, and one does not show this false by first making it mean much

[1] *Treatise of Human Nature*, Bk. III, Pt. 1, Sec. 1

more than it need mean, and then refuting this gratuitous addition.

(b) Such plausibility as Hume's argument has is largely gained by his choice of examples. When the rationalist is told that, on his own theory, the perception that X is his duty is necessarily connected with an impulse to do it, he may be tempted to say, 'Yes, this does seem to be true and is surely harmless; why shouldn't I believe it?', and only when he is securely entangled does he realize that he has strayed into a corner where Hume's web has been spun for him. But he need not have strayed there at all. If, instead of talking about the judgment of duty he had talked about the judgment of right, as applied to other people or to his own past, Hume's criticism would have had small plausibility. The judgment that one's past keeping of a promise was right, or that some tennis player at Wimbledon did right when, as reported in the morning paper, he threw away a point, is plainly not connected with any election on my own part to do the act approved. Here the insight and performance are sharply disconnected. If Hume's discussion had focused upon judgments of this kind instead of those of obligation, the rationalist would have perceived more easily the illicit burden of implication that had been foisted upon him.

(c) Hume is assuming in his argument that reason in fact never does move the will, and he assumes this on the strength of evidence given in his book on the passions. When one turns to this book and studies the evidence,[1] one again finds it indecisive. To review that evidence would take more time than we can afford. But it is worth pointing out that unless this often questioned and somewhat questionable premise is true, the argument obviously fails.

12. (2) Hume maintains, in the second place, that if the perception of rightness is a matter of reason, we shall have to say that rightness is the same as truth, and this is absurd. What reason deals with is propositions which are capable of being true or false, of being relevant to each other and contradicting each other. A proposition *about* rightness may be true or false; but if rightness or fittingness is, as rationalists claim, something belonging to the act itself, then its inherence in the act is no more true or false than the inherence of juiciness in an apple or of hardness in a stone; it is merely a fact which, as neither true nor false, is outside the province of reason. The status given to rightness by the rationalists is thus inconsistent with the way

[1] *Treatise*, Bk. II, Ch. 3, Sec. 3

in which they allege we know it. If it were merely a relation among ideas, they might well hold that it is known by reason. But they cannot maintain at once that it is a fact or relation in the nature of things and *also* known by reason.

This is a preposterous argument. If, when we know that A is B, we are knowing only a proposition and not a fact, then we can never know that our proposition itself is true. For in order to know that, we must, according to Hume, be able to perceive the agreement or correspondence between proposition and fact, and in order to do that, in turn, we must be able to see the arrangement in fact to which our proposition corresponds. Unless we can do this, we can have no knowledge, properly speaking, of the world at all. But Hume admits that we *can* grasp these arrangements in fact; in the very passage in which his argument is stated he admits that propositions may be compared with the real relations whose existence they assert, and he would not deny that reason can perceive the numerical relations among fingers and toes. But if it can do such things, it is idle to say that it is confined to the sphere of propositions or truth as distinct from fact, and idle too to say that if rightness is rationally grasped, it must fall outside the realm of fact in the limbo of the merely ideal. Thus Hume's argument proves too much. If the mere knowability of a relation is sufficient proof that it does not belong to the nature of things, we can never know or hope to know anything; and this involves a scepticism from which even Hume recoiled.

13. (3) But his chief reliance in the argument against rationalism lay in a consideration of a different kind. This was the failure of the rationalists to make clear what they meant by the rightness grasped by reason. Rightness, they said, consisted in the fittingness of act to situation, and this fittingness either was, or depended on, a relation of some kind; but then of *what* kind? Nero murdered his mother; there was an act that everyone would agree to be wrong; the rationalists would say that it was self-evidently wrong, and that the wrongness lay in some relation that it set up between agent and patient. But when they attempted to abstract this relation and place it in a clear light, it belied their claims, for it always turned out to be a relation that was morally neutral. In the case just mentioned it is obviously so. Abstractly considered, what is the relation established by Nero through his action? It is that of an offspring's exclusion from existence of its parent. Now if it is this relation *as such* that makes the action wrong, it must do so wherever it appears. And this it plainly does not. Here Hume introduces his famous analogy of tree and sapling:

'To put the affair, therefore, to this trial, let us choose any inanimate object, such as an oak or elm; and let us suppose that, by the dropping of its seed, it produces a sapling below it, which, springing up by 'degrees, at last overtops and destroys the parent tree: I ask if, in this instance, there be wanting any relation which is discoverable in parricide or ingratitude? Is not the one tree the cause of the other's existence; and the latter the cause of the destruction of the former, in the same manner as when a child murders his parent? . . . . the relations are the same: and as their discovery is not in both cases attended with a notion of immorality, it follows that that notion does not arise from such a discovery.'[1]

This result, Hume argues, is typical. When the relation in which the rightness or wrongness is supposed to consist is set forth nakedly, it always turns out to be one that holds also among objects where no morality exists. It cannot, therefore, be the locus of rightness or wrongness where morality does exist.

This again is quite unconvincing. The difference between the two cases far outweighs their likeness. There is, to be sure, an abstract biological nexus between sapling and oak which appears also between Nero and his mother, and therefore each can be described as the destruction of parent by offspring, but no rationalist ever held that what made Nero's murder of his mother wrong was the thin abstraction gained by omitting all the differences between these cases. The relation between a son who knows what he is doing and a mother with memories, affections, and hopes, is so utterly different from that of a non-sentient sapling and tree, that for moral purposes the analogy between them is simply non-existent. The relation between the human beings is different because the terms of that relation are different, almost as different as terms can be.[2] To call it the same as that which holds between the trees would be like saying that when a man and a flower both seek the sunshine, or nod their heads, or curl up and sleep, they are both engaged in the same activities. Rationalists hold, it is true, that there are types of virtue and vice which embrace many

[1] *Treatise*, Bk. III, Pt. I, Sec. I, pp. 175–6; the example of Nero occurs in the *Inquiry Concerning the Principles of Morals*, Appendix I.
[2] Cf. D. D. Raphael's *Moral Sense*, 57–60, and his discussion generally of Hume's arguments against rationalism.

resembling cases, so that if it is wrong for A to deceive B under circumstances x, y, z, it is wrong for C to deceive D under similar circumstances. But the theory that right and wrong are so independent of circumstances that if it is wrong of A to deceive B, it must also be wrong for him to catch a fish by deceiving it or to tell a lie to the lamp-post, is a theory that no sane rationalist would for a moment acknowledge as his own.

14. Hume considered these arguments, and a few others of less weight, to be decisive against the view that we perceive the rightness of conduct by reason. We have seen that they are very far from decisive. But we must now insist on the other side of Hume's attitude toward rationalism. He never meant to say that reason has no place at all in moral judgment. It does not, to be sure, have the exclusive place; it does not even have the chief place; but it does have a humble and useful office of its own. What is that office? It is to place an act in perspective so that the judgment finally rendered on it may be circumspect and well informed. When a man is choosing a profession, the final vote is cast, Hume would say, by his desire or sentiment. 'But in order to pave the way for such a sentiment, and give a proper discernment of its object, it is often necessary, we find, that much reasoning should precede, that nice distinctions be made, just conclusions drawn, distant comparisons formed, complicated relations examined, and general facts fixed and ascertained.'[1] This is reason's work. Nearly every choice we make has its effects for better or worse on our own or others' lives; it is the business of the responsible man to foresee these effects, so far as important and relevant, and to make his choice in the light of them. Only by the use of reason can this provision be achieved. Thus, while the rationalists were mistaken in holding that reason itself pronounces the moral judgment or achieves the distinctively moral insight, they were correct to this extent, that reason is the indispensable adjunct and aid to such judgment. I recently saw a Scottish farmer appear in a large field dotted with sheep among which he wanted to make some sort of selection. He had at his heels a well-trained sheep dog, and he had only to give this trusty lieutenant a word to produce a performance astonishing in its thoroughness, speed, and expertness; in a very few minutes the scattered flock was rounded up at his feet. Reason in Hume's theory is the sheep-dog of the moral faculty. Its business is to use all possible skill

[1] *Inquiry*, Sec. 1

in rounding up the relevant facts through memory, analogy, and pre-
diction, and presenting them before the judge as the material for his
decision. Hume would not have denied that this was an extremely
important service. He would only have added that the sheep dog
makes itself absurd if it tries to usurp the place of its master and do
the judging also.

15. The question then presents itself, who is this judge and master?
Here Hume sides with the 'sentimentalists'. But just as his rejection
of Clarke was carefully qualified, so was his acceptance of Shaftesbury and Hutcheson. They had said that the goodness of a man or
of his conduct—and they tended to identify the two—was a special
kind of quality, not sensible like a colour or sound, and not conceptual either, if that meant apprehensible by reason, like circularity.
As we have seen, they thought its closest analogy was with the beauty
of a picture or a statue. Hume will have none of this. There is no such
quality as beauty. There is no such quality as goodness or rightness.

'Euclid has fully explained all the qualities of the circle; but has not,
in any proposition, said a word of its beauty. The reason is evident. The
beauty is not a quality of the circle. It lies not in any part of the line
whose parts are equally distant from a common centre.'[1]

It is the same with moral qualities.

'Take any action allowed to be vicious, wilful murder, for instance.
Examine it in all lights and see if you can find that matter of fact, or
real existence, which you call *vice*. In whichever way you take it, you
find only certain passions, motives, volitions, and thoughts. There is no
other matter of fact in the case. The vice entirely escapes you. . . .'

One might be tempted to discount Hume's argument here as one
that would be made automatically by anyone who held his theory of
knowledge, since according to that theory, all our ideas are copies of
what comes to us through sensation; hence if anyone alleged an
idea of what was not sensory in character, it would be ruled out a
priori. This mechanical process may have operated in Hume's mind,
as one is quite sure it has in the minds of some of his successors. But
it would be unfair to dismiss his argument on such grounds, for we
find it startlingly strong on its own merits. Try to point out the

[1] *Inquiry*, Appendix 1

beauty of a rose as a character distinct from the factual qualities and relations that compose it, and you find the sought-for character vanishing perpetually in mist. Try to isolate in your thought a distinct quality of goodness belonging to an experience, or a distinct quality or relation of rightness belonging to an act, and again you are puzzled, tantalized, and baffled. We seem to assume that a rose is beautiful very much as it is red, and an act right in the same obvious way as it is brief or violent; but whereas we can isolate these other qualities, on reflection, with complete clearness and ease, we find the beauty, goodness and rightness so hard to pin down, so impalpable and elusive, that we are likely to end by capitulating to Hume in helpless bewilderment. It seems strange to say that qualities which artists and moralists have talked about, or supposed themselves to be talking about these two thousand years and more are so many ghosts that have never existed at all. But hard as it is to believe this, it seems even harder to meet Hume's challenge to capture one of these ghosts and produce it for inspection.

16. Of course Hume does not deny that we say anything at all when we talk about goodness and beauty. What, then, are we saying? His own answer, as usual, is admirably clear. We are not declaring something about the make-up of roses or persons or actions; we are reporting our feelings toward them. We are talking less about them than about ourselves. Murder is wrong, we declare roundly, and then, under an ancient and general delusion, we may start examining the act to find where the wrongness lies. But this is hopeless.

> 'The vice entirely escapes you as long as you consider the object. You never can find it till you turn your reflection into your own breast, and find a sentiment of disapprobation which arises in you towards this action . . . . It lies in yourself, not in the object. So that when you pronounce any action or character to be vicious, you mean nothing but that from the constitution of your nature you have a feeling or sentiment of blame from the contemplation of it.'[1]

To this the rationalist may retort, 'You are really conceding, after all, that the moral judgment is a "pronouncement", it reports the occurrence of approbation or disapprobation, and hence is capable of truth, and hence again is more than a feeling; it is, or may be, knowledge'. Hume would not be troubled. He would agree that the 'pro-

[1] *Treatise*, Bk. III, Pt. i, Sec. i, near end

nouncement' was a judgment, but would point out that the act which it reports, the actual moral estimate or appraisal, is not a judgment, is not true or false, and has nothing rational about it; it is a response of pure feeling. And it is this feeling that is the essence of the matter. The judgment only echoes it, and without the feeling would be empty, while the feeling could, and often does, occur without the judgment. The 'insight' or 'perception' that an act is right *is* simply that warm feeling about it which we call approbation. And the object of this approbation is the act itself, not some illusory quality of rightness in it; the rightness has now died as a quality, and been resurrected as an attitude of the beholder.

17. Must we say, then, that no moral approval is more reasonable or unreasonable than any other? Strictly speaking, yes. Hume is willing to admit, however, that approval may be reasonable in a metaphorical sense. The act that one approves may be conceived thinly or thickly, fragmentarily or in the context of causes and effects, and its degree of 'reasonableness' varies accordingly. The judge who presides at a murder case studies the act in the context of the agent's motives and provocations, and the record and character of the victim; his final response is to the act in an extensive matrix of circumstances; and it is in that sense, therefore, a far more reasonable response than a first impulsive reaction.

Still, the fact that all this is taken into account does not make the moral response, when it comes, one whit less purely emotional. The approval or disapproval of an act by the most reflective of justices is itself as entirely a matter of feeling, and as completely non-rational, as the gurgle of a child over a bouncing ball. We can thus see what Hume meant when he said that in moral matters 'reason is, and ought only to be, the slave of the passions';[1] it would be helpless by itself, and there is nothing else for it to serve. We can see too that if no moral choice is an affair of reason at all, it clearly follows that no such choice is, strictly, more reasonable than any other. Hume not only draws this conclusion, but drives it home relentlessly.

'It is not contrary to reason to prefer the destruction of the whole world to the scratching of my finger. It is not contrary to reason for me to choose my total ruin to prevent the least uneasiness of an Indian, a person wholly unknown to me . . . . In short, a passion must be accom-

[1] *Treatise*, Bk. II, Pt. 3, Sec. 3

panied with some false judgment in order to its being unreasonable; and even then it is not the passion, properly speaking, which is unreasonable, but the judgment.'[1]

This position is somewhat shocking to common sense; and to Hume's reputation as arch-destroyer in metaphysics it added a like reputation in ethics. But he was far too massive a presence to be exorcized by a lifting of eyebrows. His case, when it came to be examined, proved disconcertingly strong. Indeed, some of the clearest-headed philosophers now living believe that it has not yet been effectively answered, for the very good reason that it is in essentials unanswerable. Whether we agree with this or not, it would be holding Hume at less than his true worth if we took as the antithesis to him, in the pendulum movement we are tracing, any of the legion of little figures who rose to shake their fists at him. Price, to be sure, was not a little figure, and he has been unduly thrown into the shadow by Hume. Still, we shall do well, I think, to look farther forward to a critic who could meet the formidable Hume on more even terms. Such a critic we undoubtedly have in Henry Sidgwick.

18. C. D. Broad startled some readers by his judgment that Sidgwick's *Methods of Ethics* is 'on the whole the best treatise on moral theory that has ever been written',[2] but it is a judgment with which, so far as my own reading goes, I should concur. Some of the conclusions of this work, most notably its hedonism, have not carried conviction to most students, certainly not to me. But for combined subtleness, thoroughness, lucidity, and fairness, I know of no equal to it in ethical literature. Writing on ethics has often gone to one or other of the two extremes of homiletics and logic-chopping, of so strong a desire, on the one hand, to make the good prevail as to lead to a neglect of rigorous analysis and, on the other, of so strong a preoccupation with analysis that one loses sight of ethics in a tangle of logic and linguistics. Sidgwick's acuteness was equalled by his sanity and moral seriousness; and for judicial detachment—the somewhat bleak, but clear, full light in which he sees things—he stands quite alone, so far as I know, in philosophic history. It is a sad thought, but an inevitable one, that the interesting people of the world are as a rule unreasonable ones, and that a man who never raises his

[1] *Treatise*, Bk. II, pt. 3, Sec. 3.
[2] *Five Types of Ethical Theory*, 143.

voice, or allows impulse to take him a hair's breadth out of the line
of fairness and good sense, is bound to seem dull. To most types of
reader, Sidgwick is irredeemably dull, while writers with far feebler
intellectual powers who speak in tones of prophesy, like Nietzsche
and Kierkegaard, are listened to with a respect they ill deserve. But
for those who want to know simply what ethical theories make sense
and what do not, and who are bored with attempts to make the subject interesting, Sidgwick's book is supreme.

It is a main thesis of this book that moral judgments are an expression of reason. Most men assume this without question, and
though they may be mistaken about this as about other things,
Sidgwick holds that one who differs from them must assume the
burden of proof. That they do hold this conviction is clear enough;
'we commonly think that wrong conduct is essentially irrational, and
can be shown to be so by argument; and though we do not conceive
that it is by reason alone that men are influenced to act rightly, we
still hold that appeals to the reason are an essential part of all moral
persuasion . . .'[1] In a sense, of course, even Hume would agree with
this. He admits, as we have seen, that reason is an indispensable tool
for bringing before our minds both means to our ends and alternative
ends themselves. Sidgwick considers whether this is all that reason
can do in such judgment, and concludes, that it does much more.
His own views on the office of reason are scattered widely through
the five hundred pages of his book, but it will not be unfair, I think,
to bring them together under two heads, his grounds for rejecting
Hume's emotionalist view, and his own alternative to it.

19. (1) If Hume's view is correct, approval is a feeling, and the
judgment that an act is right or a duty is a statement that the feeling
is actually felt toward it—usually in the light of its consequences—
by oneself or others. According to Sidgwick this misreports what we
mean to say. Roughly, what we are really asserting is an *ought*, and
this takes us to be asserting an *is*. Suppose that three hospitals ask me
for a contribution, and I try to make up my mind which, if any, to
contribute to, and how much. I conclude that I should give a certain
amount to C, and none to the others. Now if Hume is correct, what
I have been trying to find out is the actual state of my feelings toward various courses, and when I conclude that giving a certain
amount to C is right, I am reporting the state of my feeling about it.

[1] *Methods of Ethics*, 7th Ed., 23

Sidgwick thinks that by merely inspecting our meaning we can see that this is not so.

He would say, I think, that Hume's interpretation mistakes both the subject and the predicate of our actual judgment. Our subject is the suggested act, not ourselves or our feelings about it. If we were talking about our feelings, the report of an expert psychologist as to what is actually felt would be grounds for calling the judgment true or false, whereas in fact we should take such a report as irrelevant. Again, the predicate we ascribe to the act is not descriptive of any existent thing. Hume was correct in saying that rightness was not this kind of predicate; he was mistaken in saying that if a predicate was not of this kind, it was not a predicate at all. Sidgwick held that 'the fundamental notion represented by the word "ought" or "right" is essentially different from all notions representing facts of physical or psychical experience'.[1] It was the notion of what more recent ethicists would describe as a 'non-natural characteristic', one that made no part of nature as investigated by the natural sciences. And unfortunately it was 'too elementary to admit of any formal definition'.[2] This may raise suspicions about it. But so far as these suspicions are based on an antecedent conviction that no such character is thinkable, Sidgwick would be little moved by them. In this matter he was empirical without being an empiricist; that is, he was trying to find what actually was in our thought, without any preconceived theory, drawn from the supposed origin of knowledge, as to what this must be. His first argument, then, against the emotionalist view was that if it were correct, a moral judgment would be an assertion of fact— in this case of psychological fact—and that in such typical moral judgments as that of the rightness of some act yet in prospect, we were not asserting about fact at all.

Sidgwick offered other arguments, applying some to judgments of right, and others to judgments of intrinsic good. Since for him both types of judgment were in the same sense rational while for Hume they were both non-rational, we may consider these arguments without specifying in each case the context in which they were offered.

20. (2) If Hume is correct, when I judge 'that act is right', I am reporting not a character of the act, but a feeling of my own. (He also held that I am reporting the feeling which prevails in my society,

[1] *Methods of Ethics*, 7th Ed., 25
[2] *Ibid.*, 32

shifting from the one view to the other as suited his argument, without seeing, apparently, how different they were).[1] Then when I say, 'truth ought to be spoken', and you say 'truth ought not to be spoken', we are not expressing conflicting opinions, but only reporting two coexisting facts about our feelings. There is no conflict of opinion at all. Sidgwick thinks this paradoxical and untrue.

21. (3) Indeed he thinks it so obvious that we are really expressing conflicting opinions that he believes the emotionalists must have something else in mind than what they say. They can hardly intend that we do not mean to express opinions about truth-speaking at all, for we do very plainly mean to; they must be saying that, if we knew what we were about, we should see that we could not *sensibly* mean to, that the 'subjective fact of my approbation is all that there is any *ground* for stating, or perhaps that it is all that any reasonable person is prepared on reflection to affirm'.[2] Is this, then, a tenable view?

No, Sidgwick answers, it is still untenable. There are cases, to be sure, regarded by writers like Hume as similar, where this sort of analysis might serve. If I call a certain food disagreeable, and my remark is challenged, I may content myself with insisting only that I dislike it. 'But there appears to me to be a fundamental difference', writes Sidgwick, 'between this case and that of moral feeling.' What *is* the difference? It is this, that whereas in the case of the food, my meaning is, or may be, exhausted in the report of how I feel, in the moral case it is never so exhausted; besides the feeling, I am pointing to something in the object that is taken to justify the feeling. I am not simply asserting that I happen to feel in a certain way; I am asserting—if indeed there is any reference to feeling at all—that I feel in this way because, independently of my feeling, the act is right. 'The peculiar emotion of moral approbation is, in my experience, inseparably bound up with the conviction, implicit or explicit, that the conduct approved is "really" right—i.e. that it cannot, without error, be disapproved by any other mind.'[3] In short I do not call the action right because I feel in a certain way; I feel in this way because I think the action right. And Sidgwick goes on to show that where I do not think the action right, this is reflected in a difference in my

---

[1] Cf. Raphael, *The Moral Sense*, 76–7
[2] *Methods of Ethics*, 27
[3] *Ibid.*, and cf. p. 77: 'it is an essential characteristic of a moral feeling that it is bound up with an apparent cognition of something more than mere feeling.'

feeling about it. If one became convinced that on a certain occasion—
on which, for example, one was invited to disclose the secrets of an
atomic bomb to an enemy—telling the truth was wrong rather than
right, one's feeling about it would be 'quite different in kind and
degree'. Feeling is distinct from, but follows and provides an index
to, the intellectual conviction.

22. (4) Hume was in a sense a utilitarian; he thought we called an
action right in virtue of the pleasure we believed it normally produced.
But if we asked him what we meant by calling the pleasure good, he
would say that we were referring not to some quality of worth or
value in the pleasure, but, once more, to our liking or desire for it.
This liking or desire *was* the goodness, in the only intelligible sense,
and hence its variations in intensity gave the measure of goodness.
Sidgwick saw that this theory could not be worked out consistently
with our actual ways of thinking, and he criticized the theory through
that very aesthetic analogy which was so favoured by emotionalist
writers.

We call a musical composition good, for example. Do we call it so
in virtue of *any* kind of pleasure that we may happen to like, e.g. in
blasts of loud noise or tom-tom regularity of beat or the faithful
imitation of a cuckoo, or, on the other hand, in virtue of a more
special satisfaction, a satisfaction derived from music that conforms
to a certain ideal? And if the answer is the latter, as it apparently must
be, can we rule out conformity to the ideal and fix on our feeling
alone as contributing to the goodness? If pleasure, or more strictly,
the satisfaction with which we contemplate it, is to serve as the index
of aesthetic goodness, it must be the kind of satisfaction that is taken
in a particular kind of object; and the same holds of our satisfaction
with moral goodness.

Again, when I am talking about my own feeling, it is clear that I
am myself the final judge; if I say that I take satisfaction or pleasure
in something, I have no doubt of what I am saying, and should think
it absurd to suggest that there was someone else who knew better.
But when I venture to say that a new work of Stravinsky is good, I am
surely making no such claims. I am quite ready to admit that, whatever my feelings about it, I may very well be mistaken. Hence to say
that something is good is plainly different from saying that I take
pleasure or satisfaction in it.

Nor is it true that the degree of goodness attributed corresponds to the intensity of feeling; 'connoisseurs of wines, pictures, etc., often retain their intellectual faculty of appraising the merits of the objects which they criticize, and deciding on their respective places in the scale of excellence, even when their susceptibilities to pleasure from these objects are comparatively blunted and exhausted'.[1] Indeed, there may be savages who take as intense a delight in their tom-toms as ever Schweitzer in Bach. But we should hardly take that as conclusive evidence that what they delight in is equally good. A similar line of argument applies to moral appreciations.

Sidgwick makes further relevant comments when he comes to Hobbes's suggestion that 'whatsoever is the object of any man's desire, that it is which he for his part calleth good, and the object of his aversion, evil'. In essentials, this is Hume again, since it lodges goodness in the attitude rather than the object. The obvious difficulty with it is that a man sometimes desires intensely what at the same time he knows or believes to be bad, for example, 'revenge, when he knows that his true interest lies in reconciliation'. If being desired is all we mean by 'good', how can we call this bad while aware that we desire it desperately? Furthermore, something that we very much want 'may not be found good when fruition comes'; 'it may turn out "a Dead Sea apple", mere dust and ashes in the eating'. Is the same thing, then, both good and bad, or good for a while and then bad for a while? It certainly accords better with ordinary thought to say that at first we thought it was good, but that it turned out to be really bad. Finally, many things are out of our power and we should consider it rather foolish to go on desiring them when we know they are unattainable—such things as perfect weather and perfect health. But we do not necessarily regard them as less good because our desires for them have lost the intensity they once had.

23. For these reasons Sidgwick rejects the view that judgments of right and good are either feelings or reports of feeling. Moral judgment always contains a rational element. What is this element? Here we come to the theory which Sidgwick would offer as his alternative to Hume. His suggestions, as before, are scattered widely in his book, but they are of such interest and importance, that we must try to assemble and summarize them. Professor Broad has said that reason

'includes three cognitive powers, viz. (a) the power of forming *a priori* concepts, i.e. concepts of characteristics which are not sensibly mani-

[1] *Methods of Ethics*, 108

fested in any instance and are not composed of characteristics which have separately been sensibly manifested in various instances; (b) the power of recognizing that a conjunction of attributes is an instance of a necessary connexion between these attributes, i.e. the power of Intuitive Induction, as Mr Johnson calls it; and (c) the power of inferring conclusions from premises.'[1]

Sidgwick was a rationalist in the sense that he believed that reason in all three of these meanings entered into our moral judgments. All moralists would probably agree that in forming such judgments we use reason in the third sense, in which it is equivalent to reasoning. It is Sidgwick's insistence on the other two that distinguishes his rationalism.

(1) He believed, as we have seen, that neither rightness nor goodness was a character in the natural world, that is, the sort of character that could be sensed, or occupy space. Value is not existence; ought is not reducible to is. Right and good are a priori, not in the sense that we impose them on objects in knowing them, for they may belong to acts or objects without being known to do so, but in the sense that they are not given empirically, and must be intellectually grasped. It may be protested that such characters are mere wraiths, that there is nothing in the real world answering to such a description. But is this true? No one doubts that things are really similar or dissimilar to each other, but similarity and dissimilarity are not themselves sensed. There may be a dozen eggs in a nest, but twelveness is not an empirical characteristic. Sidgwick's convictions about the non-empirical nature of rightness and goodness was the more striking because of his hedonism; he held that what made an act objectively right was the fact that it produced at least as much pleasure as any possible alternative act, and that what made an experience good was the pleasure it contained; and both these points must be empirically determined. But you could not *identify* an act's being right with its producing pleasure, for then when we said that the act producing the greatest pleasure was right, we should be saying nothing more than if we said that the act producing the greatest pleasure produced the greatest pleasure. and Sidgwick was clear that we were saying more. He took a like view about good. These moral attributes were worths or values, and values, while attaching to empirical objects, must be non-empirically known.

[1] *Five Types of Ethical Theory*, 265

24. (2) He held, again, that in morals we have a variety of insights that must be called rational because they are necessary and universal. These insights were of three kinds.

(i) First there were insights, some absolute and some comparative, about intrinsic goods. (a) Sidgwick thought that everyone makes absolute judgments about what is good, whether he admits this or not. If you ask a man why he buys a hammer, he may answer, 'to drive nails with'; if you ask him why he wants to drive nails, he may say 'to put up a shelf'; if you go on asking why, he may answer successively 'to keep some books conveniently at hand', 'to facilitate my work', 'to increase the pleasure in my work'. If you ask him why he should want pleasure in his work, he would regard that as a foolish question, because if 'why?' means 'for what further end?', as it did in the earlier questions, there is no answer to it; pleasure is the end of the line; it is wanted not because it is good *for* something, but because it is good in itself. Of course many other intrinsic goods have been alleged, and no one can avoid believing in some such good, for if we only wanted *a* for the sake of *b*, and *b* for the sake of *c*, and so on without end, there would be nothing that we wanted for itself, and the chain would end in the air. But though the question 'why?' has no answer here if it asks for some ulterior end, it is not merely pointless, for there is another way of justifying our wanting something besides showing what it leads to, namely showing that it is good in itself. We have this insight when we see, for example, that pleasure, by reason of being the sort of experience that it is, is good, and that intense pain, for the same reason, is bad. Sidgwick would say that it was a muddle to confuse such an insight with an empirical one, such as 'This lump of coal is black'. In the empirical judgment there is no insight that the coal *must* be black, while in the judgment about the intense pain, we do see that being bad is *entailed by* the nature of the pain; and again, the empirical judgment would at best entitle us to say of another lump of coal that it would *probably* be black, while we are prepared to say of *any* pain as intense as this that it will be bad. In short we are seeing a connection which, because necessary and universal, is as truly an insight of reason as the perception that shape entails size or that the diagonal of a square divides it in half. Indeed Sidgwick thought we could see by intuition 'that happiness is the only rational ultimate end of action'.[1]

(b) He would say that we have a similar kind of insight when we

[1] *Methods of Ethics*, 201

D

see that *a* is better than *b*. If one compares the pain of a finger caught in a door and the pleasure of a cool drink when thirsty, one sees that the second is better, more worth having, than the first, and here again, since, given the nature of the terms, the relation *must* be what it is, the insight is not contingent but necessary. At this point one may anticipate a certain kind of objection. Do not people differ in their valuations, and if they do, is it not the height of dogmatism for any- one to claim necessity for his own insight? This is a tiresome objection. For (*a*) there is no reason why one who holds that judgments of this kind can and do occur should hold that we never make mistakes about them, or that one's own judgments are infallible. Sidgwick was peculi- arly alive to the difficulties of distinguishing what we may call certainty, in the sense of self-evident necessity, from certitude, in the sense of emotional conviction; he laid down an admirable list of requirements that must be fulfilled before he would concede the former status to a proposition; and no one could be more cautious or less dogmatic than he in intellectual practice. (*b*) It is worth pointing out that those who object to insights of this kind do not themselves dispense with them; they only find them in other places. They insist on empirical evidence or demonstrative proof, forgetting that empirical evidence can never render a general proposition more than probable, and that the rules of probability themselves rest on the kind of insight here in question; or else forgetting that demonstration depends on logical principles, and that these too must be established, if at all, by insight of the same kind.

25. (ii) Sidgwick thinks that we may have a similar rational insight into the connection of right with duty. Suppose that, seeing my neighbour's house on fire, I recognize that my duty is to try to save it; suppose I recognize, too, that the only way to save it is to call the fire department. Sidgwick would say that in this process reason is at work in two further ways. (a) First, if I recognize that in this situ- ation an effort to save the house would be the right act for a normal man, I see also that it is my own duty to make the attempt. To see that the act would be the right one and that it is my duty to do it are not quite the same though the first entails the second. (b) Again, 'it can hardly be denied', Sidgwick says, 'that the recognition of an end as ulti- mately reasonable involves the recognition of an obligation to do such acts as most conduce to the end'.[1] Thus if I recognize that saving the

[1] *Methods of Ethics*, 35

house is the most desirable thing that at the moment I could do, it would be unreasonable of me not to adopt the means of doing it. But reason is involved here in a somewhat different way from that just noted. There, the fact that an action would be the right one entailed that I should try to do it. Here, does the fact that I should try to do it entail that I should try in this particular way? Certainly there is no seen necessity in saying that, if the house is to be saved, it must be saved through my calling the fire department. That would be a causal necessity, not a necessity of the kind in question. Sidgwick does not help us here, but he would probably say that the perception that I should try to save the house, jointly with the belief that calling the department was the best or only means of doing so, entailed that I ought to call it, or try to call it. If this seems complicated and pedantic, we may say instead merely that it would be inconsistent to recognize a duty and yet to reject the means of performing it. And to perceive an inconsistency is as truly rational an insight as the grasp of necessity.

(c) There is still another rational insight that Sidgwick thinks we have about duty. We perceive that ought implies can. 'I cannot conceive that I "ought" to do anything which at the same time I judge that I cannot do.'[1] If something is really our duty, it is something we are able to do; if we are not able to do it, it cannot be our duty. These are two ways of stating the same necessary connection.

26. (iii) We come now to another and final set of insights which Sidgwick considers rational because universal and necessary, his axioms for distributing good. Suppose that, seeing pleasure to be good, and believing that in a certain situation we should try to produce as much of it as we can, we find that, to all appearances, we can produce the same amount of it in different ways. Take a homely example. If we are holding a children's picnic and have a limited amount of ice cream, we may consider that an equal amount of pleasure would be produced by giving equal shares to each, and by giving it all to a clamorous and ravenous sub-section without letting the others know. Most persons would cast a critical eye on this last procedure. If so, it is obviously not enough to know that we should choose the largest attainable good; we must also have some principles for distributing it. Do we have any such principles? Sidgwick thought we did, and that, so far as they went, they were self-evident and certain. He called them axioms of prudence, justice, and benevolence.

[1] *Methods of Ethics*, 33

(a) Prudence had to do with one's own good, and here he found two self-evident principles. (*a*) It is a duty to elect one's greatest good rather than any lesser goods. Some moralists, for example Kant, have thought it absurd to say that we ought to do what we should in any case do instinctively, and have taken the pursuit of our own happiness as the prime example of this. Sidgwick admits the oddity of speaking of a duty to be happy, and agrees that we usually think of duty as running counter to inclination, but he believes also that duty and reasonableness coincide, and that it is sometimes as unreasonable *not* to follow inclination as, at other times, to yield to it. (*b*) Suppose one must choose between a lesser but nearer good and a greater but more remote one? In such a case, one sometimes chooses the nearer on the ground that there may be many slips between the remoter cup and one's lip, and this is reasonable enough. But if the two are equally certain, it would be foolish to choose the smaller one merely because it is the nearer; it is self-evident to Sidgwick that 'the mere difference of priority and posteriority in time is not a reasonable ground for having more regard to the consciousness of one moment than to that of another'.[1]

(b) He finds still other self-evident principles in the field of justice. (*a*) The Golden Rule is sometimes taken as such a principle, 'Do to others as you would have them do to you.' But he sees that this will not pass as it stands. There are many persons who would be glad to co-operate with you in thievery and have you co-operate with them in return. Still, the Golden Rule is feeling after a principle which, when precisely stated, does seem to be self-evident, though it is to be feared that it suffers as much in form when translated precisely as does the King James Bible. Sidgwick reformulates it as follows: 'it cannot be right for A to treat B in a manner in which it would be wrong for B to treat A, merely on the ground that they are two different individuals, and without there being any difference between the natures and circumstances of the two which can be stated as a reasonable ground for difference of treatment.'[2]

(*b*) A similar principle crops up when we are considering, not what others may claim for us, but whether some action of our own is justifiable. Here the taking of an impersonal point of view may be enough to reveal to us that an act is indefensible; 'we see that we should not think it right for another, and therefore that it cannot be

[1] *Methods of Ethics*, 381
[2] *Ibid.*, 380

right for us.'[1] Kant held that the rule of subjecting our conduct to this impersonal test was the supreme rule of right-doing, and though Sidgwick demurs, he does think it self-evident that 'we cannot judge an action to be right for A and wrong for B, unless we can find in the natures or circumstances of the two some difference which we can regard as a reasonable ground for difference in their duties'.[2]

(c) Finally, Sidgwick finds that we have self-evident duties under the head of benevolence. (a) If I believe that the welfare of others is good, as well as my own, it will be unreasonable of me to fix my eye on my own exclusively; 'I undoubtedly seem to perceive, as clearly and certainly as I see any axiom in Arithmetic or Geometry, that it is "right" and "reasonable" for me . . . to do what I believe to be ultimately conducive to universal Good or Happiness';[3] 'as a rational being I am bound to aim at good generally'.[4] (b) Strict impartiality requires us to say that the good of one individual is no more important than that of any other; the happiness of a king is not in itself more important than that of a peasant, and is not to be more thought of unless for some special reason, such as that it might be more productive of further happiness. These two principles jointly entail a further and highly exacting rule of duty, namely (c) that 'each one is morally bound to regard the good of any other individual as much as his own, except in so far as he judges it to be less, when impartially viewed, or less certainly knowable or attainable by him'.[5]

Here is a mass of moral principles which, according to Sidgwick, 'present themselves as self-evident; as much (e.g.) as the mathematical axiom that "if equals be added to equals the wholes are equal".'[6] 'I regard the apprehension, with more or less distinctness, of these abstract truths, as the permanent basis of the common conviction that the fundamental precepts of morality are essentially reasonable.'[7] Whether these principles will have commended themselves to readers as having the compelling force they had for Sidgwick, I do not know. But it can hardly be denied that the emergence of such a system was a significant fact. The most distinguished of British philosophers, Hume, had argued with great persuasiveness that in morals 'reason is, and ought only to be, the slave of the passions'. Here was a philosopher, no less acute than Hume, and in ethics far more thorough, who

---

[1] *Methods of Ethics*, 209
[2] *Ibid.*, 209; and cf. the slightly modified version of p. 379
[3] *Ibid.*, 507   [4] *Ibid.*, 382   [5] *Ibid.*
[6] *Ibid.*, 383   [7] *Ibid.*

held that not only the nature of the right and the good, but also our duties in particular cases, were rationally apprehended. The pendulum had swung back again from the emotionalist toward the rationalist extreme. Not, of course, that Sidgwick stood where Clarke had stood. Most of the rules of practice that Clarke had accepted as dictates of reason, such as those of truth-telling and promise-keeping, Sidgwick held to be utilitarian precepts, which, since they obviously allowed exceptions, could not be set down as necessary. And the maxims he did accept, as we have seen, were accepted very cautiously, and formulated with precision. On the place of reason in morals, his admirably lucid and balanced discussion seemed to many to have said the last word.

27. But it turned out, as it always does in these difficult, basic questions, that there was very much more to say. One day in the nineties there appeared in Sidgwick's study in Cambridge a young man from Finland whose interest was in anthropology. Like most other students of this subject, he had been much impressed by the diversity of moral codes that modern research had brought to light, and he wanted to know how Sidgwick reconciled the fact of such diversity with his view that moral principles were insights of reason. In cases where insights were undoubtedly rational, such as the multiplication table or the laws of logic, this diversity did not exist; Eskimos do not hold that seven and five make eleven nor the pundits of Tierra del Fuego that one can argue validly from affirming the consequent. Now if the principles of ethics were similarly insights of reason, one would expect that they too would be accepted unanimously. But it is notorious that they are not. How, then, could one combine a rationalist ethics with the anthropological facts? Sidgwick listened to the young man attentively and replied that in ethics as in other fields, education and intelligence varied. Even in mathematics, there were people who could hardly count beyond their fingers, and would be wholly helpless before an advanced demonstration. But this did not show that the demonstrations of the mathematician were not self-evident to him. It is no part of the rationalist's case that what is necessary and self-evident should appear so to everyone; indeed if this were true, the larger part of mathematics would have to be rejected, since to most people it is anything but plain. And if such variation is inevitable in mathematics, it is still more so in morals, where feeling is so much more likely to distort one's thinking. There is thus no sort of inconsistency between ethical rationalism and the anthropological facts, provided that you include among those facts the varying levels of men's intelligence.

The young man appears to have gone away shaking his head. He was unconvinced, even by Sidgwick. He dug still deeper into anthropology, read omnivorously, produced two massive volumes on *The Origin and Development of the Moral Ideas*, and became in time the first professor of sociology in the University of London. Running through all his work is his old conviction that rationalism in ethics is a superstition, that if it is approached from the side of anthropology, this theory will fade away like other superstitions. It became one of his main purposes to discredit the theory, and after he retired he published a book on *Ethical Relativity* in which the thought of a lifetime about it was summed up and used against it in concentrated fire. The name of this intransigent student was Edward Westermarck. With him we come to a philosophy that may be fairly called contemporary, and we must observe at closer range the swings of the dialectical pendulum. Westermarck's subjectivism was urged with an unprecedented mass of the anthropological learning which the penetration of primitive cultures had made possible. It calls for a chapter by itself.

CHAPTER V

SUBJECTIVISM

1. There are stages or degrees of subjectivism in ethics. Westermarck stands both logically and historically between the moderate subjectivism of Hume and the extreme subjectivism of the emotivists. Hume held (not quite consistently) that when I call an action right, I mean that people generally have a certain feeling about it. Westermarck held that when I call it right, I mean that *I* have a certain feeling about it. The emotivists hold that when I call it right, I do not mean to *assert* anything at all; I am merely *expressing* a feeling. In discussing these theories, it will be well to reserve the name 'subjectivism' for Westermarck's middle position. Although it may be very briefly stated, its force and richness can hardly be understood apart from two facts which will come out in the course of our discussion, and which serve to explain it on its negative and positive sides respectively. One is that it is an ethics of protest and reaction—of reaction against the rationalism and objectivism that we found in the ethics of Sidgwick. The other is that it is rooted in anthropology and is offered as the only theory consistent with all the newly known facts about the diversity of ethical practices. The statement of subjectivism in Westermarck's *Ethical Relativity* and his application of it to the whole range of human conduct in *The Origin and Development of the Moral Ideas* form together the most impressive defense of the position that it has yet received.

2. Since Westermarck is in reaction against objectivism, it will repay us to see at the outset what it is that he is concerned to deny. All objectivists agree that when I say 'that act is right', I am not merely expressing an attitude of my own; I am asserting that some character belongs to the act or the agent. But what sort of character is this? It is objective; yes, but in what sense? To say that it is objective means that it is independent of something subjective. But this is too vague.

Independent of what? Is the rightness that belongs to an act independent of my *thought*, or of my *feeling*, or of my very *existence* itself? Or is it independent of what *men generally* think, or of what they feel, or of their existence? Or is it perhaps independent of *consciousness as such*, human, diabolic, or divine?

(1) There have been objectivists who held this latter view. G. E. Moore once held that there would still be good and bad in the world even if every kind of consciousness were wiped out; the world would still be beautiful with no one to see it, and this beauty would be better than ugliness, even if there were no one to think so. Westermarck did not, to my knowledge, discuss this view; but he would certainly have rejected it, since he rejected other forms of objectivism that were far less extreme.

Is the objectivism he is chiefly opposing, then, the view (2) that moral values are independent of *human* consciousness? At times it seems so. The second sentence of his *Ethical Relativity* runs as follows: 'The supposed objectivity of moral values, as understood in this treatise, implies that they have a real existence *apart from any reference to a human mind*, that what is said to be good or bad, right or wrong, *cannot be reduced merely to what people think to be good or bad, right or wrong*.'[1] This is an unfortunate beginning. For Westermarck seems to be placing side by side, as having the same meaning, two forms of objectivism that are a world apart, and this suggests at the outset a lack of clearness in his own mind. According to the first of these forms, that of which moral values are independent is the human mind as such. According to the second, it is merely people's opinions about them. Now if it is really the first form that he is attacking, his subjectivism is without novelty or point, for the very persons he is most concerned to criticize would themselves accept it. Bentham, Mill, and Sidgwick, for example, would all accept it. They all held that, so far as we know, moral values have no existence apart from the human mind. Right acts, they said, depend for their rightness on effects in the way of pleasure and pain; only those beings who can feel such effects and act in the light of them are capable of right or wrong action. And the only beings we know who can feel and act in this way are men. If men were to disappear, moral values too, for all we know, would disappear with them. Thus if objectivism means independence of the human mind, Westermarck is preaching to the

[1] My italics.

already converted, and his polemic is pointless. It seems hardly credible that he should not have seen this. I think we must say therefore that the singling out of this form of objectivism as what he wished to attack was a mere slip of the pen or the mind.

(3) Is it, then, the other form here mentioned that he is attacking? According to this form, 'what is said to be good or bad, right or wrong, cannot be reduced merely to what people think to be good or bad, right or wrong'. Westermarck, as we have seen, seems to take this second form as equivalent to the first, but in truth it is extremely different. All three of the philosophers just mentioned, who would deny objectivism in the first sense, would accept it in the second as obviously true. They would say that while, so far as we know, right and wrong do depend on the human mind, they certainly do not depend on what people think about them. If an act causes as much happiness as any act that could have been done instead, then it is right, even if every human mind thinks it wrong; if it does not, then it is wrong, even if every human mind thinks it right. Right and wrong are thus independent of human opinion about them. Is this the objectivism that Westermarck wants to deny?

We have just heard him say that it is. But here again I think he is misstating his aim. It is not really human opinion on which right and wrong in the end depend, for rightness and wrongness in his sense may precede any formed opinion, and even when the opinion is formed, it is itself dependent on something else. Consider the first point. It seems almost certain that men were repelled by some actions, for example wanton attacks on themselves, long before they began to reflect on moral issues and make explicit moral judgments. Would Westermarck say that among such men right and wrong conduct had begun to appear? He would unquestionably. But if rightness and wrongness can thus exist before moral opinion is formulated, they can hardly be said to depend on such opinion. But again, even when the opinion is formulated, Westermarck would hold emphatically that it only reflects something else, which supplies its underlying ground. What is this something else? It is, of course, feeling or emotion.

(4) But whose feeling or emotion? That of the community? Readers have often supposed so, and since nearly all the practices that Westermarck describes in such instructive detail are group mores, it is natural enough to suppose so. But this would be a mistake. Westermarck rejects it explicitly.[1] To accept such a view would be to say

[1] *Ethical Relativity*, 112, 141

that when a reformer denounces the practices of the community as evil, his denunciation reflects and expresses the feeling of the group, whereas it seems clear that the feeling he expresses is the very opposite of the group's. Moral appraisals that are sincere express the feeling of the judge himself. Here we come to the end of the line. The objectivism Westermarck is attacking is one that denies the dependence of moral values on individual feeling. The subjectivism he advocates would make the moral qualities of conduct depend on the feelings of the individual persons who contemplate it.

3. Of course this view is at odds with common opinion. To most of us there is something shocking in the suggestion that slavery was really right among the Greeks merely because they felt as they did about it, or that if Hitler had so destroyed opposition that everyone left alive admired him, this would prove his conduct to have been right. Most of us believe that there are some things, for example wholesale and gratuitous slaughter, that are simply wrong, and that if some persons think or feel otherwise, what this shows is not that the act is right but that the persons are perverse or stupid. Westermarck frankly admitted that he had the plain man against him. He admitted, too, that he had the majority of philosophers against him. But he seems to have been as little moved by the one consideration as by the other, and this for the reason that the two modes of opposition are in the end the same; he thought that in ethical matters the philosophers had taken their lead from common sense. The two main questions of ethics are often said to be, What is the meaning of right? and What is the meaning of good? Philosophers have commonly held that the way to answer these questions is to look into our own mind and see what in fact we mean by these terms. And when we do look into our mind, we find that we mean by them something objective, something that actions possess regardless of our attitudes toward them. With this, philosophers suppose that they have proved that right and good really are objective. But this, says Westermarck, is confusion. They have confused *what* we mean with the *truth* of what we mean. They have confused the analysis of an assertion with the proof that in the nature of things there is something answering to this assertion. And these are wholly different. Men everywhere may believe in objectivity, they may imply it in all their moral judgments, and yet they may suffer from a general delusion. This is indeed what Westermarck holds. 'If, as I maintain, the objective validity of all moral valuation is an illusion, and the proposition "this is good" is meant to imply such validity, it must always be false.'[1]

4. But if plain men and philosophers alike are deluded in this matter, there must be strong and widespread influences at work to account for the delusion. So there are, says Westermarck. The chief factors are three, and they are not hard to discover.

(a) First, there is 'a very general tendency to assign objectivity to our subjective experience'.[2] If we feel threatened by the prospect of rain, we call the dark clouds threatening; if the lightning is a source of danger, we call it dangerous; and these words come to stand for supposed qualities in the object. We experience a sensation of blue when we look at a delphinium, or a piercing sound when we hear a train whistle, or an impression of beauty when we see a rainbow in a waterfall, and proceed to talk of the flower as blue, the whistle as noisy, and the bow as beautiful, though reflection makes it improbable that colour or sound or beauty ever exists apart from the experience of it. If these things are true, we can never argue from the common belief that a quality belongs in an object to the conclusion that it really does belong there, or even that there *is* such a quality. It is perfectly possible to explain our moral judgments without supposing any moral qualities whatever. We dislike pain; things that cause pain are therefore repellent to us; this repellingness we assign to the thing and call it bad. People act so as to pain us; we call them also bad and their acts wrong. If we go by analogy, the subjectivist explanation here is just as plausible as the objectivist.

(b) Again, there is a tendency to take impressions as objective when they are like those of others. My toothache is private because there is no evidence that, when I am having it, other people have anything like it. But if, when I report that snow is white, everybody else confirms it; if, when I say a rainbow is beautiful, everyone understands and agrees; and if, when I say that lying is wrong, everyone again understands and agrees, I assume that whiteness, beauty, and wrongness are characters in the objects and are presenting themselves alike to all of us. And it must be remembered that, however widely communities may differ about moral rules, within the limits of a given community practically everyone does agree about them. 'Society is the school in which we learn to distinguish between right and wrong.

[1] *Ethical Relativity*, 142
[2] *Ibid.*, 49

The headmaster is custom, and the lessons are the same for all the members of the community.'[1] The simplest explanation of our agreeing about such things, is to say that just as we all agree about the squareness of a box because it really is square, so we agree about the wrongness of an act because it really is wrong. Westermarck regards the two cases as totally unlike to the discerning eye, but deceptively similar to the undiscerning one.

(c) Finally, there is the immense influence of authority. Parents, teachers, the Church, the Bible, public opinion, the sages of the race, all combine to impress on us that moral principles are *true*. 'From our earliest childhood we are taught that certain acts *are* right and that others *are* wrong.'[2] To question this would be almost impious. We are extremely suggestible, and in a region where nonconformity is very rare, we are bound also to be uncritical. We come to regard the moral law, as Kant did, with the sort of awe that is given to the starry heaven. Conscience seems to ratify its absolute authority. Religion further assures us that it is the expression of the divine will. Though Westermarck was convinced that this whole notion of moral principles as true and objective was an illusion, he thought that, when backed by a weight of authority so overwhelming, this or almost any other illusion could be imprinted upon docile minds.

5. 'I maintain . . . ' writes Westermarck, 'that the qualities assigned to the subjects of moral judgments really are generalizations derived from approval or disapproval felt with regard to certain modes of conduct, that they are tendencies to feel one or the other of these emotions interpreted as qualities, as dynamic tendencies, in the phenomena which gave rise to the emotion.'[3] 'Those who first established the use of these and all other moral concepts felt disapproval or approval and expressed in the concepts their tendency to feel such an emotion in the given circumstances. This is what may be called the intrinsic meaning of the terms.'[4] The unsophisticated man does not know all this; he ascribes rightness to acts very much as he does beauty to the rose; but the sophisticated man sees that this is all one has a right to assert. For he sees, as the plain man does not, how moral concepts arise. He sees that they are home-made articles, as truly fashioned out of the stuff of emotion as the concept of fearfulness, and that there is as little presumption in the one case

---

[1] *Ethical Relitivity*, 50; cf. 109
[2] *Ibid.*   [3] *Ibid.*, 114   [4] *Ibid.*, 116

as in the other that any such quality exists. Hence the sophisticated man will correct the plain man's illusion. When he calls an act of courage or justice good, he will know what he is doing. He will understand that the moral quality lies not in the act but in his own feeling, and that all he can sensibly mean is that the act gives rise to approving feelings in his mind.

6. An interesting consequence follows from this reinterpretation of the moral judgment. We have seen that as the plain man makes it, this judgment is always false. But as the sophisticated man makes it, it turns out to be all but infallible. When he says that generosity is good, he means that generosity tends to arouse in him favourable feelings, and if it does arouse such feelings, the judgment is true.[1] Now he is in a better position to know his own feelings than anyone else in the world. Since his moral judgments are in essence reports of these feelings, and it is hardly possible for him to mistake favourable for unfavourable feelings in his own mind, it is hardly possible for his judgments to be mistaken.

7. Another odd consequence follows from this view, namely that there is no such thing as a science of ethics in the traditional sense. Ethics has sought to tell us what ends are really good, that is, what all men should try to gain, and what sort of conduct is really right, that is, what men generally ought to do. We now see that, as commonly meant, no such assertions can be true; there are no possible answers to questions of this kind, since the answers, if they came, would be nonsense. I can say, of course, that all men ought to be honest, but this turns out to mean only that honesty wakes favourable feelings in *me*. Or my statement may be a descriptive generalization to the effect that all men have such feelings about honesty. But then this is not an *ethical* statement at all; it says nothing about what is good or right or obligatory; it is a statement of psychological fact. Once I have seen clearly how my value concepts and feelings are related, I can see that a general ethical statement is a contradiction in terms. The claim it makes to universal validity is a claim that in terms of its 'intrinsic meaning' can be valid only for me. An ethics that knows its business will therefore give up moral legislation for the description of fact; it will become an adjunct, though a useful adjunct, of psychology and anthropology. Ethics as a normative science, pursuing the *summum*

[1] *Ethical Relativity*, 141

bonum with its butterfly nets of speculation, formulating solemnly 'the whole duty of man', codifying the universal rules of human conduct, will have to go.

8. We have now seen what forms the predicate of the moral judgment, that which is asserted, and it turns out to be a tendency to arouse in us certain feelings. What now of the subject? What is it that we are asserting of? We have been talking as if it were an act, but 'act' is a treacherous term. If A robs B, is the act that we disapprove the mere physical process of going through B's pockets, or this plus A's intention to do so, or both plus his motive, i.e. that which moved him to form and execute the intention, or all of these plus the character out of which the motive sprang? Westermarck argues, convincingly I think, that it is all four of these things, and that their importance increases as we go back along the line. Certainly the physical act alone cannot carry the burden of odium; if these identical motions were made by an automaton or a hypnotized man, we should not feel about them as we do. So we must include the conscious intention of the man who does them, the will to bring them about. But we cannot stop here either. If he were compelled to do them under threats upon his life, he would still be willing them, but his motive—to save his own life—would make his 'act' extremely different from that of a footpad. We must go on, then, beyond the motive to the character, the set of habitual motives that governs the life. A sudden impulsive breaking over of the traces is one thing; conduct that springs from deliberate and persistently repeated choice is another, and we feel far more strongly about it. Indeed in Westermarck's view it is character that carries the chief weight of praise or blame. There is a well known injunction to the effect that our righteous indignation should be reserved for the sin and should spare the sinner. Westermarck considers this unnatural and impracticable, for the reason that moral emotions are in the nature of the case 'reactionary attitudes towards living beings'.[1] We do, to be sure, pass judgments on what a man does, but we do so *in the light of* what he intended to do, what moved him to do it, and, above all, whether it expresses the man himself—whether it springs from the settled bent of his will.

9. Granting now that some acts arouse favourable feelings and some unfavourable, why the difference? If we see a hold-up in the street,

[1] *Ethical Relativity*, 152; cf. 85

and then, after a horrified moment, see a cameraman in the offing grinding out what is obviously a scene for a motion picture, our mood changes abruptly; why? Westermarck would answer; because one is harmless, the other not. Or, more formally, there is a wide difference in the two situations in their tendency to cause pleasure and pain. Moral approval is 'a kindly attitude of mind towards a cause of pleasure'; moral disapproval is 'a hostile attitude of mind towards a cause of pain: we approve a person who causes pleasure and condemn one who causes pain'.[1] It would have been better, perhaps, to say 'one who is *believed* to cause pleasure,' etc; do not persons often approve what causes an excess of pain, a declaration of war, for example, because they *think* it will cause the opposite, and disapprove conduct that causes a surplus of pleasure, for example the stern discipline of a parent, because it *appears* to be more productive of pain? Probably Westermarck would accept this. He points out, indeed, that many a line of conduct has been approved or condemned not because of its actual consequences, but because of theological teaching about it; 'the view that celibacy is the height of moral perfection is simply the outcome of some specific religious and magical beliefs of a rather primitive character'.[2] There are of course many other questionable ways in which conduct may acquire an aura of harmfulness or the opposite. But the point of ethical importance is that approval or condemnation is dealt out to such conduct in the light of its assumed productiveness of pleasure or pain.

Pleasure or pain to whom? To the person himself who passes the judgment, to others, or to both? On so fundamental a question, Westermarck might well have been at more trouble to be clear. On the one hand he denies emphatically that the moral judgment is based merely on the consequences of behaviour to oneself; it is disinterested in its very essence.[3] The ground of his moral condemnation is that the act tends to cause pain as such, not pain to A rather than B, or to himself rather than another. On the other hand, he holds with equal definiteness that it is our *own* pleasure or pain on

---

[1] *Ethical Relativity*, 227

[2] *Ibid.*, 256–7

[3] 'A moral judgment always has the character of disinterestedness. When pronouncing an act good or bad, I mean that it is so quite independently of any reference it might have to me personally. If a person condemns an act which does *him* harm, how can he vindicate the moral nature of his judgment? Only by pointing out that his condemnation is not due to the particular circumstance that it is he himself who is the sufferer.' *Ibid.*, 90

which these judgments are grounded; 'our retributive emotions are, of course, always reactions against pain or pleasure felt by ourselves'.[1] Sympathy and altruistic sentiment may make us spare the feelings of other people, and hence if we feel satisfaction or resentment at an action, this may well be because other people's pleasure or pain has excited our own. But Westermarck seems to take it as obvious that whatever the remote causes of our moral feelings and judgments may be, their proximate cause and ground lie always in our own pleasure or pain.

10. It is natural that if moral concepts reflect emotions, moral judgments should not be a matter of black and white, but of degree. The degree of wrongness, for example, will depend on the intensity of our indignation. This again will depend on further factors such as the amount of pain caused, and whether those affected are near or far from us. Westermarck thinks this implication of his theory an effective argument for it. For truth, he says, is *not* a matter of degree, and if in our judgment we were really ascribing a predicate, wrong, to the act, that predicate must either belong to it or not, and the judgment would be wholly true or wholly false. But he insists that this is not the way we think about wrongness; it is always wrong in degree, the degree answering precisely to the intensity of our feeling. Hence the accord between fact and theory is most happy.[2] (Unfortunately, the argument would seem to prove too much. It would equally show that brightness, loudness, and heat are not qualities that we assert, because they too are always experienced in degree; whereas it seems clear enough that they *are* such qualities.)

11. His theory here comes close to some other well-known theories, notably those of Mill and Hume, and it may be well to mark precisely the divergence. According to Mill, to judge an act wrong was to say that it produced a smaller net pleasure, or a greater net pain, than some other act that might have been done instead; and the truth of the judgment depended on a chain of hedonic consequences that took into account everyone affected by the act through a possibly endless series. According to Hume, it was not the consequences, but men's attitude towards the consequences that made an act wrong; to judge it wrong was to say that in virtue of producing less pleasant

[1] *Ethical Relativity*, 96
[2] *Ibid.*, 218

consequences than some alternative, it aroused in those who contemplated it a feeling of disapprobation. The truth of the judgment thus depended on whether most people did in fact feel about it in this way, and as Broad has remarked, the issue could in principle be settled by statistics. Hume's is thus a feeling-theory, and he is obviously closer to Westermarck than Mill is. Where does Westermarck differ from these predecessors? He would hold that to judge an action wrong is not to say with Mill that it produces less pleasure, nor with Hume that in consequence of this it arouses general disapprobation, but that in consequence of a pain in me of which I believe it to be the cause, it tends to arouse in *me* the feeling of disapproval. The truth of the judgment thus depends not on how people generally feel, but on how I feel; 'if I am right,' says Westermarck, 'in my assertion that the moral concepts intrinsically express a tendency to feel a moral emotion of either approval or disapproval, it is obvious that a judgment which contains such a concept may be said to be true if *the person who pronounces it* actually has a tendency to feel the emotion in question with reference to the subject of the judgment'.[1]

12. Since moral concepts thus depend on moral emotions, it is important to see what these emotions are. Their place among emotions generally will be made clearer by the diagram on facing page. First we divide emotions generally into retributive and non-retributive. 'Retributive' in this usage has no special connection with punishment or the requital of evil; emotions are retributive when they are a response *either* to an injury suffered or to some service rendered. Since all moral emotions fall in this first class, we may dismiss the non-retributive emotions from further notice. Retributive emotions fall naturally into two classes, negative and positive, those that consist in some form of resentment for injury suffered and those that consist in 'kindly emotion toward a cause of pleasure'. But these retributive emotions are not always moral emotions. Anger clearly is not; there is no moral complexion about a mere burst of anger at a blow or an insult. On the other hand, indignation toward the cruelty

---

[1] *Ethical Relativity*, 141–2, my italics. Cf. p. 58 and this from *The Origin and Development:* ' . . . the import of the predicate of a moral judgment may thus in every case be traced back to an emotion in him who pronounces the judgment.' I, 6. I have taken wrongness rather than rightness as the point of comparison here because the meaning Westermarck gives to 'right' is a somewhat exceptional one. He holds that, as normally used, the term does not express a feeling at all, even of approbation and hence is not typically ethical. 'Wrong' always is. *Ibid.*, 127.

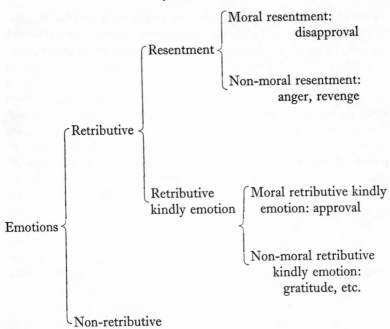

or treachery that is practised on another has the moral tone unmistakably. The same distinction may be made within those retributive emotions that are 'kindly'. If a man feels grateful to someone
who has just pulled him out of the river, there is not necessarily
anything moral about that. But, if seeing a courageous rescue by
another, he feels an appreciative glow, that again has the moral
character. What is it that marks these retributive emotions as moral?
Westermarck replies that it is impartiality. If the emotion is aroused
merely because pleasure or pain has been occasioned to oneself as
opposed to someone else, it is not moral, as we have seen; if it is
disinterested, it is. Of course it is not always easy to tell whether one's
emotion is moral or not. The best test lies in an imaginary change of
relationship;[1] if, and so far as one would feel the same way if the insult were addressed not to oneself but to another, and the person
pulled from the river were not oneself but a stranger, one is feeling
genuine moral emotions. These emotions bear special names. What
one feels in the first case is the emotion of disapproval, in the second,
approval or approbation. These terms, so often used indiscrimi-

[1] *Ethical Relativity*, 93

nately of feelings and judgments, are strictly reserved by Westermarck for the two retributive moral emotions. And these two emotions are in his view all-important, for if an action arouses approbation, it is *ipso facto* right; if it arouses disapproval, wrong.

13. From the two root terms, approval and disapproval, both of them names of emotions, Westermarck derives the other main concepts of ethics. But the two are not of equal importance. The notion of resentment determines a far larger range of ethical terms and judgments than the notion of kindliness. Take the meanings of 'right' and 'wrong'. One would naturally expect that what makes an action right is its arousing kindly emotions, just as what makes it wrong is its arousing moral resentment. This turns out to be untrue; resentment is the basis of both concepts. As regards wrong the argument is already clear, but consider right. Do we in practice confine the term to those acts that arouse in us benevolent or kindly feeling? Westermarck says no. The truth of the matter is rather this: moral rules are generally customs, and customs come in time to have something of the force of laws, that is, of commands by the community to its members. Disobedience to such commands is felt as a flouting of the community's will and naturally wakens resentment. But in mere conformity to custom there is nothing to excite feeling one way or the other; it is the norm, the established practice, what everybody expects. A man who abuses his parents is running against the current of custom; his conduct will be called wrong, and such wrongness implies felt reprobation. But when we say that the man who treats his parents in the normal way is acting rightly, do we have any corresponding glow of active approval? No. 'Right' then does not mean approved; it means merely not disapproved. It follows that 'right' and 'wrong' are not really correlative terms. 'Just' and 'unjust' are dealt with by Westermarck in similar fashion.

The terms 'ought' and 'duty' must also be redefined. What is it that makes an act one's duty, that which one ought to do? Objectivist writers have often found this in the perception that one act rather than others tends to the general good. 'Strictly speaking, however,' writes Westermarck, ' "ought" and "duty" only express the tendency of an act's omission to call forth moral disapproval and say nothing about the consequences of its performance.'[1] Thus 'duty' is like 'right' in drawing its substance from the capacious well of human

[1] *Ethical Relativity*, 125

resentment. It cannot derive this from kindly feeling, for too plainly
we do not always think of our duty with a glow of positive emotion.
Hence if it is to have any ethical meaning at all, this must come from
moral antipathy. Antipathy to what? Not to the duty itself, or it
would presumably never get done, but to the non-performance of
duty. 'Every "ought"-judgment contains implicitly a prohibition of
that which ought *not* to be done.'[1] To say that anything is one's duty
is thus to report an *un*favourable feeling about the *failure* to do it.

Though hostile feeling is the most fertile of the moral emotions,
not all ethical terms owe their meaning to it. 'Good', 'virtuous',
'meritorious', reflect the emotion of approval. '*Good*' is properly
applied not to an act but to a person, and it implies a kindly feeling
towards him as a cause of pleasure.[2] The *virtues*, such as temperance
and courage, are merely dispositions to be good in particular ways.
When we call a man *meritorious*, we are expressing the approbation
we feel for the good man, but also something more; we are saying that
he ought to be approved, which means that if his goodness passed
unrecognized, this would meet with our disapproval. It is worth
noting that in Westermarck's theory another term gets a meaning
from kindly emotion which in many ethical theories would be set
down as meaningless. This is 'super-obligatory'. If duty means only
that whose omission would arouse indignation, to go beyond one's
duty becomes both possible and easy; we all do things from time to
time which we should not be blamed for omitting, even perhaps by
ourselves. When we do these, we are going beyond our duty in
Westermarck's sense; our action is super-obligatory.

14. We now have the main features of Westermarck's theory before
us. Unfortunately, the most persuasive of his arguments for it is
one that cannot be presented with its full force in any summary
statement, because that force depends on a vast mass of inductive
evidence. The argument is based on the facts of moral diversity. It is
not, of course, new. That men differ widely in their moral convictions
and practices was perfectly well known to those who have held objectivist theories; Sidgwick was much interested in 'history studied
as inductive sociology';[3] Hegel's attention was arrested by the variety
of cultures, as indeed by nearly everything else; Kant was a student

[1] *Ethical Relativity*, 123; cf. 139.
[2] *Ibid.*, 135
[3] *Memoir*, 436–7

of anthropology; Plato must have known his Herodotus; and the conclusion so strongly suggested by the diversity of men's moral judgment was no doubt carefully weighed by all of them.

That conclusion is that in morals there is nothing objective to know. If there were, it is argued, there would be some agreement on moral issues, whereas in fact there is anarchic diversity. Men do not differ about the multiplication table; they all agree that two and three make five; and if they do, it is because the laws that govern the relation of numbers are universal and independent of the will. Nor, except on the speculative side, is there any substantial difference about chemistry and physics, for there is always an arbiter standing ready, to whom passing disputes may be taken, an arbiter whose decisions are final, namely nature. If we study such agreement, we shall find that what makes it possible is always an independent law or structure through comparison with which our personal deviations may be cancelled. Now if agreement depends on objectivity, general disagreement strongly suggests the lack of it. And in ethics such disagreement is precisely what we find. Indeed we find something like chaos. There is no custom, however sacred, and no principle, however compelling, that is not somewhere put aside as plainly unsound. How are we to explain this except by saying that the objective principles that we find in other sciences do not exist in ethics? If they did, surely there would be some signs of order, some suggestion of an agreed-upon set of principles, emerging from the chaos.

To this the objectivists have replied that the diversity can be explained in a much simpler and less violent way. This is the way suggested to the then youthful Westermarck by Sidgwick in a conversation to which we have referred.[1] Why not account for the diversity by the very simple hypothesis that some men are stupid in moral matters and others more discerning? Indeed if agreement is to be made out in science itself, it would seem to be only by taking advantage of this sort of explanation; we tacitly rule out the dissenting votes of savages on mathematics and chemistry as not worth including in our poll. If we did include them, we should have a diversity very similar to that in ethics. But it is clear how we should go about it to deal with that diversity. No one would question a judgment of Newton on the ground that some Andaman Islander shook his head over it. We should say that if the Islander failed to see, that was not because Newton's insight was false, or indeed anything less than self-evident

[1] Above, p. 102.

to a mind qualified to judge, but because the Islander was stupid or untrained. And if we are entitled to say that in science, why not in ethics? The civilized man sees clearly, or thinks he does, that to rob a stranger is wrong, and that to deprive a man of rights because he is of another colour or country is unjust. To most savages such views are absurd. Does this show that fairness is really no better than unfairness? Is it not far more sensible to say that fairness really is better, but that the savage has not reached the point where he can see it? To Sidgwick, perhaps the clearest-headed of all moralists, one could in this manner hold firmly to the objectivity of moral law while admitting to the full the diversity of moral judgment.

15. How does Westermarck reply? He replies by denying the parallel between scientific and ethical diversity. In science all who apply themselves impartially to the subject recognize certain persons as experts, and these experts on the whole agree. In ethics the experts themselves disagree. The only way one can get agreement is to set up one's own insights as authoritative and admit to the rank of expert only those who see eye to eye with oneself, a method that remains unconvincing in spite of its wide popularity. Short of this high-handed procedure, one can only concede, says Westermarck, that there is not a single proposition that qualified moralists have regarded as self-evident which is not held by moralists of equal standing to be untrue. He is ready, as one would expect, to supply chapter and verse in profusion. 'Some "moral specialists" say it is an axiom that I ought not to prefer my own lesser good to the greater good of another; whilst others not only deny the self-evidence, but thoroughly disagree with the contents of this proposition. According to Sidgwick the assertion that pleasure is the only rational ultimate end of action is an object of intuition; according to Moore, the untruth of this proposition is self-evident. The latter finds it self-evident that good cannot be defined; but others, who have no smaller claim to the epithet "moral specialists", are of the very contrary opinion.'[1] These are not bones of minor contention at the bottom of the cultural scale; they are divergences at the very top, and concern matters of the first moment. The theory, then, that would explain the variety of ethical insights as approximations by minds of differing level to a common objective truth does not cover the known facts.

[1] *Christianity and Morals*, 31–2

Is there any theory that does? One only, Westermarck holds. It runs as follows: Assume that what all men primarily want is to gain pleasure and avoid pain, and that approval and disapproval themselves consist of emotion. Assume finally that men's perception of the causal connections that actually hold is wavering and uncertain, so that it is likely to be distorted by fear and chance association, by superstition and desire. You will then have a theory that, without any need for objective moral truths, covers the facts completely.

16. As he develops this theory in his great work, two features gradually come to light that must deeply affect our estimate of it. The first is the somewhat surprising disclosure that the supposedly enormous divergences are, after all, less moral than intellectual. Westermarck goes down the list of the more important mores and finds in one after another that what men chiefly differ about is not ends but means, not the importance, for example, of the happiness, strength, and health of oneself and one's immediate family, but about the means by which these are to be achieved. And he recognizes that a divergence about means is not a moral divergence at all. Take a well known case in which the difference does seem to be moral and also to be so wide that it is beyond all bridging. Among ourselves kindness to parents is approved and demanded. On the other hand, Westermarck notes more than a dozen peoples among whom approval is actually given to the killing of parents.[1] The moral difference here seems deep and shocking. But as the circumstances unroll, this difference steadily fades. Among tribes where physical strength is all-important and weakness is misery, where the food will not go round, where the group must keep on the march, and where, above all, it is firmly believed that men retain in the next life the mental and physical faculties they take with them at death, 'what appears to most of us an atrocious practice may really be an act of kindness, and is commonly approved of, or even insisted upon, by the old people themselves'.[2] To us the shocking thing about such behaviour is the indifference it seems to show to the life and happiness of those who are normally most dear. But no such indifference is necessarily involved; in some of the cases 'the son will kiss and weep over his aged father as he prepares him for the grave. . . .'[3] No doubt as one goes

[1] *Origin and Development*, I, Ch. 17
[2] *Ibid.*, I, 388
[3] *Ibid.*, 390, quoting Fison and Howitt.

down the cultural scale, there is a falling off of imagination and sympathy just as of other capacities of mind. But if a savage, in doing what he does, thinks he is serving the best interest of his parent and the community, it is idle to say that he is living in a wholly alien moral world. He is living in the same world because seeking substantially the same ends as ourselves, though in ways imposed upon him by a harder economy and a more uncritical religion. Thus by Westermarck's implicit admission, the very research which casual readers suppose to have demonstrated moral chaos shows that there is an impressive unity and stability in man's moral nature, and that if we have regard to the grounds on which its approbation is given we shall find in its verdicts a smaller variation than in his intellectual beliefs.

17. The second feature is more important still; and here appears what seems to me an almost incredible omission in Westermarck's ethical system. To approve something, he holds, is to feel a favouring emotion toward it as a cause of pleasure; to disapprove it is to feel an opposite emotion toward it as a cause of pain. Pleasure and pain are thus the grounds, and the prospect of them the cause, of all moral emotion. It is not because acts by themselves have any value for us that they are approved or disapproved; it is because of what they lead to, because they are means to something else; and this something else which alone gives importance to the means is pleasure or pain. These and these only are what in the end we prize or disprize; pleasure is what all men everywhere want and always have wanted; pain, what they have sought to avoid. It would seem clear, then, that the question whether an act is objectively right or wrong would depend on whether pleasure and pain themselves have objective value. If, when we say 'pleasure is good', we are saying something objectively true, true independently of what we may be feeling, then the judgment 'this act is right' is also objectively true. Hence it is of the first importance for Westermarck to show that the judgments we pass upon pleasure and pain are as lacking in objective truth as those we pass upon acts.

Now what I find almost incredible in Westermarck's treatment is that on this issue, so clearly fundamental to his whole construction, he has nothing to say. He passes it over as if the problem had never occurred to him. What he would say about it if he did raise and discuss it one can only conjecture. But he would need to say something very convincing, for the view that pleasure and pain are themselves without objective value is far from plausible. Let us try to think of the most probable and plausible things that he *might* say.

He might dismiss the problem by observing that 'pleasure is good' and 'pain is evil' say nothing at all, that 'good' *means* pleasant and 'bad' *means* painful, and that such statements as 'pleasure is pleasant' and 'pain is painful' would obviously not be worth making. I will not linger over this suggestion because I think it has come out clearly enough in the long debate about hedonism that we do not mean by 'good' simply pleasant, nor by 'bad' painful. Two remarks will perhaps serve. First, as has been shown by G. E. Moore, if 'good' meant simply pleasant, the question whether pleasure is good ought to be meaningless, whereas in fact it is not. Secondly, 'good', even when used of intrinsic goods, has a far wider application than 'pleasant'; we call pleasure good, but we say the same of knowledge, love, and justice, when it seems clear that it is not their pleasantness that we are concerned to stress. One can hardly cut off discussion of the value of pleasure and pain by dismissing the problem as meaningless.

But Westermarck might dismiss the problem in another way. He might say that he was dealing with moral judgments alone, and that judgments about the value of pleasure and pain were *not* moral. Verbally, this would be correct. In his view, it is always on persons or acts, or more accurately on both together, that moral judgments are passed; pleasure and pain are obviously neither. Nevertheless to take this line would be to evade the real problem. Suppose we agree that when we call conduct right, our judgment is moral, and that when we call pleasure good, our judgment is non-moral; still on Westermarck's theory it can only be because we accept the latter that we ever accept the former; unless we took pleasure to be good, we should not approve acts that produced it. Hence it would be odd to discuss elaborately whether our judgments on acts were objective, and refuse to discuss, as irrelevant, the objectivity of the judgments we pass on the consequences of those acts. We may *call* such judgments on consequences non-moral if we like, but if the force of our moral judgments depends on them, then they are moral in effect, whatever we choose to call them.

Very well, suppose Westermarck did raise the question whether the judgments of value that we pass on pleasure and pain are objectively true or not; what would he say? One would perhaps expect him to say that they should be dealt with in the same way as moral approvals. If we follow this clue, the statement 'pleasure is good' will mean 'pleasure is something that tends to arouse in me an approving emotion in virtue of its being thought of as a cause of pleasure'; 'pain is bad' will mean 'pain is something that tends to arouse in me a disapproving emotion in virtue of its being thought of as a cause of pain'. Clearly this will not do. If we approve of pleasure merely because it is a cause of later pleasure, we shall approve of this later pleasure only because it is a cause of a still later pleasure, and we shall have no ground for approving any pleasure at all until we have completed an endless series, that is, never. On the other hand, if one stops anywhere along the line with a pleasure conceived as self-justifying, then there is precisely the same reason for stopping at the first term, and making our approval of *that* pleasure depend on something in the pleasure itself.

'Pleasure is good' is now to mean 'pleasure causes in me or tends to cause an emotion of approval', and 'pain is bad' to mean 'pain causes in me or tends to cause an emotion of disapproval'. Now that pleasure does normally cause favouring, and pain hostile, emotion may well be true. But that what a sophisticated person *means* by calling them good or bad is some fact of causation seems to me plainly false. Historians tell us that in the fifteenth century, many thousands of women were burnt at the stake as witches. When we think what this meant, even in a single case, we say that the suffering involved must have been horrible. Is it our intention, in such a remark, to say something about the character of the suffering or merely to report its causal action on ourselves? On the theory before us it is the latter. On this theory we are asserting a chain of causation leading from certain events in the fifteenth century to occurrences in our own minds. If this is really what we are doing, then the question whether our judgment is true, the question whether the experience of being burned alive in the fifteenth century was good or bad, will depend on the effect which that event has on us now. It seems to me perfectly clear that this is not our meaning. By way of test we may put to ourselves the question whether we mean to say of the suffering something that would still be true even if we ourselves were not alive. We should surely answer that we do, that whether we were alive or not could not make the slightest difference to the goodness or badness of events that occurred in the fifteenth century. If so, it cannot be the action of those events upon ourselves that we are primarily asserting. The badness asserted is something we take to have belonged to the suffering *at the time when it occurred*.

The case is perhaps clearer still of judgments of the future. Suppose a man makes a will in which he leaves a substantial amount to a small grandson of whom he is fond. If asked to explain this, he might say, 'I want the boy to be happy'. If pressed as to why he wanted him to be happy rather than miserable, he would probably say, 'Don't be silly; it is surely a good thing to be happy; one doesn't need to argue about that.' If it were then said to him that the boy's future happiness could not possibly have any value, because its value depended on its causal action on himself and he would be dead before it came about, he would regard this as stuff and nonsense. Probably most of us would agree. What he is aiming at and talking about is plainly a future good, that is, something that will be good in the future. And if this is an intelligible aim at all, the goodness cannot possibly consist in a causal action running from the future to the past.

18. What we have here essentially is old-fashioned egoism in a new guise. Pleasure is good, and pain bad, but only in their relation to me. To say that the suffering of someone else, which does not affect me, is bad is meaningless, since badness *consists* in effects on me; to call such suffering bad would be like saying of an armless man that he is awkward in shaking hands. Similarly, if other people's happiness does not in some way act on me, there is literally no sense in my calling it good. One may define goodness and badness in this fashion if one pleases; but certainly neither the plain man nor the reflective man would agree that it catches his meaning, since it would commit him in an obvious way to what he would reject as completely unreasonable. Suppose the view were to be generally accepted. Then, just as I should attach no value to other people's pleasure or pain except as it affected mine, so they would attach no value to mine except as it affected theirs. And I do not believe that anyone thinks of good and bad in a way that would require everyone else to regard his happiness or misery as something in itself of no account. To be sure there is nothing formally inconsistent in this sort of egoism. 'I can find nothing irrational or inconsistent', writes Westermarck, 'in the proposition that it is right for everybody to be an egoist, myself as well as others.'[1] There is no contradiction in your calling good what I call valueless if what each of us means by these terms is merely a relation to his own feelings. But when Westermarck goes on to say that in such egoism there is nothing irrational, we begin to

[1] *Ethical Relativity*, 33

feel uneasy. Why? Perhaps we may put it this way: if I were to ask myself why I regarded a certain state of mind in myself, for example a severe pain, as bad, while regarding as good or neutral an exactly similar pain in another, I could see, if I were honest, that its special relation to me had nothing to do with its goodness or badness, that what made it bad was its character, the sort of experience it was, its being an intense pain, not the accident of its happening to one man or to another. The unreasonableness lies in making essential to goodness and badness a relation that is plainly *not* essential. The trouble with such egoism is not that it is inconsistent, but—if one may say so—that it is stupid.

19. If Westermarck is to escape such clashes with our plain meaning, he must move on into another position. He must say that the value of pleasure and pain depends not on their relation to me, but on their relation to whoever feels them. When I call *my* happiness good, I still mean that I have a favourable feeling toward it, but when I say that *your* happiness is good, I mean, not that *I* have such a feeling toward it, but that *you* have. The misery of the women burned as witches was really bad if they felt in a certain way about it, whether the people around them felt this way or not, and regardless of whether you and I ever lived. This is a far more plausible view than the last, but still it will not serve. For, first, though pain may be made worse by our emotional attitude toward it, one can hardly believe that its evil is wholly created by this attitude. And this is still harder to believe of the pain of animals. I am sure that if my dog were struck by a car and his leg broken, he would suffer intense pain, and I am sure that the occurrence of this pain would be an evil thing. But it seems extremely questionable whether the pain would become bad only when and because the dog took up an unfortunate emotional attitude toward it, and that unless he did, there would be nothing bad about it at all. Pain exists, and is surely bad, at psychical levels at which this sort of analysis would be highly artificial.

Secondly, even if the analysis were adopted, Westermarck could not consistently accept it. It would destroy his subjectivism. For the goodness and badness of consequences no longer depends on what *I* feel about them or even whether I exist. I approve of an act, he says, in virtue of the pleasure it produces. But the goodness of this pleasure does not depend on me; it is now admitted to have value, whatever my attitude may be, if only it is welcomed by the person who experiences it. Such independence of my feeling is, as we have seen, what Westermarck means by objectivity. On such a view, not only are good and bad objective; we can lay down those universal moral laws which are one of his chief aversions, for example, 'Always so act as to produce the greatest total good.' This will now mean almost exactly what Mill meant by it, and it will give a yardstick of right conduct that can be applied in the same sense everywhere and always.

Let us sum up what we have been saying. According to Westermarck, the rightness of an act depends on its approval, and its approval turns on its believed conduciveness to pleasure or pain. We have seized on this latter point, and held it to be implicit in Westermarck's argument that the justification of the approval rests on the truth of the belief. If an act does really conduce to the largest net pleasure, must he not, on his own implicit premises, call it objectively right? That some acts do really conduce to pleasure or pain is clear enough. But might he not save subjectivism by pointing out that even if they do, the pleasure and pain they produce are themselves without objective value? We have asked whether there is any way in which he could consistently maintain this view, and we have reviewed the only ways that seem plausible. None of these was at all convincing. Our conclusion is that Westermarck leaves the objectivity of moral judgments very much where it was. It is still open to us to say, for example, that some acts are objectively right because they do in fact produce results that are objectively good.

20. He seems indeed to admit this and even to make it, in a half conscious way, the basis of his whole treatment of morals. When conflicting customs are equally approved by the groups that practice them, he certainly does not put them all on a level; he thinks that some are better than others, and he evidently considers his judgment that they are better to have a ground beyond his own feeling. On this point Rashdall remarks: 'Professor Westermarck, though he is generous to the savage, and perhaps underrates the difference between his morality and ours, never exhibits the slightest real doubt that his own ideal of life, when it is different from that of the savage, is the higher of the two.'[1] We have seen that in his view the morality of the savages who kill their parents is not as remote from our own as appears; but even so, it seems clear that he would not place it on the same level. These people were misled by superstition as to the true

[1] *Is Conscience an Emotion?* 121

consequences of their conduct; we are not; and with our release from that superstition we can see things as they are and determine our conduct in the light of truth rather than illusion. If happiness is, as he holds, what everyone wants, is it reasonable to say that conduct which produces this is objectively no better than conduct that does not? Verbally this is what he is maintaining; the fact is that he abandons it within the first three pages of his great book. He writes:

'in every society the traditional notions as to what is good or bad, obligatory or indifferent, are commonly accepted by the majority of people without further reflection. By tracing them to their source it will be found that not a few of these notions have their origin in sentimental likings and antipathies, to which a scrutinizing and enlightened judge can attach little importance; whilst, on the other hand, he must account blameable many an act and omission which public opinion, out of thoughtlessness, treats with indifference.'[1]

One who could write this does not really believe that the emotional approval of a line of conduct closes the question of its rightness. He clearly believes that the approval which springs from 'sentimental likings and antipathies' is less likely to be sound than that of 'a scrutinizing and enlightened judge' who is able to engage in 'further reflection'. And what is the point of such reflecting if not to reveal the truth about the act, in the sense of its actual consequences, the contribution it really makes to human welfare? Thus it seems to have been Westermarck's conviction, whatever his theory required, that conduct dictated by these correctly seen consequences was better —really and objectively better—than conduct chosen in ignorance of them. A main purpose of his book is to enable us to achieve this more rational conduct, a purpose, we may add, that he excellently fulfilled.

Westermarck is of course quite aware of this line of criticism, and reminds us that it has been made against him by G. E. Moore. 'He says it is commonly believed that some moral rules exhibit a *higher* morality than others, and asks what I could mean by saying that A's morality is higher than B's. He himself gives the answer: I could only mean that "A's morality is my morality, and B's not".'[2] In spite of this frank avowal, it is hard to believe that this is all Westermarck means. He argues that an advantage of his own view is that it would lead to greater social tolerance and more general self-criticism.[3] These

---

[1] *Origin and Development*, I, 3
[2] *Ethical Relativity*, 146
[3] *Ibid.*, 59

things then possess value. But is Westermarck really saying that they have value only in the sense that he has a certain emotion toward them, whose absence would render the judgment false? Would his judgment no longer be true if he suffered a paralytic stroke? Surely he means more in saying such things than his theory allows him to mean. As Arthur Murphy has remarked:

> 'the relativist is committed in advance to a refusal to deal with moral issues on a moral basis. He dare not make moral judgments except by disguising them as statements of existing matter of fact. Since the whole point of adducing the variety of codes and customs as a ground for tolerance is to provide a *reason* for one course of conduct and a basis for condemnation of its intolerant opposite, the result of this procedure can only be confusion.'[1]

21. It is time to turn from Westermarck's implicit to his explicit emphasis. He says little, as we have seen, about judgments of intrinsic value: he says a great deal about judgments of right and wrong; his main point about these is of course that they are statements of our own emotion. We do not feel approving emotions toward conduct because we see it to be right; we judge it to be right because we feel these emotions toward it; indeed to the self-critical mind, the judgment *is* simply the statement that the conduct arouses (or tends to arouse) emotions. This gives us Westermarck's views on two very important matters. It tells us first what he thinks about the *psychology* of moral judgment, about the respective parts played in it by thought and feeling; and it tells us, secondly, what he thinks is the *meaning* of the judgment, what a reflective mind means to assert in calling an act right or wrong. The two topics are very closely related. But it will be convenient to consider them separately and to begin with the first.

Westermarck's theory of moral judgment is often called an emotional theory. But we have seen that he never accepted the view held by the more extreme positivists that such judgment expresses *nothing but* emotion. It is not an exclamation merely; it is genuine judgment, with its own truth or falsity. Still, as made by the plain man, he holds that its concepts are bogus concepts, like those of the 'frightfulness' of a storm or the 'frowning' aspect of a cliff. Though they pretend to be, and are commonly taken to be, notions of attributes in the object, they are really reports of how we feel. The

[1] *The Uses of Reason*, 159

sophisticated man will see this. There will still be an intellectual element in his judgment, but it will be confined to two things, first an apprehension, usually implicit and vague, of the act as a cause of pleasure or pain, second, an apprehension, which is the essence of the judgment, that it tends to arouse approving or hostile emotion in his own mind. Westermarck's case, as we have noted, is curiously incomplete about the first of these elements. But on the second he is explicit and emphatic. He holds that while the judgment of approval is not reducible to a mere exclamation like 'Cheers!', it is reducible to a statement that I feel, or tend to feel, as I should if I did so exclaim. The intellectual element has not quite vanished. But it approximates the vanishing point, since it derives from the emotional element the whole of its distinctive meaning.

Now we must surely agree that feeling is bound up with moral judgment in manifold and intimate ways.[1] When we have granted this, have we conceded Westermarck's point that the moral judgment is essentially an expression of feeling? No, I think not, and he finds it impossible himself to adhere to it consistently. He cannot fit one of the most important of ethical judgments into an emotional theory. He recognizes that while the judgment that something is wrong involves hostile emotion, the judgment that something is right seems to involve no corresponding emotion of approval; ' . . . we regard it as perfectly right to pay a debt and to keep a promise, or to refrain from killing, robbing, or lying, though these acts or forbearances have no tendency whatever to evoke in us an emotion of moral approval'.[2] What are we to make of this? We have been told that to use moral concepts is to assert 'tendencies to feel either moral approval or disapproval with reference to that of which those concepts are predicated'.[3] We are now told that the judgment of right asserts *no* such feelings or tendencies to feel. It follows that the judgment of right is not a moral judgment at all. Since everyday right acts excite no emotion in us, one way or the other, our moral judgments about them must, on the emotional theory, have no content. I find this very hard to accept. It is not easy, of course, to be sure what we do mean by 'right', but it is difficult to believe that we mean nothing by it. Most people would think it better to start by assuming that a term so long regarded as fundamental did mean something, and would say

[1] For an enumeration of the most important of these, see below, p. 197
[2] *Ethical Relativity*, 127
[3] *Ibid.*, 90

E

that if a theory had no room for it, so much the worse for the theory. Westermarck is prepared to drop the concept rather than rewrite his theory to suit its actual meaning.

He does not, indeed, think it necessary to call the judgment wholly meaningless. He attempts to supply it with emotional meaning by connecting it with disapproval. When we say that an act is right, we are saying that the *failure* to do it would excite such disapproval, and since disapproval is an emotion, the term after all draws from emotion such significance as it has. I do not think this defence will serve. It still denies to the judgment of right any distinctive meaning. It holds that when we say an act is right, we really mean that some other act is wrong. 'Chamberlain's course at Munich was right' means 'Chamberlain would have been wrong in *not* taking that course'. But these judgments, as commonly made, do not mean the same thing. This is clear from the fact that the first can be true while the second is false. When a man says that Chamberlain was right, he is certainly not committing himself to the view that all alternative courses would have been wrong; it is often the case, so far as we can see, that any one of a variety of courses would be equally right. The attempt, then, to reduce the judgment of right to an expression of *dis*approbation for *not* acting in a given way does violence to our meaning. And unless this violent course is taken, the term remains without any meaning at all.

22. The term 'just' is dealt with in much the same way as 'right'. 'When we style an act "just", in the strict sense of the term, we point out that an undue preference would have been shown someone by its omission.'[1] The criticism just made applies here again; justice disappears as a moral concept. But there is a further difficulty. If 'just' means what Westermarck here says that it means, it is certainly not an expression of emotion merely, either positive or negative. It connotes a complex set of relations, connecting one man with others, and the agent is conceived as giving each of these others his due. This complex relationship belongs to the essence of justice. But it is evidently not included in any *emotion* that we may assert ourselves to be having. If it is replied that 'just' has no emotional meaning of its own, but draws one from 'unjust', the difficulty remains. For 'unjust' involves a relationship equally complicated and equally far removed from any mere feeling. In his concern to exalt the emotional element

[1] *Ethical Relativity*, 131

in the judgment at the expense of the intellectual, Westermarck seems here to have poured out the baby with the bath.

Another line of reply may be offered; it may be said that the work of intellect or cognition is limited to defining the object toward which the emotion is felt, and that the judgment declares this emotion. But this would imply that the characterization of the act as being in the above sense just is one thing and the judgment another, that the first precedes the second as the condition of its occurrence. In our actual thought there is no such division or precedence. When we call an act just or unjust, the set of apprehended relations is ascribed in the judgment itself and forms an essential part of its content. Indeed if this judgment were reduced to the expression of an emotion, everything that could distinguish the judgment of justice from the more general judgment of rightness would have disappeared.

This fact that the content of justice cannot be supplied by emotion raises a further doubt. We have seen that for Westermarck the distinctive note of moral emotion is its impartiality. Suppose, for example a careless driver rams my motor-car from behind, injures it badly, and makes off before I can discover his identity. Mere anger at what he has done to me is not a moral emotion. The emotion is moral only so far as it is what would have been felt toward *any* driver in similar circumstances, excluding any feeling arising from the fact that it was I in particular who was the victim. Now Westermarck is surely right in implying that the moral judgment is a universal or as-such judgment, that what it pronounces wrong is not merely X's injuring *my* car by his careless driving, but anyone's injuring anyone's car in this way. The judgment *is* then impartial and impersonal. But does it make sense to say that the *emotion* is impartial and impersonal? To split an emotion up into a personal part, directed against a certain man, and an impersonal part, directed against this *sort* of man and act, would prove no easy business either in practice or in theory. But even if it were done, is it the emotion that would be impartial? Impartiality involves applying a principle; it implies a distinction between those features on the one hand that are essential and universal and, on the other, the irrelevant claims of particular persons; and one would have thought that if anything is the special function of intelligence and beyond the power of emotion, this is. No doubt when intelligence thus comes into play, emotion is modified to suit. But emotion itself cannot distinguish the universal, or recognize the species of a genus, or distinguish the essential from the irrelevant.

Hence when the emotional theory makes impartiality the distinctive trait of moral judgment, it is implicitly giving up its case. Impartiality belongs to intelligence, not to feeling.

23. This refusal to give intelligence its due part has also distorted Westermarck's account of the judgment of duty. 'Strictly speaking,' he writes, ' "ought" and "duty" only express the tendency of an act's omission to call forth moral disapproval . . .'[1] When the inveterate toper, then, judges that he ought not to visit the bar again, he is really judging that his doing so would excite his own moral indignation. I do not find this convincing. I should have thought it not only a possibility, but a rather common occurrence, that he should see that he ought not to indulge himself further, and yet at the same time know that he is going to, and feel no indignation against himself for doing so. The issue is a somewhat treacherous one because it is no doubt true that in most cases where we see something to be our duty, we should disapprove ourselves for failing to do it, and one must resort to exceptional cases to dissociate the two factors. That they do not necessarily go together seems clear from the instance given. But even if they always did go together, they would still not be identical. One could still see that in calling something my duty, I did not *mean* merely that I should be indignant over my failure to do it. If a kindly fate should provide us with an introspective and articulate toper, I think he would agree that in saying it was his duty to stop indulging himself, he was not merely saying that he would be indignant with himself if he did not. He would say that he knew quite well he ought to stop, though he was very far from certain whether he would be indignant with himself if he did not, that his belief that he ought to stop would not be shown false merely by his failure to become angry with himself, and that even if he did become angry with himself, this would be because he saw that he ought to stop. The perception is the cause of the anger, not the anger of the perception. Westermarck has got the cart before the horse; he has made the emotional consequence of a judgment into the substance of the judgment itself.

We have been commenting on the place that Westermarck assigns in moral appraisals to the cognitive and the emotional factors. It is time to turn to a somewhat different kind of consideration. Suppose we assume that moral judgment is as largely an affair of emotion as

[1] *E.R.*, 125

he holds it is; do the implications of such an analysis fit in with the rest of what we know, or seem to know, about right and wrong? We have seen that, on the surface, they obviously do not. But we must examine this apparent conflict more closely.

The conflict resolves itself into a single large issue, which crops up in different forms. This issue is not, as it is sometimes said to be, whether moral judgments are objectively true or simply *true*; 'objective' here adds nothing. Westermarck does not deny their truth. On his theory, if I call an act wrong, what I mean is that I tend to feel reprobation for it; if I do feel this, the judgment is true; if not, false. No; the issue is not over the truth of moral judgments but over the objectivity of moral values. Westermarck maintains that these are subjective, that there is nothing good or bad, right or wrong, apart from my feelings about it. It is clear that most men believe the contrary. They are persuaded, justly or not, that these terms answer to some character in the object itself that is independent of our feelings. How large a revision would be required in their ways of thinking about morality if this view were admitted?

24. Since we have just been discussing duty, let us go on with that from this fresh point of view. We have seen that what 'ought' means for Westermarck is at variance with our ordinary meaning. But may it not be that though the connotation differs, the denotation will remain the same? It is notorious that philosophers may differ widely in what they profess to mean by such terms as 'life', 'cause' and 'right', and yet agree all along the line in their applications of them. Granting that Westermarck's definition of 'right' is different from that of most of us, would his view make any significant difference to the range of actions we take as obligatory?

It would make a very great difference. All that would be needed to remove an act from the list of duties would be to change one's feelings about it. Suppose I have agreed to pay a certain rent on the first day of each month; we should certainly say that if I were able to pay it I ought to pay it, and that my having a headache, or being in love, or feeling a dislike for my creditor, or having an aversion, however intense, to parting with my money, made no difference to its being my duty, since that does not depend on how I feel. On the theory before us, this is not true. I can erase the obligation merely by a change of feeling. All that makes it an obligation lies in me; it lies in the moral aversion I feel for the non-payment of the debt, and disappears as I get over this aversion. Is it replied that there is no danger of my getting over it, since I can see that I ought not to try? But all *this* means is that I have another aversion to trying to get over the first aversion; there is no objective ground for either; and the cure for both is the same, namely to get myself to feel in a different way.

'Not so fast,' it may be said; 'Westermarck has given us such a ground, for moral aversion is not in his view arbitrary; it is felt against an act "as a cause of pain". My conviction that non-payment should be avoided thus rests upon a judgment which is, or may be, independently true.' At this stage such a reply is mere confusion. If it really is productiveness of pain, conceived as bad in itself, that makes an act wrong, that is an intelligible view, but then, as we have seen, there is no subjectivism about it. What makes an act right for Westermarck is not the pleasure or pain it causes, but the emotional attitude which the apprehension of such consequences happens to arouse in me. I may normally be moved to sympathy by the prospect of my creditor's pain, and, as a result, moved to indignation by an act that would produce such pain; but apart from the way I happen to feel, there is no duty to have either emotion, and once I see this clearly, no reason remains why I should not try to outgrow them both. It may be replied, once more, that the payment of rent belongs to a large network of practices which must be maintained as a whole if my happiness is to be assured. But this is continued confusion. Not only may the non-payment, with its rich and immediate return, mean far more to my happiness than payment ever would through its roundabout influence on order generally, but even if payment did have such an effect, this would impose no sort of obligation on me. For obligatoriness, we repeat, does not rest on conduciveness to anyone's good, either society's or my own; it rests on my feelings; and if I happen not to feel disapproval for an act, there is no duty to avoid it. The 'ought' has really gone. It has completely vanished into 'is'. And since the 'is' has to do with my emotions, the range of my duties will depend on my emotional self-control. If I can 'condition' my emotions in a certain way, I shall not only believe that it is no longer my duty to pay the rent; it will in fact cease to be my duty. This certainly opens vistas to tired saints. Let them become sufficiently expert in applied psychology and their 'moral holiday' can begin. It can begin, furthermore, without the slightest detraction from their saintliness.

One can foresee the protest that will arise here. 'You find this implication in Westermarck only because you have left out his express proviso about what makes emotion moral. You speak of the self-disapprobation bound up with non-payment as if it were a whim that would evaporate as soon as one sees its inconvenience. But since this emotion has nothing to do with any special advantage to oneself, it is not likely to be exorcized merely by finding it somewhat troublesome. It is the sort of emotion one feels toward the evasion of debts *as such*. And however easy it might be to tone down the condemnation of oneself for such a practice, one cannot wave away one's condemnation of others. That, at least, is deep-seated and firm. And as long as it remains, the sense of duty will remain.' Does this not meet the criticism completely?

On the contrary, it gives away the case. What is apprehended when the act is thus impartially viewed is either something objectively wrong or it is not. If it is—and we have seen that Westermarck really though inconsistently implies that it is—then the wrongness clearly does not lie in my emotion, nor does the judgment primarily express emotion; it expresses an insight or a belief. On the other hand, if in the act thus viewed there is nothing objectively wrong, then my antipathy to it is groundless, and there is no more reason why I should not treat it as an inconvenience to be got rid of than any other emotion that proves a nuisance. Let us remember that for Westermarck, while speaking in the official robes of the subjectivist, there is nothing wrong whatever about rent-dodging as such apart from my emotions about it, nor, these emotions again apart, is there any obligation to feel about it in one way rather than another. Once I see this, why should I cling to a quite ungrounded antipathy which stands in the way of my desires? I had supposed duty to be a stern taskmaster imposing obligations upon my reluctant will in the name of an impersonal reason. I now see that the taskmaster is a creation of my own, and that the reason he invokes is only a wraith like himself. If I can exorcize both together by adopting a new attitude, why in the world should I not?

To the person who replies, 'Exactly: why not indeed?', I think the plain man's answer is the best one: 'Because you can see, if you look at the matter straight, that your duty to pay the rent does not depend on how you feel, but on an agreement you have made and on the bad results of breaking it.' To be sure, the emotion of disapproval is a natural and suitable attitude toward a wrong act, but its very suitability implies that the act has a character of its own that makes this suitable. To hold the emotion *constitutive* of the rightness is to make the tail wag the dog. Was it not Mr Milquetoast who said to his boy, 'Son, go down cellar and bring up some wood.' 'I won't,' said the boy, 'I don't want to.' 'Then don't,' was the reply; 'I'll be obeyed.' For duty to capitulate to the changes of feeling strikes one as a performance of about equal dignity.

25. We have been considering the strange shift that would take place in the content of duty if the emotionalist theory were accepted. There would be, if anything, a still stranger shift in the list of right and wrong acts generally. This follows from the reflection that it is all but impossible, on the theory, to make a mistake about right and wrong. Acts which, as we should commonly say, are approved mistakenly will be really right, and acts mistakenly disapproved will be really wrong, wrong in the only sense in which any acts are. Most people would say that Booth was mistaken in judging it right to assassinate Lincoln. On the theory before us, he was making no mistake whatever. If he felt an emotion of approval toward the act, it was not only right but laudable. Some people who are inclined to subjectivism deceive themselves thoroughly on this point by failing to see what the theory commits them to. 'Surely,' they say, 'if Booth felt as he did, the act *was* right to him.' What they fail to see is that the theory they are defending makes this defence irrelevant. For most of us there is merciful distinction between what is objectively right and what is subjectively right; even if we were to do something accounted monstrously wrong, like murdering a great and good man, it could always be said that if we did what we *believed* to be right, our action was right subjectively. But it is the essence of the theory before us to render this distinction meaningless. An act that is subjectively right, in the sense of being sincerely approved, *is* right, simply and without qualification.

26. We may conclude by pointing out two or three more ways in which subjectivism commits us to paradoxes. (1) It makes it meaningless to ask whether what we approve of is right, or what we disapprove is wrong. A man may, because of parental or religious teaching, disapprove most strongly of contraception, let us say, or euthanasia. If all he means by calling these things wrong is that he has an unfavourable feeling toward them, then in calling them wrong he is clearly correct, and that should end the matter. He knows that he has the feeling and since this is all the judgment affirms, to ask whether it might be mistaken would be meaningless. Yet it is plainly not meaningless. In spite of his conviction that these things are wrong, he may be willing to listen to argument about them, and come to think that his earlier judgment was mistaken. How would the subjectivist deal with this conviction of error? He would say that the new judgment—that the conduct in question is right—is true, because it reports correctly the favourable attitude now taken. This, however, casts no criticism upon the truth of the former judgment, since that too reported correctly what was felt. This is certainly a paradox. Most men would say simply that they had come to think their earlier belief mistaken, and surely this is the natural way to put it. Yet on subjectivist assumptions, it is a meaningless thing to say. Their earlier judgment reported correctly how they felt; they know it to be correct; they still know it. How then could it have been mistaken? Nevertheless, it was.

(2) Again, we attach great importance to *consistency* in moral judgments, an importance that is hardly intelligible on the subjectivist view. A man who yesterday struck a white man with his car and gave him every attention, while today, when he strikes a black man in the same circumstances, he pays him no attention whatever, would be criticized for inconsistency. But there is no inconsistency for the subjectivist. Two differing emotions are simply two events, and events are not inconsistent with each other. Neither are the implied judgments. The judgment 'I ought to help the white man' is quite consistent with 'I need not help the black man', for these judgments are merely the reports of successive states of feeling, both of which are true. 'Emotional moods vary: and if either an individual or a community were angry with a certain piece of conduct today and not angry with precisely similar conduct tomorrow, nobody would have any right to reproach them with inconsistency.'[1] But of course we do so reproach them. And if this reproach is justified, it can only be because the moral judgments concerned are more than reports of feeling. They are inconsistent because they mean to say something about conduct, and to say incompatible things.

(3) Then there is the consideration that G. E. Moore found so decisive against subjectivism.[2] We do mean at times to contradict

[1] Rashdall, *Is Conscience an Emotion?* 111
[2] Moore, *Ethics*, 100 ff.

each other about moral matters, but if subjectivism is true, we cannot even if we try. You may say that an income tax is robbery, and I may maintain that it is not. Each of us may suppose that he is contradicting the other; each of us would certainly say that he means to take exception to what the other has said. But with the worst intention in the world, we cannot bring the contradiction off. All that you are doing is reporting—quite correctly—your antipathy to this tax. All that I am doing is reporting—equally correctly—my lack of antipathy to it. Both judgments are true, and two true judgments can never conflict. The only way I could contradict you would be to say that you do not really feel what your judgment says you feel, and that, besides being impertinent and almost certainly false, is not an ethical difference at all, but one about psychological fact. So long as we confine ourselves to judgments of value, conflicts of opinion are impossible, since we are never talking about the same thing, but you about your feelings and I about mine. Moore thought this absurd. He held it to be far more certain that we really do mean to deny others' opinion at times on moral issues than that the subjectivist analysis of ethical judgment was correct. I agree.

But at the time Moore wrote, modern emotivism had not yet shown its head. Assuming that moral judgments really were judgments, it seemed absurd to say that they never conflicted with each other. But what if they were not judgments at all? What if they were pseudo-judgments, mere exclamations masking under the guise of assertions? Moore had not thought of that. And if they really were such, then the consequence he alleged against Westermarck as an intolerable paradox—that our moral judgments can never conflict—will be a perfectly natural one. They will say or assert nothing; and if they assert nothing, they obviously deny nothing. Whether this emotivist analysis is nearer the truth than the subjectivist one we shall soon examine.

CHAPTER VI

DEONTOLOGY

1. In the dialectic of reason and feeling which we have been tracing, Westermarck was supposed for a time to show the furthest possible swing of the pendulum toward the reduction of moral judgment to feeling. In fact there was a still further swing to come, as we shall see. But he had barely launched his theory before the pendulum began to swing back again toward ethical rationalism. *The Origin and Development of the Moral Ideas* appeared in 1906, and a second edition was called for in 1912. In the latter year an article appeared in *Mind* by H. A. Prichard with the arresting title, 'Is Moral Philosophy Based on a Mistake?' It attracted no great notice at the time, but it planted seeds of reflection that grew steadily and produced rich fruit many years later in the work of Sir David Ross and E. F. Carritt.[1]

Prichard's answer to his own question was that moral philosophy *was* based on a mistake. It had assumed ever since Socrates that the judgment of right or duty called for a defence, and a defence of a particular kind. We must show that the act alleged to be right conduced to someone's advantage. The advantage might be to the agent himself or to others; and it might be in increased happiness, in enlarged knowledge, or in many another good. But if our approval was to be justified, some advantage there must be. Here, Prichard insisted, lay the mistake. No such justification was necessary or possible. The reason why we should keep a promise or avoid a lie is not that someone is going to reap a profit from it. There is really no reason at all outside the fact of duty itself; the reason for acting in this way is that it is self-evidently right and obligatory. We should do our

[1] Most notably Ross's *The Right and the Good* (1930) and *The Foundations of Ethics* (1939) and Carritt's *The Theory of Morals* (1928), *Morals and Politics* (1935), and *Ethical and Political Thinking* (1947). Prichard's own *Moral Obligation* appeared only posthumously in 1949. Perhaps I may be permitted to add that I had the great good fortune to have all these men, as well as Moore, Joseph, Perry, and Dewey— of whom more later—as teachers and friends. I have sat under many lectures of Rashdall, but did not know him personally.

duty because we see that it is our duty, just as we should believe what is true because we see that it is true. No more ultimate justification can be given in either case. What is right need not be right because it is contributory to the good, for it may still be right when it produces no discernible good at all, even when it produces, for all we can see, a surplus of evil. It is because of this emphasis on right as not derivative from good that these philosophers have received their name. They are called 'deontologists' because their emphasis is on τό δέον, that which is right or binding, as distinct from that which is good.

2. We have described them as returning to rationalism in ethics. The ground for this will be evident from this characteristically clear passage from Sir David Ross:

> 'That an act, *qua* fulfilling a promise, or *qua* effecting a just distribution of good . . . is *prima facie* right, is self-evident; not in the sense that it is evident from the beginning of our lives, or as soon as we attend to the proposition for the first time, but in the sense that when we have reached sufficient mental maturity and have given sufficient attention to the proposition it is evident without any need of proof, or of evidence beyond itself. It is self-evident just as a mathematical axiom, or the validity of a form of inference, is self-evident. The moral order expressed in these propositions is just as much part of the fundamental nature of the universe (and, we may add, of any possible universe in which there were moral agents at all) as is the spatial or numerical structure expressed in the axioms of geometry or arithmetic. In our confidence that these propositions are true there is involved the same trust in our reason that is involved in our confidence in mathematics; and we should have no justification for trusting it in the latter sphere and distrusting it in the former.'[1]

This leaves us with no doubt that in Ross's view the judgment that an act is right is an expression of reason. But what is it exactly that reason is apprehending in such a judgment? Is it the rightness of some particular act? Is it the validity of some rule of action, like 'keep your promises' or 'don't lie'? Or is that which is self-evident, as Kant thought, some very abstract rule like 'be consistent', which we can apply as a test to rules of less abstractness? Ross accepts none of these views.

[1] *The Right and the Good*, 29–30

3. What he takes as self-evidently binding is *prima facie* duties. And a *prima facie* duty is a claim on us resting on some circumstance of the situation we are facing. Sometimes this circumstance is a previous act of our own. Suppose we have promised to return a book on a certain day. Then in virtue of this promise, the return of the book has a self-evident claim on us. It is not a claim that can never be out-weighed by any other claim, so that it is our duty to keep our promise though the heavens fall; that is fanaticism. But the man who does not feel that making a promise lays him under any degree of restraint must be morally blind. Similarly with other features of the situation. Sometimes what gives rise to my *prima facie* duty is a previous act of someone else. Suppose someone has saved my life at the risk of his own. Does this leave me at liberty to treat him as if he had never raised a finger in my behalf? Clearly not. Sometimes, again, what gives rise to a duty is the possibility of injustice. If I am distributing provisions at a school picnic, should I be justified in passing one boy over because he had a wart on his face? Should I be justified in doing so even if I could convince myself that by giving his share to some particularly greedy youngster, I could produce as much pleasure on the whole as if I had acted justly? Ross would say no. Justice has a claim on us merely as justice, and quite apart from any goods that it may lead to. How many sorts of circumstances give rise to these special obligations? Not many, apparently;[1] but what there are are of very common occurrence, and taken together they fill a large space in the field of our duties.

4. Now to recognize a rule as self-evidently and universally valid has in the past meant that in practice it had no exceptions. Kant held that if the rule of truth-telling passed the test of rightness at all, it allowed of no exceptions whatever. Ross has abjured such rigorism. He holds *both* that the rule is self-evidently valid *and* admits exceptions in practice. How is this possible? His answer is that what is self-evident is the claim, not the duty in a concrete case. An act is a concrete event, and such an event is never simple; it always has a diversity of aspects. Considered under one aspect, it has a certain claim upon us; considered under another, it has a different and per-haps a stronger claim. My duty is to weigh these claims against each

[1] Ross recognizes seven duties: (1) of fidelity to promises, (2) of reparation for injuries, (3) of gratitude, (4) of justice, (5) of beneficence, (6) of self-improvement, (7) of not injuring others. *The Right and The Good*, 21

other, and to choose that line of action whose total claims are greater. Suppose I am considering whether to repay a debt. On one side, my payment of the money will be the fulfilment of a promise, and that has an obvious claim upon me. On another side, my family may be in extreme need, and then my repayment of the money has the aspect of a failure to alleviate their need. Ross would recognize a self-evident obligation to seek the good of one's family as well as to fulfil one's promises. Both features lay one under a self-evident obligation, though the obligations cannot both be met.

There is conflict here, but no contradiction. And the conflict can normally be solved, for the different features of the situation will impose obligations of differing weight. Moral laws are related to concrete cases very much as physical laws are. We hold that the law of gravitation is universal; when we see a balloon rise, we do not say that the law is being contradicted; we say that gravitation is still acting on the lighter-than-air gas in the balloon, but that the upward pressure of the heavier air around it is stronger than this downward pull, and hence the balloon goes up. What is really universal is not the falling of bodies, for sometimes they do not fall, but the *tendency* to fall; this will still be present, though temporarily overcome. It is the same with moral laws. The fulfilment of promises, taken in the abstract, is always, and as such, right; and so far as any particular act is the fulfilment of a promise, it also *tends* to be right. Similarly, the securing of good to one's family is, as such, right and obligatory. But in a particular case the first of these claims may be much stronger than the second and hence outweigh it as a ground of actual duty. The relative force of the obligations may be extremely hard to estimate; the deontologists hold that we can never be sure that we have made the right choice, since we can never be sure we have exhausted the relevant aspects of our action or done justice to their several claims. Prichard used to say that our chances of ever doing the precisely right action were very low, and that if we ever succeeded, it was by luck. But our estimate of comparative claims, however fallible, is still a function of reason, and if our powers were equal to the task, we could see the solution of concrete problems as clearly and certainly as a competent mathematician now grasps the solution of a complex equation.

So far we have been dealing with what is asserted in a judgment of right. According to Ross, what is asserted is either that the agent has an obligation grounded on some aspect of his situation, or that the situation as a whole is such as to render a certain action (or perhaps one of several alternative actions) obligatory. The first judgment expresses a necessary insight, as necessary as anything in mathematics. The second contains subordinate insights of this kind, but it is not as a whole necessary, because the concrete is inexhaustible.

5. What of the other principal judgment of morals, the judgment of good? Ross is willing to go a certain distance with the subjectivist. He goes so far as to say: 'the only common fact that is present whenever we use the term "good" is that in each case the judger has some feeling of approval or interest towards what he calls good'.[1] But though this is an interesting fact of psychology, it does not imply that being approved is all we *mean* by good;

> 'it is surely a strange reversal of the natural order of thought to say that our admiring an action either is, or is what necessitates, its being good. We think of its goodness as what we admire in it, and as something it would have even if no one admired it, something that it has in itself. We could suppose, for instance, an action of self-denial which neither the doer nor any one else had ever admired.'[2]

Again, though goodness belongs only to states of mind, it is not dependent on being known; 'goodness is entirely objective and intrinsic to the things that are good'.[3] Ross holds, as Sidgwick and Moore did, that goodness is a non-sensible, indefinable quality which must be apprehended, if at all, by intelligence.

How is it related to the things that have it? We are of course talking now not about things that are good as means, but things that are good in themselves, like happiness, knowledge, or dutifulness. When we say that happiness, for example, is intrinsically good, the relation we have in mind is certainly not causal, for a cause precedes its effect, while happiness and the goodness that belongs to it are not separated by time; nor are we reporting a mere empirical togetherness, as we do when we say grass is green, for though grass could be grass without being green, happiness could not be what it is without also being good. The connection, therefore, is a necessary one. When we apprehend it, we see that anything having the nature X *must*, in virtue

[1] *The Right and the Good*, 90
[2] *Ibid.*, 89
[3] *Ibid.*, 132

of that nature, also have Y.[1] Such necessary insight may appear again in our comparison of values. We say, for example, that our delight in last night's talk with an old friend was worth more than the boredom of the night before over a recent 'thriller'; but we should not offer this as an inductive or deductive conclusion from anything; we should expect it to be self-evident to anyone whose experience was really like ours.

So far, in his dealing with good, Ross is at one with Sidgwick and Moore. But at the next step he parts company with Sidgwick, and, a step later, with Moore also.

6. Sidgwick held that it was self-evident to the reflective mind not only that pleasure is good, but that it is the only good. We can see, that is, when other alleged goods are offered us, such as knowledge, friendship, reputation, power, that they would be worthless unless they brought pleasure with them, and that such value as they have belongs to this attendant pleasure. Ross agrees that pleasure is good and self-evidently so, but he thinks it plain on examination that the goodness we attach to experiences does not vary exclusively with the amount of pleasure in them, and indeed that some things other than pleasure are just as clearly valued for their own sakes. He recognizes three of these; virtue, knowledge, and the just allocation of pleasures and pains. That these really are intrinsically good can be shown, he thinks, by ideal experiments. Consider virtue. This means action, or the disposition to act, from such motives as the desire to do one's duty or to make others happy. One can imagine a universe in which such virtue did not exist, but in which the total pleasure or happiness was the same as in another where it did exist. Would the first lose nothing by reason of its lack of virtue? Ross thinks we can see this to be false. Imagine, again, a world in which virtue, happiness, and everything else regarded as good, existed in the same amounts as in some other, the only exception being that all the people in the first were ignorant while all the people in the second were enlightened; would not the second be better than the first by reason of the enlightenment? Ross thinks it self-evidently would be. Finally, take two worlds in which, with equal amounts of happiness and unhappiness, these amounts were so distributed that in the first the virtuous people were miserable and the unvirtuous happy, while in the second the allotments were reversed. This is a quite conceivable

[1] *The Right and the Good*, 121–3

situation, however improbable in fact; and Ross thinks that the second pattern of allotment, in which virtue was attended with happiness and vice with unhappiness would be intrinsically and self-evidently better than the other. Ross thus goes beyond Sidgwick in recognizing that goodness is a necessary property of three other forms of experience besides pleasure. But there is still nothing novel about this position. With some differences regarding the number of goods recognized, it is the well known position of Rashdall and Moore.

7. From this point on, however, the deontologists strike out a new path. Since it was in reaction against the views of Moore and Rashdall that the most novel and significant part of their theory was developed, it may be well to pause for a moment over the theory against which they were in revolt.

The appearance at Cambridge of Moore's *Principia Ethica* (1903), followed a few years later at Oxford by Rashdall's *Theory of Good and Evil* (1907), had raised 'ideal utilitarianism' into something like an ethical orthodoxy. This theory was attractively simple. Of the two classical questions of ethics, What is good? and What is right?, it said that the first was by far the more important, since you could not answer the second without answering the first, while if you did find an answer to the first, you could answer the second by deduction from it. If you knew what sorts of things were intrinsically good, you could say that conduct was rendered right by the production of these things. Those who adopted this way of thinking were called utilitarians because they believed, as Bentham, Mill, and Sidgwick did, that what made an act right was its consequences; they were called, a little clumsily, *ideal* utilitarians to distinguish them from this earlier school, which had accepted pleasure as the only good; their *summum bonum* was what Rashdall called 'an ideal end or good, which includes, but is not limited to, pleasure'.[1] They recognized a variety of intrinsic goods, but held that all of these could be given places on a single scale of value. This made possible a single, simple rule of all conduct, which was taken as self-evident and holding without exception: 'So act as to produce the greatest net good.'[2]

[1] *Theory of Good and Evil*, I, 184
[2] 'The only possible reason that can justify any action is that by it the greatest possible amount of what is good absolutely should be realised.' Moore, *Principia Ethica*, 101. 'It is to my mind a perfectly clear deliverance of the moral consciousness that no action can be right except in so far as it tends to produce a good, and that when we have to choose between goods, it is always right to choose the greater good.' Rashdall, *Ibid.*, II, 39

Now it is precisely this cardinal principle of utilitarians of all schools that the deontologists reject. They think there are cases where, on a mere calculation of goods, one should clearly do act A, while, by the general agreement of conscientious persons, one should do act B instead. You have borrowed money from a well-to-do man, for example, and promised to return it on a certain day. On the way to return it, you meet a friend who is unemployed, ill, or distressed, and who would, in all probability, use the money to much better advantage than the man to whom you owe it. Is it obvious that you should turn the money over to the needy person and break the promise to your creditor? Certainly most men would not accept that. Or suppose that two neighbours of yours are in need, and you are considering to which of them, with your limited means, you should offer help. So far as you can see, their needs are equal, and they would put such help as is offered them to equally good use. In your relations with them there is only one significant difference. You recall that, on a skating party last winter, when you foolishly ventured on to thin ice and went through, it was one of these men, Jones, who, at some risk to himself, pulled you to safety. Would the fact that the consequences of offering aid would be equally good in the two cases really leave it indifferent which man you offered it to? A utilitarian of either type, it is said, would have to answer Yes, whereas anyone who really acted on that view would be thought callous to the claims of gratitude. Or suppose, once more, that the government of a certain community finds itself faced with an outbreak of lawlessness which it believes can be effectively checked only by stern measures. Unfortunately it cannot lay its hands on any of the ringleaders. It has in jail, however, a man of criminal record, who would certainly be no loss to the community, and whose connection with the recent outbreaks could be easily made out by a little skilful and entirely secret manipulation of evidence. The good to the community of getting rid of him and of simultaneously deterring future outbreaks would seem greater than that of keeping him alive to be a lasting nuisance. So he is formally condemned and hanged by way of public example. Such action might conceivably be called for by utilitarian calculations. None the less, say the deontologists, it would be obviously and monstrously wrong.

8. How would the ideal utilitarians reply? They would certainly begin by saying that on the practical issue their conclusion in all these cases would be the same precisely as that of the deontologist and the plain man; they differ only as to the ground on which this common conclusion is based. In Ross's view, it is based on a *prima facie* duty to keep promises, to pay debts of gratitude, and to do justice, independently of any good that such action may bring; and in these cases the line of duty on which everyone would agree is supposed to be indefensible on any other basis, the appeal to consequences requiring the opposite verdict. To this the utilitarian answers that it is only by irresponsible book-keeping that consequences are made in such cases to cast their vote against what common sense would say. Make your calculation more complete, and you will find that it supports rather than opposes common sense. Take the case, for example, where you have to choose between paying a debt as you have promised and giving the money to someone in need. You are not playing the game of consequences fairly if you consider only that the creditor does not need the money and the other man does, and that you will therefore do more good by breaking your promise. A breach of promise does not stop with itself; it has its own train of manifold and far-reaching consequences. They include not only the deprivation and disappointment of the creditor, but also the loss on your part of his confidence, the weakening of your habit of keeping engagements—a habit that must be firmly maintained if the ever-present temptation to relax it in one's own favour is to be avoided—and, above all, the small but appreciable lowering of public confidence that follows any deliberate breaking of such an engagement. This last is no light matter. The business of life depends at a hundred points on people's readiness to trust the promises of others, and every breach of that trust has its repercussions. Subtract from the advantages of promise-breaking all these serious ills, and you will find them clearly outweighed by the goods of loyalty to one's word. Rightly viewed, ideal utilitarianism thus has the support of common sense rather than its veto.

9. It is now the deontologist's turn. What would he answer? He would admit that promise-breaking does have consequences of this kind, and that before a decision is arrived at in any particular case they must be taken into account. He is not denying that consequences are important. He is a rationalist, but he is not a rationalist like Kant, who tried disastrously to make right-doing independent of consequences; he recognizes the producing of good consequences as one of his self-evident *prima facie* duties. What he is denying is that consequences *alone* are important. He is insisting that some kinds of action have an obligation *not* derived from them, and that, in a particular case, this may outweigh the obligation that *is* derived from them. Now there is no hope of settling this issue if, whenever such a case is offered, the other side is allowed to contrive additional consequences *ad hoc* and throw them into the scale. One must take a case where the evidence is agreed upon and where it stays fixed. Can any such cases be found?

The deontologist would say that, ideally at least, they can; he would say, I think, that they can be provided in either of two ways. First, one may imagine a situation in which all the goods and bads involved in keeping a promise and in breaking it are exhausted as far as the eye can see, and the net good on the two sides is admitted to be the same. (This is clearly a possibility, and if anyone says it is not, on the ground that promise-keeping will always have the best results, he is claiming quite unreasonable powers of prophecy.) Very well, in such a case, where there is admittedly nothing to choose in point of consequences, would the ordinary conscientious man say that it was just as permissible to break a promise, or suppress his gratitude, or punish an innocent man, as to do the opposite? The deontologists are clear that he would not. Hence they say that, in point of fact, he thinks of such actions as promise-keeping as having a rightness of their own, which they owe not to their consequences but rather to being what they are. Here I think the deontologists have the better of the argument.

They would proceed to ask, secondly, how it is that, if the rightness of our conduct does depend wholly on consequences, we should so often be sure, *before knowing the consequences*, that certain actions are wrong. Would a judge, or any other reflective man, to whom the suggestion was made that an innocent man be hanged, really have to stop and work out the consequences pro and con before having an opinion about it? Surely his opinion would come out instantly, and with a confidence that would be inexplicable if it depended on calculating results. Such considerations do show, I think, that many of our moral judgments are made with no thought of consequences. Still, the argument is less decisive than it seems. For, as Sidgwick so conclusively showed, it is possible for a rule that was utilitarian in origin and is justifiable only in the utilitarian way to come, in course of time, to seem evident intuitively. Nevertheless, the argument does have some weight. Most of us would not only say before thinking of consequences that the hanging of an innocent man was wrong; we should stick to our opinion, even when faced by evidence we could not refute that society would profit by the deed. Such tenacity strongly suggests that in justice of this kind we find an obligation that cannot be wholly accounted for by any consideration of prospective gain, personal or social.

10. Granting to the deontologists that we do feel this obligation, the question now is whether they are right in their way of explaining it. Their way of explaining it, as we saw, amounts to saying that it is ultimate and inexplicable. 'The sense of obligation to do, or of the rightness of, an action of a particular kind', says Prichard, 'is absolutely underivative or immediate'; 'our sense of the rightness of an act is not a conclusion from our appreciation of the goodness either of it or of anything else'.[1] Ross writes: 'It seems, on reflection, self-evident that a promise, simply as such, is something that *prima facie* ought to be kept . . .'[2] 'If any one ask us,' says Carritt, ' "Why ought I to do these acts you call my duty?", the only answer is, "Because they *are* your *duty*", and if he does not see this we cannot make him, unless by informing him about matters of fact; if he sees they are duties, he can no more ask why he ought to do them than why he should believe what is true.'[3]

Now we have granted that the duty of promise-keeping, for example, does not rest merely on consequences; it is better that promises should be kept, even if no later advantage accrues from it. And it may be thought that this is what the deontologists too are saying. That would be a mistake. What they are saying is that promise-keeping is our duty though in fact there is no good in it at all. According to Ross, 'If I contemplate one of the acts in question, an act, say, in which a promise is kept . . . and ask myself whether it is good, apart both from results and from motives, I can find no goodness in it. The fact is that when some one keeps a promise we can see no intrinsic worth in that. . . .' And again: 'we can see *no* intrinsic goodness attaching to the life of a community merely because promises are kept in it.'[4] It is our duty to keep promises, not because, even with other things equal, the life of a community is *better* for promises

[1] *Moral Obligation*, 7, 9
[2] *The Right and the Good*, 40
[3] *Theory of Morals*, 29
[4] *Foundations of Ethics*, 142–3

being kept in it, but because . . . the sentence cannot be completed. It is our duty, but there is no reason why. Our obligation is read off directly, and with self-evident necessity, from a set of neutral facts. So also of such duties as repaying debts, and telling the truth. Indeed most of the *prima facie* duties recognized by the deontologists rest not on the goodness of any state of things, but on the neutral and factual character of the act itself. For this reason, the ancient search of the philosophers for some single characteristic of right acts which serves to make them right is set down as misguided. There is *no* one thing that makes right acts right. Sometimes they are right because they are the keeping of promises, sometimes because they are the paying of debts. But between the rightness of an act and its tendency to bring into being any kind or degree of good there is no general relation at all.

11. Here I must dissent. This conclusion does not seem credible. We are being told that it may be a self-evident duty to choose one rather than another state of affairs even though, in respect to goodness, there is nothing to choose between them. But more; we are being told that state of things A may be definitely and admittedly *worse* than B, and that it may still be our duty to bring A into being. With a choice before us of making the world worse or making it better, we may have a moral obligation to make it worse. This is very hard to accept. A strong case has been carried too far. When the deontologists said that duty is not based always on a goodness that follows the act in time, but sometimes on the character of the act itself, they carried us with them. They did so because it seemed clear that a state of things in which promises were kept, gratitude recognized, and truth told, was a better state of things than one in which these were not done. But when we are now told that such obligations have nothing to do either with the intrinsic goodness of the acts, or of the state of things they institute, let alone the goodness of their consequences, we feel as if the mat on which we had been approaching this school had been pulled out from under our feet. The obligations that were presented to us as rational insights take on an air of caprice.

Can we offer any evidence that we are correct about this and the deontologists not? I think we can, though argument on such ultimate issues is notoriously hard.

12. (1) Perhaps an *ad hominem* argument may therefore be permitted.

Sir David Ross 'can see *no* intrinsic goodness attaching to the life of a community merely because promises are kept in it'; goodness attaches only to the motives or consequences of such conduct, not to the state of affairs constituted by its general practice. But when we come to justice, in one of its important forms, Ross is emphatic that this does have intrinsic goodness, regardless of motives or consequences. A community in which virtuous men are happy and wicked men unhappy he considers much better than one in which these allotments are reversed, even though the totals of happiness and unhappiness are the same.[1] Now the goodness admitted to be present here is not the property of anyone's experience, but of a set of arrangements between experiences. If intrinsic worth can be owned by such a set of arrangements, why should it not also be owned by that other set of arrangements in which promises are kept, or truth told, or debts repaid? If there is any fundamental difference between these situations, which would justify saying that one is self-evidently good and the other self-evidently valueless, I have failed to catch it.

13. (2) Is it really the case that to ask *why* something is our duty is meaningless? Mr Carritt says that if we see it is our duty to keep a promise, it is as pointless to ask why we should keep it as to ask why we should believe what is true. In this he is no doubt right. Once we have seen that the keeping of a promise is our duty, it would be idle to ask why we should do it, since we have in our possession already the most conclusive answer that could be given. But then this is not the situation in which the question would be asked. It would be asked, rather, by someone to whom his duty was not apparent and who wanted guidance about it. He might see that keeping a promise would bring pain to someone, and, reluctant to give this pain, he might ask, 'What ground is there, after all, for saying that to keep a promise *is* obligatory? You tell me that there is *no* ground, that if I attend and am clear-headed I shall see the obligation immediately. But for the alternative course of breaking the promise there clearly *is* some ground, namely that it will avoid pain. Am I to believe that it is my duty to do something that involves that pain, yet carries no good

---

[1] '. . . besides virtue and pleasure, we must recognize, as a third independent good, the apportionment of pleasure and pain to the virtuous and the vicious respectively. And it is on the recognition of this as a separate good that the recognition of the duty of justice . . . rests.' *The Right and the Good*, 138.

to counterbalance it? That does not seem to me, on the face of it, reasonable. *Why* should I take it as obligatory to produce that which you own to be without value? I cannot think this question meaningless, nor the asking of it a sign of obtuseness or failure to attend. I suspect that most people who do attend would agree that it is significant, and also that it has a natural and intelligible answer; namely, 'It is your duty to keep promises because the state of things in which they are kept is a better state than one in which they are broken'. A critic may rejoin that this is no more obvious to the obtuse than the proposition for which it is offered as a reason. That may or may not be true. But the point is that it *is* significant and does give a reason. It is one thing—and a not very convincing thing—to say that the keeping of promises is a duty because its obligatoriness is self-evident and another thing to say that it is a duty because it is good. If the first account is true, the reason given in the second must be an impertinence—unneeded, untrue, adding nothing to the case. And I do not think it is.

Since the inability to give a reason for duty is ascribed to the 'immediacy' of our insight, it may be well to look a little more closely at this immediacy. Take a necessary proposition of an ordinary kind, say 'whatever has shape has size'. This is an immediate insight because the first attribute entails the second directly; the suggestion that the second follows only through the intermediary of another and omitted term would seem absurd. But the parallel suggestion about promise-keeping and obligatoriness would not seem at all absurd; indeed the absurdity, if there is one, seems rather to lie on the other side, in the suggestion that promise-keeping, described as wholly valueless, should as such be obligatory. And whereas in the shape-size proposition the suggestion of a middle term is a gratuitous complication of what is plain already, the introduction of a middle term in the other clears up a puzzle. 'Act A, worthless in itself, should be done'; that seems very dubious indeed. 'Act A, *because it is intrinsically good*, should be done'; that is a different matter and makes sense at once. We are not questioning that the obligatoriness of a kind of action may be seen as rational and necessary. We are only contending that the line of necessity does not run straight from a state of things that is utterly grey, so far as worth is concerned, to a duty to produce that state; what carries the obligation is the fact that the state would be worth while, or of some positive value—in short that it would be good.

14. (3) A further point may be mentioned which has troubled many moralists about this form of intuitionism: the duties with which it presents us are 'an unconnected heap'. Philosophers and scientists alike have generally felt that they should use Occam's razor whenever they can; it is their business to reduce apparent disorder to law, and diversity of fact to unity of principle. Moral philosophy has proceeded on the assumption that, if we searched resolutely enough, we should discover behind the great variety of acts that we call right and obligatory some unifying principle that made them so. Ethics has consisted very largely of the search for that principle. To be sure, moralists have disagreed in disappointing fashion as to what the principle was; we have been variously advised to order our conduct so as to secure survival, wisdom, self-realization, power, pleasure, the beatific vision, and much else. But the difficulty and disagreement in answering the question have not destroyed the conviction that some principle is there to be found, even if only a very abstract one like the rule of producing the greatest good. Now the new intuitionism says that there is *no* such unifying principle. There is *no* common reason for calling actions right or obligatory. Sometimes they are right because they produce the greatest good; sometimes because, though they produce a smaller good, they have the character of promise-keeping; sometimes because they have the character of debt-paying; and so on. And the deontologists are surely right in saying that we cannot be sure that when we set out in search of unity we shall find it, or even that it is there to be found. The fact that a theory is simpler than another is no proof in itself that it is nearer the truth. The world has not been ordered for the ease of our understanding.

15. Are we to say, then, that there is no presumption in favour of a single ground of duty as against a heap of duties? That, I suggest, would be going too far. When we use the same word 'right' of a variety of actions, I do not think it is used either to refer to utterly different things, as the word 'mother' is to refer to a female parent and to a mould that appears in vinegar, or to some quality that is perfectly obvious to us but abstract, simple, and indefinable. 'For it is a character of that peculiar sort, like truth, beauty, and goodness, that we can seek it, as Plato says, "divining it to be something", before we know what it is . . .'[1] The analogy to truth is worth con-

[1] H. W. B. Joseph, *Some Problems in Ethics*, 71

sidering. The truth of a proposition is not, as certain realists once suggested, a simple unanalysable quality that attaches to it 'like the flavour of gorgonzola', nor can we believe that the term refers to utterly different things—sometimes it means correspondence with fact, sometimes coherence with other beliefs, sometimes success in practice, sometimes prescription by authority. However hard it is to bring to light the nature of truth, it has been the conviction of most inquirers in this field that such a nature there must be. Unless there were, the conflicts of belief that trouble us most deeply would be insoluble and indeed hardly possible. When the biologist declared it true that the human mind has evolved, he would mean, for example, that it corresponded to fact, and when the theologian denied it, he would mean that it was not sanctioned by authority. The second would not be denying what the other asserted, and there would be no dispute. But we know perfectly well that the one does intend to assert the truth of the proposition in the sense in which the other intends to deny it; they mean by truth the same thing, even though one or other must have gone wrong in formulating what he means.

Just as we must believe that there is some common character that makes true beliefs true, so we are constrained to believe that there is some common character that makes right acts right. To be sure, this may be an illusion. We may be using the same word to indicate the presence of quite different characters. But one who thus rejects the evidence of usage must at least accept the burden of proof. And most moralists would probably confess to an 'invincible surmise' that there is more to the story than an 'unconnected heap' of duties, that we can hardly have reached the end of the line when we say that what makes generosity right is its producing something of worth, while that which makes truthfulness right has nothing to do with worth, but lies in a suitability in itself worthless. That position is to be accepted only when the search for a common ground has broken down. It has been replied that this disunity is not escaped by making the right dependent on the good, since among the things to which we apply the term 'good' there is the same lack of common nature that appears among right acts. Without agreeing that this is true, we may point out that even if it is, those who hold to the primacy of good have the more intellectually satisfying case. For though they may admit that there is no common nature in what is good, the deontologists double this pluralism by saying that there is no common nature in what is right either.[1]

16. Is there any way in which the deontologists could admit a common ground for all right acts and yet keep this rightness independent of the good? One interesting suggestion, recently put forward, is somewhat reminiscent of Clarke. May it not be that all right acts are right because of their fittingness, that in one way or another they all fit the situation? We recognize that if a service has been done us, an act of gratitude is fitting, while an ignoring of the service or a returning of evil for good would be plainly unfitting. It is fitting that we should pay our debts and unfitting that we should renounce them, fitting that we should concern ourselves more for the welfare of our own family than of other people's families, fitting that we should tell truth rather than falsehood, fitting that we should acquit innocence of guilt and unfitting in the extreme that we should punish it. Even the rightness that depends on good consequences can be brought in under the formula, for in view of human needs and desires it is always fitting, so far as it goes, to add to the stock of human good. If we take this line, we can say not only that rightness has a common base, wherever it appears, but also that this base is objective and rationally apprehended, for fittingness is not a quality, still less a feeling, but a relation evident only to intelligence. Right will then remain irreducible to good, for the fittingness which makes an act right will be quite distinct from goodness.

This view does, I think, help to explain why we call some acts right and some wrong. The unsuitability or inappropriateness of treating harshly a person who has befriended us is surely a ground, whether the whole ground or not, of calling such conduct wrong, and the theory applies with special force to such cases as the condemning of

---

[1] It is the practice of some philosophers to distinguish the meaning of terms like 'true', 'right', and 'good', from the common characteristics in virtue of which the terms are applied. In support of the distinction it is pointed out that we are often sure that the term applies, though unable to report the ground on which we applied it. But I do not think it can therefore be said that we are using two meanings, one very abstract, simple, and obvious (e.g. 'true'), and the other massive and indeterminate (e.g. 'true-making characteristics'). The common characteristics in virtue of which we apply the term *constitute* what we mean by it. We are using one meaning only, and in a perfectly familiar way, though this way has provided a well-known puzzle to philosophers from Socrates on. The puzzle is that we at once know what we mean and do not know it; we know it well enough to recognize instances of it when we see them, but not well enough to say what it is in them that awakes our recognition. But this difference in explicitness of grasp is not a difference in meaning.

an innocent man; the wrongness of such action, particularly on the part of a judge, seems to consist chiefly in its being so shockingly unfitting and incongruous. Every sound theory must, I think, incorporate this insight into its account of our calling such actions wrong. My one question about it is whether it has really escaped the basing of the right upon the good, whether the fitness upon which rightness is now based is not itself approved because it is good. Fitness or suitability is, of course, a very broad notion, and it is obviously not all kinds of fitness, but only certain special kinds, that are supposed to make actions right. If a man has committed a long row of murders, and finds a chance to make a great gain out of another with small chance of detection, there is a sense in which it fits his character and the circumstances perfectly to do it again. I knew an old lady once who, when asked her view what should be done with Hitler if he were caught, said that he should be put in a cage and taken about for persons like herself, whom he had made miserable, to stick pins into; and I must confess to having felt a certain fitness in the suggestion, however absurd. Kant, as is well known, thought that if the society on some remote island were being finally dissolved and certain persons guilty of murder were still living in jail, the appropriate thing to do with them was to execute them before the community broke up. Military men think that the appropriate way to treat enemy invaders is to kill as many of them as possible; Quakers have commonly thought that for a man to kill a brother man is unfitting absolutely. We are clearly in need of a test which will distinguish the suitability that makes an act right from other kinds of it.

Sir David Ross thinks there is such a difference, but that it is indefinable; 'We can begin to define moral rightness, because we can say it is a form of suitability; but we cannot complete the definition, since if we ask what kind of suitability it is we can only say that it is the kind of suitability that is rightness.'[1] Now I strongly suspect that if we were to examine the suitabilities that were pronounced right, we should find that all of them constituted, or belonged to, a state of affairs that we recognized as good, and that if we inspected the suitabilities pronounced wrong, we should find that they were similarly bound up with states of affairs thought to be bad. How, for example, could you ever decide Kant's problem whether it was more suitable to kill the men in jail before society broke up than to give them another chance, except by considering that the two acts would

[1] *Foundations of Ethics,* 55

belong to two different states of affairs of which one was better than the other? Again, taken as mere abstract suitabilities, what possible choice could there be between the pacifist and the military view of how to treat aggressors? Both are eminently suitable in their different ways. If we are to arrive at an intelligent choice between them, we must compare not two abstract suitabilities merely, but the two vastly extended states of affairs which these acts would tend to engender, and ultimately, perhaps, the two opposed ways of life to which they belong. It may be said that this makes the problem enormously difficult. But then it *is* difficult; and when we see that to solve it satisfactorily we must judge the comparative worth of competing ways of life, we see *why* it is so difficult. Comparative fitness should be considered, by all means. But we shall soon find ourselves effectively blocked unless the schemes of things into which differing acts would fit may themselves be registered as better and worse.

17. Why should we trouble our heads over these impalpable distinctions? It is because they lie on the watershed between two conceptions of ethics, that which finds in *right* the primary notion, and that which finds it in *good*. The majority of great moralists have belonged to the latter school. Plato, Aristotle, the Epicureans, Hobbes, Hume, the utilitarians, the idealists, the evolutionists, though they had very various notions as to where the good lay, all took as the test of right conduct its conduciveness to good. But there have been moralists of weight on the other side. Christian ethics, indeed, has not taken a very clear stand, since its insistence on conformity to right, as given in divine commands, has been balanced, even in such exponents as Locke and Butler, by the teaching that this conformity is the necessary means to happiness hereafter. But in the Stoics, in Cudworth, More, and Clarke, in the immensely influential Kant, in Reid, Price, and Whewell, and now again in the recent and remarkable school of British intuitionists, we find the insistence on a right that is directly perceived by reason and owes nothing to its productiveness of good. What we have been considering is, in effect, the issue between these schools. If a single case can be adduced of an act that is seen at once to be obligatory and *not* to produce the greatest good, the deontologists—the advocates of an independent rightness—have won their case.[1]

[1] For a further consideration of this issue, see below, Chapter XII, Sec. 8–13

18. My own position in the matter is this: if the good on which rightness is said to depend is confined to consequences caused by the act and following it in time, then the dependence of right on good is not made out. The reason is that in some cases what seems to promise such consequences, for example the punishing of an innocent man for public good, is plainly wrong. On the other hand, if it is contended that the rightness of an act need have no connection with good whatever, the contention seems to me false. And it will be the more clearly false if, besides the goodness of later consequences, we take into our account the goodness of the act itself, or, I would rather say, of the pattern of life generally, with its mass of personal relations, which this act implies. If this goodness—too often forgotten in utilitarian reckonings—is included in our review, I think that rightness is always dependent on good produced, and that a duty that would leave the world no better for the doing of it is an irrational duty, indeed no duty at all. The attempt by the new intuitionists to breach this position is not, in my opinion, successful.

Have we anything better to offer? We have shown that there are some elements of paradox in saying that the right is independent of the good, but we have produced no constructive argument to show that it is dependent on it. In theory, two such lines of argument are possible, one inductive, the other a priori. The first line was developed with typical caution and clarity by Sidgwick. He undertook to show of each of the main types of virtue that, with minor exceptions and borderline cases, it conduced so uniformly to good that the connection could not be accidental; we must have come to account actions right *because* of this conduciveness to good.[1] His argument here is masterly and we shall not try to retrace it. The trouble with it is not so much in its account of the right as in its account of what is intrinsically good. Sidgwick found this in pleasure alone. But if the only thing that can be thrown into the scale as good is pleasure, the case of the deontologists against the utilitarians seems to me unanswerable. To say that in every case where we approve the keeping of a disagreeable promise or the telling of an unpleasant truth we approve it because it promises the greatest pleasure is to say something that is not only unprovable, but plainly contrary to fact. The argument becomes much more plausible, however, if the good admits other elements than pleasure, and more plausible still if it is allowed to include the good of the frame of life to which the act belongs. In that case the

[1] *Methods of Ethics*, Bk. III, Ch. 4–11

right and the good may not, after all, fall apart. When we come to discuss constructively the nature of goodness, an account will be offered that we hope will heal this breach.

The other way of arguing for the dependence of the right on the good is the way of direct insight. 'No one would say', wrote McTaggart, 'that a man ought to will the existence of anything unless the thing willed was judged to be such that its existence would be good.'[1] 'It seems to me self-evident', said G. E. Moore, 'that knowingly to do an action which would make the world, on the whole, really and truly *worse* than if we had acted differently, must always be wrong.'[2] I do not reject this appeal to intuition, and those who do reject it will usually be found to be substituting intuitions of their own; such an appeal is sooner or later inevitable. But it ought to come later rather than sooner. One of the requirements for self-evident truth laid down by Sidgwick was that the terms of the proposition should be unambiguously clear; and to say that the rightness of an action is self-evidently dependent on its production of good before one knows what one means by 'good' is courting danger. Claims of self-evidence should follow analysis, not precede it.

19. The deontologists have shown a fidelity to actual moral judgment that is probably closer than that of any other contemporary school. They have argued with great force that moral judgments are really judgments, not expressions of feelings only, and here—for whatever it is worth—common sense is undoubtedly on their side. If they were asked more particularly about the part played by reason in such judgment, they would answer, I think, that its work was threefold. (1) It may apprehend that certain experiences, or arrangements of experiences, are intrinsically and necessarily good. (2) It may infer the consequences of a suggested action. (3) It may perceive that certain acts are necessarily right in virtue of, and so far as, they have a certain character, such as that of truth-telling or promise-keeping. As to (1), I suspect that they are substantially correct, though if the notion of goodness turns out to be less simple than theirs—and Moore's—the insight that X is good will itself be less simple. As to (2), the function of deducing consequences, they are again surely

---

[1] *Some Dogmas of Religion*, 152–3
[2] *Ethics*, 181. *Cf.* also: ' . . . the assertion "I am morally bound to perform this action" is identical with the assertion "this action will produce the greatest possible amount of good in the Universe . . . it is important to insist that this fundamental point is demonstrably certain".' *Principia Ethica*, 146.

right; indeed this is hardly a matter of controversy among present-day moralists. As to (3), the alleged insight that a kind of act is right by reason of a certain abstract character, I think they are mistaken, but not wholly mistaken. The act is seen to be right in virtue of producing goodness, if not in consequences, then through being the kind of act it is. And reason is involved not only in seeing it to be of a certain kind, but also in seeing the filiation of this kind with a way of life as a whole. Truthfulness and promise-keeping do not stand alone. They are implicated in a wider order from which they draw part of whatever goodness they possess. Since we thus hold that the rightness of a kind of action is not independently grasped at all, but always derives from goodness, it is upon the notion of goodness that we shall fix our attention from now on. The next swing of the pendulum, returning to the view that rightness depends on the goodness of consequences, will compel us to look more closely at this fundamental notion of *good*.

CHAPTER VII

INSTRUMENTALISM

1. Among recent American thinkers, perhaps among American philosophers generally, John Dewey stands first. He is not the keenest philosophic critic; that place belongs, I think, to Lovejoy. He is not the philosopher whose writing, as writing, is most likely to be read in the future; that honour will probably go to Santayana. Nor is he the most learned and systematic; Royce excelled him in both respects. Nor again is he the philosopher who as a person is most influential or memorable; here one thinks first of William James. But his thought was impressively original; it was carried into every department of philosophy with an inexhaustible energy; by some interpreters it has been taken to express with peculiar fidelity the American mind; and however that may be, its influence in politics, in religion, and in education, has been incalculable. Though my own sympathies in philosophy lie in other directions, it was my good fortune to have been a pupil of Dewey and to have remained in occasional touch with him for more than thirty years. Those who disagree with another's conclusions are not usually the best exponents of his thought, whatever regard they may feel for him personally; and I do not presume to have fully understood Dewey. But his star has undergone an all too rapid eclipse, and since he was one of the most thoroughgoing of naturalists in ethics as in every other philosophic field, it will be well to take him as our representative of this type of ethical theory.

Dewey travelled far in ethics. It is sometimes forgotten that in his early days he was, like Mr Gladstone, 'the rising hope of the stern unbending Tories'. If one looks at articles he contributed to *Mind* in his thirties, one will find little in their orthodox pages to suggest what a heretic he was to be at ninety. In those days he was doing sturdy battle for the Absolute, conceived as an all-inclusive consciousness in which everything was connected organically with everything else. He thought that the business of the philosopher was to reproduce this whole as nearly as he could in his own consciousness. The business of the good man was essentially the same; as an enthusiastic disciple of T. H. Green, Dewey considered the goal of life to be self-realization, the fullest and most harmonious experience one could achieve. His ethics was thus founded on his metaphysics. Hence when his metaphysics began to crumble, as it did in the 1890s, the ethics had to be largely rebuilt. Let us try to see what happened.

It was not that at any particular time he found Green to be refuted; that is hardly the way in which philosophies get replaced. It was rather that his interest shifted from metaphysics to science, and that at this new and less lofty altitude the old beliefs turned out to be snow men that melted away. The focus of his attention shifted from the organism as conceived by Hegel to the organism as conceived by Darwin, and this change carried with it a total transformation in his view of the nature and end of thought. For the Hegelian, thought is a misty term of magnificent sweep; everything seems to fall under it; one's consciousness is mostly thought, and wherever it turns in nature, it is greeted by more thought in the form of what Dewey described as 'the universal intelligence'. But as he became more of a biologist, the metaphysician in him faltered. Thought to the biologist is not a stuff of which things are made; it is a process of thinking; and thinking is a way of behaving on the part of the organism. It must therefore be studied in the way in which we study other such activities —walking, climbing, or swimming, for example. When we set out to explain such activities, we usually ask how they came about, or what we are trying to do by means of them, or perhaps both. Now, said Dewey, if you ask such questions about the activity of thinking, the answer will force you on to a new theory of the nature of thought. That theory is 'instrumentalism', and since this forms the core of Dewey's new philosophy, we must try to see what it means.

2. Consider what first made men think. According to Dewey it was not wonder, as Aristotle supposed, but the pressure of practical need. Thinking is the sort of activity an organism resorts to, if it can, when instinct and habit break down. So long as primitive man could satisfy his hunger and thirst by instinct eked out by habit, he no doubt followed that animal pattern. But when he was faced with starvation, it was a case of think or die. If he was to go on living at all, he must devise a spear to help him bring down the elusive deer. Thought is a means, a device, an instrument, engendered by biological need to secure the satisfaction of that need. Now it is the essence of Dewey's theory to say that this account of how thinking first came about holds of thinking today. Why does anyone now think? The answer is roughly, because he has to. The sleepy flow of habitual response is blocked, and a way must be found of getting round the obstacle. You are going out; shall you take your coat? You must have a look at the weather and attempt some forecast. You come home, fumble in your pocket, and find you have forgotten the key; what shall you do to get in? Thinking springs from conflict, says Dewey; it is always the response to a challenge. It first appeared as a means devised by nature to help the organism adjust itself to surroundings that were frustrating. In its latter-day activities it has managed to disguise itself under imposing masks of impersonal science, speculative philosophy, and other adventures in *reine Vernunft*, but the shrewd naturalist will not be taken in. He will see that beneath all the disguises, thinking remains in essence an instrument of organic adjustment. Dewey has written a book called *The Influence of Darwin on Philosophy*, and someone has said with point that in writing the title he wrote his own description.

We may well note that by thought Dewey means what most of us would call reflective thought. It is of course common to speak of thought as present in perception and recognition; when we recognize a post-box for what it is and drop a letter in it, there seems clearly to be more in our mind than sensation, and it is natural to call this surplus 'thought'. Dewey regards this as a major mistake. For him there is no such thing as immediate knowledge or immediate inference. Post-boxes, so long as there is no question about them, are simply given things, and he calls them data. To distinguish within such things between sense-data and the non-sensible seems to him a falling back on the perverse old notion that thought is a kind of non-sensible stuff. To perceive a pillar-box is to respond to a given whole unquestioningly. To think is to deal with a problem, to surmount a barrier that halts and flouts us.

3. But if thinking is to be seen as it is, we must ask not only what brings it about but what it is for. Dewey's answer is that its true end is implied in its beginning; and what that is we have just seen. Thought is called into existence by a block to our activity; it reaches its end when that block is surmounted or removed. The ideas that suggest themselves when we are in difficulty are really plans of action, devices for relieving the tension, tools for restoring the adjustment between organism and environment. The thought of the savage was a proposal to make a spear as a means of getting the stag; your reflection about the weather was a means of insuring that you stayed dry; your ideas about getting into the house were merely practical substitutes for the key, and designed, like it, to effect an entrance. And if thought is thus always generated as a means to restoring a situation to harmony, its achievement of this end is all we can intelligibly mean by truth. Truth in short means success, success in removing the particular frustration which thought was invoked to deal with. The test of truth does not lie in self-evidence, or in the intellectual grasp of necessity; Dewey devotes much of his *Quest for Certainty* to trying to show the illusoriness of such notions. It lies in the satisfaction of bringing some divided situation to harmony, a satisfaction which always involves, in his view, a course of physical action. Instrumentalism, then, is the theory that thought is an instrument of organic adjustment whose truth lies in its success.

4. Why talk about Dewey's instrumentalism when our topic is his ethics? Because the ethics of his later days, like his later logic and his philosophies of religion, education, and politics, is the by-product of his instrumentalism, and unintelligible without it. He once held that thinking in science and thinking in ethics were directed toward different ends and must be treated in different ways. He came to think this a blunder, and to hold that the future of ethics and the hope of moral sanity lies in seeing that thinking is the same process in both, that moral judgments are essentially statements of fact and as capable of scientific testing as other statements of fact. He was an empiricist and anti-rationalist in ethics as in logic. Logic for Dewey is not a study of self-evident and changeless principles to which valid thinking must conform; all such principles he regards as themselves hypotheses, to be tested by the way they work out; satisfactory working replaces both truth and self-evidence as fundamental in his system. Logic is thus for him a 'theory of inquiry', a study of the process by which doubts are satisfactorily removed. Ethics is the same study with a more restricted subject-matter. Most ethical studies have been concerned with the principles conformity to which makes an act right, or with the nature of the *summum bonum*. Dewey's ethics is concerned with neither, for he regards such concepts as futile attempts to impose fixities upon a flux. Ethics for him is the study of how to solve problems where values are involved. It is the theory of ethical inquiry. The reader approaching his logic or ethics for the first time is likely to be bewildered. He has expected a study of the laws of thought and of the construction of a deductive system, and he finds a study of the psychology of thinking. He looks for a reasoned argument about the right and the good, and gets instead a description, full of humane insight, but tantalizingly remote from classical ethics, of how impulse and instinct in fact flower out into habit, choice, and will.

Dewey has described these processes over and over again, in his *Logic, Quest for Certainty, Experience and Nature,* and *Theory of Valuation.* These accounts are all, to my mind, extremely obscure. The obscurity is not merely a matter of language, though Dewey's habit of writing sentences composed as far as possible of abstract nouns makes for heavy going; the trouble is that he was in reaction against logicality itself as this had been traditionally conceived, with its sharply delimited concepts and its self-evident finalities; and his attempt to make these over into suggestions for action resulted in what, to more orthodox beginners, seems like a perpetual blurring of distinctions, a perpetual stress on what is slightly beside the point. On the other side, every critic of instrumentalism has been accused with wearisome iteration and only too probably with justice, of getting the position wrong. Dewey often urges the importance of keeping close to the concrete. It will be fair enough, then, if in setting out his view on moral judgment, we follow a somewhat unusual course. Instead of stating his view in the abstract, we shall take a simple case of moral choice and ask how his account of it would differ from that of more traditional moralists.

I am a university student, let us say, and someone gives me a ticket to a concert, which he cannot use himself. I am interested in the concert and should like to go. But it happens that my room-mate is a musician of parts who has tried to get a ticket without success. What should I do? Most sensitive people would think it right, and perhaps a duty, that I should give the ticket to him, on the ground that, at a small cost to myself, I could give him much enjoyment. With this Dewey would no doubt agree. But his account of what goes on in settling even a simple question like this differs from the one commonly received.

5. (1) He differs as to how moral problems arise. He holds, as we have seen, that they always arise from a psychological conflict. In the case in question, it has been my habit, when something is given to me, to use it for my own pleasure, and that is my first impulse when I am given the ticket. But, living in close association with my room-mate, I have also been in the habit of taking his pleasure and convenience into account. Here the two habits conflict. If I pursue my own advantage, I must sacrifice his; if I pursue his, I must to some extent sacrifice my own. There is an inner rift; I am drawn in both directions at once. It is some such division and tension, Dewey would say, that gives rise to every moral problem.

Does he really differ here from other moralists? Yes and no. To say that every problem involves a conflict between one's inquiring self and stubborn fact seems hardly more than tautology. But Dewey's view is distinctive in at least three ways. For one thing, he holds that a moral problem concerns what the thinker is to *do*. Most people would say that they often deal with moral problems that require no action at all on their part, as when they read in the newspaper that New York dockworkers have gone on strike, and wonder whether that is justifiable. Again, since the conflict is over what to do, it always has regard, Dewey thinks, to the future, not the past. And this has an air of paradox, since most of us would say that we were raising a moral problem in asking whether Brutus did right in killing Caesar. Thirdly, Dewey differs from most moralists about the parties to the conflict. Most of them would probably say, as Kant does, that the conflict is between the sense of wanting to do something and the sense, however vague and variously grounded, that one ought to do something else. Dewey's accounts of this conflict vary. In his earlier days, the conflict was a contradiction between judgments; later it was a maladjustment between organism and environment; sometimes it appears as a psychological strain or tension; sometimes it is a mutual inhibition of habits; sometimes— and this seems to be his latest teaching—the situation itself is tensional and conflicting, and demands restoration to harmony. (This I do not understand. How a situation, as distinct from people's wants or needs or beliefs about it, can have tensions or make demands, is not clear; I think Dewey must be talking in metaphors.) The conflict, then, that in Dewey's mind gives rise to ethical reflection is more narrowly conceived in two respects than it is by most moralists, and more vaguely conceived in another.

6. (2) What makes a problem a moral one? For of course not all problems, even problems of practice, are moral. If in cashing a ten-dollar cheque, the teller asks you whether you will have two five-dollar bills, or ten ones, or some small change as well as paper, the issue is not felt to be moral. But there is one condition which, if fulfilled, would at once turn your choice into a moral one, namely that it should involve a conflict of values. Suppose you know that three minutes later you are to take a bus to the station, and that your only change will be what you are now getting. To give a harried bus driver a ten-dollar bill for a fifteen-cent fare is to make oneself a nuisance, and if it occurs to you, as you stand at the teller's window, that this is involved, the choice is no longer indifferent. It becomes moral because it involves competing values. 'All the serious perplexities of life . . . come back to a conflict of goods.' (*Quest for Certainty*, 253.) A moral choice is always a choice between better and worse. Here most moralists would agree with Dewey, though the deontologists, as we have seen, would not.

7. (3) In holding that a moral conflict is a conflict between values, what does Dewey mean by a 'value'? Is it a quality that exists in things, independently of our knowing or feeling? Not at all. Take away human needs and feelings, Dewey would say, and there would be nothing of value left in the world. A value is a satisfaction. But what is it in human nature that a thing must satisfy as a condition of having value? Dewey is careful on this point, and if we are to be clear about his position, we must distinguish two attitudes of mind—enjoying on the one hand, and prizing or desiring on the other. The first does not involve values; the second does.

To enjoy something is simply to take delight in it. There is no reflecting about what it means, or what caused it, or what it will lead to. A child's pleasure in a bright new stone, a man's pleasure when he hears that he has been left a fortune, Dewey mentions as examples. In such experiences, he will not admit that, properly speaking, there is any value at all. Why not? It is hard to believe that he could come by such a view through looking directly at the facts; one can only suspect that his instrumentalist theory of knowledge is here moulding his theory of value; nor is it very difficult to see how. If you conceive truth as the successful surmounting of an obstacle in practice, you will go on to deny, as Dewey does, that there is any truth in common perception, since that offers no obstacle to surmount.

The good instrumentalist will want to make value, like truth, some-thing achieved in action; and if he does, there will be no immediate valuation any more than immediate knowledge. In speaking of the man who hears that he has been left a fortune, Dewey admits that 'there is enjoyment'. But if valuation is defined in terms of desire and interest, he goes on, 'there is no valuation, and in so far, no "value", the latter coming into being only when there arises some desire as to what shall be done with the money and some question as to the form-ation of an end-in-view'.[1]

Value then is not relative to enjoyment, but to desire. How does this differ from enjoyment? It differs as a process of active seeking does from one of passive relishing. It is an activity or effort, Dewey says, and is 'marked by energy expended to secure the conditions that are the source of the gratification'.[2] And this arises as we should now expect, only when there is some need or act that calls it into activity; 'valuation takes place,' we read, 'only when there is some-thing the matter; when there is some trouble to be done away with, some need, lack, or privation to be made good, some conflict of tendencies to be resolved by means of changing existing conditions'.[3] When the man who heard about his new fortune began to ask what he would do with it and to want certain things that he could get with it, value first came upon the scene. The mere having of a concert ticket is of no value. But when, in trying to settle the doubt what to do with it, I imagine myself at the concert listening to an accomplished performance, the desire is aroused to go. Then the concert has value for me.

Now if all value depends on desire, it is important to be quite clear what Dewey means by it. Most philosophers mean by it a conscious experience, a feeling of being drawn toward something thought of, a mental as distinct from a bodily affair. The desire may lead to outward behaviour that will help realize it, or it may not, but the desire is one thing and the behaviour another. Dewey will have none of this. He insists that he is a behaviourist, that for him the desire *is* the behaviour. He objects to introducing into the account of valuation any reference to feelings at all, on the ground that 'the word is brought in from an alleged psychological theory which is couched in mentalistic terms or in terms of alleged states of inner

[1] *Theory of Valuation*, 37
[2] *Ibid.*, 14
[3] *Ibid.*, 34

consciousness or something of that sort'.[1] The ground of this objection is that no assertion is fully warranted unless it can be verified by scientific method, that this method requires what it deals with to be open to public inspection and that feelings taken as mental are not open to such inspection. The desire in which valuing consists must therefore be regarded as 'an active relation of the organism to the environment' which 'takes place in the public and observable world'.[2]

8. (4) Granting now that the desiring or prizing of anything is what confers value on it, is this prizing ever mistaken? Dewey says No. Only judgment can, in the proper sense, be mistaken, and to find something of value is not the same thing as to judge it to be of value. The first may occur without the second, and the second without the first. A mother prizes the welfare of her child, but in doing so she is not necessarily making assertions about how precious the child is. If a question arose in her mind as to whether it was precious, she would no doubt say at once that it was. What is it that such judgments assert? Dewey's answer supplies our fourth point about this theory, which follows from the third. Such judgments, he says, 'are always propositions about matters-of-fact'; 'they are valuation-propositions only in the sense in which propositions about potatoes are potato-propositions'.[3] To say that a thing is of value is to say that someone desires it; and to say that is to say that someone acts toward it in a certain way. Usually this someone is oneself. To say that the concert is good is thus normally a statement of fact to the effect that one acts toward it in a way that would make an observer report that one liked it. What if one says that a concert is good while giving no signs of acting in this way?—for this does seem to happen. In such a case one presumably means that other people act so. On Dewey's view one never means what most people would probably say they meant, namely that the experience of enjoying a concert is worth while in itself. The question, whether something is of value is a factual question to be settled by looking and seeing; 'that a mother prizes or holds dear her child . . . may be determined by observation'.[4]

9. (5) But suppose the question now arises, not whether someone

---

[1] *The Theory of Valuation*, 10
[2] *Ibid.*, 16, 14. Again: 'since desires and interests are activities which take place in the world and which have effects in the world, they are observable in themselves and in connection with their observed effects.' 19
[3] *Ibid.*, 19   [4] *Ibid.*, 20

does prize a thing, but whether he ought to prize it, whether he is attaching the *right* value to it. This brings us, fifthly, to what Dewey regards as the purest and most typical value judgment, the judgment of appraisal, the valuation of a value.

Suppose that, wanting to go to the concert and also to further my friend's enjoyment, I find that both wants cannot be satisfied. What do I do? I appraise them. I ask myself the question, Which of these two values, or desires, is the more important? How am I to settle that? There is no more crucial question for any writer on ethics. Dewey's answer to it is this: that to appraise something is to present to ourselves the means we must adopt in order to reach it and the further consequences to which it tends, and to allow our desire to be remoulded in the light of this enlarged situation. Let us see more concretely what this means.

I have the desire to go to the concert, and hence for me the concert has value. How much value? Is there any sense in saying that I can intuit the amount directly, or by placing it on a scale of satisfactions? According to Dewey, none. What I must do instead is to consider the causes and effects of the satisfaction. First I must consider the causes, that is, the means I must adopt if my desire is to be fulfilled. I find that the concert is to be given in a distant part of the city, which would take some two hours to reach, and that if I am to get there, I must go partly by underground and partly by bus, with the connections uncertain, or else take a taxi, which in view of the distance would be expensive. In the light of these means, my valu-ation of the end undergoes a change; my desire flickers and threatens to go out. Nor does this end the matter. The revaluation continues as I turn from means to consequences. For going to a concert is not so simple a matter as occupying a seat for an hour or two; it is a stage in a longer process which unfortunately involves getting myself home at the end. Even if the affair is over at eleven, I shall not be at home till well past midnight, which probably means a bleary-eyed following day. And that day I may have to devote to construing Mr Dewey, an exacting enough business for the most clear-headed day. When I contemplate the concert in this lurid context of causes and conse-quences it looks very different and I find that my desire has vanished.

I then turn to the alternative. Unfortunately, the difficulties my room-mate would have in attending are the same as mine, and as for the consequences, they will no doubt be worse. The poor man has recently had the flu, and his artistic temperament has cursed him with an excitability that would keep him awake afterward half the night. I consider that it would be an indiscretion for him to go, and no kindness in me to tempt him. When placed thus in their contexts, both my desires get reappraised at zero or rather less.

What this reappraisal has done, however, is not to remove the conflict, but to redraw its lines. I still have the ticket. I no longer want to use it, or want my friend to use it, but neither do I want to throw it away. I am forced into reflection again in order to find a way out. Suddenly I have it. It occurs to me that my old friend Middlemarch lives in that part of the city, and that he would no doubt like to go very much. I slip the ticket into an envelope with a note of greeting, and that is that.

This is typical of what happens when a moral problem arises in Dewey's world. The attempt to appraise the competing values by placing them in their context of means and consequences alters those values; sometimes it gives a clear advantage to one, sometimes to the other; sometimes, as here, it abolishes both, reconstitutes the parties, and compels us to go hunting for a new way out. When this further way suggests itself, it becomes in turn the object of another desire.

10. (6) Now if this reconciling course of action is thus the object of desire, it is of course itself a value. We must therefore ask, sixthly, how *this* value is appraised. It presents itself as good to us, but how do we know that it is not a snare and a delusion? Still, since it has emerged out of the process of taking all the involved circumstances into account, it would seem that we could hardly appraise it in the same way. Dewey answers that every appraisal or re-appraisal must in the end be tested by results. What sort of results? The results required to bring this particular conflict to harmony. Desire always springs from conflict, as we have seen, and what it seeks in every case is to remove the conflict. The test of its goodness, then, is whether it does in fact bring about the harmony it was invoked to produce. That this really is the end being sought in ethical reflection and practice is of course a point of the first importance, and we should have it in Dewey's words. 'The end-in-view', he writes, 'is formed and projected as that which, if acted upon, will supply the existing need or lack and resolve the existing conflict.'[1] Ends are 'means to unification and liberation of present conflicting, confused habits and

---

[1] *Theory of Valuation*, 34

impulses';[1] 'an end is a device of intelligence in guiding action, instrumental to freeing and harmonizing troubled and divided tendencies'.[2] 'The end-in-view of desire is that object which were it present would link into an organized whole activities which are now partial and competing.'[3] The true value of this end, as it presents itself to our desire, will then be tested by the extent to which it brings this satisfaction. And this is a matter that can be observed. In our model case, there was the desire and the tendency to make use of the ticket somehow; there was also the desire and tendency to avoid subjecting myself or my room-mate to great inconvenience. Sending the ticket to Middlemarch satisfied both desire-tendencies at once, and brought the conflict to a harmonious close.

11. (7) Have we reached the end of the line? Can I say that with the removal of the conflict I have reached a good of definite amount, in terms of which I can measure all it cost? Even here, Dewey says, we do not really come to rest. Every good, every end, is tentative and provisional. Though the settlement of the conflict marks the end of one chapter, it also opens another; it releases energies which must themselves be strategically used and is therefore as truly a means as an end. Ends, says Dewey, are not terminating points; 'they are re-directing points in action':[4] 'there are no fixed self-enclosed finalities'.[5] Does this imply that there are no such things as intrinsic values, or ends in themselves? Yes, Dewey would answer—here is our seventh and final point—this *is* what it implies. The good does not lie beyond the process in some El Dorado or Vale of Avalon in which all our strivings cease; it lies in the process itself; indeed it *is* the process, so far as this is a process of releasing and integrating energies. 'The sole meaning of aims and purposes' is 'to liberate and guide present action out of its perplexities and confusions',[6] and to this enterprise there is no end that can be internally set. Accordingly, Dewey sometimes describes the goal and test of right action as lying in progress. This he defines, none too clearly, as 'present reconstruction adding fullness and distinctness of meaning,'[7] or, a little more in detail: 'progress means increase of present meaning, which involves multiplication of sensed distinctions as well as harmony,

[1] *Human Nature and Conduct*, 229
[2] *Ibid.*, 231   [3] *Ibid.*, 250
[4] *Human Nature and Conduct*, 225
[5] *Ibid.*, 232   [6] *Ibid.*, 261   [7] *Ibid.*, 281

unification'.[1] To the question what is the test whether apparent progress is really progress, Dewey would answer that no test is possible except that of still further progress. He will admit no ends whose value is not determined by the fact that they are also means.

12. These are the bones of the theory. Of course one learns nothing from them of the wealth of psychological description and sensible ethical commentary with which Dewey covers them. We have been concerned only with his answer to the central question, How is one to go about it to find what one ought to do?, which resolves itself in his hands into, How is one to find what is good? What are we to say of the theory?

My main criticism of it, as it is of other theories like positivism that allege themselves to be empirical, is that it is not empirical enough. Instead of looking at moral judgment directly, Dewey seems to look at it through the lenses of a preconceived theory of knowledge, a theory that unfortunately does not inspire confidence. Instrumentalism as a description of how thinking is commonly aroused and the stages it goes through may be illuminating; Dewey, like James, is at his best as a psychologist, and when he sets himself, as he did in his little book called *How We Think*, to produce a psychology of thinking, he is admirable. But instrumentalism as a logical theory seems to me scarcely more than an oddity.[2] At any rate, we can see that where the theory most directly affects Dewey's ethics, it makes him say some very strange things.

13. (1) Take at once the three most typically instrumentalist points, that thinking always arises out of a conflict, that what it offers us is a proposal to act, and that what it is aiming at is therefore future consequences. We make many ethical judgments, I think, in which no one of these features can be found.

In the course of reading Froude's great history lately, I came to his dramatic account of the divorce of Catherine of Aragon by Henry VIII. Innumerable thoughtful people have branded Henry's action as monstrous. Froude goes into the matter painstakingly and concludes that in view of all the circumstances Henry was justified. Which view is nearer the truth? As an issue between right and wrong,

---

[1] *Human Nature and Conduct*, 283
[2] For a defence of this statement I must refer the reader to my *The Nature of Thought*, I, Ch. X.

this is clearly an ethical problem. And in a sense it involves a con-flict, for there is so much evidence on each side that one may find decision difficult. But the conflict is here very different from the sort Dewey has in mind. It is not a conflict between impulses, habits, or desires, but between masses of evidence which seem to make for different conclusions. So far as one can see, there are no impulses present to do contrary things, no habits pulling one in opposite directions, no desires to do incompatible things at once, no block to organic behaviour which must be surmounted. Of course I may be interested in the question primarily for the light it may throw on some practical problem of my own, or of a friend, but I need not be; and even if I were, the question whether Henry did right is not the same as the question what I should do now.

14. (2) Instrumentalists deny this. They say that even in judgments about the past what we are really doing is trying to lay out a course of action for ourselves. 'Ideas', they say, 'are statements not of what is or has been, but of acts to be performed'; Dewey tells us that he con-ceives of 'all knowledge' as 'an instrument for further action'.[1] If I judge then that Henry was right, what I am really doing is solving a problem of how *I* should act *now*. Here again—and this is my second criticism—Dewey's instrumentalism has surely made him mis-describe the facts. *What* is the course of action which, in judging about Henry, I am supposed to be adopting? I cannot conjecture. No doubt there are actions I might perform that would help me indirectly to solve my problem, such as going to the library and getting down other histories, but such behaviour would not itself settle the problem. Strictly speaking, any action I may take is irrele-vant; what *is* relevant is the evidence which that action may turn up. Dewey is advancing here a theory of the most radical kind re-garding what we are about when we think; and a difference of opinion at this level is almost beyond the reach of argument. The difference concerns not merely the point at issue, but also the meaning of every assertion advanced on either side. It is for each of us to examine as well as he can what he is trying to do in judging. In cases where the problem before us is what to do next, it is plausible, though I think inaccurate, to say that all we mean by determining truth is finding a means to an end. But when we are trying to settle what was or would

[1] *The Quest for Certainty*, 160, 263

be right, to identify the interest in knowing with the interest in doing seems to me a confusion between two aims that are each definite and quite distinct.

The fundamental trouble with pragmatists is that they disown this distinction. They want to absorb all the uses of thinking into its use as a biological tool. Now we need not deny that what first drove men to ethical thinking, and indeed every other kind of thinking, was practical need. The man faced with starvation must either make a spear or die; and if he is not too dim of wit, necessity will prove the mother of invention. But granting that his thought is an instrument of action, it does not follow, even here, that it was wholly or merely that. Practical need rouses his sluggish attention and starts it looking for the means of making a weapon. But when he goes on to note that this sapling is straighter than that, and has fewer branches to cut off, he is interested in the facts about it, and this interest in knowing is already different, though not discriminated, from the interest in doing.

Through the mass of instrumentalist writings there runs the assumption that because it is practical need that brought thinking into play in the first place and usually does today, therefore thinking in its very nature is a tool of this need, with no end of its own. To recognize a purely theoretical goal and try to reach it by reflection seems to the pragmatist the symptom of an incipient disease. The whole history of moral philosophy therefore carries a taint. The entire succession of moralists from Socrates to Ross have been pursuing a will-o'-the-wisp. They have been trying to determine the characteristics of right action as such, as distinct from bad; and since there is no conceivable course of action that could settle this question, it is unreal and meaningless. Those who supposed themselves pre-occupied with it did not understand themselves; their thought was really a tool to some other and disguised end prescribed by their social class or by their need for 'rationalizing' practical deficiency, a need more readily brought to light by the psycho-analyst than by the philosopher.[1] Now it must be admitted that the treatment of speculative philosophy as a psychological abnormality has gained some support within the philosophic community itself since Dewey wrote, though this theory of philosophy shows a singular reluctance to apply the theory to itself. Suffice it to say that if I had to decide which is the more likely, that moral philosophers generally before 1900 were pursuing

[1] Cf. the argument of Dewey's *Reconstruction in Philosophy*.

illusions or that there is an error somewhere in the instrumentalist account of thought, I should feel compelled to choose the latter.

15. (3) Moral problems, then, do not always grow out of a conflict of desires, nor are they always practical problems, in the sense of being problems of what to do. It is worth noting, thirdly, though this has been implied already, that ethical problems do not always have to do with the future. The instrumentalist says they do. This follows from his view of ideas as 'anticipatory plans and designs'.[1] Like some of the more extreme of present-day positivists, Dewey holds that in thought about the remote past it is 'the present or future' that 'constitutes the object or genuine meaning of the judgment',[2] and that the truth of such judgment lies in what he calls the interlocking of two sets of future consequences, those of the past event on the one hand and those of my present belief on the other. On this point the criticisms of Lovejoy and others seemed to many to be decisive, but they apparently left Dewey unmoved. In discussing moral judgment he writes: 'The reference in blame and every unfavourable judgment is prospective, not retrospective.'[3] It seems to me on the contrary that if I say Henry did wrong in divorcing Catherine, my reference is clearly retrospective, not prospective. It may be true that if I blame him, it is on the ground of consequences which came after his own decision and which he might have foreseen, but these can hardly include consequences that after four centuries are still to come, and the case would be unaltered if they did. For when I say that Henry did what he ought not to have done, my reference is surely to an act long past and to a guilt belonging to that act at the time. Henry's act did not wait for its guilt till we turned our attention to it; unless he was guilty when he lived and acted, he was never guilty at all.

16. (4) These are comments on Dewey's ethics as applied instrumentalism. Now for some further comments. Is it true, then, fourthly, that when we say anything is good, we mean that it is desired? Dewey would say that it is, if we mean by desire the desire that leads to active seeking. He would say that my prospective presence at the concert

[1] *Quest for Certainty*, 160
[2] *Journal of Philosophy*, XIX, 313
[3] *Human Nature and Conduct*, 315–6. 'It is as causes of future actions that excuses and accusations alike must be considered.' *Ibid.*, 18

has value, so far as it arouses an active desire to go. Now it is true, I think, that nothing would have value in the absence of some kind of experience. Would a prehistoric boulder on the other side of the moon have any sort of value? I think not. Nor do I understand how a sunrise can have any value if no one sees it, except as meaning that something exists which under the right conditions would give rise to a valuable experience. There is even a sense, yet to be seen, in which all that is good is so because it contributes to the satisfaction of impulses. But to say that value—all the goodness and badness in things—is derived from our desires and dependent on them seems to me untrue.

Take another simple case of conflict and active desire. Jones retires to his room at bedtime, and discovers that his dog has been in the room. The little pest has climbed with muddy feet on the fresh white counterpane, has left dirty traces all over it, and in the course of pawing it up has managed to tear a gaping hole in it. Jones is devoted to his dog, but this is too much. His habit of making allowances for his pet tends in one direction, his angry desire to find the offender and give him a drubbing tends in the other. Let us suppose that the second, however unreasonable, wins, and he works off his anger by beating the dog unmercifully. He wants to hurt him and he does. Now if it is true that something becomes good by being the object of desire, the pain of the dog is made good by Jones's desiring it. That I cannot accept. Is the amendment offered that the dog's pain may more properly be called bad, because men are normally averse to it? This may be more humane, but it is still not true. The truth is that the goodness or badness of the dog's suffering does not depend on whether we or others desire it or dislike it; the misery of a solitary dog, crayfish, or earthworm, if these creatures are capable of misery, would be evil even if it were the only sentient being in the universe and even if it were itself below the level of desire. If this is true, to say that values and disvalues generally derive from desire must be untrue.

When we say that something is good, then, we do not mean merely that it is desired. This conviction becomes stronger when we realize that we can judge a course of action to be good while at the same time acting in the opposite direction. Men have been known to take another drink or to embezzle money in the consciousness that what they were doing was wicked. Suppose the question arises in their own minds whether they regard embezzling or excessive drinking to be good or

bad. On Dewey's view, this is to be settled by observing their behaviour. If they actively drink to excess or embezzle, then they must
regard these things as good, for this is all that so regarding them
means. Is not Ovid's insight a shrewder one that we may see and
approve the better while actually doing the worse? It is, I suppose,
generally sound that one can judge what a man regards as really
good by observing what he does, that actions speak louder than words.
But to say that a man's valuations are so accurately reflected in his
conduct that the two can be identified implies that we never act
against our better judgment. And we sometimes do.

17. (5) But fifthly, Dewey not only admits but insists that the goodness or badness that belongs to anything in virtue of the desire it
first awakens is not final. We are able to appraise these values, and
we often find that what seemed at first glance to be very desirable
indeed has little value; our desire to attend the concert, and hence
the value of the concert, dwindle as we think of it. What is the method
of this appraisal? It is the method of means and ends. Every end, says
Dewey, falls in the flux of experience; it has causes that lead up to
it and consequences entailed by it; and to appraise it is to revise our
desire in the light of the values involved in its causes and effects.
'The position that ends have value independent of appraisal of means
involved and independent of their own further causal efficacy'[1] is
branded as a major confusion. 'The *value* of enjoyment of an object
as an attained end is a value of something which in being an end, an
outcome, stands in relation to the means of which it is the consequence. Hence if the object in question is prized *as* an end or "final"
value, it is valued *in this relation* or as mediated.'[2] 'Propositions in
which things (acts and materials) are appraised as means enter necessarily into desires and interests that determine end-values.'[3]

Now it is true that when we are considering whether it is worth
while to pursue some end, we usually go about it by weighing the
value of the end against the disvalues of the means, and perhaps of
the later consequences. We want very much to hear the concert, but
when we consider the whole course of action involved in attending it,
we see that the discomforts and inconveniences outweigh the advantages and the proposal loses its attractiveness. To many readers

[1] *Theory of Valuation,* 43
[2] *Ibid.,* Italics in original.
[3] *Ibid.,* 35

Dewey seems to be talking mere obvious sense like 'look before you leap'.

As a matter of fact he is saying something quite at odds with common sense. Common sense believes that you can look at the disvalues of the means, then at the values of the ends, and weigh them against each other. Dewey seems to hold this impossible, because the only way you could appraise *either* means or end is to see them as interdependent, as parts of a single proposal. He is inveighing, he tells us, against the very belief 'that there are such things as ends having value apart from the valuation of the means by which they are reached'.[1] If this is true, the weighing against each other of means and ends whose values are independently fixed is out of the question. If the value of the end depends on that of the means, and that of the means in turn upon that of the end, you cannot tell the value of A till you find that of B, but since to find that of B you must already know that of A, you can never fix the value of either, and comparison is impossible. To attach value to an experience or to anything else simply in itself would be, Dewey thinks, entirely arbitrary. Since, apart from causes and consequences, there is no way of appraising what is desired, there is nothing to prevent one's taking it as justifying any means at all. In illustration he takes Charles Lamb's whimsy about the origin of roast pork, to the effect that the first roast pork resulted when a Chinese house burned down with some unfortunate pigs inside; whereupon certain gourmets, discovering the delights of roast pork, proceeded to build more houses with pigs in them and burn them down in order to get more roast pork. 'Now,' says Dewey, 'if ends-in-view are what they are entirely apart from means, and have their value independently of the valuation of means, there is nothing absurd, nothing ridiculous, in this procedure . . .'[2]

The first comment to make upon this is that it is at odds with the facts. We are constantly assigning values to means and ends independently, and weighing them against each other, to all appearances successfully. I do not know why it is impossible to contemplate at this moment the delights of roast pork and to assign some value to them without any reference whatever to the means that might enable one to achieve them. To say that I cannot so value them without committing myself to the corollary that it would be all right to burn

[1] *Theory of Valuation*, 36
[2] *Ibid.*, 40

houses down to get them seems to me astonishing reasoning. If the case seems somewhat fantastic, take a very commonplace one. Near the house where I have spent many summers in Vermont lies Burke Mountain, with an observation tower on top. This commands a magnificent view of the countryside, from the White Mountains on the east to the Green Mountains on the west; and in company with friends I have sometimes made the ascent for the sake of the splendid outlook. Now climbing Burke Mountain puts some tax on wind and limb. One soon learns by not wholly pleasant experience that it requires an effort which in a lazy mood, or in illness or fatigue, is to be avoided. When one considers, therefore, whether to make an ascent to the view on a certain afternoon, one would be silly beyond words to think of the view alone, and not of the cost of getting it; the view and the effort are parts of one enterprise whose worthwhileness as a whole depends on the values and disvalues of its parts. But to go straight from this to the conclusion that no value can be placed on the view at all apart from the thought of the climb and its attendant discomforts—which is what Dewey is saying when he denies 'that there are such things as ends having value apart from the valuation of the means by which they are reached'—seems clearly illicit. The value one attaches to the view may remain completely unchanged, whatever may be one's means of achieving it. There happens to be a motor road up Burke Mountain, and if Dewey's account is correct, the view, which is my end, ought to have two quite different values on Wednesday when I climb the mountain, and on Thursday when I ride up at ease in a friend's commodious Lincoln. But surely *its* value is the same. Indeed it is because it does remain the same that I can weigh it so readily against the disvalues of the varying means.

18. What is it that has led Dewey to this strange theory that we can attach no value to ends in themselves? There seem to me to be two errors at work, both connected with his instrumentalism. The first is that a judgment of value is a tool for the securing of consequences. We have seen that, according to the instrumentalists, judgment in its essence is such a tool. Hence if a kind of judgment were to appear that halted in the immediate and stopped with the here and now, if my judgment that the view was glorious were really a means to nothing and was tested by nothing beyond the view itself, instrumentalism as a theory of judgment would have run on a disastrous reef. If the theory is to be kept intact, an analysis is therefore necessary that will prevent any judgment from absorbing itself in the here and now. The judgment of value, even of intrinsic and immediate value, must be a process of flight, not of perching. Ends, however seemingly self-validating, must be seen as links in a chain; the instrumentalist never really knows; as Lovejoy says, he is always about to have known. In short what Dewey seems to me to be doing here, of course with transparent honesty, is rewriting what experience tells us about the independence of ends from their means in the interest of an antecedent theory of thought.

Secondly, behind Dewey's account of appraisal is his insistence that judgment always deals with some specific situation, not with generalities or as-suches. To most of us it would make sense to say that the view we should get from a mountain top would be worth having in itself, that we could say this without reference to what might precede or follow the experience, and that to insist on considering these was to confuse the worth of an experience with the worth-whileness of trying to get it under such and such conditions. Dewey seems at first reading to be making just this confusion. But he is too sophisticated for that. He is not confusing two different judgments; he is deliberately denying that the first kind of judgment is meaning-ful, or therefore, a judgment at all. If the question is whether you should ascend under such and such conditions, the decision does obviously have to be made in the light of a sequence of experiences which will include both means and ends. But if the question is whether a certain kind of experience is worth having as such or in itself, we have a problem which could not possibly work itself out in any sort of action, and a problem of this kind is in Dewey's opinion a pseudo-problem. And because it is a pseudo-problem, the judgment that tries to solve it must be put down as a pseudo-judgment. Just as the Dewey of later years virtually ceased to talk about truth and spoke instead of warranted assertibility, so he is reluctant to mention values, as suggesting something fixed and outside the process of actively remoulding things, and speaks instead of 'valuations'. Strictly speaking, there are no values; there are only more or less successful activities of valuation. To talk about the value of an ideal state of things, considered in itself, is therefore to talk idly. I do not think that Dewey adheres to this theory consistently, or that anybody could. As has been remarked by Professor Mitchell, when he writes on politics, he attaches great value to projected social arrangements, regardless of his degree of clearness as to the means of ushering them in. 'Dewey is no more able than Plato was to show how the necessary conditions are to be realized. If Plato could not show how philosopher-kings are to be found, neither can Dewey show how we can have academic freedom in state-supported schools, free art depending on popular approval, free dissemination of information through commercial publishing and broadcasting, industrial democracy along with private enterprise, or free science supported by industries or tax-supported universities.'[1] For him all these ends were worth working for, even if we did not now see the means to them, and would be worth having at the price of any number of different means.

19. In insisting that ends do have values of their own, dependent on neither means nor consequences, I do not want to suggest that these values are final and unalterable. Although Dewey does seem to have stressed out of all proportion the special means-end relation, he is surely right that the new relations in which we place things may affect profoundly the values we attach to them. The man who returns in middle age to the garden where he played as a child sees in it something very different from what he saw in childhood; his estimate of its size, its variety, its mysteriousness, its attractiveness, has changed because he now sees it against the background of an immensely larger world of which in his childhood he was unaware. This is the way, not the way of means and ends, by which our present valuations are in fact revised. If we outgrow our childish taste for comic strips, moving picture 'westerns', and certain kinds of novel, it is because we can now see them in perspective, a perspective in which their infantile notions of what is true and important are incongruous at a hundred points with the human nature we have come to know. In the same way, truths and attitudes that seem trivial at first may move from the periphery of importance to the centre as we come to see their implications for thought and life as a whole. Not that this change is a matter of explicit thinking; the man who returns to the garden may never have thought of it in the interval; the shift in value of 'childish things' may come to him as a surprise. No one has described this process of re-appraisal more finely than John Henry Newman, and I will indulge myself in the pleasure of quoting his famous paragraph on how even fugitive fragments of verse may change their significance for us with the passing years.

[1] E. T. Mitchell, *Ethics*, Vol. 55 (1945), p. 289

' . . . consider, too, how differently young and old are affected by the words of some classic author, such as Homer or Horace. Passages which to a boy are but rhetorical commonplaces, neither better nor worse than a hundred others which any clever writer might supply, which he gets by heart and thinks very fine, and imitates, as he thinks, successfully, in his own flowing versification, at length come home to him, when long years have passed, and he has had experience of life, and pierce him, as if he had never before known them, with their sad earnestness and vivid exactness. Then he comes to understand how it is that lines, the birth of some chance morning or evening at an Ionian festival, or among the Sabine hills, have lasted generation after generation, for thousands of years, with a power over the mind, and a charm, which the current literature of his own day, with all its obvious advantages, is utterly unable to rival. Perhaps this is the reason of the medieval opinion about Virgil, as if a prophet or magician; his single words and phrases, his pathetic half lines, giving utterance, as the voice of Nature herself, to that pain and weariness, yet hope of better things which is the experience of her children in every time.'[1]

It is by focusing our experience as a whole on a poem or novel that we judge it. An inferior work we outgrow; a masterpiece, as someone has said, is a work contemporary with every age; its significance is not only maintained but deepened when placed in the appraising context of fuller experience. At times Dewey too seems to say this: 'to think,' he writes, 'is to look at a thing in its relations with other things, and such judgment often modifies radically the original attitude of esteem and liking'.[2] Excellent. But when he goes on to say *what* relations, out comes the stock instrumentalist answer: the 'meaning' of an intuition of value is identified out of hand with 'the consequences which will accrue from acting upon it'.[3] And this, we must repeat, it is not.

20. We have been considering Dewey's doctrine that valuation is a process of active desiring, and that it gets revalued through being set in a prospective chain of means and consequences. But such valuation remains only tentative. It is still a proposal to act in a certain way, a way that is attractive in prospect but has still to be tested in practice. It is this test in actual practice that validates or refutes all our judgments of value, and it is therefore extremely important to see what it

[1] *Grammar of Assent*, 5th ed., 78–9
[2] Dewey and Tufts, *Ethics*, 291
[3] *Ibid.*, 295

consists in. Unfortunately, to see this is not easy. But Dewey makes two assertions about it which are repeated so often that we may be sure he attaches weight to them. One is that the test is the same kind as that used for scientific judgments; the other is that the consequences which serve as test must take the form of bringing a prior conflict to a close. Let us look at these requirements.

Dewey insists that he is a naturalist, and by naturalism he appears to mean the theory that every legitimate question can be dealt with by the methods of physical science. He thinks that ethics must either adopt the methods of such science or forfeit its claim to intellectual respect. What these methods require he sometimes states in a disarming way. Scientific method, he says, 'after all is but systematic, extensive, and carefully controlled use of alert and unprejudiced observation and experimentation in collecting, arranging and testing evidence'.[1] Of course we are all for that. If we pause anywhere, it will be over the words 'observation and experimentation'. Does Dewey mean that problems of value are *merely* problems of fact, that questions of duty, of right and wrong, of better and worse, are to be settled by observation in the same sense that the question can be so settled whether a chair has four legs? The answer is Yes, he does. What is being appraised is valuations, and 'valuations are empirically observable patterns of behaviour',[2] not mental responses but bodily ones. A mental response in the old sense *would* be unobservable. But then there are no such things as mental responses in the old sense. 'Conceptions derived from a mystical faculty of intuition,' he writes, 'or anything that is so occult as not to be given to public inspection and verification (such as the purely psychical for example) are excluded.'[3] 'Personally, I doubt whether there exists anything that may be called *thought* as a strictly psychical existence';[4] and if there did, it could not count in a scientific test, since 'the first requirement of scientific procedure—namely, full publicity as to materials and processes'[5] would rule this out. Dewey is content to describe himself as a behaviourist. When he talks about processes of valuation as successful or not, he is talking about activities that are as public and palpable as the rolling of billiard balls.

When we appraise, then, we are appraising processes that are (a)

[1] *Naturalism and the Human Spirit*, 12
[2] *Theory of Valuation*, 51
[3] *Logic*, 19   [4] *Ibid.*, 21
[5] *Theory of Valuation*, 22

active and (b) physical. A word must be said about each of these characteristics.

21. (6) (a) To report that we find value in anything, Dewey says, is to report that we do things about it. The question at once suggests itself, Do I not often find value in things without *doing* anything about them, but by merely enjoying them? Dewey admits that there is value in what he calls 'consummatory enjoyments', that is, experiences in which we realize that a conflict is being harmonized. He admits also that there exist 'enjoyments of things directly possessed *without* desire'.[1] For example, 'take the case of a child who has found a bright smooth stone. His sense of touch and sight is gratified. But there is no valuation because no desire and no end-in-view, until the question arises of what shall be done with it . . . The moment he begins to prize and care for it he puts it to some use and thereby employs it as a *means* to some end, and, depending on his maturity, he estimates or values it in that relation, or as means to end.'[2] One could hardly have selected an example, I suggest, that would bring out more clearly the artificiality of the instrumentalist account of value. In that account, the child's natural and simple remark that the stone was wonderful would not be a statement of value at all because it would contain no suggestion of the use to which he could put it. It is only when a problem arises regarding this use, and he can view the stone as a means to an end, that he can make a significant report of value. Surely no one thinks of value in this limited means-end way, and it is hard to believe that Dewey normally did. Note that in the last sentence quoted he puts the two things involved in their right order in spite of himself. Speaking of the child he says, 'The moment he begins to prize and care for it he puts it to some use', suggesting that the prizing leads to the use, not that the finding of a use leads to the prizing. When he holds that in none of our 'passive enjoyments' does prizing take place, Dewey implies, since value depends on prizing, that nothing rightly called value is present at all. I cannot accept that conclusion. Many people, perhaps most, if asked for cases in which, beyond any question, they were finding things of value, would mention the experience of listening quietly to great music, or following with absorption the unfolding of a tale, or watching a superb piece of acting. These are not, at least not necessarily, cases of consum-

[1] *Theory of Valuation*, 37
[2] *Ibid*, 38. Italics in original

mated desire, nor are they cases in which we find use for something in practice. For all that, they are instances of the experience of value; they are instances *par excellence* of that experience.

22. (7) (b) But if the experience of value is not to be found in the mere enjoyment of something, where is it to be found? It is to be found, Dewey answers, in active desire, and this means doing something; it consists in bodily behaviour. These processes, he tells us, 'are to be considered in terms of observable and identifiable modes of behaviour'; if they are described as 'affective-motor', 'care must be taken not to permit the "affective" quality to be interpreted in terms of private "feelings" . . . the word "liking" is used as a name for a mode of behaviour (not as a name for a private and inaccessible feeling). . . .' 'If there are "feelings" existing in addition, their existence has nothing to do with any verifiable proposition that can be made about a valuation.'[1] Dewey's naturalism here reaches its extreme point. Mind is banished, if that means anything different in kind from bodily behaviour. If the word 'mental' is to be kept at all, he thinks, it should be reserved for the sort of organic response that is made to the doubtful *as* doubtful.[2] Even 'sensations in immediate consciousness', he says, 'are elements of action dislocated through the shock of interruption'.[3]

I must confess that there is no part of Dewey's theory which I find it harder to understand or sympathize with than this. To call it empirical is to abuse a respectable word. Looked at empirically, there are no two things in the universe more obviously different than a sensation of pain and a bodily movement, and to suppose that this difference can be somehow transcended by lumping them together under the head of 'action' or 'organic response' is mere delusion. Why should anyone want to say such things? Apparently in this case because it is required by what Dewey sometimes calls 'the primacy of method'. He has convinced himself, like the positivists, that if a statement is to be meaningful, it must be verifiable, but unlike the more critical of them, that to be verifiable means to be publicly verifiable. It follows, then, from this method that any statement not publicly verifiable will be meaningless. Now an assertion that I am

---

[1] *Theory of Valuation*, 13–14, 15. 'The test of the existence of a valuation and the nature of the latter is actual behaviour as that is subject to observation.' *Ibid.*, 54
[2] *Quest for Certainty*, 225
[3] *Human Nature and Conduct*, 182

feeling a pain or finding something of value, if this is the report of a private experience, is not publicly verifiable. Hence it cannot be a meaningful, and is neither true nor false. In all this I find nothing even faintly plausible. It seems to me one more instance of something too common in extreme empiricists, namely the twisting of what experience reports in the interest of a method seemingly adopted a priori.

Is it true that my valuation of my friend, of Mr Eliot's criticism, or of my new pipe, consists in my behaviour towards them? No doubt liking and desiring do normally take effect in action; if I like my friend, I write to him occasionally; if I like Mr Eliot's essays, I buy or borrow his books; if I like my pipe, I shall probably smoke it. It must be admitted, further, that unless my liking for something did display itself in some observable way, either by doing such things as these or by making remarks, no one would have any means of knowing whether I liked something or not. True enough; but that is not at present the point. The point is whether by liking or desiring something I mean on the one hand a feeling or attitude, something distinctively mental and conscious, or on the other hand a bodily change. On this point I cannot hesitate. Liking is a feeling and exclusively that. If consciousness were abolished, I think it would take all value with it, even if every bit of bodily behaviour in the universe remained precisely what it is.

Now it is notorious that we cannot refute the behaviourist when he says all he means by mind is bodily process; for he is in a better position than we are to say what he means. All we can do is to point out the consequences of such identification and ask him in the light of them whether he has not been confused as to what he does mean? I do not propose to list again the paradoxes he falls into;[1] it will be enough to fall back on the ideal experiment suggested long ago by a psychologist of insight who was himself a trained scientist but would have had little use for the 'scientific method' of some of his successors. Imagine a human body, James suggested,[2] that was like other human bodies except in the one respect that it had no trace of consciousness, that is, of the sensations, feelings, and ideas which, because 'private and inaccessible', are dismissed by Dewey. It opens its eyes and seems to look at things, but it sees no shapes or colours. It steps on tacks, and reacts sharply with the appropriate remarks, but never feels a

---

[1] Cf. *The Nature of Thought*, I, Ch. IX
[2] *Journal of Philosophy*, Vol. 8, pp. 130, 322

twinge of pain. It goes to college, attends lectures, sits in the front row taking notes copiously, passes its examinations, and winds up with a *summa cum laude;* only it never has an idea. It meets a comely damsel. It says all the right things, sends strategic chocolates and seasonable flowers, plays the perfect squire and cavalier, always with a light in its eyes, and responds like a weathervane to the thoughts and moods of its inamorata. It is irresistible; the lady is transported. Then comes an evil day. Some well meaning soul whispers to her the truth. The perfect lover will go on with his perfect love; in that she may rest secure. There is just one little point she should know about— it would, of course, make no difference, for it is quite unobservable and hence irrelevant. Her lover happens to lack consciousness. It is true that in the old-fashioned sense he has never seen her, never heard her words or attached a meaning to them, never recognized her when present, never remembered her in absence. And of course he has never liked her. But since this liking was in any case an un-verifiable hypothesis, a truly emancipated girl would not miss it. His behaviour has been, and will be, exactly as if he did have feeling about her. Her situation therefore is unchanged.

James, if I remember rightly, thought this utter nonsense, and so do I. The next time the automaton appeared, to look at her with its sightless eyes, address her with its meaningless words, and attempt its galvanized embraces, she would run from it as a grisly horror. So long as she could believe that behind the acts there was fondness for her, the fact that this was not visible to the eye would be nothing to her. With all that they expressed removed, they would be the acts of a Frankenstein monster.

This simple common sense expostulation seems to me the most effective comment on behaviourism, and it is likely to succeed where technical argumentation will not. For behaviourism is less a tech-nical doctrine than a temporary lapse from common sense under the influence of some idol of tribe or marketplace. It is to my mind at once revealing and depressing that a mind of Dewey's calibre should have succumbed to it. In any case when he says that in talking about valuations we are talking about bodily responses, I can only demur.

23. (8) It is not in the mere observing of such behaviour, however, that the test of an appraisal lies; it is in the apprehension of it as performing a certain office, which is, to use Dewey's words, to 'supply the existing need or lack and resolve the existing conflict', to bring about the 'unification and liberation of present conflicting, confused habits and impulses'. What strikes one first about these statements is their vagueness. Are there not innumerable ways, of bringing conflicts to an end, some of them moral and some not? A man feels a strong desire to lie abed in the morning, and the desire gives such behaviour value. He begins to wonder whether the behaviour is justified; there is a conflict within him between his laziness and his sense of duty. He may conclude after reflection that he ought to do his duty, and may do it; this brings the conflict to an end. On the other hand, he may decide that he will give himself a holiday, and may turn over and go to sleep; this too brings the conflict serenely to an end. If the test is merely the bringing of a conflict to a harmonious close, either of these consummations is as good as the other; in short we have no test at all, since we can solve and remove a conflict without doing so morally. If the test is that we should solve the conflict in the right way, the proposal is that we should recognize the right solution by its rightness, which is not helpful. To such criticisms the instrumentalist would probably answer that he had never suggested that *any* way of solving a conflict was a successful one; only that way was the right one which brought to rest the *specific* tension, which removed the *particular* conflict involved.

Now when someone proposes a test for conduct, how is the test to be tested? I know of no other way than by asking whether it squares with the actual judgments of sensitive and thoughtful men, which means in practice ourselves when we seem to be judging most responsibly. If a course of action fails conspicuously to conform to the test and yet is rated high by all of us, if a course of action fulfils the test and yet is rated low by all of us, one is bound to suspect the test. It is not difficult, I think, to show that the instrumentalist test meets neither requirement. Take two cases that have lately been much in the contemporary mind.

We may recall that the life of Kierkegaard was one of continual conflict. He wanted to devote himself altogether to his studies; he wanted also to marry Regina Olsen; and between the two desires he was torn in two. This conflict he never solved. He jilted Regina without ceasing to love her, and he continued to tear himself in eloquent pieces through a long succession of volumes. Suppose that he had settled the conflict as men have done so often, by some sort of 'higher synthesis' of the two desires—by marrying Regina, for example, accepting a local professorship, and supporting a wife and family on the proceeds. It seems not at all unlikely that if he had done this there would have been far more 'linking into an organized whole of activities which are now partial and competing' than he ever in fact achieved. Would this, therefore, have been the more desirable course? On the theory before us it obviously would; unresolved conflict seems to supply what evil means. But is this, after all, quite clear? Professor Kierkegaard in carpet-slippers, with Regina knitting at the table and his children round his knees, would not have been Kierkegaard. It was his unending inner conflict, his chronic storm and stress, that made him what he was by perpetually feeding the flames of his passionate self-analysis. It was not *in spite of* inner conflict and suffering that he achieved such distinction as he did; it was because of these; and if the conflict had ended in peace, as it gave some promise of doing at twenty-seven, it is not improbable that we should never have heard of him or his work. No doubt he *desired* the removal of the conflict, and perhaps he would have welcomed it when it came; but this only shows once more how impossible it is to equate the desirable with the desired. It seems to me at least an arguable thesis that it was better for Kierkegaard and the world that his road should have wound up hill all the way, though such a suggestion must make nonsense if value is to be measured by the removal of conflict.

Look now at a case in which a conflict was solved so successfully as to make a man a battering-ram of uninhibited power. The case is the more enlightening because one knows where Dewey stood politically; he was the most devoted and steadfast defender of democracy and a gallant foe of authoritarianism in all its forms. For Hitler and all he stood for, Dewey's abhorrence was unequivocal and profound. Was the test Dewey offered as a philospoer an adequate base for the condemnation he so generously felt as a man? In the early pages of *Mein Kampf*, the author describes how he emerged from the bitter conflicts of his youth. He writes: 'My ideas about anti-semitism changed also in the course of time, but that was the change which I found most difficult. It cost me a greater internal conflict with myself, and it was only after a struggle between reason and sentiment that victory began to be decided in favour of the former. Two years later sentiment rallied to the side of reason and became a faithful guardian and counsellor.' 'I now realized that the Jews were the leaders of Social Democracy. In the face of that revelation the scales fell from my eyes. My long inner struggle was at an end.'[1] Hitler was looking for

[1] *Mein Kampf*, Eng. trans., 58, 62

an objective which, in the words of the ethical theory before us, 'would link into an organized whole activities which are now partial and competing', which would be a 'means to unification and liberation of conflicting, confused habits and impulses'. Can it be denied that he found precisely that? His life from this time forward was a supreme example of it. 'Good', for the instrumentalist, 'consists in the meaning that is experienced to belong to an activity when conflict and entanglement of various incompatible impulses and habits terminate in a unified orderly release in action.'[1] In this case they did so terminate, and if such 'unified orderly release in action' is an achievement of goodness, then Hitler was achieving goodness. From this conclusion one can only suppose that Dewey would draw back as heartily as any of us. What these examples seem to show is that there is a great gulf fixed between the instrumentalist formula for value and the test we actually use. It is not the solving of conflict *as such* that makes a course desirable, nor the maintenance of a conflict *as such* that makes it undesirable.

24. To all this it may be replied that the justification of conduct for Dewey does not lie in the solving of individual conflicts, but in dealing with them to the advantage of society. In Dewey and Tufts' *Ethics*, it is said expressly that the end in terms of which present desire is to be appraised is the satisfaction of desires in the 'long run', and the desires of others as well as one's own.[2] Sometimes Dewey protests against taking the conflicts and satisfactions of which he is speaking as those of persons at all. Thus when Russell objected that he made truth dependent on personal satisfaction, Dewey replied:

'by changing doubt into private discomfort, truth is identified with the removal of this discomfort. The only desire that enters, according to my view, is desire to resolve as honestly and impartially as possible the problem involved in the situation. "Satisfaction" is satisfaction of the conditions prescribed by the problem. Personal satisfaction may enter in as it arises when any job is well done according to the requirements of the job itself; but it does not enter in any way into the determination of validity, because, on the contrary, it is conditioned by that determination.'[3]

Instead of speaking of a conflict of desires in Jones's mind, Dewey

[1] *Human Nature and Conduct*, 210
[2] *Ethics*, 200
[3] *The Philosophy of John Dewey* (ed. by Schilpp), 572

preferred to speak of 'situations' as conflicting and problematic, and as making those demands the successful meeting of which is the test of truth and rightness.

Now this places beyond doubt that it is not one's proximate good that is to be sought, nor even one's own good in the long run, but the long-run good of humanity. This is excellent, and in accord with Dewey's public-spirited practice. But (a) it then becomes difficult to understand his constant emphasis on the solution of this particular problem in its own way. When he writes as a psychologist or biologist, he has in mind the problems of adjustment of some individual organism, and insists that any solution that is to satisfy must remove the particular conflict which that particular organism is facing. Is Kierkegaard now to be told, for example, that he had best not remove his conflict at all, since it is in the interest of the larger social value that he maintain it? If so, then the rule to proceed by overcoming specific conflicts seems to be suspended.

(b) What is to take its place? If Dewey had answered: 'the rule of producing the greatest happiness on the whole', or 'the completest practicable fulfilment of human impulses', or even 'the widest possible removal of personal conflicts or tensions', the rule would have been intelligible, however hard to apply. I do not find it intelligible if it reads, 'bring into harmony the conflicting demands of the situation'. Situations do not, as such, make demands or exhibit conflicts. Demands are imposed on persons by their own ends or ideals in the light of the situation they are in, and the only moral conflicts are those within or between human beings. In his desire not to make truth and goodness relative to personal demands, Dewey speaks as if situations broke themselves into halves, and these halves then fell into conflict with each other and made demands of their own. There is a touch of mythology here. And if the advice to remove individual conflicts is not enough to give moral direction, neither is the advice to remove men's conflicts generally. 'There is no such thing as the single all-important end,' says Dewey; ends, as we have seen, are 'means to unification and liberation of present conflicting, confused habits and impulses'.[1] This seems to mean that such liberation and unification is *ipso facto* good and is itself the end. The trouble with this is partly that it is so vague, partly that its goodness is itself open to question. How could one apply such an end in the making of a particular choice? And on the face of it, some liberations

[1] *Human Nature and Conduct*, 229

and unifications of impulse seem good and some not. How can they give what we *mean* by 'good'?[1]

25. It may seem absurd after this spate of criticism to say that Dewey was, after all, on the right track. His theory as he presented it was heavily involved with instrumentalism in logic and behaviour-ism in ontology, and any theory that entails either of these, let alone both, is bound to end in insolvency. Nevertheless, two at least of Dewey's main theses seem to me sound and important, and there is no reason why we should not free them from their entanglements and take them with us. (1) He is right, I think, in insisting that moral choice should be directed not to conformity with rule but to the production of good. (2) His conception of good, however vague, is a step forward. He is a naturalist in ethics in the large sense in which Aristotle was. Goodness is not for him a non-natural quality in-hering in things regardless of their relations to human needs and desires; it is bound up with these so intimately that its very meaning is in satisfying them, and so fulfilling human nature. Here again I think he is right on a point of the first importance. Not that the good can be defined in Dewey's manner as the solution of conflict or the harmon-ization of desire, but that the goodness of things does bear some relation to their satisfying actual need, impulse, or feeling. What that relation is we have yet to determine. The most influential of recent attempts at an answer will be considered in the next chapter.

[1] One of the main difficulties in interpreting Dewey is the extreme generality of his statements, which often admit of translation into the specific in many different ways. We are sometimes told, for example, that the over-all end is progress, and on looking for the definition of progress, we find, 'Progress means increase of present meaning, which involves multiplication of sensed distinction as well as harmony, unification.' (*Human Nature and Conduct*, 283). How this could be used as either end or test it is not easy to see.

G

CHAPTER VIII

EMOTIVISM

1. Emotivism marks the farthest swing of the pendulum in making moral judgment the expression of feeling. To be sure Hume had made it so in a sense; 'reason is and ought only to be the slave of the passions'. But this was less radical than it sounded. Hume believed that in judging an action we should invoke the aid of reason in inferring consequences; he believed that a judgment of right was an attempt at knowledge, and was true or false. It either was or was not the fact that people generally, observing a certain action in the light of its consequences, felt a favouring feeling towards it. If they did, the judgment was true; if not, it was false. Westermarck carried the subjectivist swing one stage farther. He agreed with Hume that moral judgment was a report on feeling, but the report now was not on how people generally felt, but on how the agent felt. Emotivism carries the movement one stage farther still. It holds that the function of moral judgment is not to report emotion, but to express it. A moral judgment *says* nothing at all, in the sense of asserting or affirming. Perhaps the clearest, as well as the most familiar statement of the theory is that of Professor Ayer:

> 'The presence of an ethical symbol in a proposition adds nothing to its factual content. Thus if I say to someone, "You acted wrongly in stealing that money," I am not stating anything more than if I had simply said, "You stole that money." In adding that this action is wrong I am not making any further statement about it. I am simply evincing my moral disapproval of it. It is as if I had said, "You stole that money," in a peculiar tone of horror, or written it with the addition of some special exclamation marks. The tone, or the exclamation marks, adds nothing to the literal meaning of the sentence. It merely serves to show that the expression of it is attended by certain feelings in the speaker.'[1]

What are called moral judgments are thus really exclamations. The

[1] *Language, Truth and Logic*, 2nd ed., 107

judgment that a thing or a man is good or an action right, is the expression of a warm or approving feeling about the object, and is roughly equivalent to 'Cheers!' or 'Good for you!' The judgment that anything is bad, or that an action is wrong, is the expression of repulsion or abhorrence, and is roughly equivalent to 'Boo!' or 'Shame!' The theory has therefore been christened—presumably by way of booing it—'the Boo-Hurrah theory of ethics'.

So stated, it is attractively simple. But we must be careful not to oversimplify it. When it is said that value statements express only feeling, the words 'only' and 'feeling' need comment. The emotivist would not say that nothing but feeling is being expressed in such statements as 'that was a courageous speech', 'that is sheer thievery', 'that is a bare-faced lie'. All of them, indeed, state facts: 'courageous' suggests that danger was being firmly faced; 'thievery' says that what, under the law, belongs to someone else has been taken; 'lie' indicates that a false impression was deliberately given. Here are unquestionably moral judgments stating unquestionably empirical facts. But the emotivist has a reasonable answer. These statements, he would say, are hybrids, combining both fact and value statements. *So far* as they are value statements, they do merely express emotions —of admiration for courage, and of disapproval for lying and thieving.

Again, when these latter are said to express only *feeling*, the term must be taken with some latitude. If the theory implied that the only feelings expressed were simple liking and disliking, it could be overthrown by a moment's introspection. But these feelings are of enormous variety. Indeed the whole great spectrum of qualities that value judgments seem to take as inhering in objects—'comic', 'charming', 'wicked', 'noble', 'horrid', and the rest—are withdrawn from the object only to turn up in another guise. as qualitatively different feelings that may be felt toward it. Furthermore, some emotivists, like the linguistic analysts who are their successors, would include among the 'feelings' expressed much that, in the technical sense, is not feeling at all. Carnap takes the distinctively ethical element as a command; 'truthfulness is good' means 'tell the truth'; Stevenson would say that this statement, at least in many instances could be translated into 'I approve of truthfulness; do so too', in which the ethical note is sounded in the exhortation at the end; and he would recognize also a wide variety of 'affective-conative attitudes' which are not so much emotions as recurrent desires or dispositions of will. The emotive theory may thus be regarded as a protest against intellectualizing judgments of value, made on behalf of our non-intellectual self as a whole.

2. The theory when offered in Mr Ayer's provocative version of 1936 produced a minor storm among moralists. It was repudiated as making morals a matter of taste or even of caprice, and implying that nothing was really better or worse than anything else. We shall have to look into these charges. Meanwhile it is worth noting that emotivism is not itself a rootless or merely capricious theory. In our study of the dialectic of British thought, we saw that one important current of that thought had been setting in this direction for three hundred years. Beginning with the recognition by Shaftesbury and Hutcheson of the close affinity of the moral judgment and the aesthetic, it runs on through Hume and Westermarck with a force that renders the emergence of an emotivist conclusion all but inevitable.

This historical pressure, however, seems to have had little to do with the appearance of the theory in Britain in the middle thirties. The theory was proposed by the logical positivists, whose roots were not in Britain but in Vienna; and it seems to have been adopted less because of an independent study of moral judgment than because of the exigencies of their theory of knowledge. The positivists had committed themselves to the view that every statement that is cognitive, that is, capable of being true or false, must be one or other of two kinds. It must be either empirical, and then it was a statement of fact that could, at least in theory, be verified in perception, or else it was an a priori statement, and then it was true analytically, that is, it would be self-contradictory to deny it. Having satisfied themselves that this dichotomy was exclusive and exhaustive, the positivists, who were not primarily interested in ethical questions, were confronted with the problem what to do with judgments of good and right. Where, in their table of judgments were they to put the statement, for example, that pleasure is good? Goodness is not a sensible quality whose inherence in pleasure can be observed, like the spots on a leopard. Nor is it an a priori judgment, positivists would say, for when people have denied that pleasure was good—and, oddly enough, there have been such people—they were not merely contradicting themselves. The statement that pleasure is good, then, seems to be neither a statement of fact nor a statement of analytic necessity. It follows, if one accepts the positivist classification of statements, that it is not a statement at all. But if it has no cognitive meaning, what can it express?, for it is not meaningless utterly. There seems to be only one thing left for it to express, namely emotive meaning. It must be an exclamation or interjection, expressing, not a proposition that is true or false, but the speaker's feeling or attitude.

3. The emotivist analysis, then, was a by-product of the positivist account of knowledge. But it was more than that. When the positivists turned to the closer study of moral judgments, they found a mass of facts that added immensely to the plausibility of their theory. Even a casual inspection of such judgment reveals that feeling plays an exceptionally intimate and important part in them, a part that non-emotivists themselves cannot but acknowledge. We shall be better prepared to do justice to the theory if we mention the chief roles that, by general admission, feeling plays in moral judgments.

(1) Feeling accompanies such judgments in a peculiarly regular and intimate way. When we say something is bad, we normally feel some repulsion for it; when we call an act wrong or a man wicked, we do it with a stirring of indignation; one does not call another a scoundrel to the accompaniment of an affectionate smile. So invariably do feelings of approval and disapproval attend expressions of right and wrong that the terms 'approval' and 'disapproval' are as naturally used of the feelings as of the alleged assertions.

(2) Again, moral 'judgments', unlike most others, are matters of degree, and vary with the intensity of the emotions felt. Approval passes over by degrees into admiration and reverence; condemnation is not a flat denial of rightness or goodness, but something felt with all degree of force from gentle distaste to blazing and implacable anger. Where the 'judgment' thus varies with the feeling, it is not unnatural to take the one as really expressing the other.

(3) Moral 'judgments' are under the influence of feeling in a way that has no parallel among the judgments of science, empirical or mathematical. No one would attempt to alter a chemist's view of the constituents of sugar, or a geometer's view as to whether a circle touching all sides could be inscribed in any triangle, by working on his emotions. But that *is* notoriously practicable in regard to moral estimates. If A detests B, it is almost impossible for him to regard B as other than detestable, though if he comes to know and like him, his estimate of him will probably follow suit. How likely is it that a judge, however masterly his summing up, will convince the mother of

a criminal that her son deserves the gallows? Fiction and real life are full of illustrations of how 'judgments' are fixed by attitudes, instinctive and acquired; if a sample item is wanted, one may take the infrequency with which, in American legal history, male juries have been willing to bring in capital verdicts on women offenders. Such facts do not prove, to be sure, that moral judgments *are* merely feelings. They do show that these veer with feeling in a way that renders their intellectual independence suspect.

(4) Philosophers from Plato down have been struck by the resemblance between moral judgments and aesthetic; to many, perhaps to most, the likeness of judgments of goodness to those of beauty has seemed much closer than to those of logic or mathematics. Now there is little difficulty, either for the philosopher or the plain man, in accepting aesthetic statements as expressions of feeling. It seems obvious that 'comic' and 'sublime', and plausible that 'beautiful' and 'ugly', report our own impressions rather than characters existing in things. And the aesthetic analogy suggests a like interpretation of moral judgments.

(5) In a very large number of statements that are commonly taken as moral, the emotive analysis would be accepted by almost everyone. Is it not plain enough that when we call a person irritating, or disagreeable, or repulsive, or attractive, or likeable, or admirable, or a hundred other things of the kind, we are hardly, even in appearance, giving a descriptive report of his qualities, but are telling rather how he strikes us, whether he 'rubs us the right way'? It is hard to draw a line between such characterizations and such others as 'noble', 'honourable', and 'good', which would be taken as unequivocally moral. Hence the suggestion is strong that we should carry the analysis over to moral judgments generally.

4. It is time to turn from the reasons why the theory may have commended itself to the question of real moment, whether it is sound. Any assessor of it has to face one awkward difficulty at the outset. The emotive theory is supposed to give the correct use or meaning of statements like 'this is good', but is it what people actually mean that is being supplied, or what, if they were self-critical, they would or ought to mean, or something else? We get no clear and firm answer. Hence there is too much truth in Mr Mabbott's comment, 'we slide from the statement that an analysis tells me what I mean to the view that it tells me what I would mean if I were clear on the matter; and thence to the view that it gives me what I would say I meant after a course of treatment aimed at "re-adjusting" my "psychological mechanisms", and thence finally to the view that what I mean is what I would say if my errors were corrected and the view I held were true.'[1] Perhaps the fairest course is to assume that the attempt is to give the plain man's meaning, as held not naïvely and crudely but self-critically, that is, with a desire at once to clarify what is actually meant and to fit it in consistently with our other meanings.

Now it seems to me clear that the theory, so conceived, will not do. There are many considerations that lead me to say this, but they all seem to belong to three general types of difficulty. (I) The theory makes goodness external to that which has it; (II) it leaves no basis in the object for either favouring or disfavouring; and (III) it makes reflection about values far more irrational than in fact it is.

5. (I) Consider, first, the way in which the theory makes the goodness of anything fall *outside* what is good. It tells us that when we say '*x* is good', we are expressing not the character of the object but a feeling or attitude on our part. The object, then, has no goodness of its own; the only sense in which goodness attaches to it is that one or more persons are taking a favourable attitude toward it. This goodness is adventitious. It is, so to speak, conferred by the accident of someone's taking the attitude. Now there is one kind of value judgment of which this analysis is plausible, namely that passed upon a physical thing. When we taste a peach and say 'this is good', or, looking at the weather, say, 'what a dreary day!', we do not need much persuasion to agree that we are talking not about qualities these things would have if nobody were aware of them, but of experiences they induce in us. For my own part, I should agree that the abolition from the world of all forms of consciousness would abolish value also; I cannot enter into the thought of those who hold that in a world devoid of experience, the addition of a crater on the moon would add to the goodness of things, or its removal detract from this. I should agree, then, with the emotivists so far as to say that the goodness or badness of physical things lies not in the things themselves but in the experiences aroused by them. Only experience, or situations involving experience, can be intrinsically good. But to say this is not, of course, to grant the emotivist theory; it is only to

[1] *Aristotelian Soc. Proc.*, Vol. 49 (1948–9), 142–3

narrow the issue down to the meaning of 'this is good', when applied to experience. And when so applied, I think the theory breaks down.

6. (1) The plain man, i.e. one's ordinary self, sits at the table and says, 'This peach is delicious'. The goodness of the peach lies not in the peach, we agree, but in the man's enjoyment of it. Very well; his enjoyment is good. When we say that, what do we mean? The emotivist tells us that we are saying nothing about his enjoyment; we are only expressing our own favouring attitude toward that enjoyment. The only goodness involved in the case, so far as our statement is concerned, lies in *our* experience, not in his; it came into being with our expression, and lapses when we turn our attention away. As a report of our meaning, this is absurd. Whatever the goodness of an experience may consist in, it is something that belongs to the experience itself, and attaches to it in virtue of what *it* is; to say that when we call an experience intrinsically good, we are expressing only something that attaches to it as externally and accidentally as the attitude of some chance observer, is plainly at odds with our intention.

It may be replied that the goodness of the man's enjoyment lies in an attitude taken by himself. If this means that the goodness of the *peach* lies in his response to it, or someone else's, we have agreed that this is true. If it means that his enjoyment of the peach is itself an attitude the experience of which is intrinsically good, we agree again, though with some demur about calling enjoyment an 'attitude'. But of course neither of these things is what the emotivists are saying. That the man's enjoyment can be good in itself is precisely what they deny. To call it good is not to ascribe goodness to it, but to express an attitude that occurs in one's self. Yes, yes, they may say, but whatever attitude other people may take toward the man's enjoyment, it is clear that he himself takes a favourable attitude toward it, and thus it does in a sense have a goodness that is independent of what others may feel. But consider what this means. It means that the man's enjoyment is in no sense good until he becomes self-conscious about it and makes it the object of a further response. To say that there was any goodness in his enjoyment while he was merely surrendered to it would be to talk metaphysics, to ascribe a non-sensible property to it. The enjoyment becomes good, in the sole legitimate sense, only when he comes to contemplate it and take up toward it a favouring attitude; then, and only then, would a statement that it was good express anything at all. This is an extraordinary view, whether as analysis or as psychology. As analysis, it is incorrect, since a man who says, 'What a good time I am having!', means to say how much enjoyment he is having, not—primarily at any rate—to express a secondary attitude he is taking up to his own enjoyment. As psychology, it is myopic, because the point at which the enjoyment becomes good, in the only sense the theory will allow, is the very point at which such a statement begins to lose its applicability, since, when enjoyment becomes self-conscious, it begins to go.

7. (2) Consider, again, the case in which we are calling good or bad something that happened in the past.[1] The positivist view (a) forbids us to hold that if our statement had not been made, there would have been anything good or bad in the event when it occurred, and (b) requires us to hold that if the event had not occurred, all the good or evil that our judgment expresses would have come into being anyhow, by reason of our attitude. Both these implications conflict flagrantly with the intention of such judgment.

Let us take a slightly out-of-the-way example which, though selected to bring out the point, could be duplicated a thousand times over in the thought of ordinary life. You are taking a trip at sea, and you come out on deck some morning to find that in the course of the night the ship has struck a whale whose body is found across the prow. It has evidently made a violent struggle to disengage itself, but was too deeply wounded, and failed. A reflective and compassionate man might naturally remark that such intense suffering on the part of an innocent creature was a great evil, or a very bad thing. According to the emotivists, when we say this we are ascribing no badness to the whale's past suffering; we are only expressing our present feeling. Is this interpretation plausible?

(a) Suppose first that our remark had not occurred; would that have made any difference to the badness of the animal's past suffering? The plain man would be bewildered by such a suggestion. How could the accident of someone's coming to know and remark about that suffering after it was over affect the character of the suffering when it occurred. What if nobody had learned of the incident at all; would the animal's suffering then *not* have been bad, or indeed one whit the less bad? To most of us it would seem absurd to say so. If suffering is really bad, it must be bad when and where it occurs, not at some

---

[1] Here, and at two other points in this chapter, I reprint, with minor changes, some paragraphs which appeared in *The Philosophical Quarterly* for January, 1951. I do so with the kind permission of the Editor.

later time when it has ceased to exist, and in some other mind that
is not suffering at all. Yet this last is, in effect, what emotivism tells
us. It says that apart from the accident of someone's coming on deck
and finding the whale's body, it would be meaningless to say that
anything evil occurred. Whatever may be the force of this theory, it
is certainly not implied in what the plain man means to say. When he
says that the suffering was bad, he means to say something about the
past misery of the beast, something that characterized it while it was
going on. This is evident, I think, from the most casual inspection
of our meaning. But there are also indirect ways of showing it. Consider the mystification we should feel if anyone replied to the remark
about the badness of the suffering as follows: 'There was nothing bad
in the suffering; still, now that you mention it, there is'; or 'It was
touch and go whether the suffering should be bad or not, for it was
the merest accident that the body was discovered'; or 'The suffering
in the case occurred about 2.00 a.m.; but there was nothing bad about
it till five hours later'. We should think any of these replies idiotic;
why? Because they all assume that what is expressed by 'bad' can be
separated from the suffering by an interval of time. Yet the emotive
theory does in effect say this, since it insists that what we are saying
about the suffering is exhausted by our present attitude.

(b) We have tried an ideal experiment, namely removing the value
judgment made about a past event and asking whether we should
recognize on reflection that this removed also what we meant when
we said the event was bad. Clearly we should not. Let us now try the
experiment the other way about. Let us remove the event and keep
the statement. When I came on deck this morning, the second mate,
not averse to widening the eyes of landlubbers with his inventions,
tells me about the whale with every appearance of truthfulness. I
remark, as before, that it was a sorry thing for the poor beast to
suffer so. The remark is made, of course, under a complete misapprehension. No whale was struck; no struggle ensued; no suffering
occurred. And since there was no suffering, there was none of the
badness that attends such suffering. So at least the plain man would
say. But not the emotivist. He must hold that there is precisely as
much evil in the case if the suffering did not occur as if it did, provided
only I make my remark about it. There was nothing bad in the suffering
itself; what 'bad' expresses is my present feeling exclusively; hence
if that feeling exists, the only badness the case admits of is still there
in its entirety.

Once more, this seems to me absurd. There is no sort of analysis that can extract it from what the plain man actually means. The best way of settling this is to ask whether, when he discovered that the event had never happened, he would recognize that in saying something bad had occurred, he had been in error. If the emotivist is right, he would not. Since he had not meant that anything bad had happened, no discovery that an event had not happened would call for a revision of what he had meant. His remarks merely reported present feeling, which is equally real, whether the past event happened or not. He would certainly not swallow such an account. He would say, 'If what I thought bad never happened, then of course I was mistaken; the badness cannot remain when there is nothing left to be bad; you can no more take away the suffering and leave its badness than you can take away the cat and leave the grin.' He would be clear that, following a wrong lead, he had made a mistake, whereas the emotivist would say that, since he had not judged at all, this was impossible. To be sure, the emotivist would admit an implied mistake, a purely factual one, to the effect that suffering occurred when it did not. Is this enough? No. For the plain man is saying not merely that suffering occurred, but that something bad occurred, and he is quite clear that if nothing bad occurred, he was mistaken in supposing it did. If on this point there is no conflict between his judgment and the fact, how account for his relief when he discovers that the incident never took place? Why rejoice in the non-occurrence of something if there was nothing bad about it?

8. Troubled by the paradox of placing the value of an experience at a time when the experience no longer exists, the emotivist may take a different line. He may say that the suffering *was* evil at its own time and place, but only in the sense that the suffering animal took up a disfavouring or disapproving attitude toward its own suffering; hence what it would have expressed in the words 'this is horrible', if it had been able to speak, did in fact exist. But this will not do either. (i) Though it puts the evil, in a sense, in the animal's experience, it still makes it adventitious to that in the experience which alone we recognize as evil. The evil lies in the suffering, not in some process of mind external to it. (ii) As an excursion in animal psychology, the suggestion that a line can be drawn between the creature's suffering and its attitude toward this seems speculative, unverifiable, and improbable. (iii) In any case, when *we* say the suffering was bad, we certainly do not mean to speak about one section of the animal's mind, more especially not about a process distinct from the suffering. And (iv) even if the animal was capable of conferring badness in this way upon its own experiences, the theory would prevent our saying so. As soon as we came to the word 'bad', it would stick in our throats. We could not, if we tried, make it mean anything whatever about the misery that went on there in the past; its sole use is to express a feeling in our own mind. Thus goodness and badness are effectively dispossessed from the only place where, according to ordinary thought, they can be located.

The emotivist may try another tack. He may suggest that when we say such suffering was bad, we mean that it was potentially bad, in the sense that *if* it were to act causally on someone capable of a disfavouring attitude, it *would* produce such an attitude. But, once more, this is no part of our meaning, nor even consistent with it. It takes as only potential evils that we undoubtedly mean as actual. Consider one bit of evidence. Even the very plain man now knows that human history on the earth has been limited, and that strange 'dragons of the prime tore each other in their slime' for aeons before the first man appeared. He knows that a wholesale destruction of life and an enormous mass of misery attended the slow emergence of the race, and he has no doubt that it was evil; the occurrence of such masses of gratuitous evil is one of his stock difficulties when he starts thinking about theism. Would it make sense to him to say that all this evil was potential merely, that in all this misery there was nothing actually bad, but only something that had the power of producing a disfavouring reaction in human nature when, after the lapse of some millions of years, men achieved the power of contemplating their racial past? As an exegesis of current meaning, this is fantastic.

I have taken animal suffering deliberately because, while we are clear that it is intrinsically bad, that badness can hardly be constituted by the beast's own attitude toward its suffering, and hence must fall, on the emotivist theory, at a distance from this in space and time. The paradox of dislocated value is thus brought out with especial clearness. But it is needless to resort to the animal mind if anyone feels that it is too treacherous a territory. For the emotivist is cut off by his theory from admitting that there has been anything good or evil in the past, either animal or human. There have been Black Deaths, to be sure, and wars and rumours of war; there have been the burning of countless women as witches, and the massacre in the Katyn forest, and Oswiecim, and Dachau, and an unbearable procession of horrors; but one cannot meaningfully say that anything evil has ever happened. The people who suffered from these things did indeed take up attitudes of revulsion toward them; we can now judge that they took them; but in such judgments we are not saying that anything evil occurred. We are not saying so because, under the theory, that is impossible; if we supposed we were saying so, we should be mistaking emotive meaning for cognitive, and trying to convert a statement expressive of feeling into the characterization of fact. That we are forbidden to do. This prohibition presents us with a clear alternative. Which of these two things is the more certain: that the emotivist analysis of value propositions is correct, or that some things in the past have been bad? Most of us would say the latter. But if the latter statement is true, if it is even capable of being true, then the emotivist analysis is false. That analysis, when first presented, has some plausibility. But when this is balanced against the implied unplausibility of setting down as meaningless every suggestion that good or evil events have ever occurred, it is outweighed enormously.

9. For the above line of argument I have been taken to task by an able writer whose own theory is somewhat different from emotivism and more plausible. When offering essentially the present argument some years ago, I took in illustration a rabbit which, after struggling vainly, had died in a trap, and supposed a compassionate person to have remarked on discovering it that it was a bad thing that the little animal should have suffered so. And I argued, as in the present case, that such a remark must be taken as attributing badness to the pain when and as it occurred. Professor Edwards finds several confusions in the argument.

(i) He says: 'Only a philosopher writing in a vacuum, could ever suppose that anybody would really in this situation say, "It is a bad thing that the little animal should suffer so." ' What one would really say is, 'This is terrible' or 'Something dreadful happened here' or 'The poor animal!' or maybe 'What wicked traps these people put up!'[1] Now I attach no great importance to the verbal form in which the remark is cast, and should be quite ready to argue the case with one of Mr Edwards' alternatives. But why does he find the form I used so objectionable? Apparently because he thinks this leaves it

[1] Paul Edwards, *The Logic of Moral Discourse*, 201

obscure whether one is making a value statement such as 'intense pain is evil' or a statement of moral condemnation such as 'whoever set this trap is wicked'. But the form of words I selected was chosen, in part, precisely to exclude the latter interpretation. To say that animal suffering is a bad thing is not necessarily to say that some one is wicked, and to charge the statement with the possibility of obscurely meaning this is not very convincing. Nor do I think that the kind of judgment here made is at all unusual. The person who, looking back on the course of nature and history, says of such things as the Lisbon earthquake, or Indian famines, or the deaths of Keats or Chatterton, or the senility of Kant, that they were great evils is making a perfectly natural remark, which does not on the face of it blame anybody.

10. (ii) Suppose we have got it clear that the judgment made is that an experience of intense pain was intrinsically bad, not a judgment of moral condemnation. The question now is, What is asserted in it? Mr Edwards says,

> 'The occurrence of this intense and prolonged suffering is what we primarily wish to assert by means of this sentence. To be quite accurate, it is not the complete referent. We also assert, I believe, that the pain suffered by the rabbit was pointless or unnecessary. By this I mean that either the killing of the rabbit did not have any useful results such as helping to rid the neighbourhood farmers of a nuisance or that, it if did, the same results could easily have been achieved without subjecting the little animal to such extreme agonies.'[1]

This introduction of needlessness or pointlessness as part of what we mean by calling the pain bad betrays a confusion of the two kinds of judgment which I had myself just been charged with confusing, on somewhat slender grounds. Intense pain is bad in itself; it is not the less bad because it may produce good results, or worse because it is needless. What we have in mind when we speak about its needlessness is the moral character of the person who inflicts it. When we say that the pain of the rabbit was needless, we are criticizing the action of the farmer, who could have reached his end by other means; when we say the Lisbon earthquake was needless, we probably mean that it was needless on the part of a Deity who had the power to prevent it. But it is confusion of instrumental with intrinsic value to say that part of what we mean by the goodness of pleasure is its

[1] Paul Edwards, *The Logic of Moral Discourse*, 202

serving some end beyond itself, or by the intrinsic evil of pain the failure to serve such an end. Such failure may be part of what we mean by instrumental badness; it has nothing whatever to do with making something intrinsically bad.

11. (iii) The passage we have just quoted from Mr Edwards begins by saying regarding the judgment that an intense pain was bad, 'The occurrence of this intense and prolonged suffering is what we primarily wish to assert by means of this sentence.' This seems to me questionable. No doubt our statement *implies* that the pain occurred, just as the statement that Brutus's killing of Caesar was wrong implies that Brutus did kill Caesar. But it would be a mistake to say that 'what we *primarily* wish to assert' by 'Brutus's killing of Caesar was wrong' is that the event occurred, and it is similarly mistaken to say that 'what we primarily wish to assert' by 'the suffering of intense pain was an evil' is 'such pain occurred'. The emotivist tells us that when we make these value judgments about the past, we are asserting nothing but descriptive characters. In view of the alliance between positivism and emotivism, it may not be unfair to recall how unstable the positivist theory about judgments of the past has been. Leading positivists once held that a judgment of the past was really about the future events that would 'verify' it. This they soon abandoned. But they clung for some time to the view that in talking about another's pain, past or present, we are talking exclusively about his bodily behaviour, his gestures, groans, and grimaces. This too they abandoned. They would now hold, I take it, that it is significant to talk of another's pain, though not of the badness of his pain, to talk of Chatterton's and Keats' having had certain powers and dispositions which were in fact terminated by their deaths at the age of seventeen and twenty-five respectively, though it is not significant to say that in this there was anything evil.

Now if their theory attempts to set out our actual meaning, they may as well abandon this too; for it is plain that our judgments of the past do mean to assert goodness and badness of past persons and events. Is it seriously suggested that when we call St Francis a good man, we do not mean that he was good during his lifetime? The plain fact is that we do mean that, and that if the emotivists tell us we cannot mean it, there is something wrong with their analysis. When we say that the Black Death was a great evil, would the meaning we wish to assert be adequately conveyed by a statistical or sociological survey, the size of several Britannicas, but containing no suggestion that anything good or bad had occurred? However difficult it may be to say what 'bad' means, we surely do not mean to express by it merely something that is happening in us now; we mean to say something true about what happened then.

Mr Edwards sees that this conclusion is unavoidable, but tries to protect emotivism by offering an amended version. He says that 'good' and 'bad' are not expressive of feeling simply, but perform a double function; they are *both* descriptive of fact *and* expressive of feeling. The term 'good', as applied to a man, *means* (i.e. has as its 'referent') his being truthful, gentle, loving, free from envy and pleasure in another's pain, etc., and these are observable facts. At the same time it is a vehicle for expressing a feeling of approval for these traits. To say, then, that St Francis was good is in fact a descriptive judgment ascribing to St Francis certain factual traits and also expressing our feeling about them. The judgment 'St Francis was good' would thus state a proposition about the past which is as objectively true as any proposition about an eclipse or a tidal wave.

This theory is certainly nearer our actual meaning than is pure emotivism. Whether it reports our actual intention will depend on where the line is drawn between the descriptive and emotive components in the judgment. Mr Edwards says that being truthful, gentle, and loving are to be included among the purely descriptive characters. But are they really such? They seem to me already tinged or tinctured with positive value. Suppose that these and the other qualities included in the meaning of 'good' were denuded altogether of such value suggestions, and we were then asked whether the aggregate of them gave what we meant in saying that St Francis was good. We should know that when, on a certain occasion, he made a statement, the statement bore such and such a relation to fact, that when he saw a man wearing garments fewer by so many than the average and differing in their texture in such and such ways, he felt an emotion of a certain kind and intensity, and placed certain of his garments in the hands of the object of his emotion. Mr Edwards seems to me right that when we call St Francis good we do assert or at least imply that he did things of this kind. But that is not all we mean to assert. Plain men confronted by such a summary would probably say, 'Yes, this is all true enough, but we meant to say also that Francis was a good man, and you seem to have left this out.' And if they were told that this sort of catalogue exhausted all that was true about Francis when he lived and all we could say about him now, that whatever in our judgment went beyond this expressed nothing but the glow of our own feeling, they would, I think, rebel.

They would rebel too, I suspect, against the interpretation placed on their judgment that intense pain in the past *was* evil. To be sure, pain and pleasure are not easy to analyse, and it is hard, perhaps impossible, to draw a line within them between the aspects of fact and value. But that the aspects are different aspects and that both are there seem clear. Every experience is an event that has a describable character, has causes and effects, and lasts for such and such a time. Jones, on looking out the window at 10 a.m., has a sensation of green of such and such an intensity which lasted for thirty seconds. That is a purely descriptive statement. A rabbit, caught in a trap at 10 a.m., had a sensation of pain of so many degrees of intensity, lasting with fluctuations till at 7 p.m. the organism ceased functioning. That again is a descriptive statement. Would this, or any extension of it in like terms, supply what we mean to say when we speak of the rabbit's suffering as terrible? I cannot think so. Was this aspect of it which we denote by 'terrible' actually there in the past experience? We clearly mean to say so, and cannot doubt that it is true. That is why we object to people's causing such experiences, why we shudder at them now, and why we seek to prevent their repetition in future.

Does Mr Edwards deny this? Instead of giving a mere yes or no, he answers with a distinction. The pain as a describable event did occur in the past; but no value or disvalue attached to it, for in the verbal ascription of such values we are only expressing present feeling. The immediate protest that such a view arouses he would meet by including among the descriptive attributes the 'extreme agonies' of the animal. Now it is obvious that 'extreme agony' is not a merely descriptive term; it means horrible suffering, and is therefore heavily value-charged. Mr Edwards is thus in a dilemma. If he says that we can ascribe such a character to the animal's experience, and say that it was really there whether we are aware of it or not, he has abandoned emotivism. On the other hand if he divests the descriptive characters of every trace of value, and tries to make us say that the suffering when it occurred was entirely neutral, since any mention of value is merely expressive of present feeling, his interpretation is a misinterpretation; it destroys the main point of what we are saying. One cannot save emotivism by compromises of this sort; for the conflict only breaks out again in one's new middle ground.

12. (iv) Mr Edwards charges my argument with a further confusion. I said, it will be recalled, that if emotivism is right, no badness would come on the scene till some observer made a remark expressing his feeling about the past pain, and that this dislocation of value from what it belongs to is absurd. I will quote what I take to be the essential part of Mr Edwards' criticism.

'... on certain occasions people make such fundamental moral judgments as that stealing or convicting an innocent man is wrong ... Now is it not preposterous to maintain that in such cases the goodness or badness, the rightness or wrongness depend on the existence of the approval or disapproval in a human being? ... Here again the reply is ... that the position which Blanshard attacks does not have the alleged consequences. The two positions which he now confuses are as follows:

P_1—when a person makes a fundamental moral judgment of the form "x is good" he feels approval towards x; and this approval (i) produces the quality of goodness in x, and (ii) is a necessary condition for its continued existence so that when the approval ceases the goodness disappears with it.

P_2—when a person makes a fundamental moral judgment of the form "x is good" he expresses his pro-attitude towards x.

The position here advocated and the position of the logical positivist is P_2 and not P_1. I do not know of anybody who has ever held P_1. It is a bad dream dreamt up by Blanshard. He so strongly believes, it seems, that "x is good" always asserts that x has a feature of some kind that he cannot, in stating the views he attacks, conceive that anybody else does not accept this.'[1]

Now I did not say that P_1 was the position consciously advocated by emotivists. I said that this was what their position amounts to when interpreted by one who believes that we are saying something significant in referring to past evils. This I should like to repeat, and I am grateful to Mr Edwards for the stimulus to make it clearer.

I hold that if people call Henry VIII a bad man or say that something in the past was an evil, they mean what they say, namely that the man or experience *was* bad when it occurred. The emotivists deny this. They do not deny it, to be sure, in the form of saying that the character of badness attaches to the present act of retrospect.

[1] *The Logic and Moral Discourse*, 207–8

They do not deny it in that form because they regard that form as meaningless; they hold that there is nothing good or bad in people or events at all. But the plain man thinks there is; we have been driving that home with tiresome iteration. When he hears the emotivist say that to call anything bad is only to express one's feeling about it, he wants to know what that implies for his own way of thinking on these matters. He sees that if the term 'bad' denotes nothing, and merely expresses a feeling, then past acts and experiences were not bad at all in the sense in which he thought they were. This is a perfectly straightforward inference. But if there is no badness in things or persons, what has become of it? Has it simply evaporated out of the universe? 'Not quite', answers the emotivist; 'the term "bad" still has meaning, but emotive meaning only; that is, it expresses a feeling existing in me here and now.' 'But doesn't that imply', asks the plain man, 'that the only badness the theory admits of is a badness depending on my feeling, coming into existence with it, and passing away with it?' Again, that is a legitimate deduction, and the answer is Yes. The emotivist may at once protest, as Mr Edwards does, that this language is incorrect, since it assumes that there is such a thing as badness that comes into existence and passes away, and the emotivist is not saying that; what comes and goes is not a character denoted by 'bad', but the emotion *expressed* by it. This of course is true, but as an answer to the plain man's point, it is trifling and evasive. The issue he is interested in is whether something he calls good or bad really is so, in the sense of being so independently of how he thinks and feels. The answer emotivism gives to this question is an unequivocal No. If he then says, 'I see; you are putting the goodness and badness in the attitude rather than the object', it does seem to me a wilful missing of his point to say 'Oh no, not at all; we are not putting goodness and badness in the attitude because there has never been any goodness or badness to put anywhere.' He is surely entitled to reply, 'but you *are* putting these qualities in the attitude in the only sense in which the question has any importance for me, and in the only sense in which you allow my words to have any meaning'. That is what the plain man is trying to say, and he is right in saying it. His language is obviously exceptionable in the sense that his use of 'good' and 'bad' to denote anything is outlawed by the theory he is criticizing. But note (a) that in my own statement of his criticism care was taken to make even the language unexceptionable; I made it clear by repetition that I was speaking of 'badness in the only sense in which it was involved at all'. And (b) the very fact that it is so difficult to state the theory in ordinary language without violating it is an additional witness against it. If it were really in accord with ordinary meaning, the emotivist would not have to cry out in protest when others put it in the language most natural to them.

13. (v) Mr Edwards seems to suppose that if one holds to an objective goodness or badness, these characters must be conceived as 'non-natural qualities'. There is no good reason for this. To be sure, Moore, Ross, and Ewing have held that goodness is a quality of this kind. What they have meant by this is that it is not a quality like square or rough, which can be sensibly apprehended, and would be included in a list of qualities constitutive of the object's 'nature'. I too think that goodness and badness, as commonly thought of, cannot be analysed as a sensible property that can be seen with the eye or pointed at with the finger. It has become fashionable of late to take those who hold such views as harbouring dubious loyalties to an antiquated metaphysic, if not of doing secret obeisance to the supernatural in some form. 'Most of us would agree', said F. P. Ramsey, 'that the objectivity of good was a thing we had settled and dismissed with the existence of God. Theology and Absolute Ethics are two famous subjects which we have realized to have no real objects.' Just like that! Unfortunately I do not find these matters so simple. I think that there is an objective goodness. I think that this goodness must be analysed in naturalistic terms, though not in the naïvely dogmatic and restricted terms alone permitted by positivism. There is nothing novel about such a position. The goodness talked about by Aristotle, Butler, Sidgwick, and even Green is a natural goodness, even if it cannot be seen or touched; to speak of an experience as good, for example, in the degree to which it is a fulfilment of human faculty is perfectly legitimate, whether the notion goes beyond sense or not.

As soon as one realizes that goodness may be at once objective and naturalistic, Mr Edwards' polemic loses much of its force. For he thinks of objectivism as linked to non-naturalism and this again to a bigoted supernaturalism. 'Intuitionism and, more generally, all forms of non-naturalism in ethics from Plato to Ross, have fundamentally had one and only one purpose: to help support the morality of self-denial and sin. . . . I do plead guilty to the charge of undermining morality in the sense of undermining the moralities of the fuddy-duddies and the sour-pusses.' I do not wish to say that there is nothing in this whatever. But as applied, for example, to the chief defender of non-natural qualities among recent moralists, G. E. Moore, one can hardly imagine anything wider of the mark. Nor is it, I would add, a fair example of Mr Edwards' standard of controversy.

14. (3) The charge I have elaborated at such length is that emotivism dislocates values from the place where they belong. If what we have said is true, a very curious consequence follows: emotivism would afford the perfect justification for 'the perfect crime'. Jones, let us say, is a wealthy old bachelor, and I am his veteran manservant. It would be a simple matter for me to alter his will so that it should leave me the bulk of his fortune, and almost as simple to deposit that in his cup which would send him painlessly off into the sleep that knows no waking. I am an expert in these things; I am universally trusted; and I am confident that I can cover every trail that might lead to my detection. I carry the plan through with triumphant cunning. In the present theory, what is my status? The answer must be that I have committed no crime at all; I have done no wrong; I have produced nothing bad. Of course my victim would have had much to say along these lines if he had been accorded an opportunity, but he was not; his feelings toward me, so long as he entertained any, were entirely benignant, as everyone else's continue to be. As for his murder—but no; after all, no murder was committed. That is a harsh word expressing disapproval, which no one feels toward me. The one person who knows of the act, namely myself, regards it, on the contrary, as an act of far seeing strategy, causing no pain to anyone, consummate in its expertness, and rich in the fertility of its benefits. To say that in the absence of all unfavourable attitudes my act was wrong, or my own resolution wicked, or my benefactor's death an evil, or my gains ill-gotten ones, would be meaningless; for the only use of these words is to express attitudes, and the attitudes do not exist. It is literally senseless, then, to say that an undetected wrong is a wrong at all. Needless to say, I am not attributing to the emotivists, who are harmless and kindly persons, any exceptional leaning toward the more *recherché* branches of crime. I am saying that if, like the rest of us, they called such conduct wrong, even though it was never discovered, they would have no ground for doing so. For any ground on which they might justify it would admit that evils exist *apart from* our attitudes, and that emotivism denies.

15. (II) In thus denying that there is any goodness or badness in objects apart from our attitudes toward them, it also denies by implication that an attitude of favouring is ever more *appropriate* than its opposite; and this again conflicts with universal convictions. We think that approval is appropriate to what is good and disapproval to what is bad; but if the only goodness and badness involved depend on these attitudes, if they have no existence or meaning until these attitudes are taken up, then there is nothing in the object itself that could justify either, or could make one more appropriate than the other.

Consider a case. There is a well-known painting called *Vae Victis*, which represents the end of a gladiatorial combat in a Roman arena. The victor stands with upraised sword, his foot on his prostrate opponent, who is mutely appealing to the spectators for mercy. It was the custom of those days to let the spectators decide the fate of the vanquished; if they wanted mercy shown him, they turned thumbs up; if they preferred to see him killed, they turned them down. In the picture a group of elegant Roman ladies, with languid amusement, are turning their thumbs down. It is a grim scene. Why does it so jar the spectator? I suppose because of the incongruity between the horror of what was going on in the arena and the attitude of the on-lookers. Bored amusement, languid approval, is hardly the fitting attitude with which to greet the bloody and painful extinction of a life.

This, I think, is the natural explanation of the picture's jarring us. And the difficulty with emotivism is that it cuts the ground from under such explanations. It holds strictly and technically that there is nothing bad in death and pain, and nothing wrong in inflicting either on anyone. Nothing answering to these value words enters the scene until someone assumes an attitude, and even then it enters only as an emotional response that happened to be aroused by these events. But if this is true, why is either attitude more fitting than the other? As far as value is concerned, the object is neutral; it is mere naked fact, as little good or bad as the law of gravitation. As such, there is nothing in it that would justify either approval or disapproval. If an attitude of favouring, or the reverse, is to be appropriate, there must obviously be something in the object to make it so, and if, independently of the attitude, the object is wholly valueless, what is there left to favour or condemn? On the emotivist theory, nothing. Hence both attitudes are arbitrary, and equally arbitrary.

We may go further. On this theory, why should the gentle spectators not have their little amusement? Their attitude may be unfitting, but it is at least no more so than its opposite, for there is nothing bad in itself in suffering, death, or the infliction of either; and they can actually make these things good, in the only sense in which anything is good, if only they take a favouring attitude. And if they can supply the materials of optimism thus cheaply, it seems silly not to do so. Indeed to the wistful reformer an alluring programme opens up for making the world over, a programme which has much in common with that of Mrs Eddy. If all that we mean by the goodness of things lies in our attitude toward them, we need only take that attitude in hand to make all well. We had supposed that suffering and death were evil; they are not; they will become positive goods in the only legitimate sense if we can get ourselves to feel and to ejaculate how splendid they are. Now there is no doubt some truth in this doctrine. Cheerfulness and courage do mitigate evils. But the suggestion that they place in our hands a magic wand with which we can wave out of existence evils which mankind have always found as stubborn as granite boulders seems to me irresponsible. A man does not exorcize all the evil of his own insanity, for example, by developing euphoria about it; indeed such cackling incomprehension may make the tragedy worse.

We may be met by the reply that we have misunderstood how the emotivists would deal with our example. We have assumed them to hold that there is no evil in the fate of the vanquished gladiator apart from the attitude of the spectators, and this assumption may be repudiated. For after all, that fate is repugnant to *him*, and thus to him still evil, regardless of what the spectators feel. But such a defence is inadequate. For, first, if the evils he is facing are made so by his own attitude, he may uproot them by changing it; let him greet his own death with a cheer, and there will be nothing evil about it. This is silly. Secondly, even if his attitude persists unchanged, and his situation still seems intolerably evil to him, this gives no ground to the spectators for calling it evil. If they apply this word to his fate, they find that all it expresses is their *own* feeling about that fate; they cannot concede or understand that, apart from this feeling, there was the smallest evil in it. If this is offered as a statement of what plain men mean at any level of intelligence or self-criticism, it seems to me grotesque.

16. (III) Emotivism involves a further consequence that, from our particular point of view, is even more important than those we have considered: it takes ethics out of the sphere of the rational. Moral judgments have always been supposed to be *judgments*. As such they have been included in the general province of knowledge and reason. They were either true or false; one could pertinently call them clear, or precise, or vague, or confused; they were either consistent or not with themselves and with other ethical beliefs; one could argue for them by producing relevant evidence; one could say that in accepting a belief about the wrongness of national aggression, or the duty of paying one's taxes, one was taking a *reasonable* view, and that if one differed from another about such things, there was a truth to be found, which formed the ultimate court of appeal. Common sense has no hesitation about all this. Indeed the wisdom that it has traditionally ascribed to the philosopher is primarily ethical wisdom, not so much a knowledge of the ways of nature as an insight, gained by much reflection, into the relative value of things and the true ends of living. The right and the good have been thought to be most clearly seen by the man who views them reflectively and dispassionately. To wrong another is to treat him unreasonably; and although the temper of the saint is not that of the rationalist, most men would be reluctant to think that the selfless heroism of a Francis Xavier or a John Woolman was really out of harmony with reason. The plain man may be said to be a rationalist in morals without being an intellectualist; that is, he believes that the good life is in accordance with reason and defensible by it, though not, for the most part, consciously directed by it. The main tradition of western philosophy takes the same view, but with a stronger intellectualist leaning. The three great Greeks held that reason displayed itself as truly in the choice of ends as in adoption of means, and went so far as to maintain, with some minor differences, that virtue *is* knowledge. Though most of their successors went less far, still all the elements of rationality that we just noted in common-sense ethics would be accepted by Aquinas and Descartes, by Locke and Butler, by Kant and Hegel, by Green, Sidgwick, and Spencer.

The crux of the issue is whether when we call something right or good, we are saying anything at all, in the sense of making any sort of assertion. To most persons it will seem curious to hear that we are not. And if the emotivist proposal is put forward as an account of what we ordinarily intend, it hardly merits discussion. It is really useless to tell us that when we pronounce a judicial decision unjust or the return of a lost article right, we are saying nothing that we mean to be true. On the question whether it *is* true, we may be ready to listen to discussion. On the question whether we mean to say something true, we may reasonably claim to be in a position of some advantage, and we cannot hesitate for a moment. If when we said returning the lost article was the right thing to do, someone asked whether we meant to say it was *true* that this was the right thing to do, we should regard the question as so strange that we should wonder how it could be asked. True? Why *of course* we mean that it is true. But the emotivist is not satisfied. He holds that we may be mistaken about our own meaning through assimilating it to what is really unlike it. If we start with the notion that rightness or goodness is a quality like squareness, which can really belong to things, we shall naturally suppose that in moral judgments we are ascribing this quality. But suppose that no such quality exists or can be conceived, and that all we have a right to assert is that we feel in a certain way; then we *must* be deeply mistaken about what we mean. How is the emotivist to show that we are thus mistaken? He has two lines of argument. One is to show that the goodness we suppose ourselves to be asserting is strictly unthinkable, and that since we cannot assert the unthinkable, our 'judgments' of value are not assertions at all. The other is to show by psychological analysis that in such 'judgments' the ethical component is reducible to an expression of feeling.

17. The first of these arguments will not detain us long, for we have considered it in another connection.[1] It is the argument drawn from the verifiability theory of meaning. Logical empiricists as we saw, developed a theory about all propositions outside the sphere of logic and mathematics to the effect that their meaning consisted in their mode of verification. When we asserted anything, we were referring to the experience that would attest the assertion as true. And when we examined the sort of experience that would supply the attestation, we always found it to be sense experience. We could say then that only assertions that referred to actual or possible sense experience had meaning. And it seemed clear that when we called the return of a lost article right or obligatory, or the achievement of understanding good, the terms, 'right' and 'good' did not refer to any sort of sense experience. They must, therefore, refer to nothing; they are meaningless.

[1] *Reason and Analysis*, Ch. 5

This neat and expeditious way of disposing of everything in metaphysics, theology, and ethics, that does not fit into one particular philosophy of science no longer carries weight with us. We found that the theory was compelled to dismiss as meaningless whole classes of propositions whose significance was far more certain than the truth of the theory that would impeach them. If we can refer to nothing but sense experience, all assertions about time, causality, number, and degree, all such statements as 'I believe X' or 'I remember Y', or 'I don't understand Z', all statements of scientific law, all contrary-to-fact hypotheticals, even the statement itself that all unverifiable propositions are meaningless, must be held devoid of meaning. The theory is both dogmatic and naïve. If anyone proposes to carry it over into ethics and use it as a measuring-rod for ethical judgments, we need ask only one question. Was the theory framed with ethical propositions in mind? If not, then to apply it in Procrustes fashion is quite foreign to the empirical spirit. If the theory did include ethical judgments in its review, then its claim must be that independent examination will show them to be asserting nothing. This is the second line of argument. Is it more successful than the first?

18. I cannot think so. But we must be careful to see what it is exactly that the emotivist is denying. He does not deny that ethical statements are assertions in any sense. Indeed, as Mr Stevenson showed in his *Ethics and Language*, every ethical statement, when taken in context, is charged with a mass of both descriptive and emotive meanings. When I say 'I ought to return that article I found', I am obviously implying a variety of factual judgments about my having found something, about its being a material article, about the possibility of my returning it, and so on; and the words 'I ought' may express sarcasm, fear of criticism or of the police, desire to gain approval or to make the loser happy, or many other things. Mr Stevenson did useful work in patiently running down many kinds of descriptive and emotive meaning that ethical judgments may involve, in singling out the emotive elements from the factual or descriptive, and, among emotive meanings, in distinguishing the ethical from the non-ethical. Such a review is most helpful if taken as preparing for, rather than settling, the crucial question. That question is, Is the distinctively ethical part of the statement—for example 'I ought' in the statement above—simply an expression of feeling, or is it also an assertion? The emotivist says it is the former; it is essentially an interjection which, as expressive of feeling only, is neither true nor false.

I do not believe this. But one cannot contentedly stop with mere disagreement. What is philosophy for if not to help toward agreement on questions of this kind? It is hardly believable that intelligent persons, brought up in the same culture, and applying such terms as 'good' and 'right' apparently in the same way to the same things, should yet be using them in senses poles apart. If they think they are, it seems probable that at least one of them has mistaken what he means.

19. But then how is he to be shown that he is mistaken? If a man insists that whenever he calls another man good, he means that the man should be put in jail, is there any way of *proving* that he is wrong? None, I fear. He is asserting a fact to which he has access and we have not, and, for all our arguments, the last word must lie with him. But if candour exists on both sides, and agreement that one may be mistaken even about one's own meaning, there is hope. For in these circumstances there is an effective method for dealing with disagreement. It is the method used in disagreement on other fundamental questions such as the nature of truth. If A says that the truth of a belief means for him its good consequences, and B says it lies for him in its correspondence with fact, it would seem at first that the difference was hopeless, since any arguments A might bring for his position would be offered as true only in a sense that B must regard as question-begging and irrelevant, and so of B's arguments in the eyes of A. What are they to do? They might, of course, turn on their heels and walk away. But if they are sensible, they will be more patient. They will run over a set of propositions that both accept as true, and see if there are not some among them that would exclude one interpretation of truth, while consonant with the other. This method has, in fact, convinced nearly all philosophers that the pragmatic definition of truth is a mistake. Ask a candid man whether he believes it true that Samuel Pepys, as recorded in his diary, took a walk on a certain afternoon. He will say yes. Then ask him where the practical consequences are in which the truth of his belief consists, and if heaven has been kind to him in respect of native endowment, his pragmatism will begin to wane. Of course it may not be possible to find any case that is absolutely decisive, and as long as any loophole exists, some men will go on insisting that Shakespeare was Bacon. But if one conception of truth fits in with ordinary meaning and usage while another can be made to fit only by trimming and squeezing, the first should have the preference. Similarly, if it appears that an objectivist interpretation of 'right' and 'good' does fit with ordinary meaning, and an emotivist interpretation subjects it to continual strain, then our vote should go to some form of objectivism. I think this is the state of the case.

We have seen some of these strains already. The implication of the emotive view that the 'goodness' of an experience falls outside the experience itself in a reaction of the contemplator is unplausible in the extreme, particularly when the experience is past and the reaction present; and its further implication that no attitude of favouring or disfavouring is more fitting to an object than its opposite is likewise at odds with general belief. But we have to do now with its ability to explain, or explain away, our stubborn and inveterate conviction that moral judgments may be *rational*, that is, that they are assertions which may be assented to, disagreed about, argued for, and perhaps proved. Let us look at a number of points at which the theory impinges on this conviction.

20. (1) The theory implies that no statement of right or good is ever true. Suppose I say 'the discovery of anaesthetics had very good results'. Of course this statement has various descriptive or cognitive meanings, which it is admitted on both sides may be true. But we are talking about the statement that the results were *good*. Regarding this statement the emotivist says that it does not state anything at all about the results in question. If that is correct, then, as we have noticed in another connection, what we said would not be rendered untrue if no such results had occurred. But we can see that it *would* be rendered untrue, and therefore that we *must* have been making an assertion capable of truth or falsity. It may be replied that what would be rendered untrue is not the statement that the results were good, but the implied factual statement that certain results did occur. I agree that this statement would be thus rendered untrue. I do not agree that the value statement would not also be rendered untrue. That this is a distinct statement is shown by the fact that the two may be falsified independently. If the results we had in mind did not in fact occur, but others we should call equally good, we should say that the factual statement was in error while the value statement was not.

If the results we had in mind did occur, but further examination convinced us that they did not have the value we supposed, we should say that the factual statement was true, but the value statement mistaken. It is thus not one component only that can be confirmed and falsified, but both; and since judgments alone can be confirmed of falsified, both must be set down as judgments. It may be replied, again, that if I discover that no 'good' results occurred, I do not say that my judgment of good was untrue, but only that my feeling was inappropriate. I do not accept this, but let us see where it leads. *Why* would the feeling of approval be then called inappropriate? The rational answer is, 'because, whereas I had assumed the results to be good, I now see that they were not'. 'Inappropriate' here *means* inappropriate to the character of the object. Hence the feeling could not be seen to be inappropriate unless the character of the object were first known. The approval is seen to be inappropriate because the object is seen not to be good.

21. (2) The theory implies, again, that no two persons ever use the word 'right' or 'good' in the same sense and that no one of us ever uses it in the same sense twice. This is hard to believe. Suppose two persons of good will devote themselves to setting up a home for old people. They are asked independently why they do it. A answers 'Because I think it a very good thing that these people should be freed from anxiety.' B gives the same sort of answer. The emotive theory implies that when the two men call this freedom from anxiety good, they are not using the term in the same sense, that there is no one character that they mean to ascribe to the experience they both refer to, and therefore that on the side of value they have no common end. The reason why they cannot be using the term in the same sense is that they are not using it in any sense at all, if this means some ascribable character. The only meaning with which they are using 'good' is an emotive meaning, and that differs in the two cases. For A it is an exclamation expressing *his* liking or approval; for B it is an exclamation expressing *his*; their emotions are different, and since their emotions *are* their meanings, their meanings must be different too. Now, granting that people can use the word in this way, it seems to me clear that in cases like this they do not. A and B mean to say something about freedom from anxiety; if you asked them, they would certainly say they meant the same thing, and were seeking the same result in the way of good; and I do not think that any semantic mauling can destroy this identity. Suppose that when they had got their institution under way, and the inmates were enjoying the freedom secured for them, both of these founders died. It would surely be legitimate to say that the good they meant and sought was living after them. If they could be brought back to look at their work, and found a numerous group of old people enjoying this freedom from anxiety, they would say, 'Yes, it is because we thought this state of things would be good that we worked as we did; it was precisely this good that we were both trying to bring into being.' On the emotivist theory, this account would be unintelligible. All that either of them meant by the goodness of such freedom died with him, for the meaning was exhausted in his own emotion, and of course his emotions ceased when he did.

22. (3) On the emotivist theory, no two of us ever agree in ethical belief. The only agreement possible in matters of good or bad will be agreement in attitude. This point is close to the one just made, but is worth separate notice. To see how an emotivist argues, we shall do well to cite a passage—it must be a rather long one—from Mr Stevenson.

> 'In the example,
> > A: X is good.
> > B: Yes, that's true.
> we should *not* be likely to take B as saying the equivalent of,
> > (a) "Yes, when you uttered 'X is good' you really did approve of X"
> . . . We should be more likely to take B as saying the equivalent of,
> > (b) "Yes, X *is* good."
> In other words, B may use "That's true" in order to repeat A's words after him, as it were, to signify agreement—but where the agreement would be in attitude, rather than (as it would be for usage (a)) in belief.'

Mr Stevenson thinks that agreement here means something quite different from what it means in a parallel case in science.

> 'A: Crows are always black.
> B: That's true.
> Here B's reply is equivalent to a repetition of A's words—equivalent to B's having asserted, "Yes, crows *are* always black"—and one does not feel that "true" is being used in any unnatural sense. The ethical usage, as previously illustrated, is unusual only in that it is tantamount to repeating a man's words after him in a *particular way*—a way that changes their descriptive meaning and retains their emotive effect. When B uses "true" with the effect of repeating A's remark, "X is good", he

is not talking about A's approval, as A was, but rather about his own; so their respective utterances of the words have different descriptive meanings. And B may use "true" in this context in a way that keeps some of the emotive effects of "good". This usage, being possible only when the rather colloquial indicator terms are used, is not found in science; and indeed, it is of no use unless agreement in attitude (or some analogue of it) is in question.'[1]

Let us see what this strange passage comes to. Suppose I say 'crows are always black', and you say 'that's true'. In this case you are agreeing to the truth of what I said. Suppose now I say, 'cultivation of mind is good', and again you say 'that's true'. In this case, the one thing you must not do, Mr Stevenson tells us in effect, is to take 'true' as meaning what in the other case you have just taken it to mean. When you say 'that's true', you may mean any one of three things, the first two stressing descriptive meaning, and the third emotive meaning. (a) You may interpret my statement descriptively, understanding that when I say 'cultivation of mind is good', what I mean is 'I approve of cultivation of mind'; and then in saying 'Yes, that's true', you are telling me that you think I have correctly reported my own state of mind. Mr Stevenson's remark that this meaning is not likely is, I should say, an understatement. Our real choice, he thinks, is between the two remaining possibilities. (2) You may, when you say 'that's true', mean to report that you too, like me, are experiencing an emotion of approval when you contemplate cultivation of mind. This too is a factual statement, reporting your own emotion. But (3) you may not be reporting or stating anything at all; you may be merely expressing through a virtual exclamation your feeling of approval.

Now it will be noted that no one of these three interpretations suggests that what I mean by 'that's true' may be simply 'that's true', that what I intend by it is to express my assent to a judgment you have just made, that 'cultivation of mind is good'. This interpretation, so conspicuous by its absence, is surely the most natural one of all. Let any reader ask himself whether it is not the only one that gives, in straightforward fashion and without twisting his sense, what he would normally mean. Certainly it seems so to me. Indeed this interpretation seems so much the most natural as to raise one's suspicion of any technique that excludes it. If the result of rigorous linguistic analysis is to offer the plain man a choice between a number of

[1] *Ethics and Language*, 169–170

meanings no one of which he can recognize as his own, and to tell him he must mean what it is quite obvious to him that he does not mean, then I think the verdict must be not that the plain man is excessively dim-witted, but that semantic technique would profit by an infusion of common sense. Of course if what the semanticist wants to show is that there is and can be no such character as good in the world, we should listen with interest to a metaphysical argument designed to show it. And if his aim is to discover what people actually mean, the study of the language they use is undoubtedly helpful. What is distinctly unhelpful is analysis in the service of metaphysics, or in that of the denial of metaphysics—it is the same thing. And it is hard to see how the most obvious of the plain man's meanings could in the present case be passed over unless such preconceptions were unconsciously at work.

23. (4) We have seen that on the emotivist theory no two persons can ever agree in an ethical belief. It is also true that in this respect they can never disagree. This is a further violent paradox which reflects its incredibility on the theory unless a very strong case is made for it. What kind of case is offered? It consists in holding that where disagreements in belief occur, they concern matters of fact, and that ethical disagreements are all disagreements in attitude. Now that some disagreements which would ordinarily be called ethical are really differences in attitude does seem to be true. If two persons are motoring together and, whenever A drives, he is reluctant to break the speed limit, while B does so without hesitation, they are differing in their ethical attitude. But are all ethical disagreements of this kind? Clearly they are not. In disagreements of this kind the attitudes differ without contradicting each other. A's reluctance to exceed the speed limit is simply a different fact coexisting with B's readiness to exceed it; they are in no way logically incompatible with each other. But in many ethical disagreements we do plainly intend to deny what other people are saying, and such disagreement, therefore, involves a genuine conflict of belief. Two friends, A and B, receive a call from their government into the armed services. Both receive it reflectively, and they discuss with each other the pros and cons of what they ought to do as exhaustively as they can. A ends by going into service, B by refusing 'on conscientious grounds'. No doubt they are differing in their ethical attitude. But is there no difference of ethical belief? The emotivist would say there is none. He holds that when A says that armed service is right and B that it is wrong, 'there is no logical contradiction. The opposition is in attitude, not in belief. What A is trying to do is not to question the truth of what B has said about his attitudes, but rather, as we have repeatedly seen, to *redirect* B's attitudes.'[1] That an attempt at redirection is here being made is probably true, though it is surely not always true; witness judgments of the past. But to *reduce* the ethical element to an expression and redirection of feeling seems to me to take inadmissible liberties with what the disputants would say they meant. Neither would have the slightest question in their minds that they did differ in their conclusions, and on a specifically ethical point. And they would undoubtedly express their difference in the verbal form of conflicting propositions: 'the armed service of one's country is right'; 'such service is wrong'. The semantic technique that would go behind both this explicit profession and its linguistic form and tell the men that they did not differ and never meant to differ, in moral belief, must be very 'powerful' indeed. Where does its persuasiveness lie?

It lies in the curiously seductive plausibility of saying that statements which are normally accompanied by a certain feeling and normally understood to express it, do nothing but express it. The man who says that armed service is wrong does say so with a feeling of disapproval, and his critic who says it is right says so with some feeling of positive moral approval. Can we not on closer inspection resolve their apparent conflict of belief into this difference of feeling towards a practice which, on the factual side, they seem to conceive in the same way? 'Armed service—cheers!' 'Armed service—horrible!' Many readers of emotivist literature are inclined to comment, 'Well, they *are* saying that, aren't they?', and score a point for emotivism. But it is such a point only if the objectivist cannot say it too, and he does say it. If the emotivist is really to score, he must show that neither disputant really intends to deny what the other man has said. And I do not think that any semantic manipulation can conjure that intention away. The difference between the two persons is not parallel to that of two persons who taste an orange and say, one of them, 'I like it', and the other, 'I don't'. One man's liking it is perfectly compatible with the other's disliking it. But if, when A says, 'the armed service of one's country is right', B says, 'no, it is wrong', he surely *means* to differ in a manner other than this. He means to say 'I differ with you in such a way that if what I am saying is true,

[1] *Ethics and Language,* 155

H

then what you are saying is not'. When he says that armed service is wrong, he means that it is wrong in a sense *exclusive* of its being right; the suggestion that when he calls it wrong, he does it in some sense that would allow it also to be right, would seem to him bewildering and absurd. What he says and what his critic says are not merely different; they are incompatible; they are understood as such by both parties; and they are expressly offered as contradicting each other.

24. (5) Again, if the theory is true, no one ever makes a mistake on a moral question. In the disagreement about entering the service, neither man was mistaken, though each thought he was contradicting the other. If the man who started by calling it wrong changes his mind and comes to accept it as right, neither what he said before nor what he says now is mistaken. When communists said on June 6, 1941, that Britain was engaged in a wicked war of imperialistic aggression, and, the next day, after the invasion of Russia, that she was fighting nobly and defensively on behalf of democracy, neither statement, so far as it contained any ethical strictures or approvals, was in error. Indeed, regarding a thoroughgoing emotivism we must go farther. A Sicilian bandit is no more likely to be in error on moral matters than the Pope, or a child than his father. The emotivist may protest against such examples. He may point out that, though what they attribute to him is strictly true, an unwary reader might assume that the emotivist did recognize a scale of objective values and that his own values were low on that scale. Such an imputation would, of course, be unjust and is not at all what is intended. If the emotivist says that the child is no more likely to be mistaken than the father, it is because he holds that on moral matters there is no objective better and worse to be mistaken about, and no assertions to be mistaken. But while that explains why moral judgments are supposed never to be mistaken, it does not remove the paradox of this belief. Most persons are clear that in growing from childhood to maturity they have corrected earlier misconceptions of what is fair in sport, of what honesty calls for in money matters, and of where over-riding of parents' wishes may be justified. Indeed we could all mention particular cases of having found ourselves out in error. Who does not have lurking in his memory the sort of occasion on which he said, too late, 'I thought I was paying that porter plenty, but I certainly should have given him more.' If someone objected, 'What you now say is no nearer the truth than what you said then; you made no mistake before, and you are correcting nothing now; you have merely changed your feeling about one of your past actions', one might well reply, 'To me, who after all did the thinking and feeling in this case, it does not look that way at all. I remember calculating carefully how much I ought to pay that porter in view of his time and effort. I simply got it wrong. My feeling about paying him what I did has changed; yes. But my feeling about it has changed because of seeing the mistake I made.' Probably an analyst could show that the change of view was closely dependent on new items of a factual kind that reflection had brought to light. That would be interesting but not relevant to the present point. For the moral judgment that concludes the reflection is not a noting of one more such item. It is the judgment that, in the light of these new items, my earlier judgment of right was mistaken. As Carritt says, 'feeling is incorrigible except by habituation, but moral judgments are corrected by thought'.[1]

25. (6) The belief that we can correct, and continue to correct, mistaken notions in morals implies that progress is possible, that the moral ideas and practices achieved by one age in individual or communal life may be better than those of an earlier age. Emotivism implies that such judgments are without objective meaning. A grown person may look back regretfully on many snap judgments and impulsive actions of his youth and say he has put away childish things, but he is not seeing *that* these earlier responses were wrong or mistaken; he is only expressing his present feeling about them. And there is nothing in the fact that one feeling comes later than another in time to make its object better than that of another, or to give it special authority. Nothing is really better than anything else, if that means independently of how one feels about it. What is called progress would as justly be called retrogression if our feelings about past and present were reversed. The suggestion that the later attitude has achieved a higher level of moral discernment or response is itself an emotive expression, voicing the feeling of the time but with no authority over feelings that went before or might come after. This is certainly in conflict with our belief about the possibility of moral advance. So far as this belief is to the effect that progress is inevitable, and that what comes later is necessarily better than what went before, it is entitled to very little respect, because it is based on

[1] *Moral and Political Thinking*, 185

very little knowledge. But so far as it is a belief that progress is possible, the case is otherwise. Most of us think we have actually known some progress. We are confident that in certain fields we have not only achieved truer conceptions of what is right and good than we once had, but that by conforming our practice to these conceptions we have made this also really better. And by 'really better' we mean not merely that we have a stronger emotion of approval toward it, but that it is such as to justify that approval to any impartial eye.

Emotivists have sometimes sought to provide for judgments of progress by making some emotional responses more significant than others. They point out that the response made by a mature, well-unified, and thoughtful personality is likely to be more stable and lead to less frustration and conflict than that of some brash adolescent. This is true. But it obviously implies that stability, and the absence of frustration and conflict, are in some sense *better* than their opposites. Or they suggest, as Westermarck did, that ordered knowledge, impartial judgment, and the mastery of nature are better than the absence of these things. Would they be willing, as Westermarck professed to be, to admit that all they were saying in calling one culture higher than another was that it was their own? A statement of betterness, made by an emotivist, would not be an assertion that anything was better, but an expression of a value preference. And why should that preference be given priority over another and opposite preference? To say that one liking or approval is a better, or more exalted, or more precious feeling than others, would be merely to express a feeling *about* a feeling, and this, the emotivists hold, tells us nothing about the object. To say that it *reveals* the object as better, as a nearer approach to what is really right in conduct or really good in experience, would admit into ethical judgment that element of insight which emotivists and positivists want above all things to exclude.

26. (7) Another and most important implication of the emotive theory is that one can never give relevant *reasons* for or against an ethical judgment. Here is a criticism that has often been repudiated, and must be made with care. Since moral judgments commonly have both emotive and descriptive meanings, and the descriptive component is a statement of fact for which it may quite well be possible to give reasons, emotivists have sometimes protested against saying that their theory excludes reasoning about such judgments.

Verbally the protest is justified; in substance it is not. What it amounts to is that one can argue for the factual component of such a judgment, which no one questions, but not for the ethical component, which substantially admits what we have just been saying. Let us see how the theory differs from ordinary belief on this head.

Modern man would claim some advance over ancient Assyria in respect to the treatment of prisoners of war. Suppose that he could catch an ancient Assyrian by the beard and expostulate with him about the practice of torturing prisoners for his own pleasure. How would he go about it? Could he offer any relevant *arguments* to show that the Assyrian practice was wrong? He would have no doubt that he could. He could say that to act in this way was to produce gratuitous pain, or at least pain that was far greater than any pleasure it produced, and that this was wrong; he could also show that it was to indulge one's impulses to hatred and to satisfaction in others' misery, and that this too was wrong. If then asked why these should be called wrong, could he continue the argument? Yes. He would say that to produce intense pain gratuitously was wrong because such pain was evil, and that to take satisfaction in inflicting it was wrong because this sort of satisfaction was evil. If he were asked to give reasons for these judgments again, he would probably be nonplussed. He has arrived here at judgments that he would be content to regard as self-evident. But at any rate he has offered an ethical argument. He has produced relevant evidence for a judgment of right by showing its connection with other judgments of right and ultimately with what he would take as self-evident judgments of good.

How would the emotivist comment on this apparently ethical reasoning? He would criticize it, I think, at three points. He would say (a) that none of these judgments, so far as genuinely moral, are assertions at all. We have discussed this contention already and will not now return to it. Further, and in consequence of (a), he would hold (b) that no moral 'judgment' ever implies or entails another, e.g. that it is not true that one can *deduce* the wrongness of torturing prisoners from the wrongness of gratuitously producing pain, and (c) that no factual judgment ever entails an ethical one, e.g. the fact that an experience is intensely painful does not entail its being bad.

27. Now in both these last respects emotivism is in conflict with assumptions universally made in ethical thinking. Take the first step in the argument offered above for the wrongness of torturing prisoners.

Put formally, it is a syllogism: any act which gratuitously produces intense pain is wrong; the torturing of prisoners does this, therefore such torturing is wrong. The major premise here, however reached, is an ethical statement if anything is. From this major, together with a factual minor, the ethical conclusion seems to follow necessarily, and so far as I know, everyone but an emotivist would take this as a case of supporting an ethical conclusion by an ethical reason. Indeed ethical propositions seem so plainly to entail and be entailed by other ethical propositions that, if this is to be denied, an extremely convincing substitute account of what is going on here will have to be provided. The next step in the above argument offers a new feature. When one is asked why the gratuitous causing of intense pain is wrong, the natural answer is, 'because such pain is evil'. Here again is an ethical reason for an ethical assertion. But the character of the premise is now different. What sort of assertion is one making in saying that intense pain is intrinsically evil? It does not seem like an empirical assertion; we do not say that it is only highly probable that an intense pain will be intrinsically evil, as we do that the next swan we see will be white. Such pain is evil by reason of its nature; we can see from what it is that it must be bad, as we cannot see from anything we know of swans that they must be white. The proposition is, therefore, necessary. But it is not a vain repetition either. It is not as if we had said merely 'pain is pain', for evil is not identical with pain; it may appear where pain is not. The relation most naturally suggested is that of genus and species; pain is one form of evil. And the relation of genus and species is a necessary one. The implication is that characters commonly taken as factual or descriptive, such as that of intense pain, may *entail* a value character such as goodness and badness. Thus, in some cases at least, we seem able to argue for ethical judgments with complete rational cogency.

28. What sort of substitute does the emotivist offer for this account? Essentially it is one in which psychological 'conditioning' takes the place of rational connection. If two parties differ over the legitimacy of torturing prisoners, neither party is making a judgment to begin with, and since it is only judgments that can be supported or refuted by evidence, reasoning about the moral issue is strictly out of the question. What passes for reasoning here is really a process of calling up varying aspects of the conduct discussed, or its causes or results, which themselves, when thought of, awake emotional responses, and thus of fortifying or nullifying the original attitudes by the play of these associated feelings. Suppose, however improbably, that someone did actually maintain that the torture of prisoners was legitimate, and you set out to dislodge him by argument. You might say (I do not suggest that this is the only argument available): 'Don't you admit that such an act would cause far more misery to the victims than pleasure to the torturers?' 'Yes', he would say if he were candid, 'I do admit that'. And if he were so bereft of imagination as never to have thought of that aspect of the matter, and had been conditioned to dislike the causing of pain, he might be won over. But if he were, says the emotivist, it would not be reasoning that did it. There may, to be sure, be some inference of a non-necessary sort in seeing that torture would cause more pain to victims than pleasure to imposers, but the vital step, in which it is claimed that such conduct is wrong, contains no reasoning or insight at all. If your opponent has been conditioned to feel antipathy for such conduct, he will feel it, but simply and solely because of this conditioning, which might have been otherwise, and not by virtue of any sort of rational process. As a firm old sceptic, Santayana, puts it, 'these strange and irrational pronouncements of spirit, calling events good and evil, are . . . grounded on nothing but on a creeping or shrinking of the flesh'.[1] Suppose one had been conditioned to feel, not this 'creeping or shrinking', but attraction instead; what sense could your claim that this conduct was necessarily wrong conceivably bear for him? None whatever. You might, of course, say, 'But you surely wouldn't feel favourably toward the inflicting of intense pain on yourself, would you? 'No.' 'Then it is inconsistent, isn't it, to favour it when inflicted on others?' 'Not in the least', comes the reply; 'liking and disliking are emotions, not judgments, and are therefore inconsistent neither with each other nor with anything else.' 'But surely', you persist, 'even if you find no inconsistency in liking the infliction of pain on others, you can see that it is wrong, because of the badness of what you are inflicting.' 'Sheer confusion', comes the answer; 'what you are trying to connect here as ground and consequent are really two psychological facts which, as they are not judgments at all, have no kind of logical linkage; and your apparently self-evident ground, namely that intense pain is evil, since it is only an exclamation of antipathy, has no necessity either.' As a last despairing shot, you try: 'But this antipathy to pain is not an accident, is it? It is not something that might

[1] *Scepticism and Animal Faith*, 280

have been otherwise if people had been conditioned differently; it is something that men, being what they are, *must* feel in the nature of the case. So, after all, pain to us *is* necessarily evil.' 'More confusion' is the reply. 'When you say "pain to us is necessarily evil", all that means is that we do generally feel aversion for it. If this is a result of conditioning, it obviously might have been different. If it is a result of our original nature, it still might have been different, for causal laws are *de facto* conjunctions only; there is no necessity in them; men in Mars may, for all we know, be at this moment rejoicing in the intensest kind of pain. So if you mean by reason the grasp of intelligible necessity, there is no trace of reason in your argument from beginning to end.'

It follows from all this that when the emotivist argues an ethical case, he is doing something extremely different from what other people suppose they are doing. Instead of arguing for a conclusion, he is trying to work on another person's emotions. Since 'the supporting reasons', as Mr Stevenson says, 'have no sort of *logical* compulsion' and are 'related to the judgment psychologically rather than logically',[1] moral reasoning becomes psychological strategy. Santayana puts it baldly. If you want to prove to another man that knowledge is good, you ask him whether he would like to be an oyster, with pleasure but no ideas. This, says Santayana, is not a reason but an *argumentum ad hominem*, but unfortunately 'there can be no other kind of argument in ethics'.[2] But then is there no difference between being rationally convinced of the rightness of a course of conduct and being emotionally persuaded about it? Are we to say that the closeness, range, and accuracy of thought with which a moralist like Sidgwick supports an ethical conclusion are simply irrelevant to that conclusion and add nothing to its weight? If so, what is the difference between a reflective moralist and a mere propagandist?

Mr Stevenson is creditably troubled by this question and devotes a chapter to it. His conclusion is that 'when the terms are *completely* neutralized, we may say with tranquillity that all moralists are propagandists, or that all propagandists are moralists'.[3] Both, objectively seen, are urging conclusions that are equally non-rational and equally incapable of rational support. To be sure, Mr Stevenson protests repeatedly against the natural enough notion that this is a

[1] *Ethics and Language*, 30, 113
[2] *Winds of Doctrine*, 147
[3] *Op. cit.*, 252

cynical view; 'the practical problem is not to avoid all persuasions', he says, 'but to decide which to avoid and which to accept'.[1] 'Persuasion is unquestionably a tool of the "propagandist" and soap-box orator; but it is also the tool of every altruistic reformer that the world has ever known. We must not banish all doctors to rid the world of quacks.'[2] True. But there *is*, then, a distinction between doctors and quacks, moralists and propagandists, though, looked at 'neutrally', there appears to be none. What is this distinction? I have been unable to discover what it is, unless it is perhaps that the doctors and moralists are those whose attitude agrees with one's own. They are not, of course, men whose ethical views are more rational, or better grounded, or in better accord with nature, or with the sentiments of mankind, for none of these things is relevant evidence that what such men regard as better is really better; indeed to talk of the 'really better' is held to be nonsense. But if so, is not every quack a doctor, and *no* doctor better than any other? Mr Stevenson says that the practical problem is to decide which persuasion to avoid and which to accept. Admirable. And just *how* does one decide? The Ku Klux prophet offers one counsel; the humanitarian offers another. What can a decision between these counsels mean if, before the decision, they are both neutral, and, after it, whatever one happens to have favoured is made right by that very fact? If anything can be rendered right, in the only permitted sense of right, by one's favouring it, what ground has an emotivist for talking about quacks at all? The Ku Klux clansman favours his own morals as warmly as the saint or the philosopher does his. On the emotivist theory no decision between them is possible, if this means a decision on grounds; for in the end the verdict of right given by the philosophic moralist is, and must be, as truly the reaction of non-rational feeling as that of the fanatic. It is admitted that the philosopher takes into his account a wider area of facts. But his decisions are in no logical sense based upon those facts, and no way of feeling about them is more just or right or rational than any other.

On this all-important point of the support of moral judgment by argument, emotivism and common sense—even self-critical common sense—are on opposite sides of a very wide chasm. Can the emotivist afford to brush this fact aside by saying 'so much the worse for common sense'? No, he cannot. The meaning in men's actual judgments is

[1] *Ethics and Language*, 250
[2] *Ibid.*, 164

what we are discussing; in the end it is the only compass in ethics. If this compass is thrown overboard and one is allowed an arbitrary choice in defining ethical terms and contriving ethical systems, one finds oneself on an open sea without moorings or bearings, and going nowhere. To his credit the emotivist has seen this. He does not want to be arbitrary. What he professes to offer is an account of the actual meaning of self-critical minds in talking about moral problems. Hence his divergence from such minds must be for him a serious matter.

29. (8) Implicit in much that we have been saying is a further implication of emotivism which many would regard as the most obvious and important of all. It allows no objective court of appeal to which ethical disputes may be carried. If this were merely an argument from unfortunate practical consequences, it would hardly be worth stating, for one does not prove an analysis to be incorrect by showing that its acceptance would be inconvenient. But that is not what the present argument says. It says that there is a general conviction in men's minds about the possibility of settling disputes with which the emotivist view is inconsistent, and hence that, as an analysis of their meaning, it is incorrect.

Let us try to be clear about this. Of course, even science has no actual court of appeal in the sense of a group of experts whose judgment is everywhere accepted. Russian and American biologists, for example, differ widely, and with no recognized body to arbitrate between them. But no biologist on either side would take the thought seriously that there is really no common court of appeal, in this or any other science. That court is simply the nature of things as revealed to men's inquiring reason. The notion would not enter their heads that if a biologist in Petrograd said one thing and a biologist at Woods Hole said another and contradictory thing, they could both be right, or that in this conflict there was no truth to be ascertained. Obviously there is and must be such a truth. Furthermore, the principles of logic, mathematics, and scientific method are not transmuted when one crosses national frontiers. If truth is everywhere one, so also in general is the method of finding it. Hence if there is a difference of opinion, the procedure for settling it is plain enough; it is for the people on both sides to apply more rigorously the method accepted in common as the means of arriving at common truth. Thus scientists would continue to travel the same road if they never met at all. They know that where they differ they may have recourse to a court whose jurisdiction is universal and whose authority is absolute.

If the emotivist is right, the situation in ethics is the opposite of this. Even if moralists did meet in regular convention, even if there were a recognized world court of morals, there would be no principles on which it could proceed. The essence of justice is impartiality, and unless there are principles that can be applied without respect to persons and are valid independently of personal likes and dislikes, a court of justice is impossible. That there are such rules is assumed by those who administer courts or make use of them. Even those who are condemned by them do not, in general, question these rules. The man indicted for murder or forgery does not bring in a plea that these acts are right, but only that the facts of the case do not admit the classification of what he did under these heads. The parties before a court agree that there are principles standing over against their individual feelings and actions by which their conduct may be judged; it is the impersonality of these rules that is their protection; if a judge showed himself not bound by them and gave decisions on personal impulse or feeling, he would come to be regarded as a feather in the wind, or, like Jeffreys, as a capricious ogre. Indeed the very notion of *adjudicating* moral claims without objective principles of right and wrong is as unthinkable as the notion of judging a debate if there are no rules of evidence or laws of logic. Now the disquieting thing about emotivism is that it cannot recognize such principles.

Take a case. A certain nation, A, brings a charge against another, B, of unprovoked aggression. It does so on the assumption that such aggression is wrong, that rational persons and civilized governments will perceive that it is wrong, and that in theory at least it is possible for an international court to settle the matter by bringing home the wrong-doing to one party rather than the other. Unfortunately, if emotivism is correct, no such assumptions are warranted. There is no objective right or wrong in the case at all. There are no common moral principles, such as the wrongness of aggression, that can be brought to bear in its settlement. A says that what B has done is wrong, and if A feels as he does about it the action *is* wrong, in the only admissible sense. B says the action was an admirable example of rational foresight in caring for an expanding population, and if B feels that way about it, the action is right in the only admissible sense. And, regardless of the facts of the case or the feelings of the litigants, any verdict the court may please to give as to the rights and wrongs of the case will be unexceptionable, since there is nothing objective to check it by, and it expresses faithfully what the court feels. In a moral world of this kind, the very notion of impartial justice is without meaning. There can be no verdict in accordance with deserts because there are no deserts. There is no real guilt, no real innocence. This seems to me ethical anarchy.

30. Mr Eliot remarks that 'the most important question that we can ask is whether there is any permanent standard by which we can compare our civilization with another, and by which we can make some guess at the improvement or decline of our own'.[1] There are emotivists who would agree, and who do not like the dusty answer that their philosophy requires them to give to this question. Bertrand Russell is one of these. He sees no way of escape from emotivism. When he comes in his *History of Western Philosophy* to the famous debate between Socrates and Thrasymachus, he finds himself, in principle, on Thrasymachus' side.

'Plato thinks he can *prove* that his ideal Republic is good; a democrat who accepts the objectivity of ethics may think that he can *prove* the Republic bad; but anyone who agrees with Thrasymachus will say: "There is no question of proving or disproving; the only question is whether you *like* the kind of State that Plato desires. If you do, it is good for you; if you do not, it is bad for you. If many do and many do not, the decision cannot be made by reason, but only by force, actual or concealed".'[2]

Is this, then, the conclusion to which we are compelled? Russell thinks it is.

'Nietzsche's hero differs from a Christian saint, yet both are impersonally admired, the one by Nietzscheans, the other by Christians. How are we to decide between the two except by means of our own desires? Yet, if there is nothing further, an ethical disagreement can only be decided by emotional appeals, or by force—in the ultimate resort, by war. In questions of fact, we can appeal to science and scientific methods of observation; but on ultimate questions of ethics there seems to be nothing analogous. Yet, if this is really the case, ethical disputes resolve themselves into contests for power—including propaganda power.'[3]

[1] *Notes Towards the Definition of Culture*, 18
[2] *History of Western Philosophy*, 138–9
[3] *Ibid.*, 137

On this view it is hard to see how an international law or 'obligation' could have any binding force. I do not wish to overstate the case. I do not think the view would rule out international laws and courts and governments altogether; it would rather change their basis in a Hobbesian manner. Hobbes was an early emotivist who held that 'whatsoever a man desireth, that for his part he calleth good'. In a state of nature, therefore, he had no obligation to do anything he did not want to do, for an action was made right by the fact that he wanted to do it. But since all men are egoists, Hobbes held, they will all want to exploit each other for their own ends. Since this tended to make the life of each 'solitary, poor, nasty, brutish, and short', they concluded, each for his own advantage, to set up a power with jurisdiction over them all, and give it their joint obedience. Here then we have a pattern for a court and government possessing great power (Hobbes made it absolute), and yet with no recognition of objective right or wrong anywhere in the system. Why is this not a valid pattern now? One must agree that it would be better than nothing. But any structure that cuts the connection between morality and law, as this does, is likely to be unstable. The members who agree to obey are bound by nothing but self-interest to keep their word. If they can exploit others to their own satisfaction without being detected and punished, there is no reason, legal or moral, why they should not. If they are powerful enough to defy the government, national or international, there is no ground on which they can be validly criticized for doing so; they have no obligation if they do not feel that they have. Nor does the government. Once in power, it can do no wrong. Its obligation is identical with its preference. A policy ordered on these principles would, as we have suggested, probably be better than chaos. But if it has nothing better to base itself on than moral anarchy, it will gravitate toward political anarchy as well.

31. We have argued that the emotive theory does not give an accurate account of our actual moral beliefs. It is worth pointing out that it does not give a true account of what emotivists themselves believe when they are off their guard. When Russell, for example, is deploring a supernaturally grounded morality, he has no hesitation in ascribing to value judgments a high degree of certainty: 'the evil of being burnt alive is more certain', he says, 'than any proposition of theology'.[1] Is this not a curious opinion for one who holds that

[1] *Unpopular Essays*, 44

value statements, being exclamations, are not capable of certainty at all? Russell is one of the most effective defenders of the appeal to reason in human affairs, and the force of his defence is enhanced by a noble record of courage. There is at times a stirring ring in his words that reminds one of that 'saint of rationalism', John Stuart Mill, who happens to have been his godfather. 'The power of reason is thought small in these days', he writes, 'but I remain an unrepentant rationalist. Reason may be a small force, but it is constant, and works always in one direction, while the forces of unreason destroy one another in futile strife. Therefore every orgy of unreason in the end strengthens the friends of reason, and shows afresh that they are the only true friends of humanity.'[1] 'We have a right to hopes that are rational . . . If we allow ourselves to be robbed of these hopes for the sake of irrational dreams, we shall be traitors to the human race.'[2] Again, 'Whatever sexual ethic may ultimately be accepted must be free from superstition and must have recognizable and demonstrable grounds in its favour.'[3] Admirable, all of it. But how can the same voice tell us that regarding the ends of life and the great issues of right and wrong, reason has nothing to say? Russell's main plea as a social and political reformer has been that reason should be heard against the irrational promptings of prejudice and sentiment. Russell's main argument as a moralist is that in the ultimate decision of these issues reason is impotent and the verdict must be given by sentiment. Russell the moralist describes the plea made by Russell the reformer as nonsense.[4] He is in need of defence against himself.

Other emotivists have had similar trouble with consistency. 'Thus they employ their supposed discovery that no moral judgment is *really* anything more than the expression of a bias of the person who utters it as a basis for the claim that no moralist has a "right" to impose his own biases on others, and vigorously condemn those who violate this maxim of their moral doctrine.'[5] They may reply, of course, that in protesting against one man's imposing his prejudices on others, they are only expressing their own dislike of such conduct

---

[1] *Sceptical Essays*, 123
[2] *New Hopes for a Changing World*, 189
[3] *Marriage and Morals*, 24
[4] He admits with characteristic candour that he is not happy about his ethics: 'in feeling I am not satisfied. I can only say that, while my own opinions as to ethics do not satisfy me, other people's satisfy me still less.' *The Philosophy of Bertrand Russell*, 724.
[5] A. E. Murphy, *The Uses of Reason*, 141

and are not suggesting that there is anything wrong with his attitude in any other sense; indeed he has a perfect 'right' to impose his biases on others, in the only admissible sense of 'right', if he feels in a certain way about it. This is consistent, but one wonders if there is not some rationalization in it. Indeed one finds all too many occasions for such wonder in the writing of emotivists. In commenting on the work of one of them, Professor Paton says: 'I fail to understand why he consistently assumes agreement in attitude to be good. He even assumes that "enlightened" argument is better than argument which is not enlightened. In so doing he seems either to be assuming unconsciously some objective standard of goodness or else to be introducing personal preferences into a "neutral" analysis in which they should have no place.'[1] Of course an attitude arrived at as a result of enlightened argument is more likely to be 'rooted in fact', but then for any thoroughgoing emotivist 'rooted in fact' means neither necessitated by fact nor appropriate to fact; indeed such an attitude is no better than any other, except in the sense that I happen—for no *reasons* at all—to be drawn to it. Emotivists do not like the criticism that their theory places on a level the moral response of the reflective judge and that of the man of impulse; it is perfectly possible, they say, to consider the former better, in the sense of being ethically more weighty. If this means what everyone else would mean by it, namely that the judge achieves a fuller and more objective appraisal of the values involved, they are no longer emotivists. If it means what they say it does, it expresses nothing but another non-rational preference.

32. Are these lapses into inconsistency mere inadvertencies, or is there something incoherent in emotivism as such? I think that as it is actually maintained, there always is this latter kind of inconsistency. The theory is put forward as true, and as the only theory that will do justice to the facts of moral experience. In inquiring into these facts, in seeking a theory that will comport with them, in defending this theory by argument, is not the emotivist assuming that it is better to know than not to know? He may answer, of course, that he happens to like knowing, but is not assuming that, apart from this liking, it is any better than ignorance. But is that true? He acts very much as if he thought it better for others too, regardless of what they may happen to feel. He is certainly not content to leave others in their

[1] *In Defence of Reason,* 200–1

ignorance. Why is he so eager to put his argument before them, to expose the errors of alternative theories, and to get people to see the truth of his own account? He may reply that it is because he thinks that if others come to know the truth, they will respond to it emotionally as he does. But why should he want them to do so? Is it because their doing so would be good? If he says yes, meaning what most people would mean by this, namely that their knowledge would have a worth of its own, regardless of what *he* might feel about it, then he has deserted his theory again. If he says no, then what is the point of his efforts? He is trying to induce in others an experience that he does not admit to have in itself any value at all, and his effort to induce it is the product of a non-rational whim. He may reply that it gratifies his love of power to exert this influence over other minds. But he would take no satisfaction in convincing them of what was *not* true, even if the delusion were pleasant to them; his satisfaction depends on thinking that he is doing them some good, that it is *better* for them to know the truth. If he found them insisting that they would rather remain in ignorance and error, what would he say? Would he say that since they happened to like that state, ignorance and error were their good? I think not. He would more probably expostulate with them on the ground that it could not be anyone's good to remain in such a state, and that if they were not interested in the truth, they ought to be. That is good sense, but it is not emotivism.

Let us be clear what we are saying. There is no necessary contradiction, so far as I see, between affirming the emotivist theory as true and denying that knowledge has, as such, any value. There *is* a contradiction between what the emotivist is asserting and what is normally implied in his act of asserting it. The logic of the case is rather like that of the Cartesian *cogito ergo sum*. The real force of Descartes's argument lies in the contradiction that would be involved in denying that one's own thinking existed. But there is no self-contradiction in the *content* of this assertion; the proposition 'no thought exists', taken by itself, is unexceptionable. But taken together with the fact that it is actually being asserted, there *is* a contradiction; it cannot be true at once that no thought exists and that I am actually thinking that no thought exists; in making one's assertion, one is doing something which, when recognized for what it is, cuts the ground from under the proposition asserted. The emotive paradox is similar. In urging upon myself and others the knowledge that knowledge in itself is valueless, I am implying that it does have a value denied in my assertion about it. The position, to take another example, is a little like that of the psychological hedonist, who may protest that when he talks and acts as if the happiness of his family were important, he is interested in nothing but his own happiness; he holds that his scheming and sacrificing for their advantage show no desire for this advantage, but only a tendency on his part to find his own satisfaction in acting *as if* he had a desire for it. This is clearly a logical possibility. But most philosophers who have considered it have thought that, whatever its holder may profess, he was really belying his theory daily. He would not find his own happiness in promoting that of others unless he really did desire theirs as well as his own. In like fashion I think that emotivists are deceiving themselves about their meanings. Both in seeking the truth and trying to make it prevail, they attach an importance to knowing which belies their profession that they regard such knowledge as intrinsically worthless. A distinguished logician has written: 'those who deny the character of cognition and the possibility of truth to value-apprehensions must find themselves, ultimately, in the position of Epimenides the Cretan who said that all Cretans are liars. Either their thesis must be false or it is not worth believing or discussing . . . whoever says what is incompatible with his own presumptive attitude in saying it must either be joking or he reduces himself to absurdity'.[1] Professor Lewis is surely right.

[1] C. I. Lewis, *Analysis of Knowledge and Valuation,* 373

CHAPTER IX

THE LINGUISTIC RETREAT
FROM EMOTIVISM

1. We have dealt with emotivism at length because it is the most arresting and influential ethical theory of the past quarter century. In the pure form in which we have discussed it, however, there are probably few moralists who would still subscribe to it. The decline of its popularity is largely due to the recognition of three deficiencies in it.

In the first place, its denial that there is such a thing as moral judgment at all was in too flagrant an opposition to ordinary meaning. This was admitted by some emotivists themselves.

'Certainly' wrote Mr Ayer, 'the view, which I still wish to hold, that what are called ethical statements are not really statements at all, that they are not descriptive of anything, that they cannot be either true or false, is in an obvious sense incorrect. For, as the English language is currently used—and what else, it may be asked, is here in question?—it is by no means improper to refer to ethical utterances as statements . . . when someone wishes to assent to an ethical verdict, it is perfectly legitimate for him to say that it is true, or that it is a fact, just as, if he wished to dissent from it, it would be perfectly legitimate for him to say that it was false.'[1]

If Mr Ayer continues to hold an emotivist view,

'this does not mean that all ethical statements are held to be false. It is merely a matter of laying down a usage for the words "proposition" and "fact", according to which only propositions express facts and ethical statements fall outside the class of propositions.'[2]

Where does this leave us? It is 'legitimate' for the plain man to go on talking as if moral judgments were true or false; it is also legitimate

---

[1] *Philosophical Essays*, 231–2 (1954)
[2] *Ibid.*, 233

for the emotivist to talk as if they were not. But the plain man's usage is legitimate only in the sense that it reflects the ordinary use of language; Mr Ayer's usage is legitimate in the sense that it reflects the truth, namely that moral 'judgments', however taken by the plain man, are cognitively meaningless. It seems to me idle in such a case to say, as Mr Ayer does, that he is merely recommending a new usage. The new usage implies that plain men and most moralists have been fundamentally mistaken about what they meant when they made moral judgments. One can state this issue, as one can any other issue, as if it were a verbal question, the question in this instance whether a moral judgment shall be *called* a proposition. But the issue of moment here is not what it shall be called, but what it is, and behind Mr Ayer's new usage is an ethical theory which he admits to run counter to the common one.

But to those among the analysts who had a higher veneration for common usage, this was taking too large a liberty. Moore had said, and the later Wittgenstein more emphatically, that one must not play fast and loose with actual meaning; and if it could be shown that we actually did, in our moral statements, mean to say something true, to argue about moral beliefs and contradict them and make inferences from them, then emotivism could not offer itself as a correct analysis of common meaning. We must amend it into closer conformity with this meaning.

2. Secondly, it soon became plain that the emotion of the emotivists was by no means a simple affair. One of the complaints against them was that they seemed to reduce the moral attitude to one of mere liking or aversion, whereas moral approval and disapproval, even if emotions merely, had qualities of their own. Indeed, on further examination they looked less and less like emotions at all. What was expressed in moral judgment might be any one of a wide variety of attitudes—an entreaty, for example, an excuse, a wish, or some form of command. These were not primarily cognitive states; so those who placed them at the heart of the moral judgment were still aligning themselves on the whole with emotivism. But they insisted, and with justice, that they were not mere or pure emotivists. They had subjected the non-rational attitudes expressed in such judgment to a more discriminating analysis.

3. Thirdly, it was widely held that emotivism had gone too far in its dismissal of *argument* in morals. Stevenson's kind of emotivism did not permit one to say that any kind of conduct was, strictly, more reasonable than any other, or to defend any moral pronouncement by logically relevant means. All one could do if one differed from another was to bring causal pressures to bear upon him—including, to be sure, the recital of facts—in the hope that they would change his attitude. But since he had asserted nothing, there was nothing for one's arguments to be relevant to; it would be absurd to try to establish logically one's own emotion, or to disprove his. This situation was felt by later analysts to be awkward in the extreme. It was too plain for denial that men did argue about moral issues, and that at times they succeeded in justifying their views by evidence universally felt to be relevant. To be sure, one could never prove a moral judgment in the same conclusive fashion as a statement in geometry. But to say that repaying a creditor was no more reasonable, in the sense of justifiable by reasons, than cutting his throat was an outrageous position.

To anyone studying the place of reason in moral judgment, this last line of retreat from emotivism is, of course, particularly interesting. Unfortunately, we cannot attempt to deal with it fully. Though the important books on ethics in recent years have been all too few, the spate of articles has been prodigious, and (apart from the dreariness of writing that protests continually its concern with verbal usage), to deal with the nuances of the many minute departures of recent years from emotivism would hardly be possible. We shall merely indicate with brief comment a few of the more significant lines which the retreat has taken.

4. One mild rising against emotivism we have already noted. Mr Edwards has seen that such terms as 'good', 'right', and 'ought', usually express more than a feeling or an attitude. *What* more they express depends, he holds, on the context of their use. If I speak of a good (or nice) steak, I mean that it is tender, done to the degree of rareness that I like, and so on. If I speak of a man as good, I mean that he is kind, gentle, free from envy, and so on. The term 'good' *both* expresses my feeling *and* refers to these qualities. Since, then, in calling something good, I am asserting certain qualities to belong to something, I can defend my judgment in the same way as if I had said it was square or made of wood. If challenged, I shall point to the existence of the denoted qualities; the best conceivable reason for my judgment's truth is the presence in the object of the qualities my words refer to.[1]

5. This is a move in the right direction. It formally concedes that value judgments are really judgments, not interjections merely. But its break with emotivism is too half-hearted to be a real advance. The emotivists had already owned that when we use value terms it is because of the recognized presence in the object of certain qualities, but they had declined to include these qualities in the meaning of the terms. Mr Edwards' new proposal is that they should be so included. But is the advance more than verbal? The emotivists had distinguished between descriptive and emotive meanings and said that we could give reasons for the first, but not for the second. Mr Edwards would extend the meaning of 'good' to include both these types. But within this extended meaning he would draw precisely the same distinction as that already drawn by the emotivists, and would hold, as they do, that for the descriptive meaning we can give reasons, and for the emotive, not. And since the value meanings fall exclusively on the emotive side, he stands, as regards reason in moral judgment, precisely where the emotivists did.

He is reluctant to think this, and holds that he has made a genuine advance. Stevenson had held that if one offered reasons for a moral statement, they had a causal relevance only; they might tend in fact to win over an opponent, but since one had submitted no proposition, one had said nothing to which one's 'reasons' could be logically relevant. Edwards holds that on his view they *would* be relevant, since the meaning of 'good', 'right', and 'ought' will now contain a factual component, and for this factual part of the statement reasons may be offered.

Where is the advance? The emotivists do not deny this. Edwards would be going beyond them only if he showed that logically relevant reasons could also be offered for the value component in the statement. This he cannot do, for he concedes as completely as they do that the value side of it is emotive purely, and that one can offer no logical grounds for an interjection. He thinks that 'Stevenson's theory concerning the nature of moral disputes is altogether mistaken',[2] since it implies that 'settlement' of them means merely the achievement of similar attitudes, and 'reasons' are merely causes acting upon the

---

[1] Paul Edwards, *The Logic of Moral Discourse*, Ch. 7–9.
[2] *Ibid.*, 180

emotions. But when one examines the new senses of 'settlement' and 'reasons' which he proposes to recognize, one finds that they apply as exclusively to the factual side of moral statements as Stevenson himself contended. If one wants to attack the value side of an opponent's statement, there is still only one way to do it. The statement, on that side, expresses nothing but an attitude; attitudes cannot be proved or disproved by reasons; they must be worked on through causes; and the most effective causes are often such as sensible men would repudiate as irrelevant. Mr Edwards is rightly repelled by the emotivists' assimilation of ethical reasoning to propaganda, and does his best to avoid it. I share to the full his repugnance to it. What I cannot understand is how or why so clear-headed a writer can have supposed himself to have escaped from it.

6. A position similar to Mr Edwards' has been suggested by Mr Urmson in an able and much-discussed article 'On Grading'.[1] Mr Urmson holds that to call things good or bad is to grade them, and that we shall get needed light on how these terms are used in morals if we consider their use in the professional work of grading, for example the grading of apples. If we do, we find that for admission into each grade there is a set of criteria; to be labelled as 'super', for example, the apple must be of a certain size, ripeness, and colour. Whether we speak about a good apple or a good gun, a good cricketer or a good man, we are grading the object before us, and in doing so we are making conscious or unconscious use of certain criteria. Mr Urmson thinks that in all these cases we are using the word 'good' in the same sense,[2] but that the criteria used in applying it differ from case to case. Ordinarily when we disagree about the goodness of something, we can discuss the matter profitably, because we do not really differ either as to the meaning of 'good' or as to the criteria for applying it, but only as to whether one or more of these criteria are present. If you call Jones a good man and I disagree, you can point out to me that Jones does in fact pay his debts and is in fact kind to his children, despite what I have heard to the contrary; and when I am set right as to these facts, I shall presumably 'grade' him as you do.

7. But suppose we have different criteria for calling things 'good'; what then? Suppose that a sensualist and a scholar are taking about

[1] *Mind*, Vol. 59 (1950) 145–169
[2] *Ibid.*, 162

the value of knowing Latin, or the things to which such knowledge gives access. Or suppose a communist and a democrat differ as to whether Jones is a good man. Here the very criteria on which they would base their use of the word may be different. 'When there are differences of opinion about what grading criteria to adopt in a given situation, is there not a right and wrong about it . . . or are we to say that the distinction, for example, between higher or lower, enlightened and unenlightened moral codes is chimerical?' 'Certainly', Mr Urmson writes, 'we do not want to say this'. But if we really differ about our criteria for higher and lower, how can we proceed? 'Of course we cannot, when debating what criteria to use for moral grading, grade the criteria morally',[1] since it is precisely the criteria for such grading that are under dispute. Can we cut the knot by recognizing one code as more *enlightened* than another? But then 'enlightened' is again a grading word. Mr Urmson seems almost ready to give up the struggle. 'Clearly when we debate which of two moral codes is more enlightened there is no ultimate court of appeal, no umpire, unless some agreed revealed religious code is treated as a *deus ex machina*'; and in this he plainly does not believe. But is it the case that we really do differ in our criteria for enlightenment? Here Mr Urmson finds grounds for hope. No doubt a complete and definite list of such criteria would not be agreed upon. But would any sober person deny that a culture is enlightened so far as it contributes to the health, wealth, and happiness of those who live under it? Mr Urmson appears to think not. On such criteria for the goodness of competing codes men generally do seem to agree.

8. Now granting that in grading codes we use the same ultimate criteria, what is the relation in a given case between these criteria and the label 'good' which they carry with them? Granting that under code A there is more health, wealth, and happiness than under B, are we to say that these things *entail* the greater goodness of A, either analytically or synthetically? Or are we to say that they merely *cause* in fact an emotion of approval? To say that the criteria *abc are* the goodness, or entail it analytically, is naturalism. To say that they entail the goodness *synthetically* is, in substance, intuitionism. To say that they merely *give rise* to a favouring emotion is emotivism. Mr Urmson rejects all three. He thinks they all miss the relation between the criteria and the label. The affixing of the label 'good' is not the

[1] *Mind*, Vol. 59 (1950), 168–9

making of a judgment *either* analytic or synthetic, nor is it 'a squeal of delight'; it is an act, a doing something, the making of a choice, together with the committing of oneself to similar choices in like situations.

9. What is interesting about this theory is its evident retreat from emotivism toward the view that moral judgment can be defended by reasons, combined with a clinging to the emotivist view that 'x is good' is not a judgment at all. Consider the first point. If the communist and the democrat differ as to whether a man or a culture is good, they can compare their criteria for assigning this label. If they find among these criteria one that is admitted by one party but not by the other, they can discuss whether its inclusion is enlightened or not. And on the criteria for enlightenment, they will substantially agree; if the presence of the disputed factor clearly involves more health, wealth and happiness, the disputants will—if candid—agree that it should be retained. Mr Urmson thus believes that the choice between good and bad is not arbitrary but objectively based, and that it can be defended by insights that are all but universal. A belief that health, wealth and happiness are bad can be set down by virtually universal agreement as the mark of an unenlightened mind. Suppose we ask why—as Urmson does not. Surely the answer is that it is so obviously false. We should say that anyone who really thought health, wealth and happiness to be bad or of no account was either stupid or mentally twisted. Our major criterion for being enlightened is the power to see what is true. On this interpretation of his view, Mr Urmson is moving back precipitately toward a cognitive ethics. There is hope of agreement because when it comes to the ultimate issues of good and bad, enlightened minds will render identical verdicts, and they will do so because they will apprehend a common truth.

10. Unfortunately, what he offers us with one hand he takes away with the other. Having raised our hopes by suggesting that 'good' and 'bad' are assigned on objective grounds and can be defended in the last resort by appeal to criteria of enlightenment which are the same for all men, he goes on to say that the application of the terms is not a rational or cognitive process at all, but an *act*, all too vaguely conceived. But how can enlightened insight be more *relevant* to an act than to an emotion? An act is not true or false; no evidence can prove or disprove it, or render it more or less probable. Hence Mr Urmson's position remains to me less than clear. The statement 'happiness is good' seems to be a rational statement, in the sense that it shows an enlightened solution of the criteria for goodness. But this same statement is not really a statement at all, but an act of choice which, as non-cognitive, is neither rational nor irrational. How these two sides are connected I do not see.

One suspects some want of consistency. 'X is good', as the affixing of a label, is taken to be not a judgment, but an act of choice. The statement that criteria *abc* are the right ones for the affixing of the label does seem to be a judgment, which can be argued for by showing that its rejection would be unenlightened. But is not the selection of the criteria *abc* as the 'right' ones as much an act of choice as the selection of 'good' as the right label for them? If 'x is good' is not a judgment, but an act, so is '*abc* are the right criteria for good', and then there would seem to be no room for rationality anywhere in the original statement or in the statements supporting it. On the other hand if '*abc* are the right criteria' *is* a judgment, though a selective one, then there is no reason why 'x is good' should not be one too. Both statements are equally judgments, and equally capable of truth or falsity. Such criticism may, indeed, rest on misunderstanding; Mr Urmson presents his view only in brief outline. In any case the theory is interesting as typical of post-war linguistic ethics. There is a manifest desire to escape emotivist irrationalism, coupled with an equally manifest desire to refuse moral judgments the position of judgments at all. Its equilibrium is therefore unstable.

11. The same double desire is evident in the ethics of another writer of the linguistic school, Mr R. M. Hare. His book on *The Language of Morals* is an admirably clear and careful statement, and fortunately for the interest of his readers, it is more concerned with matters of substance than would be gathered from his insistence on talking about 'the peculiarities of sentences' and 'the behaviour of words'. We may well ask the same two questions about his position that we asked about Mr Urmson's: What is it that is expressed in such judgments as 'X is good'? and, in what sense can they be supported by reasons?

Mr Hare loses no time in answering the first question. There is a fundamental difference between what is expressed by descriptive and by prescriptive language, and a statement of 'good', 'right', or 'ought', is of the latter kind. A descriptive statement is one that makes a true or false assertion, such as 'you are going to shut the door'. The simplest form of prescriptive statement is an imperative, such as 'shut the door'. Are all moral judgments imperatives? Mr Hare seems to hold that they are. He is not an emotivist; '*x* is wrong' is not an expression of felt disapproval merely. It expresses, rather, something like 'Don't do *x*'. The distinctive feature of moral judgment is that of prescribing or guiding choices. When I say '*x* is wrong' or 'you ought not to do *x*', I am uttering a kind of general instruction or imperative designed to prevent people from choosing *x*. More surprisingly Mr Hare treats the judgment of good also as essentially imperative. At first, indeed, it looks as if he were going to deal with it in a different way, for in discussing it he takes as his motto the definition in the *Oxford English Dictionary:* 'Good . . . the most general adjective of commendation . . . ', and says that the one constant office of the term, which holds equally whether we talk of 'a good fire-extinguisher', 'a good sewage-affluent' or 'a good man', is this one of commending.[1] But it soon turns out that commendation itself is a kind of imperative; 'to commend is to guide choices'.[2] Its primary work is to urge upon others or myself the choosing of one kind of thing or action rather than another.

12. This being Mr Hare's answer to our first question, how would he answer the second? Can we support imperatives by reasons, or call one more rational than another? He is eager to show that we can, and he uses two principal means of doing so. The first is to revive the distinction between the meaning and criteria of 'good' with which Mr Urmson has made us familiar. He holds that though the primary meaning of 'good', that is, its commendatory one, remains the same through every context, its secondary meaning that is, the criteria for applying it, vary from case to case; 'good fire-extinguisher' does convey information, and a different kind of information from 'good sonata' or 'good man'. And regarding the facts thus secondarily asserted when we call something good, it is plainly possible to offer evidence, just as it was in the theories, so similar at this point, of Mr Edwards and Mr Urmson.

Mr Hare's own device is more original. He holds that the imperative itself can be analysed into two parts, and that one of these parts turns out to have most of the logical features of an ordinary

[1] *The Language of Morals,* 102, 118, 140
[2] *Ibid.,* 129

indicative statement; it can be defended, contradicted, and used as a basis for inference. 'You are going to shut the door' is an assertion. 'Shut the door' is an imperative. But they clearly have something in common: both of them are *about* the same thing, namely your shutting the door in the immediate future. We could recast them in the forms:

Your shutting the door in the immediate future, yes.

Your shutting the door in the immediate future, please.

The first part of these sentences, which is the same for both, Mr Hare calls the *phrastic;* the second part, which varies, he calls the *neustic.* 'The utterance of a sentence containing phrastic and neustic might be dramatized as follows: (1) The speaker points out or indicates what he is going to state to be the case, or command to be made the case; (2) He nods, as if to say "It *is* the case", or "Do it". He will, however, have to nod in a different way, according as he means one or other of these things.'[1]

Now if we fix our eyes on the common phrastic above, we see that it gives to the imperative containing it all that is necessary to serve as a basis of rational discussion. The imperative can be contradicted, as in 'Your *not* shutting the door in the immediate future, please'; it can be supported by reasons, as when we say the room is too cold; it can be declared unreasonable, as when we say the door is fixed, and so cannot be moved. Indeed a logic of imperatives that is very like the logic of indicatives has been shown to be possible.[2] In reasoning about imperatives, the most important point to bear in mind, however, is that though facts may be introduced in support or objection, no imperative conclusion can be drawn from factual statements only; there must be at least one imperative in the premises. From the premises, 'You ought to prevent needless pain', and 'This is a case of needless pain', it follows that you ought to prevent it. From the minor alone, 'This is a needless pain', no statement of obligation follows.

13. Mr Hare's ethical theory is the most completely elaborated that we have so far had from the linguistic moralists. Is his conception of moral judgment as an imperative an advance over the emotivists' view of it as an interjection, or Mr Urmson's as an act of choice? A little, perhaps. But it has failed to satisfy some of those who most firmly agree with him that moral 'judgments' are not really judgments.

[1] *The Language of Morals,* 18
[2] G. H. von Wright, 'Deontic Logic', *Mind,* Vol. 60 (1951) 1ff.

Mr Braithwaite, for example, has pointed out that to recast 'Lies are always wrong' into 'No lies being told by anyone, past, present or future, please', is not plausible.[1] We plainly do make moral judgments about the past—a fact, indeed, that we have found fatal to both the instrumentalist and emotivist theories. I suspect it is also fatal to imperative theories. For we cannot intelligibly be said to *command* something to be done in a past that we know to be unalterable. Nor again can we sensibly enjoin an avoidance of lying on persons we know to be beyond our reach, like our descendants of a century hence, though our moral judgment is clearly meant to be universal. Mr Hare himself suggests a further difficulty which, though he does his best to answer it, seems to me unanswerable.[2] Is it not possible to say to someone meaningfully, 'You ought to do *x*, but don't'? Here the moral statement and the command, far from being identical, are in conflict with each other. I may be convinced, for example, that you ought to make your will in favour of Jones, but want very much that you should enrich me instead, and may do all I can to that end. The difficulty is the fundamental one that appraising an action as right or wrong is simply different in intention from the attempt to guide future choices. 'If I censure someone for having done something', says Mr Hare, 'I envisage the possibility of him, or someone else, or myself, having to make a similar choice again; otherwise there would be no point in censuring him.'[3] No practical point, perhaps, but is my only interest in making the judgment the interest in getting something done? If it were, the censure spoken silently, of a man I was sure was incorrigible, would not really be censure at all, since it is not an attempt to get either him or myself to act. Yet it may carry a full and unequivocal moral meaning. Both censure and commendation may retain their moral point when a command would have no occasion and no sense.

14. Does Mr Hare deal more successfully with the other issue of importance, as to the support of moral judgment by reason? His thesis is that we can get at the neustic, so to speak, through the phrastic. Let us see how one would go about it to support a moral judgment. We have a friend who never opens a newspaper. We say to him, 'You really ought to look at a paper now and then.' 'Why should I?' he

[1] *Mind*, Vol. 63 (1954) 257
[2] *The Language of Morals*, 163 ff.
[3] *Ibid.*, 129

asks. 'Because you ought to take some interest in politics.' 'Why should I interest myself in politics?' 'Because you are supposed to be able to cast an intelligent vote.' 'But why should I trouble to vote?' 'Because if people don't trouble to vote, they can't make a democracy work.' 'Why should they care whether democracy works?' 'Because if it doesn't they'll soon find themselves with something very much worse. Some set of persons, hungry for power, will probably take over, and exploit them unmercifully; they will cut down their right to criticize at home and involve them in trouble abroad.' Here arguments, more or less relevant, are offered for an imperative. Mr Hare would no doubt remind us of two points about them. First, the arguments are never merely factual, for no *ought* follows from an *is;* one premise at least must itself be an imperative. Secondly, every moral judgment is really a judgment of principle. In saying to my friend 'You ought to read the papers', I am saying by implication, 'Anyone circumstanced as you are should read them.' What these requirements amount to is that if I am to argue for my judgment, I must bring it, as a particular case, under an imperative principle, which may be very sweeping and complex. In the present case the major premise is something like, 'Whatever steps are necessary to avoid the destroying of civil liberties and the mutual trust of nations should be taken.' Then—with the help of subsumptions—'Your reading the papers is such a step; therefore you ought to take it.' A fully adequate major premise would involve the description of a whole way of life. For

'a complete justification of a decision would consist of a complete account of its effects, together with a complete account of the principles which it observed, and the effects of observing those principles . . . Thus, if pressed to justify a decision completely, we have to give a complete specification of the way of life of which it is a part. This complete specification it is impossible in practice to give; the nearest attempts are those given by the great religions . . . Suppose, however, that we can give it. If the inquirer still goes on asking "But why *should* I live like that?" then there is no further answer to give him . . . We can only ask him to make up his own mind which way he ought to live; for in the end everything rests upon such a decision of principle.'[1]

15. This is admirable—up to the last step. Mr Hare is surely right that we do argue in this way for our moral judgments; we do plainly

[1] *The Language of Morals*, 69

argue from principles, and we may see, if we are fortunate, that these principles hang together in some large view of how life should be lived. But when we come to a conflict between two conflicting ways of life, is that the end? Is the choice between them a matter, not of rational judgment, but of a non-rational decision or act of will? Mr Hare thinks it is. If a Greek of the fourth century BC were to meet a Hebrew prophet of the same period, they would soon find themselves in conflict about ultimate and intrinsic values—about the value of knowledge, of holiness, of athletic sport, of the experience of beauty, of contrition for sin. Regarding such differences Mr Hare would say, in terms as unqualified as the emotivists', that to talk of an objective decision, of either party's being *really* right or wrong was meaningless. Even in theory, there is no ground on which a judge could stand in arbitrating the difference. All that either party could do would be to announce a commitment, to issue an imperative to himself and others which, as essentially an expression of preference, was beyond rational vindication or criticism. At this point the linguistic moralists of Britain make a curious *rapprochement* with the existentialists of the continent. The ultimate act of moral choice is, for both alike, an act of will responsible to nothing beyond itself.[1]

The linguistic moralists consider that they have left emotivism far behind. A moral judgment as Hare conceives it can be supported by arguing from its coherence with an extended system of principles, and one can say to anyone who disputes it, 'you must either accept the judgment or reject all that it implies'. This looks like an impressive advance. The trouble is that having carried us this grateful distance beyond emotivism, these moralists pull us back at the last step with an irrationalism that calls the whole advance into question. For if the imperative 'you ought to read the papers' rests on a wider system, and this system in turn on a non-rational commitment, then all the commitments that depend on it are similarly in the end indefensible.

Why not be content with this? We gave our answer in the last chapter. What we have here is a free use of reason on the lower slopes with a surrender to unreasoned decision at the summit. On this summit the imperativist and the emotivist join hands. We have seen what to think of emotivism. We could not believe that when the adherents of different ways of life, the communist for example and the democrat, differed about the value of individual freedom or happiness, they did not differ in belief at all. We have the same trouble

[1] The resemblance was pointed out to me by Professor H. B. Acton.

with imperativism. What we are concerned about is whether our moral judgments are really judgments, and it makes very little difference whether, if this is denied, it is on the ground that they are interjections or on the ground that they are commands. Emotivism and imperativism alike deny the chief thesis we are concerned to support, and we reject them for much the same reason. Both hold that the ultimately differing parties—the communist and the democrat, the Greek and Hebrew—are not really differing in opinion or belief; that neither denies what the other is saying; that neither is making a mistake; that neither is nearer the truth than the other, because in such conflicts there is no truth to be found. On such a theory, as we have seen, neither can make a value judgment of the past without a distortion of meaning; neither, strictly speaking, can offer arguments that are relevant to the final decision; neither can distinguish, in the end, propaganda from moral reasoning. If Mr Hare met an opponent of the Christian way of life, in which I take it he believes (or, rather, to which he has made a non-rational commitment), he would no doubt set out in his able fashion its doctrines of love, sin, and forgiveness, and its attitudes toward art, sex, and science, exhibiting these as some sort of connected whole. Having done so, he could only say, 'Take it or leave it.' His subscription to the Christian way of life as a whole is neither more nor less reasonable than its rejection; since it is not a judgment but an act of will, it of course does not *follow* from anything that has been presented, nor does his opponent's opposite subscription; and if he wants to change his opponent's attitude, his only recourse, so far as I see, is to psychological pressures. These things I cannot accept. The ultimate reason is merely that a judgment, even about intrinsic value, is too plainly a *judgment*— not an expletive nor yet a command. The case for this has been stated in part in the last chapter. The rest of the case lies in an alternative account of the meaning of 'good', which will presently be offered.

16. Among the linguistic moralists, the writer who has gone most extensively into the way moral judgment makes use of reasons is Mr Stephen Toulmin. To him this is the most interesting question in ethical theory. It is plain enough that moral judgments are not, like scientific judgments, true or false in any straightforward sense; their function is 'to alter one's feelings and behaviour'.[1] Yet we must face

[1] *An Examination of the Place of Reason in Ethics*, 130

the arresting and undeniable fact that we do offer reasons for them, and that these reasons are confidently appraised as relevant or irrelevant, good or bad, and often as conclusive. This fact is enough in itself to impose a veto on both subjectivist and emotivist ethics. The subjectivist says that '*x* is right' means 'I approve of *x*'. But it would be absurd to offer *arguments* in favour of the thesis that I am having a certain emotion. The emotivist says that '*x* is right' is an exclamation *evincing* feeling and not reporting it. But again it would be absurd to adduce arguments for an exclamation, whereas everyone does offer them for moral judgments. Mr Toulmin would say nothing so monstrous as that common sense and common usage might be mistaken in these matters; for, lively as his sense of humour is, he takes with great seriousness the tables of the law delivered to Wittgenstein about the inviolability of usage. People do in fact argue about their moral judgments; hence any theory that would forbid their doing so must be in error.

It might be inferred from these linguistic loyalties that when people said 'x is good' Mr Toulmin would take them to mean 'x is good' in the most straightforward sense. But not so. It is curious to recall, in passing, what moral philosophers have done when confronted with this simple statement. Moore argued that it should be taken at face value, as a judgment ascribing a quality, and often true. Westermarck agreed in this interpretation, but since the truth of the judgment, so interpreted, collided with his ethical theory, he held that common sense was on this point universally mistaken. Mr Ayer, though insisting that philosophy consisted of definitions and that its definitions were to be tested by reference to usage, also admitted that 'x is good', was commonly meant to assert what was true; but since the acceptance of such truth would collide with his ethical theory also, he 'recommended' a different use of 'good'. Mr Toulmin, much influenced likewise by Wittgenstein, takes still another course. He holds that ordinary men do not really mean to ascribe a property at all, as the objectivists have claimed. He offers, so far as I can discover, three arguments for this view.

17. In the first place, the sort of property objectivists have talked about neither exists nor can be conceived, and it is queer to charge the plain man with making daily use of something so elusive. Mr Toulmin runs over the possible types of property and finds that goodness is not among them. A property must be one of three kinds.

It may be a 'simple quality' like the red I now see in a flower; or it may be a 'complex quality' like 257-sided, whose presence can be checked only by some appropriate routine like counting; or it may be a 'scientific quality' like 'radiating such-and-such types of electromagnetic wave'. Properties of the first two of these types are directly perceivable; those of the third are not. Mr Toulmin proceeds to argue, successfully I think, that goodness, not being directly perceivable, is not a property of the first type or of the second. The argument that it is not of the third type never materializes,[1] though one would have supposed that it was precisely in this category of the three mentioned that goodness was most likely to fall. But even if it falls in none of these categories, the argument will not carry much weight with those against whom it is chiefly directed. Moore, Broad, Ross, and Ewing all take goodness as belonging to none of these types, but as being, or at least involving, a *non-natural* character. Mr Toulmin's argument is of the form: all properties are of kinds *a*, *b*, or *c*, goodness is none of these; therefore it is not a property at all. Such an argument is of no weight unless the major is shown to be exhaustive. And those who have held that goodness belongs to none of these types but to a fourth type, *d*, will not be much moved.

18. Secondly Mr Toulmin argues, the plain man has been misrepresented. Moralists of traditional types have assumed without inquiring that he agreed with them, that because in saying 'x is good' he used an adjective, he must mean by it what adjectives usually mean, namely some kind of attribute. But if we take the trouble to ask him whether he means what Moore, for example, makes him mean, his answers give no colour to this interpretation. Suppose, says Mr Toulmin, that I am talking to a Moorean philosopher about a common friend who by general agreement is a man of the highest character.

    ' "Surely," I may say, "if ever a man knew what goodness was, he does!"
    "I imagine that he does," the philosopher will say.
    "And yet," I may reply, "I have asked him whether, when making up his mind what to do, he is conscious of observing any 'non-natural property', any 'fittingness', in the action he decides on, and he says he isn't. He says that he does what he does because there's a good reason

---

[1]On p. 13 it is deferred to Chapter 9 but, if it appears in this chapter, I have not identified it.

I

for doing it, and that he isn't interested in any additional 'non-natural properties' of his actions".'[1]

Surely this result is not very significant. Philosophers have found it hard themselves to say what they mean by good; and when the ordinary man is suddenly confronted by the meta-ethical question, which he has never thought of asking, whether he is referring to some kind of 'non-natural property', it is only to be expected that he should hesitate or say No. But an opposite result could no doubt be gained with equal ease by merely rephrasing the question. If one were to ask him whether in saying it was good to have an educated mind he meant to say something true, he would presumably say 'Of course I do'; if then asked whether he could verify what he meant by means of eyes, ears, or hands, he would probably say 'No'. Where meanings are so vague, and those who use them are so little practised in analysis, it is only too easy, with the help of some verbal legerdemain, to extract the answer one wants.

19. Thirdly, Mr Toulmin thinks that when objectivists have taken moral judgments to ascribe a character to an object, they have been moved by an argument which, if brought clearly to light, can be seen to be fallacious. They have had the experience of differing with others as to whether a proposed action was right, and they have supposed that this difference was possible on one assumption only. If two people differ about the colour of something, one saying it is red and the other denying this, what are they differing about? Obviously whether the quality redness does or does not belong to something. What are they differing about in the moral case? Surely, in the same way, over whether the quality rightness does or does not belong to an act. Thus if their difference is to be intelligible there must be a quality of rightness to which both alike are referring.

This conclusion, says Mr Toulmin, does not follow. There is another way of interpreting such differences. 'All that two people need (and all that they have) to contradict one another about in the case of ethical predicates are the *reasons* for doing this rather than that or the other.'[2] When a person differs from another as to whether an

---

[1] *The Place of Reason in Ethics*, 23. Mr Edwards gained similar negative results when he asked his classes in ethics whether intuitionism reported accurately what they meant by 'x is good'. *The Logic of Moral Discourse*, 100
[2] *Ibid.*, 28

action should be done, what he is saying is that there are better reasons on his side. Mr Toulmin apparently holds that the *meaning* of 'x is right', so far as it has a cognitive meaning at all, is merely that there are *valid reasons* for doing x. The judgment seems to be at once expressive and assertive—to express approval—as yet undefined—and to assert that this approval has adequate reasons behind it. Mr Toulmin's third argument against objectivism is that this alternative account of moral judgment is a more plausible account than the one it offers us. We must therefore now ask how plausible it is.

20. If to say that something is right is (on the cognitive side) to say that there are valid reasons for it, we may well ask what is meant by a valid reason. How are we to know one when we see it? Mr Toulmin answers that there are only two kinds of valid argument for a moral judgment, each appropriate to its own set of circumstances. Suppose we are choosing between two courses of action one of which accords with the accepted rules of the community, while the other conflicts with them. In this case we should be offering a valid argument for the first if we showed that it did so accord while the second did not. Suppose on the other hand that an accepted rule itself is called in question, or that two accepted rules are found to conflict. It is clear that some further mode of validation must be found, for the question now is how we are to validate an accepted rule itself. Here, Mr Toulmin says, the only valid argument is one that appeals to 'the general requirement that preventable suffering shall be avoided'.[1] It is only 'a natural and familiar extension' of this requirement to say that we should aim also at the greatest general happiness.[2]

In Mr Toulmin's discussion, these two ways of validating judgments sometimes appear as methods employed at different levels of civilization, the appeal to established rule being the natural method in fixed and primitive communities, and the appeal to general happiness superseding it as societies become more 'open' and self-critical. But they are also discussed as if they were independent and equally valid types of justification. This seems to me unwarranted. The head-hunter would no doubt justify his headhunting by saying that it was the accepted practice in his community; the Moslem would justify his polygamy and the Christian his condemnation of it by the same sort of argument; and if the argument is valid at all, it is presumably

[1] *The Place of Reason in Ethics*, 142
[2] *Ibid.*, 160

valid universally. 'Primitive ethics', says Mr Toulmin, 'is "deontolo-
gical",' but it is clear that he does not mean that the rules it lays down
are binding because self-evident, as Ross maintains, for many of
these are admittedly mere taboos. And to say that an action may be
validated as right by the appeal to an accepted taboo is most unplausible. Such an appeal can provide at best only a provisional
justification which must be reviewed by a superior court before it can
be granted real legitimacy.

21. Mr Toulmin virtually admits this. He goes so far as to say that
it is the avoidance of needless misery that gives the notions of obligation, right, justice, and duty their meaning.[1] The only *conclusive*
validation for any course of action lies in showing that it leads to this
result, or to its 'extension', the greatest happiness. The new interpretation of 'x is right' which is to supersede the confusion of objectivism is thus that it expresses an attitude (yet to be defined) combined
with the assertion that it can be validly defended, which assertion
means in turn that the action will conduce to happiness or the avoidance
of misery. This latter part of the doctrine seems a very tame result of
so much analysis and so much defiance of traditional ethics. It is
essentially a return to Sidgwick. Of course Sidgwick's defence of
utilitarianism is a powerful one, far more so than anything here
attempted; but if it is to be made plausible at this time of day, it
must be defended against many objections that are now too familiar
to need repeating. Why, for example, are we not offering a valid
argument for a course of action if we show that it would increase
human knowledge or understanding, even if it left the amount of
happiness unchanged?

22. So far, then, as Mr Toulmin would reduce 'x is right' to 'good
reasons of a utilitarian kind can be offered for x', his account is both
incomplete and something of an anachronism. We must now ask
what it is for which these reasons are offered. One can hardly say, as
Mr Toulmin does seem to be saying at times, that '*x* is right' means
nothing but 'there are valid reasons for "*x* is right" '; we must know
the meaning of that '*x* is right' which the reasons are offered *for*.
    It is difficult to discover what Mr Toulmin's answer is. Indeed he
seems to give two different answers, both of which, unhappily, involve his theory in incoherence. On the one hand he insists that the

[1] *The Place of Reason in Ethics*, 160

judgment '*x* is right' is really a judgment; the emotivists and imperati-vists are mistaken in making it the expression of an attitude merely; it is a statement about an object. What does it assert? It asserts that the act is *worthy* to be approved. In its objective force this statement is on a par with the statement that a conclusion is logically valid, which means not that someone believes it, but that it is *worthy* of belief.[1] This contention calls for two comments. First, as Mr Broad has pointed out in an admirable review,[2] 'there is nothing particularly new or startling in this aspect of the theory. It has been very fully developed by, *e.g.*, Sir W. D. Ross and by Dr Ewing'—and, he might have added, by himself. But, secondly, this view is inconsistent with Mr Toulmin's principal thesis, namely that 'x is right', on its cognitive side, is an assertion that there are valid reasons for doing x. He has insisted that when two people differ in opinion as to whether x is right, their difference is exclusively over whether there are valid reasons for doing it. This cannot be true if the judgment is to be interpreted in the present way. For two people might agree that x is right in the sense 'worthy to be approved' who disagreed flatly as to the reasons that would validate it, and even as to whether there were such reasons; and they might disagree over whether x was right while agreeing as to the kind of reasons that would justify it. Indeed it is absurd to talk of reasons at all unless there is a difference between these reasons and the conclusions for which they are offered. Mr Toulmin speaks as if the conclusion collapsed *into* the reasons for it.

But then on the other hand this whole view that when people differ on moral issues they are differing as to reasons seems to have been offered precisely to save the emotivist-imperativist thesis that moral judgments are not in the strict sense judgments at all. For if people could and did contradict each other over 'x is right' when used with its traditional meaning, there would be no occasion or warrant for this new doctrine that such contradiction concerned only their reasons. And if 'x is right' is now to be taken as the expression of an attitude, either of feeling or of command, then 'the place of reason in ethics' remains thoroughly obscure. For you cannot validate an emotion by reasons as you can a proposition; and as we have seen, you cannot prove or disprove a command. Mr Toulmin, like Mr Hare, is eager to show, as against irrationalists in ethics, that some moral judgments can be validated by reason, and others invalidated.

[1] *The Place of Reason in Ethics*, 71
[2] *Mind*, Vol. 61 (1952) 100

But Wittgenstein had announced in passing that 'there are no ethical propositions',[1] and Mr Toulmin feels constrained to accept this in the sense of holding that 'ethical utterances' are not descriptive, nor therefore true or false in the sense of corresponding to anything in the actual world.[2] But the whole force of his insistence on 'validating' moral judgment through reasons was drawn from the underlying assumption that these reasons were *relevant*, and that ethical conclusions could be established or overthrown by them. He argued against the emotivists that they must be wrong because these reasons were constantly given, and felt to be relevant, though they could not be relevant to an emotion. If this argument is valid at all, it is equally valid against the position he is here urging.

23. We have selected a very few of the linguistic moralists for critical attention, and there are others that we might have taken equally well. They are obviously an able group. But for that reason we may perhaps be permitted a gesture of protest against what we conceive Wittgenstein to have done to their generation. In reading such men as Sidgwick, Moore, and Ross, we might and often did disagree with them, but we knew where they stood on fundamentals. They had an eye for the essential points, and argued about them with a force and lucidity that left us with an exhilarated feeling of getting clear on major issues. In reading the linguistic analysts, one has a feeling of being led over interminable flats to no firm conclusion and in no fixed direction. It is as if the very idea that there were any fundamental issues or crucial points had been repudiated. Every statement, we are told, has its own logic. Hence to talk about ethical statements generally is rash; and even to talk about 'x is right' or 'x is good' is misleading since it assumes that people mean by these words the same thing. It is safer to say that statement A is very like B, and B very like C, and C very like D, and D again rather like A, though in somewhat dissimilar respects from those in which A is like B; but to crystallize these likenesses into definite class statements is dogmatic and misleading. Mr Urmson thinks that 'x is good' is like a process of grading, but on such essential questions as what is meant by affixing the label and whether the criteria for affixing it can be rationally chosen, we found it hard to get clear guidance. Mr Hare is convinced that value judgments are like commands, and also that they

---

[1] *Tractatus*, 6. 42
[2] *The Place of Reason in Ethics* ,78 ff.

are like judgments. At the all-important top level, the likeness to judgment seems to fail, and at lower levels, for example, in value judgments of the past, the resemblance to commands likewise fails. It is significant that Mr Hare should be less disturbed by the first dissimilarity than by the second. Mr Toulmin argues elaborately that moral judgments are like expressions of feeling, that they are like reports of feeling, and that they are like statements of fact, but also that in manifold subtle ways they are unlike all of these; and his ultimate view seems to be an unstable alliance between something like emotivism for the meaning of 'x is right' and utilitarianism as the way of establishing it.

The school has not yet touched bottom. Linguistic moralists still talk about moral judgments as such, presumably by dint of ancient custom. But if the later Wittgenstein is right, this is rash generalization. The 'logic' of ought-statements is so different from that of right-statements, and both from that of good-statements that it is shocking to lump them together; and the logic of 'happiness is good' —a statement itself shockingly alien to common usage—is so different from that of 'wine is good' or 'we had a good vacation' that it is shockingly naïve to assume a common denominator. The natural terminus of the movement is a situation in which its slogan is taken seriously and every statement (or sentence) is assigned a logic of its own. The assumption of older moralists that one can profitably study the meaning of good or the nature of obligation as such will have been exploded. What had been supposed to be major identities will have dissipated themselves in innumerable minute differences, and ethics will have become a level plain extending as far as the eye can see and littered, it is to be feared, with dry bones. If that consummation is not reached, it will be because the direction of the movement is discerned, and good sense calls a halt to it.

24. The revolt, when it comes, will have small patience with two tenets of linguistic ethics. One is that meta-ethics has no ethical implications and may be discussed in a logical vacuum, antiseptic to moral commitments. This doctrine, however popular, is untrue. To adopt certain meanings for 'right' and 'good' as the valid ones is also to elect a way of life. The person who believes that 'right' means 'productive of the greatest pleasure', as Mill did, will not only think differently; he will, if sincere, act differently, from the person who believes, as Paley did, that it means 'concordant with the will of the

Christian God', or, as Kant did, that it means 'consistent in principle' or, as Nietzsche did, that it means 'conducive to the interests of me and my class'. To be sure, we have said more than once that the correctness of an analysis is not to be judged by the desirability of its consequences. But in dealing with fundamental notions like right and good, correct analysis itself requires that one should see the implications of one's theory for men's actual valuations. If defining 'right' in a certain way would commit one to calling right a range of acts that are generally condemned as wrong, that is evidence against the correctness of the analysis. Meta-ethics cannot be pursued responsibly in divorce from ethics.

25. There is another favourite of the linguistic moralists that is also destined, one suspects, for a short life. This is the attempt to resolve ethical discussion into a discussion about language. The attempt has not yet been carried remorselessly through, and if it were, ethics would have few readers. What students of ethics have always discussed, and what they are still chiefly interested in, is types of conduct and character, qualities of motive and attitude, the tests for right and wrong, the ends men have proposed to themselves, the comparative values of these ends, and the nature of value itself. These are of course not primarily questions about the usage of words. Like every problem whatever, they may be discussed, not wholly unprofitably, as if they were questions of language. Just as one can say that Hume, in reflecting on how the billiard balls acted on each other, was really concerned with the word 'cause', so one can say that Mill, in discussing the test of right action, was really concerned with the word 'right'. But this is hardly even a half truth. For (a) it was his *concept* of right, his special theory about what in an action made it worthy of approval, that alone gave his words the slightest importance; (b) he could have set out the same theory in another language, or in other words of the same language; (c) if the actual usage of words is taken as a guide in these or other matters, it is likely to prove inadequate, erroneous, and contradictory,[1] as linguistic moralists have had to admit; witness Mr Ayer's concession that emotivism conflicts with ordinary usage and his 'recommendation' of an unorthodox usage none the less; (d) in conceptual analysis, language must follow the distinctions of thought, not thought the set of labels that language happens to provide. If these things are true, then (e) to call the study

[1] *Cf.* my *Reason and Analysis*, Ch. 6 and 7

of ethical theory a study of the *language* of morals is tiresomely misleading. It suggests that the study is far more trivial than in fact it is, and more so than the linguistic moralists themselves in practice take it to be.

So far as one can see, these moralists have achieved no clear view jointly or singly, as to the meaning of 'good', 'right', or 'ought', or as to what moral judgment expresses, or how it may be validated. Acute as they are in dissecting and differentiating the meanings of words, their writing on ethics has tended to be academic, unimaginative, and flat. Their somewhat disdainful references to emotivism, like their similar references to logical positivism, convey a deceptive impression of the distance they have travelled from the doctrines prevalent in the thirties. They are still enmeshed by these doctrines; and they are unlikely to escape from them while they maintain their parochial reverence for the gospel according to Wittgenstein. Nevertheless in one respect we owe them much. They loosened the moorings that tied ethics for a time to emotivism. None of those we have studied has broken with it cleanly; none of them has conceded that a judgment of good, or right, or ought, is a judgment in the straightforward sense at all. But they are once for all beyond the doctrine that moral judgments are mere explosions of feeling. They admit that in some sense such judgments may be more or less rational, and that they may in some sense be rationally defended. Thus their work is more than a retreat from emotivism. It is an able attempt, however abortive, to find a place for reason in ethics.

CHAPTER X

THREE THEORIES OF GOODNESS

1. We have held that the fundamental moral judgment was the judgment of good, not of right. In discussing the emotivists and their linguistic successors, we found reason to think that this judgment was irreducible, in the sense that it could not be resolved away into the expression of an emotion, a command, or any other non-cognitive attitude.

But if it is a judgment, what does it assert? Presumably a character of some kind belonging to the subject that is called good. What sort of character? Some moralists of eminence have thought it a character like yellow, which could belong to its subject even if there was nothing else in the world; others have held that it is a relational property like loved-by-Smith, which could belong to something only as this was related to something else. In this chapter we shall examine the most influential view of the first type, and then the two most plausible views—themselves widely different—of the second type.

There is no doubt that the most influential advocate in recent times of the first position is G. E. Moore.[1] 'Good' was for him the name of a simple 'non-natural' quality present in everything that is good intrinsically. Of course what he is considering is not instrumental goodness, the value of something as a means, but the intrinsic goodness of that which is good in itself or good for its own sake. There are many kinds of things that we regard as thus intrinsically good. There is the good man, the good picture, the good holiday, the good dessert, the good walk, the good scientific theory. Do we mean the same thing by 'good' in all these cases? The assumption that we do merely on the ground that we are using the same word is not quite safe. Sometimes when we use the same word there is no common element at all, as when we speak of the pile of a carpet and a pile of stones; some-

[1] *Principia Ethica*, Ch. I

times the common element could be ferreted out only by the help of analogy, as when we speak of a black night and a black crime, or a weighty pendulum and a weighty argument. Nevertheless Moore did think that whenever we used 'good' of intrinsic goods we were using it in exactly the same sense, that is, were referring to exactly the same quality in all these various subjects. The goodness of a good man and of a good dessert are *based*, it is true, on very different characters, but the goodness itself is identical in each.

How are we to define this identical quality? That, says Moore, is impossible. The reason is not that it is so bafflingly complex, but on the contrary, that it is so bafflingly simple. If we are to define anything in logical fashion, it must be at least complex enough to enable us to single out within it a genus and species, as when we say a square is a plane figure that has four equal sides and angles. But try that process on goodness. You can start by saying 'goodness is that quality which—' but how are you to go on? You can only say 'goodness is that quality which is—goodness'; there is no way of describing it except by itself; it is unique. Not that this sort of uniqueness is anything unusual or queer; it is possessed by innumerable other qualities such as sour and cold and painful and yellow. These are all perfectly familiar; yet they are indefinable because they are unanalysable, and unanalysable because they are simple.

2. The great danger here, Moore thinks, is that of confusing goodness itself with the *qualities in virtue of which* we call something good. It is a significant fact that goodness is always based on these further qualities as they themselves are not based on anything further. If someone were to remark that the sky was blue, we should think it absurd to ask, 'In virtue of what do you call it blue?' for one sees it to be blue directly. But if he were to remark that a man or a holiday was good we might quite naturally ask what it was in the man or the holiday that made him think so, and he might as naturally answer, 'Because the man has such an unfailing sense of duty' or 'Because the holiday was so pleasant'. Good, then, is a peculiar kind of quality. It is not grasped directly like blue; it is always arrived at indirectly by means of other qualities. Hence it does not belong to its subject as these other qualities do. They are part of its nature in a sense in which it is not. A psychologist describing a man's characteristics would note in his description a strong devotion to duty, but he would never include as an item alongside it the goodness of this devotion, any more than a photographer of the Parthenon would record its architectural goodness as a separate term along with the details of light and shade. For this reason Moore called goodness a *non-natural* quality. But since it is always based in this way on natural qualities, nothing is easier than to mistake them for it. Dutifulness is good; Kant says it is the only thing that is morally good; and shortly we find him arguing that in morals being dutiful is what goodness means. Mill thought that pleasure was good, and indeed the only thing that was good; and, sure enough, we soon find him arguing that 'good' *means* pleasant. This, Moore says, is gross confusion and the tag he has attached to it of 'the naturalistic fallacy' has become part of the stock in trade of ethics. Once we have seen the fallacy, once we have clearly marked the distinction between goodness and what Broad has conveniently called 'good-making characteristics', we shall see that all the attempts to identify goodness with any of these characteristics—with pleasure, or self-realization, or length and breadth of life, or any other—may be dismissed without discussion. Goodness may inhere in these characters, but it never *is* any of them. It is never anything but itself, a simple, highly abstract, non-spatial quality, identical in nature as one passes from the goodness of a man to that of a sunset, a dessert, or a poem.

3. I cannot accept this theory, and will content myself with mentioning two difficulties only. (1) Those who consider it carefully keep reporting that they have great trouble in catching or verifying this quality of goodness, that it is as elusive as a will-o'-the-wisp. Conspicuous among these are of course the logical empiricists, though their testimony has to be discounted by reason of their curiously a-priorist empiricism, committing them to recognize no quality that cannot be presented in sense. But other writers of discernment who are bound by no such commitment have reported the same difficulty, for example, Joseph, Taylor, Paton, and Ewing.[1] Indeed Moore himself has felt it, and felt it keenly. At one stage in his later thought he confessed himself to be drawn as sharply to the emotive theory as to his own original view of good as a quality, which could only mean

---

[1] For Joseph and Taylor see *Aristotelian Soc. Proceedings*, Sup. Vol. 11, 1932, 'Is Goodness a Quality?' For Paton see *The Good Will*, Ch. II. For Ewing, see *The Definition of Good*, 147, 159

that he was himself uncertain whether there was any such quality.[1] The difficulty has nothing to do with indefinability, for there are plenty of indefinable qualities about whose existence no one can doubt, like yellowness and pain, nor can it be merely a matter of nonsensibleness, for there are some wholly non-sensible characters, such as number, that belong to things indubitably. Nor is the difficulty that in thinking of good one seems to be thinking of nothing; all the writers just mentioned, for example, are clear that in using the term they are referring to something belonging to the object. The difficulty is that they cannot find the simple character required. And when a large proportion of the acutest minds that consider the matter find themselves either uncertain that they have even detected this quality or else certain that they have not, one's confidence that there is such a thing is bound to be affected.

4. (2) The theory makes goodness too abstract. It draws too sharp a line between goodness and good-making characteristics. In insisting that nothing that makes the good man good, or the good dessert or person or sensation good, shall enter into their goodness, that this quality is something sharply distinct, whose nature, when displayed in these characteristics, can be singled out and set over against them, this account is introducing a division that exists only in theory, not in the facts.

Consider a case or two. Pleasure or happiness is commonly taken as a clear case of the intrinsically good. But can one draw a line within a given experience of pleasure between the pleasure and its goodness? Moore apparently thinks that one can, that the pleasure and the goodness are sharply distinct, though connected synthetically by a relation of entailment, as colour and extension are in 'what is coloured is extended'. I cannot think that this has caught the true relation between them. That relation is more intimate. The goodness of being happy is not some isolable quality supervening upon the happiness; the happiness is itself a kind of goodness; we call it *a* good, as we call love an emotion, meaning, I think, that it is one of the forms in which goodness presents itself. Or take pain. By scrutinizing a pain, can

[1] This attitude was only temporary. He held it in the early forties, when for six months he was my guest in the USA. When I asked him later (in 1950, as I remember) whether he still felt equally drawn to the two positions, he answered with an emphatic No; he was now more inclined to think his earlier view the right one. In 1955, I put the same question again, and received the same answer, still more emphatically given.

one distinguish in it two different components, the pain on the one side and the badness on the other, as one can the redness and the extension of a given object? That does not seem very plausible. To be sure, badness and painfulness are not the same thing, for not all bad things are painful, but the badness of the experience lies in the pain in a more intimate sense than that in which the extension lies in the colour. For an experience to be intensely painful is a way of being bad; colour is not a kind of extension, it only entails this. Or take still another type of experience. We say that an educated mind is good, or (to avoid problems about 'dispositions') that our final grasp, on a certain evening, of just how the Michelson-Morley experiment led up to the theory of relativity was an experience very much worth while. Is it really possible to isolate within this experience a hard little qualitative pellet called goodness, quite distinct from the understanding itself, but absolutely identical with the goodness that we have previously found in a chocolate eclair and The Moonlight Sonata? Surely goodness is not present in this external way. The goodness of the insight is not something outside it, to which one travels on a bridge of inference. Of such an illumination of mind it would be as true to say that it was an experience of good as that it was a good experience; it does not carry goodness on its back as a rider; such goodness as it has belongs to it through and through. It is itself a species or manifestation of goodness.

5. The reply may come that even if happiness and understanding are manifestations of goodness rather than experiences to which this attaches, it does not follow that the common goodness cannot be distinguished and marked off from that in which it is embodied. The genus does not lose itself in its species. Even if not separate, it remains different and distinct. It is the element of identity that preserves itself through diversities, and in each of them it keeps a hard imperviousness to its environment, like a diamond that appears first in rock, then in mud, and then in a silver setting. This is the doctrine of the abstract universal, often associated with the name of Aristotle, though Aristotle himself was unable to hold to it. That it is not wholly unplausible is shown by its stubborn longevity. If one divides the genus billiard-ball into the species white billiard-balls and red, one may say with some credibility that the generic qualities of size and roundness are a distinct and unvarying group in both. But if one takes the genus colour, and tries in the same way to put one's finger on a common colour or colouredness, which is neither red nor blue nor yellow, but a changeless component in all of them, one cannot do it; the species red and the genus colour so interpenetrate that no wedge can be driven between them. Similarly, if one tries to conceive of life or mind as an identical something in the insect and in Goethe, one will once more be defeated. So of goodness.

If we may pursue this technical point for a moment, it was this very instance of goodness that Aristotle took to illustrate the deficiencies of the mechanical kind of logic when applied to ethics. Goodness, he said, may be of many kinds. It is true that 'the conception of whiteness appears the same in snow and in white lead. But the conceptions of honour, wisdom and pleasure, are distinct and different in respect of goodness. "Good" then is not a common term falling under one idea.' Indeed 'there are as many ways of predicating good as of predicating existence'.[1] This parallel between goodness and being is illuminating. Aristotle taught that there were ten categories, or ultimately different kinds of being, in the world. In a sense, therefore, they were the species of which being was the genus. But one has only to ask what exactly it is that characterizes this genus to see that if it really is a genus, it is one of a very queer kind. Can one conceive of mere being as such, which is not this or that kind of being, which is not anything rather than anything else? Such being, as was pointed out later by Hegel, is virtually indistinguishable from non-being. On consideration, Aristotle declined to call this shadow a genus at all. It became clearly conceivable only in its differentiations, and in these it was itself so profoundly differentiated that what distinguished quantity from quality, for example, was far more significant than anything they had in common. Now goodness is like being in this respect. Aristotle remarks in the *Ethics* that goodness is so deeply differentiated that each category has its own special forms of it. The goodness of a fine waterfall which is a substance, is not that of wisdom which is a quality, or of utility which is a relation; they are almost as different as the kinds of being in which they are embodied. And if one refuses to admit into the goodness of wisdom anything that is not equally present in the waterfall and in utility, one will fail to catch the specific goodness of wisdom. *That* goodness one can know only through entering into wisdom. To be wise *is* to realize goodness in one of its forms. If this is true, and it does seem to be so, then the goodness of wisdom does not lie in an abstract quality

[1] *Nicomachean Ethics*, Bk. I, Ch. 4. Welldon's trans.

identical in all good things. If it did, I could learn what the goodness of wisdom was by tasting a chocolate eclair, since when I call this experience good, I have in mind the same simple quality that makes anything good. Such a consequence is absurd.[1]

The conclusion suggested is that goodness is objective without being an objective quality. That the goodness of Emerson's wisdom should depend on the contingency of my thinking of it and approving it, as the emotivists in effect are telling us, is absurd. The opposite view, that this goodness consists of an extremely abstract non-natural quality attached to the wisdom is, if not absurd, at least unconvincing. The goodness is 'more deeply interfused' with the experience, belongs to it in a more integral and constitutive fashion. To see this is an advance. But we are still far short of what we want. Granted that goodness belongs in this way to the objects that have it, we want to find if we can what goodness is in itself. What is it more exactly that distinguishes what is good from what is not?

6. Moore can help us at this point. In another part of *Principia Ethica* than the one we have been considering, he discusses whether an object could be good apart from anyone's consciousness of it, and he uses an illustration that will suit us all the better because it is so well known.[2] Let us imagine, he says, that by a turn of our hand we could create one or other of two worlds. The first is a world that is utterly beautiful, in which all the colours and shapes and sounds are in harmony with each other, and everything in gross and detail is such as to arouse delight. The other world is the antithesis of this; it is one vast heap of putrescence and filth in which everything is of the sort to disgust and repel. Before we make our choice, there is one condition that must be laid down. This is that in neither world is the element called consciousness to be admitted. The colours, shapes, and harmonies are to be there in the beautiful world, but nobody is ever to see them or hear them. The foulness and ugliness of the other are also to be there, but since no one will become aware of them, no one will ever be offended by them. Both worlds alike are to exist outside the range of human or any other experience. Which would you choose to create?

---

[1] I owe the suggestion of this line of thought to H. W. B. Joseph. See Arist. Soc. Proc. Supplementary Vol. 11 (1932), 140 ff. and his *Some Problems in Ethics*, 75 ff. The difficulties with the abstract universal I have dealt with more fully in *The Nature of Thought*, Vol. I, Ch. 16.

[2] Pp. 83–4

Moore in his *Principia* has said he would choose the more beautiful world. It would be better that it should exist, he thought, even if there were no mind to respond to it in any way. But in the years that followed he continued to reflect on the matter and, with his remarkable freedom from prejudice even in favour of his past self, he reversed his judgment, declaring that there would be no ground for choosing either. Colours unseen, sounds forever unheard, harmonies that no one perceived or rejoiced in, if such things could be conceived, as he thought they could, would at any rate be totally valueless. What would be bad about filth if it never did or could in any degree offend? Moore's final conclusion was, then, that a universe without consciousness would be a universe without value. With this I think we must agree. There is no way of proving it except the way of ideal experiment which he adopted—the way of asking oneself whether, if all modes of consciousness were banished, anything we should call good or bad would remain? Of course there are persons who would answer this differently. Thomists, for example, continue to hold the obscure view of Aristotle that each material thing is a more or less complete actualization of what it is potentially, a more or less perfect embodiment of its special form, and is, so far, good. The disappearance of a boulder on some unheard of dark star would therefore be a loss of value to the world. Of course one may conceive of value in this way if one wishes, but it carries one quite out of touch with ordinary meaning; most men would say it made no difference whatever to the amount of good in the world whether such a boulder existed or not. Take any example of what we ordinarily regard as good or bad, imagine consciousness away, and the values vanish with it.

7. Whatever is good, then, must stand in relation to consciousness. But in what relation? Several have been suggested..It has been held that if anything is to be good, it must be a *state* of consciousness, an *object* of consciousness, an object of a particular *kind* of consciousness, and a *fitting* object of a particular kind of consciousness. To the first two of these we shall devote a word or two only. The last two deserve fuller attention.

As to the first, is it true that only states of consciousness are good? Certainly our first impulse is to say No. We call sunsets and operas good, for example, and it would be odd to hear them described as conscious states. Still, we should probably agree on reflection that it is only when in fact they are such states that they have any value. The sunset we prize is of course not that of a physicist, which consists of a mass of light waves of varying frequencies, and which no one would think of describing as good or bad; it is rather an array of colours which presumably have no existence except as seen, and in any case no value except as seen and enjoyed. And it is not the opera as a set of marks on paper that has value, but the opera as heard and delighted in.

What of the second suggestion, that whatever is good must be an *object* of consciousness? This too is exceptionable. A man who is wise and kindly without ever thinking of his own virtues and without being recognized by his neighbours for what he is, is not less good because his virtues are unnoticed.

This has been questioned by those who hold the third type of theory as to the relation between value and consciousness, namely that to be good or bad is to be the object of some special kind of consciousness. There are many possible forms of the theory. What is good may be identified with whatever is the object of one's desire, as by Hobbes; or of one's approval, as by Westermarck; or of the general approval, as by Hume; or of the interest of anyone at all, as by Perry. Most forms of this theory wear their refutation on their face. If anyone says, with Hobbes, that 'good' means 'object of my desire', it is enough to point out that I can meaningfully judge the serenity of Buddha to have been good in spite of the fact that, since it is in the past, it cannot now be the object of any sane desire. If anyone says, as Westermarck does, that 'good' means 'approved by me', one need only point to my unquestioning belief that there are, and have been, all sorts of good things in the world that I have never heard of, and therefore cannot think of with approval. Hume's view that 'good' means 'generally approved' is refuted by the single fact that there have been reformers who were convinced that their causes were good, even though they knew them to be disapproved of by almost every living soul.

8. To my mind, the most persuasive of these theories is that of Professor Perry whose *General Theory of Value* defends the view that a thing is made good or bad by being the object of anyone's interest. And 'interest', as Perry uses it, is a very wide term, covering liking, approving, pursuing, willing, admiring, and a host of cognate attitudes, together with their opposites. This view avoids the emotivist extravagance of saying that in judgments of good we are asserting nothing at all, for it holds that 'good' is not an interjection, but the name of a relational property; 'in my view', Perry writes ' "good" *means* the "feeling toward" or more precisely, "the being felt toward" '[1] and the existence of a feeling is as much a fact as that of Gibraltar; assertions about it are obviously true or false. The theory though relativist, likewise avoids the subjectivism of views like Westermarck's, for the interest that is creative of value need not be one's own; if anyone anywhere loves or hates something, wants it or admires it or detests it, that is enough to clothe it with value. Perry writes: 'in order to create values where they did not exist before it seems to be sufficient to introduce an interest. The silence of the desert is without value, until some wanderer finds it lonely and terrifying; the cataract, until some human sensibility finds it sublime. . . .'[2] To the question, what is good?, then, he answers, 'any object of any interest'.

9. Is this the insight we are in search of? Unhappily, I cannot think so. While Perry's books are a mine of helpful reflections about value, and his own position seems to me not far from the truth, it will not serve as it stands. It is clearly at odds with our common meaning. What we commonly mean by goodness may be present, and believed to be present, while interest is absent, and interest may be present when value, or at least any corresponding value, is absent.

(1) Do we not often say that things have been good or bad at times when we have every reason to believe that no one felt anything about them? We have already illustrated this in commenting on the emotivists. Consider the vast weltering mass of prehistoric animal pain, when life, as Dean Inge says, was 'a conjugation of the verb "to eat" in the active and the passive'. Was all this wretchedness free from anything bad till badness was posthumously conferred upon it, at a distance of a hundred milleniums, by a sympathetic palaeontologist? Or are we to say that the badness lay in the sufferers' 'negative interest' in their own pain? But we are surely much more certain that their suffering was bad than we are about their ability to perform the process that Perry regards as essential to their badness, namely cognizing the pain with a 'negative interest'. Or if pain is too treacherous a topic, consider the case just mentioned of the good man whose goodness is not thought about, or therefore felt about, by anyone,

[1] *General Theory of Value*, 133
[2] *Ibid.*, 125

even himself. We should certainly not regard his goodness as something that sprang into being when first appreciated. His case is typical of a very large class which Perry has perhaps not considered sufficiently. All cases of value, he says, can be symbolized by S-R-O, in which S is an interested subject, O an object, and R the relation of interest that links them. The connoisseur in the gallery looks at a Titian with delight, and the Titian therefore has value. But what of the connoisseur's experience of the Titian as opposed to the picture itself? Does not S-R-O as a whole have value, so that anyone would say it was well that it should have occurred? Presumably Professor Perry could admit this only if there were another subject S^1, who could contemplate this experience of S with satisfaction, and whose relation to it could be symbolized by S^1-R-(S-R-O). But it is clear that for the great majority of our experiences no such observer exists, and therefore that most of the things of whose value we are certain namely experiences, as distinct from the objects of those experiences, must, on the theory, be valueless. This is hard to accept.

10. (2) And just as objects may have value in the absence of any interest in them, so interest may be bent upon them without producing the appropriate values. On Professor Perry's theory, everything we admire or desire is good. What leaps to mind when we hear this is that people often admire and desire what is trivial or even bad; a boy may admire with all his heart the swaggering bravado of a movie hero which more mature persons regard as thoroughly cheap. Perry admits that this is 'the most popular objection' to his view, and much of his discussion may be read as a reply to it. If I have understood this reply, it is in substance as follows: To talk about the true or real value of such bravado is meaningless, for there is no such thing; the only value it has it takes from people's attitudes toward it. If the boy admires it, it is good for him; if his parents dislike it, it is bad for them; its 'true' or 'objective' value is a myth. When the parents say that the boy is admiring something bad, they must therefore be taking someone else's dislike, presumably their own, as authoritative, and using this as a basis from which to condemn what he admires. Have they any justification for this? Certainly not in the sense that the object as now enjoyed by the boy is not really good, for his enjoyment so far constitutes its goodness and makes it an unalterable fact. But they could legitimately say this, that if the boy could look at his hero with the knowledge and interests possessed by themselves, or by most mature and thoughtful persons, he would *dislike* it. Such persons prize considerateness and intelligence, with which swaggering bravado goes ill; they therefore find it a bore and a nuisance. It is wrong to say that the boy likes what is bad; strictly speaking, that is a contradiction in terms. It is correct to say that he is liking what mature and thoughtful persons dislike, and what he himself will presumably dislike eventually. But *this* statement is perfectly compatible with the theory. Does this reply meet the point?

We must agree, I think, that the statement 'such bravado is bad' does imply that a mature person, assumed to be able to see things clearly, would regard it as bad. But is that what we *mean* by the statement? Clearly not. For (a) we should certainly say that if the mature man so regards an object, he does so because it is bad; not that it is bad because he does so. (b) The suggested reading would turn the remark into a curiously unlikely conditional statement. What we should ordinarily mean by it is surely something like this, that an attitude of swaggering bravado is in normal circumstances a bad thing. To this the suggested reading would tack on 'provided it is in fact disliked by mature persons generally'. But we should surely grow restive if anyone tried to saddle us with such a condition. We were saying that this attitude was bad; period. There is no such 'if' about it. (c) We may significantly call the attitude bad while knowing perfectly well that mature persons generally regard it as good. We sometimes believe that the estimate even of the mature persons of our time of the goodness or badness of war, or of intellectual achievement, or of the way to treat animals, is a mistaken one. And this would be impossible if what we *meant* by goodness was the fact of their favour.

11. I have tried to give the most plausible answer possible on Professor Perry's theory to the objection that since one may like what is bad, the liking cannot make a thing good; and this answer seems insufficient. It would be even more insufficient if he had taken certain other tempting lines. He might have said that in judging that the boy was liking something bad, we were merely reporting that we ourselves disliked it, but he sees that to interpret value judgments in this individual way would invite anarchy by putting all such judgments on a level.

But has he escaped this objection after all? He is clear that there must be some means of revising and improving our value judgments, of weighing one liking against another, if we are to avoid ranking every adolescent enthusiasm on a plane with the insights of maturity. But the only revision open to us, on his theory, is that which comes not from 'insight' into what is really better, but from a change in our likings, a change not justifiable by anything but further liking. Any object is better than another if it has won a more intense, a preferential, or a more inclusive interest. 'An object, wine, is better than an object, water: (1) if the interest in the wine is more intense than the interest in the water; (2) if the wine is preferred to the water; and (3) if the interest in the wine is more inclusive than the interest in the water,'[1] that is, if it sums up a larger number of interests. An object that awakes any part or the whole of this triple liking in fuller measure than another is, so far, better than it. It is almost as if Professor Perry had said that the experience of an intense preferential, and inclusive interest were better than another, though he could not say this consistently. What he does say is that goodness depends on *de facto* favouring or liking. Whereas Moore and Ross hold that goodness is a 'consequential' quality, following necessarily from the nature of the object, Perry holds that it is connected with the object only contingently, through the chance of its being liked; a thing is good not because of what it is, but because someone happens to like it.

12. Now it is certain that goodness, in our ordinary thought of it, does not sit as loose to things as this. Do we think, to use Bentham's old case, that pushpin becomes as good as poetry if only people like it as much? If two men organize their lives, the one around the game of pushpin and the other around poetry, so that their interests in their respective objects are equally intense, preferential, and inclusive, is it therefore meaningless to question whether the objects they are engrossed in are equally good? I do not think most people would take this as obvious; I suspect they would take it as untrue. Or suppose that two men devoted themselves, with interests equal in these ways, the one to astronomy or metaphysics, the other to counting and measuring the rocks on a New Hampshire farm; would the knowledge gained, because equal in interest, be regarded as equal in value? Again I do not think so. We seem to have a stubborn conviction that whatever may be the facts of men's interest, some things are worth their devotion and others not, and therefore that our interests should be

[1] *General Theory of Value*, 616

adjusted to, and appraised by, the goodness, not the other way about. We are not prepared to admit even that if the race generally should come to favour something, that would settle the question of its goodness. Suppose that in the next world war our 'proud and angry dust' were to raise such effective dust-storms as to force the gibbering remnant of us that remained into a troglodyte existence, where science and art had lost their interest, moral sensitiveness was sneered at as effeminacy, and love derided in any but its animal forms. Would the fact that these things, formerly prized so highly, were now regarded with indifference or aversion, settle anything about their value?

It might be replied, to be sure, that if we were to compare the troglodyte existence with the old life before the deluge, we should see that the latter gave fuller scope for the arousing and fulfilment of interests, and was therefore better. But what would 'better' mean here? If it meant that a life whose capacities were more fully realized was really or objectively better, the theory is being deserted. If it meant that people actually liked such a life better, a troglodyte could disprove it by pointing to the fact that his contemporaries did not like it better; and if it were retorted that he ought to prefer a life that fulfilled his likings more inclusively, he could rejoin, and I fear unanswerably, that he happened not to like such a life, and that in that case there was no ought about it. Between such ultimate differences in liking, the theory before us would not admit even the theoretical possibility of saying which was right, or that either was right, or that one was more nearly right than the other. The fact that one is off with an old love and on with a new does not show that the new object is better, unless one means merely that it is liked more; and what is liked more may become bad overnight if one's feelings about it shift again. Valuations may be revised, but only by further feelings, which are themselves judged only by still further feelings, and so on without limit; and the revisions may with equal propriety (because in no case with any propriety) intensify what is already felt or reverse it altogether. To seek the good is rather like shooting at a target blindfold and hearing that one is getting nearer and nearer the mark, only to find, as the blindfold drops for a moment, that there is no target there at all and that every shot may be regarded, according as one is disposed, either as a bull's-eye or as a miss.

Now it may be that there is no one meaning of 'good' that would fit all the cases in which we take things as intrinsically good. But to break completely with common sense is to throw overboard the most useful compass we have and we must keep to it as long as we can. And we have seen that common sense would reject the suggestion that things are made good merely by our own feeling about them.

13. Still, we must not go too far. Common sense would not reject feeling as unimportant; indeed I think it would regard this as indispensable. Leave feeling out entirely, and, as we saw in the experience of the Stoics and the younger Mill, the goodness of life, as most of us conceive it, would go too. The pursuit of knowledge, the cultivation of art, the attempt to better oneself or one's community, is simply impossible when the wind of interest dies out of one's sails. There is no savour left in the salt when desire fails; the pitcher, as the Old Testament Preacher said, stands broken at the fountain and the wheel broken at the cistern. Why turn one's hand or lift one's finger if nothing can possibly come of it that one could welcome? As James once said, all the art on the walls of the Vatican would have no value for a stray dog lost in the halls, for it is unable to notice, or if it notices, to take the slightest interest in such things. Perry and the emotivists are right in stressing that interest is a condition of goodness. Where they have gone astray, I venture to think, is in *identifying* interest with goodness. In the end one gags at the paradox that one can make hatred and ignorance good if one is depraved enough to like them. Most men are convinced that hatred and ignorance have a character of their own which appoints some attitudes towards them as fitting and others as unfitting. They would say that if we like them, that does not transmute them into something good, but merely reveals how blind we are.

14. This brings us to the other type of theory that would make of goodness a relational property. It has been stated persuasively by Dr Ewing in *The Definition of Good*. With much of what we have said about the simple-quality theory and the interest theory I think Dr Ewing might agree. But he finds important truth in both. Moore is clearly right, he thinks, that typical judgments of good mean to say something true of an object, something that would still be true, however one felt about it. On the other hand, Perry is clearly right that feelings and desires are bound up in a peculiarly intimate way both with the making of these judgments and with what they assert. How are we to reconcile the objectivity of the judgment with this curious involvement with feeling? The strength of Dr Ewing's suggestion lies in its resolute attempt at justice to both of these all but irreconcilable demands. The suggestion is that when I call anything good, what I mean is not that I favour it, or that anyone else does actually favour it, but simply that it is fitting and proper to favour it, that the thing called good is a 'fitting object of a pro attitude'. 'Pro', of course, means favouring. 'Attitude' is a blanket term which 'covers, for instance, choice, desire, liking, pursuit, approval, admiration.' 'When something is intrinsically good, it is (other things being equal) something that on its own account we ought to welcome, rejoice in if it exists, seek to produce if it does not exist. We ought to approve its attainment, count its loss deprivation, hope for and not dread its coming if this is likely, avoid what hinders its production, etc.'[1] To say that an action is good is to say that it is a fitting object of moral admiration or approval. To say that an experience is good is to say that it is worthy of being sought and prized. To say that pain is evil is to say that it is a suitable object of aversion.

15. Dr Ewing is convinced, and with reason, that this theory has great advantages. For one thing, it thins the region of controversy between the naturalist and the non-naturalist in ethics to the narrowest possible area. The naturalist is the person who thinks that ethical characters such as good and right reduce without remainder to the sort of observable characters dealt with in physical or psychological science, for example that 'good' means actually desired by oneself, or by people generally. The non-naturalist is the person who thinks that this reduction cannot be carried through. Dr Ewing is a non-naturalist.[2] But he is inclined to think that there is only one ethical term that holds out against such reduction. This is what he calls 'fittingness'. When we interpret 'x is good' by 'x is a fitting object of favour', the fitness of attitude to object is a relation, but it is not like *before*, or *larger than*, or *part of*, which are commonly thought to belong to empirical science. The fitness or fittingness of a favouring attitude to a pleasure, for example, is not an empirical relation at all. It is a relation of synthetic necessity apprehended by intuition, which is itself a form of reason. One sees immediately that, pleasure being

[1] *The Definition of Good*, 149
[2] In his recent *Second Thoughts in Moral Philosophy*, which has appeared since this chapter was written, Dr Ewing has amended his view in a sense more sympathetic to rationalism. Though his position has not changed fundamentally, the reader should be warned that the criticisms which follow are concerned exclusively with its formulation in *The Definition of Good*.

what it is, a favouring attitude toward it is appropriate, and a disfavouring attitude is not.

But though this relation must be set down as non-natural, it is the only term of this kind that Dr Ewing finds it necessary to introduce, for all other ethical terms can be defined by means of it. Thus the controversy between Moore and Ross over whether ought depends on good is cleared up with singular ease. Dr Ewing agrees with Moore that it is always our duty so to act as to bring the most good into the world. But he then turns round and defines good in terms of ought; what is good is what ought to be favoured, in the sense that it would be fitting to favour it, that its nature calls for such favour. There is thus no conflict between good on the one hand, and ought or right on the other; you may say that either is primary as you wish; and the parties to this ancient controversy may both go away happy. The only ethical term that might make a show of resistance against reduction to fittingness is 'ought' in its specifically moral sense, the 'ought' that means 'it is my duty to do this'; but even that he thinks may be brought into line by a double dose of fittingness: the judgment would now mean, first, 'it would be fitting for me to do this' and second, 'if I do not do it, I shall be a fitting object of disapproval'.[1] Thus Dr Ewing is not asking the naturalist to admit into his universe a pantheon of dubious divinities—good, right, wrong, ought, sin, guilt. Let him admit this one relation of fittingness, and he will be troubled by no more importunities from the non-natural realm.

16. The theory has a second great advantage: it gives empirical and ordered meanings to a vast range of value terms. Besides the generic 'good' which is now to mean fittingly favoured, there are multitudes of sub-terms for special forms of good—admirable, beautiful, lovable, charming, sublime, noble, honourable, and so on—and there is an even more extensive armoury for the forms of evil. If all these terms were taken as meaning characters in the object, each with a quality quite distinct from that of our feeling about it, the task of distinguishing these qualities would become impossible. Try to say what lovable means without reference to the quality of love, and you are lost. On the other hand, define it as 'such that love may be appropriately felt for it' and the definition, however vague, is in terms of a perfectly familiar relational property. So of the other value qualities. Taken as out there in the object, independent of all attitudes toward

[1] *The Definition of Good,* 168

it, they return to the mysterious status of Moore's indefinable good; they are virtually or wholly characterless; and trying to relate them to each other is like trying to round up and classify the clouds on a breezy day. But everyone knows what it feels like to love or admire or reverence or desire; everyone knows many degrees of such feelings; everyone knows the difference, however hard it is to define, between approving something morally and appreciating it aesthetically. Once the value qualities are allowed to borrow content from the attitudes specially appropriate to them, the chaos of these qualities falls into an order determined by the degrees, affiliations, and mixtures of these attitudes themselves.

17. Finally, as Dr Ewing points out, the theory accords most happily with the way moral beliefs arise. We do not come to think uncleanliness, lewdness, idleness, and ignorance bad through achieving an intellectual insight into the necessitation by these things of an objective quality called 'evil', but rather through catching the way people feel about them. In childhood, if our mother abhors a certain person and shows it, that is enough for us; he is bad, and we are ready to do battle against him whether we know anything about him or not, just as a faithful dog acts on the principle 'whoever my master is against is a limb of Satan and fair game for me'. It is true that as we grow up we amend these attitudes in the light of further knowledge. But this does not mean that growing up morally is a process of ascent out of the fogs and clouds of attitude to the passionless sage, sitting atop a snowy and rational peak. A graduation from feelings and desires would be a graduation right out of the moral life. What actually happens is that, beginning with a mass of likes and aversions picked up by the contagion of sympathy, we little by little correct them, partly through contact with people who feel otherwise, partly through learning more about the objects and finding that our feelings hardly suit them. Moral judgment is at first almost pure prejudice, in the sense that it is an expression chiefly of ungrounded, or ill grounded, feeling. In the educated mind it never remains that wholly. In conversation with Charles Lamb, a friend happened to name another man: 'I h-hate that man', Lamb stammered out. 'Why I didn't suppose you even knew him', remarked the other, in surprise at such an outburst from the friendliest of men. 'I d-don't', said Lamb. 'I c-can't h-hate a man I know.' Changing knowledge changes our attitudes, clearly. But it does not cause them simply to deliquesce and vanish. They remain present, and they remain essential, from first to last. Dr Ewing is right, I think, in insisting that the judgment of good, even in its most sophisticated form, does imply that its object merits the favour, or would satisfy the feelings, of a reasonable man.

We may concede to the theory these important points of strength. May we then accept it without further ado? Unfortunately, there are difficulties through which I cannot quite see my way.

18. (1) First, the conviction persists that if it is *fitting* to favour an object, this is because the object is good already. And if it is thus good, its goodness cannot be exhausted in the fittingness of possible favour. The account of good here given seems to presuppose another good in the object, of which that account could not be repeated. To put it more concretely: a man by discipline of mind and character achieves what we call wisdom, and we say of this wisdom that it is good. That means on the view before us, that his state of mind may fitly be favoured. Is it an intelligible question to ask why it should be favoured? I cannot help thinking that it is. On the theory before us, it is not. For according to that theory, the only answer we could give is 'because wisdom is wisdom'; we could not say 'because wisdom is good', because all 'good' means is that it should be favoured, and we should therefore be explaining why wisdom should be favoured merely by saying that it should be favoured. The question why it should be favoured is thus unanswerable because really meaningless. One can say that a state of mind should be favoured in virtue of its wisdom; one cannot say that the wisdom should be favoured in virtue of anything at all; to see that wisdom is good *is* to see that it should be favoured. One either sees that it should be, or one does not; and if one does not, no reason can be offered why it should. I must admit that I am not content. It still seems to me truer to say that we favour the object because it is good than to say the object is good because we may fittingly favour it. Are there any crucial considerations that may help us decide this issue? I suggest the following.

Consider what the object is like independently of any attitudes actual or possible. What is being thought of, let us say, is the wisdom of Emerson. Was it good or not? Obviously and by definition, not. On the theory, all objects, considered apart from a possible favouring or disfavouring, are neutral as respects value, for it is only in relation to such favouring that they get their value. So considered, then, nothing is better or worse than anything else. Emerson's wisdom is a matter of fact; so is the dullness of Peter Bell; and as mere natural facts, they are on a level. We now ask whether it is fitting that one of these states of mind should be favoured over the other, and the answer given is Yes. This answer is even taken as expressing a necessary insight; wisdom requires favouring in virtue of what it is. And yet on the terms of the theory itself, it is hard to regard this answer as other than arbitrary. If the goodness of wisdom lay in its own nature, as Joseph, following Plato, contended, and I, following both at a due distance, should also contend, then the favouring of it would have the rational character that Dr Ewing wishes to preserve in the moral judgment. But if the wisdom has no goodness apart from the reference to favouring it, just why should it be favoured? Dr Ewing is of course alive to the difficulty, and he gives a straightforward answer to it.

> 'It will be objected against me that it is only fitting to approve, or have a pro attitude towards, what is good because we first know or believe it to be good, and that if we did not believe it to be good, there would be no ground for such an attitude, so that the attitude would not be fitting. The answer is that the ground lies not in some other ethical concept, goodness, but in the concrete factual characteristics of what we pronounce good. Certain characteristics are such that the fitting response to what possesses them is a pro attitude, and that is all there is to it.'[1]

My difficulty is to see how a pro attitude could be fitting merely to 'concrete factual characteristics', and Dr Ewing seems at times to feel this himself. Thus he writes: 'A principal objection made by me against naturalist definitions of "good" was just that, if "good" were defined naturalistically, it would be no more rational, right, fitting to pursue the good than the bad and that good would carry with it no moral obligation to pursue the good.'[2] Now unless I have misunderstood, the naturalistic qualities here said to offer no ground for favouring or pursuit are the same qualities which, in another context, we are told require a favouring response. And it seems clear that they cannot be both. If these factual characteristics do deserve a response of moral favouring or disfavouring, an important part of Dr Ewing's case against naturalism, which seems to me very effective, will have to be abandoned. If they do not, can he say, as he does, that they are 'such that the fitting response to what possesses them is the pro-attitude'?

[1] *The Definition of Good*, 172; and cf. 157, 176
[2] *Ibid.*, 178

The phrase 'such that' is puzzling. What does it mean? At one point Dr Ewing suggests that 'I might well admire something just because I thought it worthy to be admired',[1] with no idea of what it was in the object that was admirable; but he adds immediately that if this thought is to be justified, the qualities that are admirable must be pointed out; a blank cheque could hardly be honoured at the bank where our admirations are stored. If Dr Ewing were to explore the implications of 'such that', he might find them carrying him to a fuller objectivism than that which he now holds. The moral judgment emerges from his account a remarkably ingenious bridge, with the agent's favour at one end, a non-natural relation of fittingness or congruity forming the imposing span, and the other end resting on nothing visible to the ethical eye. To some relations of fittingness natural qualities could indeed give support. The roundness of the hole is fitting to the roundness of the peg; the shape of the shore fits exactly the shape of the ocean; between two notes in tune there is congruence in frequency of wave. But in these fittings there is no goodness. Goodness comes only when in the object there is something that answers to favour, something 'such as' to require and deserve it. And you cannot fill that blank called 'such as' with neutral natural qualities, with round holes or coastal inlets or physical frequencies; you cannot even fill it with St Francises or with the giving of all one has to feed the poor, if these are considered solely as natural events. As such, they are mere facts, none of them better than any other. If saintliness and generosity are such as to merit favouring, it must be because there is something in them that goes beyond their 'factual characteristics' and equally goes beyond a mere blank cheque on our favour. What is this? I think we must answer, a goodness that they have already. Unhappily the nature of this goodness eludes us still.

19. (2) This is the fundamental objection to a theory that seems to me very nearly right. But it may be well to mention one or two others that are perhaps less objections than difficulties. For one thing, considering how important it is, the relation of fittingness is left unfittingly obscure. Dr Ewing thinks that to say 'wisdom merits favour' is a synthetic necessary proposition, thereby attracting around his ears a Pandora's box of buzzing cavils from those who hold that there are no necessities outside logic and only analytic necessities inside it. His refusal to flee before this cloud of gnats I find admirable,

[1] *The Definition of Good,* 157

meaning more, I think, than merely that to admire it would be fitting. But to say that a relation of congruity between an object and an emotion may carry necessity in it is in these days a courageous thing to say, and even though true, needs explanation. To be more specific, Dr Ewing objects, as I do, to the idea of an abstract identical goodness in St Francis, the Moonlight Sonata, and a chocolate eclair. But for all one knows, he holds that the fittingness of our favour for these three is itself identical, that the fittingness that marks our favour of a generous deed is the same as that which marks a ready responsiveness to humour, a due appreciation of music or painting, religious reverence, and the hatred of cruelty. Furthermore, I gather he would say, with Professor Broad and Sir David Ross, that the act of a man who performs a rescue at sea 'fits the situation'. I think he would say that the relation is an internal one, in the sense that the agent has it to the situation in virtue of the nature of that situation. If so, does it vary as its terms vary? And how is its necessity related to that of logic and mathematics? I speak as one who is convinced, as Dr Ewing is, that the current exclusion of rational necessity from all domains except formal logic is an unfortunate passing fashion. But just for this reason, I should like to see the case against this, which is surely a powerful one, more fully developed.

20. (3) Thirdly, if goodness were the same as fittingness of favour, they could never fall apart, but it seems to me that occasionally they do. Favour and disfavour include, as we have seen, many kinds and intensities of attitude. I think Dr Ewing would say that if one of our children were starving, our judgment that this was bad would mean that the strongest aversion toward it, acute grief about it, and energetic efforts to remove it, would be fitting. Now there happens to be another child starving in central China. To feel nothing about this would certainly be unfitting if we knew its plight. On the other hand, perhaps no one would say that the suffering had the same claim on our feelings as that of our own child. There are many feelings, felt with great intensity, that are obviously suitable in the case of our own child, which we could hardly be expected to show about one that was remote and all but unknown. Now if to call anything bad *is* to say that it is the fitting object of anti-attitudes, then when we call the remote child's starvation bad, we must mean that it is a great deal less bad than our own child's starvation, since the attitudes fitting in this case are less various and less intense. But if it were put to us expressly that this was what we meant, I think we should say 'No, I didn't mean that at all; what the Chinese child is going through may be as bad as anything my own child is suffering, or even worse; I cannot feel as keenly about remote evils as I do about those nearer home, and have no sense that I ought to, but I can still recognize quite clearly that those evils are as great as those near by.' In short, the judged badness may be the same while the fitting attitudes differ; the one, therefore, is not the same as the other.

Dr Ewing is aware of this difficulty. His reply would be, I take it, that the respect in which the attitudes may fittingly differ is not that in which their fitness determines goodness. 'To speak of the good of two persons as equal means that, other things being equal, neither had more claim to pursuit than the other; but if I have a special relation involving obligation to one person which I have not to the other, other things are not equal.' In the case of my own child I have a duty arising out of its nearness, its being mine, and my being able to help; in the other case, I have admittedly no such duty. But this difference in duty arises from taking into account much besides the respective sufferings of the children. If we confine ourselves to these sufferings, we find that the attitude of aversion appropriate to the one is the same as that appropriate to the other, and thus the fitting attitudes tally with the degree of judged badness.

This is surely an effective reply when the difference of attitude is a difference of duty. I am not clear that it is equally so where duty is not involved. We read in the morning paper about a train wreck three miles off, in which many lost their lives. We note that no friends of ours were involved, and there is nothing we can do about it, yet we are much stirred. We then go into our study and read about certain 'old unhappy far-off things and battles long ago' which involved, we know, much more misery than the wreck of yesterday. About these gigantic far-off ills we feel only a gentle melancholy, and we are not, in our own eyes, guilty of impropriety in so feeling. Here the amounts of evil assigned to the events are the reverse of what they ought to be if the degrees of aversion accepted as fitting in our attitudes were the measure of badness. Again, suppose that two persons, oneself and another, perform actions of equal courage or moral goodness. It is certainly fitting that one should admire the action of the other man. Dr Ewing agrees that it would be unfitting to indulge in the same admiration for oneself.[1] Fittingness and goodness seem once

[1] *The Definition of Good*, 155

more to fall apart. Dr Ewing, I am sure, has considered this difficulty, but I am not clear what his answer would be.

21. If the criticism we have offered is well founded, the goodness of anything is not defined or exhausted by the fitness of favouring it. Favouring it will be fitting if it *is* good, but that is not what its goodness means. To say that something deserves to be favoured is to say that there is already in the object something that lifts it out of neutrality and justifies taking a positive rather than a negative attitude toward it. That in the object which makes it fitting to favour it can hardly be the fittingness itself. We are therefore thrown back again upon our apparently endless search.

But we have made some progress. We have seen that the fundamental question of ethics is what is meant by 'good', and in this chapter we have considered three theories of what it means, offered by three very able moralists. So far as we could make out, they were all partly wrong and partly right. Moore was wrong in holding that goodness is a simple unanalysable quality, but right in holding that when we talk about the goodness of someone's pleasure or the badness of someone's pain, we are talking about something objective, in the sense of belonging in the object, and not merely in our attitude toward it. Perry was wrong in holding that value consists in interest, but he was right in holding that for the person who has no feeling about an object, that object has no value, and hence that there is no value in the world except as relative to consciousness. Ewing was wrong in reducing goodness to the appropriateness of favour, though he was right in holding that goodness does not vary with attitudes actually taken. We have now a conundrum set for our solution. The goodness of an experience is an objective character of it, not reducible to feeling and not necessarily variable with feeling, and yet in some sense dependent on it. What sort of character is this? We shall try to suggest an answer in the next chapter.

K

CHAPTER XI

HUMAN NATURE AND GOODNESS

1. There are two ways of studying our processes of valuing things, an internal way and an external. We turn in this chapter to the external way. So far we have followed exclusively the internal one, which proceeds by analysing meaning, and have considered many suggestions as to what the treacherous word 'good' means. We have seen that though it is one of the commonest words in the language, analysts are deeply divided about its import. Some think it means a simple indefinable character, the same in all good things. Some think that 'x is good' means x is pleasant, some that I like it, some that people generally like it, some that it *means* nothing at all, but is expressive of an attitude, though if they do say this, they promptly divide again as to what this attitude is—an emotion, for example, a desire, or a command.

Now one can only suspect that when acute analysts differ so flatly and so widely about a common term, they are looking for a sharpness of definition which is not there to be found. G. E. Moore sometimes spoke as if for such common-sense terms there was one primary and definite meaning, which could be captured with complete distinctness if only one made the necessary effort. In dealing with the linguistic philosophers, both in our earlier volume and in this one, we have been able to find no good reason for this assumption. Indeed there is something absurd in the notion that the most tortured problems of speculation can be cleared up by catching the meaning with which plain men use common words. The fact is that plain men use these words as one would expect them to—effectively enough for their purposes, but most loosely and uncritically for the philosopher's purpose; and the more fundamental the term, the more vaguely they use it.

The words 'hammer', 'nail', 'cup' and 'saucer' they use with some exactness. The words 'life', 'feeling', 'thought' and 'good' they use with such a wealth of woolly meanings that the attempt to extract any precise and common significance is misguided effort. Such vagueness and ambiguity are entirely natural. A term that is at once important and of frequent recurrence is used in widely differing circumstances; it acquires voluminous and various associations; its use may become charged with feeling; and both meaning and feeling are diversely modified as it is applied in different situations. In the end a term like 'good' comes to carry a vague cloud of cognitive and other meaning, so that philosophers who offer a dozen conflicting analyses can do so with equal plausibility. In such circumstances, what are we to do?

It may be thought that we should simply acquiesce in this diversity. Why not take the hospitable course of saying that all the cognitive, emotive and imperative meanings offered by all the analysts are equally present and equally primary? Because it would lead straight to self-contradiction. When two people differ as to whether an experience is good or an action right, it is idle to say that the cognitive and emotive meanings, for example, are both primary, for if one says the first, one is saying that this is a case of differing opinions; if one says the second, one is saying that it is not; and if one says that they are equally primary, one is saying both that it is *and* that it is not. Democracy in this matter is mere incoherence. And analysis, if it will not carry us all the way, will at least carry us part of the way. It is good enough, as we have seen, to deal fairly effectively with the claims of emotivism and imperativism. But after such theories have been dealt with, we are still faced with a variety of more or less plausible conceptions of what goodness means.

2. It is at this point that the second way of approaching the matter may help. This is the external way. It has been employed illuminatingly by Hobhouse in Britain and in a varying manner by Parker, Dewey, Perry and Pepper in America. I do not mean the method of behaviouristic study, though Dewey and Perry dallied with that method; for a behaviouristic study of values is inept and strictly impossible. What I mean is the method of which Aristotle was the pioneer, a study of goodness that places it in its wider human and biological context. Aristotle would have regarded Moore's attempt to make goodness of unvarying meaning, identical in a symphony, a mathematical intuition and the taste of a sandwich, as essentially misguided, for there was no suggestion in it of how deeply goodness was implicated with human nature and faculty. Looked at from the inside, goodness might easily appear to be such an abstraction. Looked at from the outside, from the point of view of an observer of the human and animal scene as a whole, this abstraction would seem singularly thin and rootless. Man is a creature of impulses, needs, and faculties; what he seems to be bent on is the fulfilment of those impulses, the satisfaction of those needs, the realization of those faculties. The suggestion of the external approach is that good is as various as they are, and that to conceive of goodness rightly, when cut off from these roots in human nature, is impossible.

Goodness may be studied either as the predicate of a judgment or as an object of pursuit. It was of course clear to Aristotle that we pursue some things merely as means to others, and it was these others in which he was interested. The intrinsically good is what is prized and pursued for its own sake. We may study such goods directly by asking ourselves what it is that above all we want. But the fact is that we do not know what we want with any clearness and definiteness. Hence we must fall back, Aristotle thought, on the consideration of what kind of beings we are. We occupy a certain place in the scale of living things; we have powers and impulses that make some ends natural for us and others impossible. It would be futile for a man to set his heart on acrobatic prowess that would be easy for a monkey, or an aquatic or aeronautic prowess that for a fish or a bird would be effortless. The main principle of the life of reason, for Aristotle as for his modern disciple Santayana, was that every ideal fulfilment had its natural basis and every natural impulse its ideal fulfilment. Neither could be understood in separation from the other. We could no more know what man essentially was without knowing what he was striving to become than we could know what an acorn was without knowing that it was in potency an oak. On the other hand, we could know the appropriate end only in the light of actual powers. The two lines of inquiry must therefore advance together, each set of results serving as a check on the other.

The external approach has been ignored by recent analytic philosophy. This I think is a mistake. Value is so fundamental in human life that its true character can be seen only against the background of human nature. If the intrinsically good is that which this nature finds in itself attractive, it is reasonable to suspect that its attractiveness has something to do with its answering that nature's needs and demands. I am convinced that if we find certain things good, it is not merely *because* they fulfil needs; such fulfilment enters into the very meaning of goodness. A sound theory of value can be developed only from an understanding of the soil or setting in which value arises.

3. The kind of consideration on which we are embarking is so different from our earlier analyses that it may be well to set down briefly and at once the view of goodness that will gradually emerge from it. We shall hold that only experiences are directly or immediately good. When they are good intrinsically, they perform a double function: they fulfil an impulse, drive or need, and in so doing they give satisfaction or pleasure. Both components, fulfilment and satisfaction, are necessary, and they vary independently of each other. But both are always partial in the sense that they apply to a limited set of needs; and they are always provisional or incomplete, so that goodness is a matter of degree. It is to be measured against an ideal good, which is the kind of life which would fulfil and satisfy wholly.

Every point here is controversial. It is obvious that this view of goodness and the good is bound up with a theory of how the mind is constituted, of how values arise in experience, and of how they are connected with needs and impulses. Instead of launching at once into controversy, it is better, even at the cost of moving slowly, to set out the background from which our view emerges. I shall do this in a series of propositions, with a brief commentary on each.

4. (1) *Conscious process is goal-seeking from the beginning.* A vast mass of evidence, which it is needless to review, has been marshalled by Ward and James, McDougall and Woodworth, Freud and the Gestaltists. From the outset the stream of consciousness has a direction, and does not merely meander; it is carried along by seekings and strivings. The infant at the start *is* very largely an impulse to suck and to avoid discomfort. The chief interest of things, when they begin to be discriminated, is as cues for action; the ball is something to bounce or roll, the cat to be felt, pulled about, and stroked, the blocks to be piled up, the gleaming bits of glass to be triumphantly seized. Some of these adventures turn out well, that is, they provide experiences that satisfy; and when the opportunity comes to have them again, the impulse is strengthened by its past success. Sometimes the experiments turn out badly; the piece of glass gives a stinging cut. These adventures serve to define the end of the impulse. The child does not know what it wants; it merely sends out exploratory horns as a snail does, ready to draw them back instantly or to explore further according to the encouragement received. A satisfying experience is a signal to go on with the exploration so long as it continues to satisfy, and a sting or an ache is a warning not to try *that* sort of experiment again.

So far, there is nothing beyond the reach of the animal mind. That mind is moved by impulse and instinct, but apparently never, in the full sense, by desire. It is time to define some of these terms. Impulse is an 'urge' or felt tendency toward a certain course of behaviour. Instinct is such an urge based on a pre-formed structure of the organism. Desire is again such an urge but now with a consciousness of its end.

The greatest advance of the human over the animal mind lies in its escape from perceptual to free ideas, and the advance from perceptual to free desire parallels that escape. Take the first form of advance. A dog can obviously think, if that means that it can attach meaning drawn from its experience to what is given it in sensation; even a moron among canines can recognize its master or tell a bone from a stick. But the most brilliant of canine thinking remains perceptual; that is, it remains anchored to sense. So long as the master is present, or even something sensibly connected with him—his shoes, his voice, the door that he went through—the animal mind can read the sign; and it may be restless and despondent when the master is away. But careful observers seem to agree that there is one thing it cannot do: it cannot sit down and think about its master, still less elaborate its thought of him, in the absence of a sensible sign to wake the idea and hold it. Man *can* do that; that is largely what makes him man.

Look now at the parallel escape into free desire. Lloyd Morgan's classic chick, after a single bitter experience of orange peel placed among its wheat, eyed suspiciously the next piece of orange peel offered it. Animals on the higher levels may learn quickly even complicated mazes that have led to getting food, and take alarm at signals that even remotely portend pain. In this sense they can desire perceptually just as they can think in this way; the two are forms of the same power. But like the independent thought of the absent, desire proper, the power to 'look before and after and pine for what is not', seems to be the prerogative of man alone. When the dog sees food in the offing, its mouth waters; when Pavlov's dog heard a bell rung that had been associated with getting food, its mouth still watered; man alone, in the absence of food or bell, can make his mouth water at will by dwelling in imagination on the delights of the gourmet or gourmand.

5. (2) Thus *desire grows out of the experience of satisfaction and is limited by it*. When the child seeks the nipple of the bottle, it is from 'blind' impulse, but having done this with satisfaction, it now has something to desire. It could not have manufactured this desire out of nothing. Desire must live chiefly on the spoils that impulse brings home from its adventures. Strength and variety of impulse are therefore the materials of the good life in the sense that the child who is interested in doing little or nothing will lack the clay out of which ideal goods can be modelled. The experience of things done variously, eagerly, and with zest, supplies us the palette of colours with which to paint our future, and we are likely to paint this in bright or sombre colours, to 'greet the unseen with a cheer' or meet it timidly and fearfully as our early experiments in living have been successful and remunerative in satisfactions or niggardly and rebuffing. Bertrand Russell has suggested that the most important years of a man's life are the years from one to two. Whether the numbers are right or not, it is certain that our early years are the momentous ones not only for the acquisition of habits but also for the accumulation of a capital of 'goods'. Hence Dewey's humane insistence on freedom for the small experimenter. Hence too, the importance of praise judiciously given. Since our satisfaction lies largely in the *belief* that we are doing something well, whether we are doing it thus or not, the current of many a life has no doubt been turned for better or worse by the pleasure of finding that in solving equations, in doing a dance, in repairing a car, we have cut a happy figure in others' eyes. Hence, once more, the truth of the ancient saw that all work and no play makes Jack a dull boy. We have already noticed Mill's account of how, because he was cut off from the activities that in boyhood are interesting, he found himself on the threshold of manhood incapable of desiring anything. Ruskin's *Praeterita* tells a significant story of how the values of a life were determined by carefully canalizing a child's activities so that it should find its satisfaction not where most boys find them, but along pre-appointed and adult channels. To be sure, we should think twice before wishing Mill's or Ruskin's boyhood otherwise if that was the price of their being what they were. The point is merely that the human mind is extremely plastic and can be engineered into responsiveness to strangely different realms of value.

6. We must add that not all the attractiveness of things is based on successful dealings with them. The Gestaltists have shown that some patterns in nature have an appeal for us that is native, not acquired; and Drever pointed out that there is such a thing as congenital emotive meaning, in the sense that a chick, for example, finds some things interesting and inviting even before impulses have had any play with them; from the start it finds grains of wheat interesting and marbles indifferent. And as James reminds us, when the chick becomes a hen and regards its nest of eggs as fascinating and 'never-to-be-too-much-sat-upon', this is no result of earlier discovery. Instinct, as McDougall insists, is a tendency to notice and feel as well as to act, and it invests some things with an aura of attractiveness that never has to be learned. Nature leaves more to learning and less to prior appointment as it goes up the animal scale. But even in man it loads some dice. J. B. Watson showed that we do not *acquire* our fear of loud sounds, but find them fearful from the outset. Mozart was confident that tones, those of church bells for example, meant more to him in the way of excitement than to other men, and Ruskin thought the same of his responsiveness to shapes and colours. They may or may not have been right, but it is obvious that at certain times of our lives we begin to find interesting what we had not found so before, not because impulses have sallied out and met with success, but because they have ripened inwardly. The boy who has been indifferent to girls finds at a certain age that they have become unaccountably interesting. And these budding satisfactions shape his desires.

It would be a mistake to infer, however, that desire can only repeat and echo past satisfaction. It must start from there, but once given its cue, it may develop the cue very richly, and spin vast and complicated dreams of what more of the same would be like. For example, though a person who had in no degree experienced romantic love could not in any definite way even desire it, since he would not know what to desire, still a very limited experience of it—or of pride or jealousy or ambition—may provide a capital which, imaginatively invested, will yield astonishing returns. Not all, we may be sure, that came out of the drab parsonages of Steventon or Haworth could have come out of the actual experiences of Jane Austen or the three young Brontës. And it is heartening to recall that the mind which added such riches to the empire as to lead Carlyle to propose the intriguing question 'Shakespeare or India?', was one whose experience at first-hand was sharply limited.

7. (3) Just as desire grows out of satisfaction, so *our ideas of what is desirable grow out of what we desire.* If we were to list at any given time the goods we genuinely prize, they would be the things that satisfy us as reflected and developed in desire. For the boy who has enjoyed games and wants more of them, games are good. If he has got nothing but boredom from poetry, and wants no more of it, poetry to him is worthless. He knows, of course, that there are people who find it good, just as he knows that there are people who find trigonometry true, and he therefore accepts the goodness and truth of these things on authority. But they are not good or true for him. Nothing is really desirable to us that we are incapable of desiring. And whatever we do desire presents itself to us as, so far, desirable or good.

This raises a question that is theoretically important. When we see how straight the line runs from satisfaction through desire to good, and then reflect how largely our satisfactions are the product of contingent factors like native interest and early success, the question is bound to arise whether the whole realm of our goods is not a chapter of accidents. Might not most or all of what we call good have been indifferent to us if fate had taken a slightly different turning? Most young Americans find baseball absorbing. But suppose that the immortal Cobb and Ruth themselves had tried their hands at it prematurely and been sharply rebuffed; is it not wholly possible that they should have turned to other things and found baseball distasteful to the end? Or take a more radical supposition. Suppose, as Clarence Day does in *This Simian World*, that human nature had emerged, not from the Simians but from the felines, so that in the instinctive stratum of our being we were akin to the tigers rather than to the apes. In such a world our satisfactions and hence our desires, and hence again our stock of desirables, would be very different from what they are. What would become of all the values connected with human gregariousness, the values of love, friendship, and communal life? Would not St Francis be an absurd figure and Christian ethics a kind of lunacy? Would not the great hero probably be some tremendous human 'cat that walked by itself', a glorified, more ruthless and less sociable Captain Kidd?

Such reflections are no doubt chastening to those who confound the values of Main Street with the eternal verities. But if this line of thought is supposed, as it sometimes is, to conduct us to a wholesale scepticism about values, it must be pointed out that it is based on defective logic. It is true that nothing is good for us if we can take no

satisfaction in it. It must hence be admitted that even love and understanding would be without value for us it we found no satisfaction in
them. And it is easy to argue that since, when you add satisfaction
you have goodness and when you subtract it you do not, the goodness
lies in the satisfaction solely, and hence all that is good in human
goods could be generated or abolished by redirecting our satisfactions.

But the case is not so simple. Such an argument confuses a necessary
with the sufficient condition of goodness. You cannot argue validly
that because a certain factor is necessary to a certain result, it is
therefore the only contributor to that result. For instance, you cannot
argue that since giving water to a plant makes it grow, and with-
holding water makes it die, water is the whole secret of its life and
growth. By such logic you could equally prove that the whole secret
lay in air or light or soil, any of which conclusions would contradict the first. The truth is that these things are all equally necessary,
and taken alone, equally insufficient. Similarly, it is true that the boy
who, through some chance rebuff, takes no interest in music, will find
no good in it. But what exactly does that show? Does it show that the
whole good of the music, even as he experiences it, lies in the satisfaction he takes in it, so that the goodness depends solely on his
liking or disliking it? This clearly does not follow. All it does show
is that the boy's satisfaction in music is one condition of his finding
it good. Similarly with our case of instinct. If nature had turned out
even more 'red in tooth and claw' than she has shown herself to be
and had spawned a tiger with human craft and cunning, it might
have regarded St Francis with indifference or contempt except as a
somewhat unappetizing form of prey. But while we are endowing
our super-cat with so much cunning, we might as well give it enough
to see its own inconsequence in arguing from the lack of satisfaction
in the Franciscan life to the worthlessness of that life for those who do
find it satisfying. We saw long ago that the goodness of music or love
does not lie in an abstract quality, identical in both, which somehow
attach to them. Neither is it exhausted in the fact that someone finds
them satisfying. The goodness is a function of the satisfaction plus
something else.

8. (4) Thus, *what makes things desirable is not exhausted in the fact
that they are desired, or what makes them satisfactory in the fact that
they satisfy.* The very notion that the goodness lies in the satisfaction
or pleasure alone as distinct from the object, shows that one is trying

to introduce into a value experience a kind of distinctness of parts that is found only outside it. There is no trouble in distinguishing the water you give to the plant from the later growth to which it contributes. But can you distinguish in the same sharp way within an experience of music, for example, the enjoyment from what is enjoyed, so that you can locate the value of the whole in one part rather than the other? If A and B sit side by side listening to Beethoven, and A is utterly indifferent while B is deeply stirred, are we to say that B hears exactly what A heard, only with the addition of a stirring emotion? That is surely to put the case too mechanically. The music and the appreciation of it are so blended that B would probably say that A *could* not have heard what he did without being stirred. On the other hand, the notion that A or anyone else could know what B found good in the experience merely by knowing in the abstract that he was enjoying something and without any notion that *what* satisfied him was music, and indeed this particular music, would seem grotesque. What has value is neither the music nor the satisfaction as abstracted from each other, but the two in this particular union. Whoever experienced that union would be in possession of the value.

Hence when it is suggested that if we had been equipped with different instincts, we should have valued different things, and therefore that all goods are in the end biological accidents, that if man had been a super-tiger rather than a super-ape, Christian love would have been valueless or bad, we can see that confusion is at work. Such a being might be unable to experience this love; and if so, it would not know what was meant by it, and thus would not find it good. This is all true. But that something is not good because it is not found good by someone who does not know what it means is an extraordinary argument. The evidence does not show that if the creature did experience such love it would not find it good. Indeed if what we have just said is true, it would necessarily find this good. For love is not the sort of experience in which satisfaction and that which satisfies can be marked off and set over against each other. To love in the sense in question and to find satisfaction in the love are inseparable. The notion that some super-cat might have the one without the other and hence find the experience worthless is thus not strictly thinkable. It seems to be thinkable only because one stays outside the experience and thinks of it as the wrong kind of whole. To anyone who actually had it, its goodness would be undeniable.

We have said that our desires grow out of our satisfactions, and that our inventory of ideal goods is drawn up by our desires. We must qualify this later to make clear the sense in which the desirable exceeds the desired. Still, what we genuinely desire is a fairly reliable index to what we take as good. It has often been held that in our inventory of goods there is only one kind of article. What we desire, it has been argued, is satisfaction—not the experience of knowing or loving or doing, but the feeling of pleasure or satisfaction in it; and then the step is short to saying that since satisfaction is the only thing desired, it is the only thing that is good. To be sure, the inference is not a compelling one. It is conceivable that everyone should in fact desire pleasure and pleasure only, and also that there should be things other than pleasure which, if we came to know about them, we should desire and regard as good. But this mere theoretic possibility has not weighed greatly with moralists. The doctrine of psychological hedonism, that we desire only pleasure, seems always to have been accompanied by ethical hedonism, the doctrine that pleasure is the only good; that one is the real foundation of the other. To see that the first is false is to leave the other baseless. And psychological hedonism *is* false. It ought to have died once for all of the wounds inflicted on it by Butler. But it seems to be as irrepressible as the phoenix, and has cropped up again and again, to be successively scotched with elegance by Sidgwick, Rashdall, Broad, and many others. For anything I shall say of it here, it may go on with these reincarnations; the criticisms already offered seem to me decisive. We desire to eat food, and not merely to have the pleasure of eating; we desire to hear music, and play games, and understand, not merely to gain satisfaction out of objects and activities themselves indifferent. And if our goods reflect the content of our desires, we see again that those goods are not exhausted in pleasure or satisfaction. They consist of satisfying experiences as wholes.

9. (5) *Our major goods answer to the main types of impulse-desire.* One major drive has been much studied by philosophers, namely the impulse to know, and its career may serve as a suggestion of what we should probably find if we studied other drives in similar detail. Instinctive curiosity, which passes on at a higher level into the desire for understanding, is a distinguishable impulse with an end of its own. That end is not at all what the pragmatists have supposed; it is not an impulse to do something to things, for example to make them over into something more satisfying to our non-cognitive impulses; that is to confuse the impulse to know in fatal fashion with impulses of a different kind. Knowing is of course an activity, but its end is contemplation, not action. The desire to know is the desire to see things as they are. Now such seeing is and must be more than a mere registry of fact. What we want is not only to know, but to understand, that is, lay hold of the connections among facts that make them intelligible. Thought at its simplest is judgment, and in the most rudimentary judgment we are grasping a linkage between terms. That linkage as it stands may be unintelligible to us. 'That cat purrs'; with this we have entered the field of judgment. But from the first there is awaking within such judgment the spirit of inquiry; we have connected the purring with the cat; can we connect it more specifically with anything else about the cat? In short, why does the cat purr? With that question we have begun our career in science and philosophy. The intellectual quest from the lowest judgment to the most complicated theories of modern physics may be regarded as one persisting effort to answer the question, Why? To answer it calls for a continually widening knowledge and a continual re-ordering of that knowledge in the direction of consistency and interdependence of parts, for the end sought by the theoretic impulse is an intelligible whole. Every advance toward such understanding brings satisfaction. We repeat, however, that it is not satisfaction merely that the impulse is seeking, but that which will satisfy it, namely this particular kind of light. But neither is it light merely; for what is the point of a knowledge in which one takes no satisfaction? What is sought is something which, because of its special character, fulfils the aim of the cognitive impulse, and which because of this fulfilment, satisfies. This double service of fulfilling and of satisfying is what makes knowledge good. It is also what makes anything good.

How many of these conative drives of impulse-desire, with their varying ends, can be distinguished in human nature? The point is a controversial one which we shall make no attempt to settle. Even if our list were perfect as of the present date, nature would probably antiquate it by evolving others. And such a listing is the less necessary because in any case the ends are not wholly independent of each other. Take the well known principle that one should not multiply entities beyond need,—the principle of 'Occam's razor'. Is that an intellectual or an aesthetic requirement? It is both. Bertrand Russell has contended that the satisfaction derived from an 'elegant' mathematical proof is as much aesthetic as intellectual. And yet one can hardly deny that there is an aesthetic impulse with its own special end, distinct from the cognitive. Both impulses require for their satisfaction a certain structure in their objects, but that peculiar implication of parts that gives intelligibility is not necessarily the same as the harmony and proportion that satisfy the sense of beauty. Such harmony and proportion satisfy us in a way that logical system does not; because they do, we seek more of them; and, as present and satisfying, they constitute what we call beauty. Beauty is therefore a good. It is true, though somewhat dangerous, to say simply that beauty is good, for that may suggest that goodness is an attribute which beauty may assume or put off; whereas the truth is that beauty *is* goodness; it is a form of goodness, the way in which some things are good. Subject to further explanation, we may say that goodness is satisfactoriness, which consists jointly in the fulfilment of impulse-desire by the content it demands and the attendant satisfaction. *A* good is what *is* thus satisfactory. *The* good is what would be satisfactory in the end. The demand of the theoretic impulse is for understanding, the demand of the aesthetic impulse for what we have called, somewhat roughly, harmony and proportion; as the one is fulfilled, we gain the good called knowledge; as the other is fulfilled, the good called beauty. Both goods are good as being satisfactory. They are goods of different kind as being satisfactory to different trends of impulse-desire.

10. It is implied here that within each type of impulse-desire goodness is autonomous. The impulse to know, for example, is governed in its development by its own implicit standards, and it is for its own court to judge how far the impulse has won success. If knowledge is a good at all, then, other things equal, the more of it the better. But nothing standing outside it can say what is to pass as better within its own jurisdiction. That is for the logical sense to determine by its own special tests. Critics have often done violence to the forms of goodness by weighing them in alien balances. Dewey appraised the good of Platonism in terms of social consequences, whereas the good that Plato was aiming at was the vision of truth, and the value of any such vision must be fixed by the canons of truth. Tolstoy would have us judge a poem by its moral influence, Lenin by its utility in the class struggle. Both views are surely myopic. So far as art is under constraint from something outside the aesthetic ideal, it is not art at all, any more than the plea of an attorney retained to prove a case is to be called scientific inquiry. We return here to

Aristotle's view that goodness, like being, differs profoundly as one passes from category to category,[1] or as we should prefer to say, from form to form of impulse-desire; and there are probably none of us to whom the Aristotelian warning against mixing categories would not at times prove helpful. In the west, and particularly in the Puritan tradition, goodness has sometimes been conceived in exclusively moral terms, and the special goods of understanding and taste dismissed as inconsequential. It is an advantage of the view here offered that it would outlaw such parochialism. Goodness has many mansions. Hellenism, with its insistence on form, intellectual and aesthetic, offers a lease on some of these mansions which Hebraism has not cared to take up. It is a singular fact that in the religion of the west, though nature is conceived as the work and expression of Deity, the scientist who unravels that work and the artist who discloses its beauty are hardly considered to stand even in the forecourt of the temple, while the man who cultivates conscience as the *vox Dei* is supposed to inhabit the inner sanctum. Such partisanship among values suggests defective education. It is conceivable that if their education had been more catholic, some of the saints who have been obscurantists would have joined Erasmus in exclaiming 'Sanctus Socrates, ora pro nobis'.

11. (6) *In the realization of the good, that which is coming to be directs the process of its realization.* This sounds mysterious. It is in fact a matter of everyday experience. We may illustrate it again from the achievement of intellectual good, since that has a special interest for us. A man sets out to solve a problem of arithmetic, the problem, let us say, of how many yards of carpet, two and half feet wide, he needs to cover a square floor of a certain area. Is the process of solving this problem a hit-or-miss bungling through, in which, if the right answer at last appears, it comes by luck? Not if the mind is competent and the problem really engages it. In such a mind, the end in view appoints the path to the solution. Since the end in this case *is* clarity on an abstract problem of space and number, it will resist intrusions by the man's ailments or affairs of state; and since the area and width of strip are precisely known, the calculations are kept within the narrow lane leading to the length of the strips and their number. The man knows what he wants, and yet in a sense he does not know. The Greeks found in this a diverting dilemma, which seemed to show that the

[1] See above, p. 271

quest for knowledge was impossible. If a man knew what he was after in seeking the answer to a problem, then there was no problem to answer. If he did not know what he was after, he could not recognize it when he saw it. Hence in neither case did the search for knowledge make sense. The solution is to distinguish between a general and a special meaning of 'know what one is after'. In our example, the man clearly knows in general what he wants; he wants to know how many yards it will take to cover a certain area; but he does not know this definitely for that is the particular figure he is in search of. He knows, that is, the conditions that must be fulfilled, and this knowledge both governs the course of his seeking, and enables him to identify the answer when it comes.

Here is a case in which the process is controlled by a purpose that is as fully explicit and definite as a requirement can be while yet leaving something to be known. But in most teleological processes the end is much less explicit and definite. Take the process of writing a poem. It would be absurd to say that such creation was not a purposive process at all, but who knows, when the impulse comes and he begins to write, what exactly he is going to produce? He is rather like the sculptor who, when asked, as he chiselled away, what he was making, replied, 'That is as it may turn out'. This inability to specify the end does not imply that the process is purposeless or blindly mechanical, for the poet may go straight to his end in a way that astonishes himself, rejecting impertinent suitors for his notice with a curiously sure sense of what he is about. Plainly the process is governed by purpose, but by a purpose that only defines itself in the course of its realization.

This gives the type of those impulse-desires of which we have been speaking. The problem about the carpet was one of the countless little problems that theory undertakes to solve as an aid to practice. But theory is not tied to practice. It has a career of its own, as we have just been seeing. In that career, it does not proceed at random, and even advance by trial and error implies a standard by which error may be found out. Thought carries its compass and criterion within itself. It blunders and gropes; its self-guidance in the early stages is so feeble that it often goes quite off course; it is pushed about and browbeaten by other interests which are more blustering and insistent. But it is not to be put off entirely. Its movement from youth to maturity in the individual, from barbarism to science in the race, is the movement toward an end which, as we look backward, we can see to have been

implicit from the beginning and to have gained explicitness and definition with advance. That it is this sort of movement is an insight
that we owe perhaps to Hegel, and one in which he was surely right
against the exponents of a mechanical evolution. There is such a
thing as implicitly directed intellectual advance, in which the ideal of
reason, though imperfectly formed, works within the process to
extend knowledge and order it. What that ideal is we see only dimly.
In the great tradition of rationalism which runs from Plato down
through Spinoza to Hegel and Whitehead, it has presented itself as a
system in which nothing is merely an accident, but is connected
intelligibly with everything else by necessary relations. But, as is
almost pitifully obvious, no systems yet devised, even by these
masters themselves, have come within many leagues of the ideal; and
no sooner is a system achieved that seems to approximate it than the
ideal itself is revised, so that the quest of it must be reorganized.
Some of the most significant studies of recent philosophy have concentrated on these very points of what a satisfactory system would be,
and what necessity means; and because the ideal itself is in course of
such critical examination, it has seemed to some impatient observers
that philosophy has lost all sense of direction and is merely marking
time. I cannot accept this view. Such periods of self-examination are
what we should expect. The ideal of knowledge is projected from a
moving base, and after times of rapid advance, such as that which has
recently occurred in logic and mathematics, it is natural and indeed
necessary that the end toward which we are moving should be re-
examined in the light of the advance. Such scrutiny does not imply
scepticism. It implies, in fact, the reverse. Criticism *is* the application
of standards, which are present, if only implicitly, within the critical
process.

12. (7) Hence *the good or desirable always outruns the desired*. We
have said that, subject to a qualification, the inventory of our goods
could be drawn up from our desires. It will now be evident what this
qualification must be. We cannot, as Mill did in an unguarded
moment, simply equate the desired with the desirable. To be sure, it
is tempting to say roundly that a man either desires something or not,
that if he does desire it, it is for him a good, and if not, it is indifferent or bad. The desirable and the desired will then coincide.
But, as so often with neat dichotomies, this does not correspond to
the facts. Desire is not the sort of experience that either has a definite

object or does not exist at all. Much of life is a seeking for we know not what. Our reach continually exceeds our grasp. We cannot say that what we desire exhausts the desirable, because (a) there is so much we do not care about which we recognize we might very well care about, and (b) so much that we now find attractive whose attraction will inevitably fade as our desires grow beyond it.

(a) We may illustrate again from the good of knowledge. Everyone knows that in the last few decades physics has made remarkable advances and opened up great realms unknown before. Most people have at least heard of the new discoveries, if only through their daily paper. Can it be said that they have any desire to understand them? Not, certainly, a very effective one. In some cases it might lead them to borrow a book from the local library and try to puzzle it out; in a much larger number of cases it would not outlast a brief popular article, and no doubt in a good many it would flicker out before the end of that. Can these later persons be said to desire an understanding of such matters? It is not likely that if they were asked to list their desires, it would occur to them to include this in their list. On the other hand, if they were asked whether they regarded such understanding as a good thing, they would pretty certainly say yes. It is clear therefore that we cannot reduce the desirable to what we are conscious of desiring.

Yet that there is a connection with desire seems also plain. Everyone has known the delight of suddenly seeing through a difficulty and having some crooked thing made straight; the point of Archimedes' shout of 'Eureka' is not simply lost on us. We know that we have picked up a few pebbles only on the shore, and that a limitless sea stretches before us; we cannot surmise what a full exploration would reveal; but we know that, whatever it was, it would be continuous with what we now know; and since in our little knowledge, we find fulfilment and satisfaction, we are confident that in its extension we should find more. Without seeing in detail what full understanding would be like, we see the direction in which it lies. Do we desire advance in that direction? Yes and no. No, if that means, Do we desire a future good anticipated explicitly and definitely? Yes, if the question is the rather more complicated one whether the impulse to know is still alive in us, whether we continue to take satisfaction in its fulfilment, and whether we recognize that we should find further fulfilment good. In short, the desirable outruns the desired if that means what is explicitly desired at the moment. It is identical with the desired if that means what fully developed impulse-desire would find satisfactory.

Because this unformed desire does not know definitely what it wants, it usually shows itself in a negative form, the form of a persistent dissatisfaction with what one has actually achieved. 'Man never is, but always to be blest'. The point could be illustrated from every kind of human activity. There are achievements in sculpture and music which enthusiastic admirers have acclaimed as perfect; but it is safe to say that no such claim would be made for them by their creators. A student of the manuscript of Beethoven's *Fidelio* found that the composer had made nineteen revisions of a certain passage, one pasted on top of another, and that at the nineteenth he was trying the first again; it seems hardly likely that he would have claimed final perfection for any of them. The good man seeks to be just in his dealings with others, but it is notoriously the best men who feel most keenly the breadth of the interval between what they have done and what they might have done. In the artisan's adjustment of means to ends, in the use of speech, in social tact, in citizenship, perfection remains indefinitely far away, do what we will. Now the dissatisfactions that spring from this perpetual falling short are not those of the spoiled child, or the weakling who complains of his luck; they are the growing pains of human nature. They have been called, and perhaps with justice, 'divine discontent', because there is at work in them a demand that exceeds any imaginable limit, a demand that becomes, indeed, more imperative as advance proceeds. In this illimitable demand lies the reason why the desirable so far outruns the desired.

13. (b) Just as the existence of this over-desire shows that there are goods or desirables that we do not now desire explicitly, so it makes it all but certain that some of the things we do desire will in time seem *un*desirable to us. No actual good is absolute, if that means one in which we should be contented to rest permanently. One may see this by looking at the continual transformation that goes on as the various trends of impulse-desire work themselves out. Take again the cognitive impulse with its germane goods. At fifteen we believe many things that at fifty we believe improbable or untrue. We found some genuine light in them, and satisfaction; they were therefore, to that extent, satisfactory or good. They were probably never refuted, for that is not the way, as a rule, in which intellectual advance takes place.

Professor G. E. Moore, in a sketch of his life that one wishes were longer, has described how, as a boy, he held a set of ultra-evangelical religious beliefs which seemed immensely important to him, and how, driven by a sense of duty, he distributed tracts along the promenade at a seaside resort in order to promote these beliefs. It is an arresting picture for those who knew only the Moore of later years. These vivid beliefs seem to have disappeared rapidly, not in the way in which tenpins disappear, by successive sharp eliminations, but in the way snowballs disappear in the sun. What seems to happen in such cases is that one acquires a mass of new knowledge which renders the old beliefs increasingly unplausible, and that the implications of the new knowledge, perhaps without any explicit reflection, insinuate themselves throughout the structure of the older beliefs like the progeny of the deathwatch beetle. Then one wakes up one morning to find that the riddled structure has quietly collapsed. There is no use in trying to patch the fragments together again; the structure can never be what it was. It is better to build anew. Except time itself, there is nothing as little resistible as the immanent logic of advancing knowledge.

So everywhere else. The desired becomes the undesired and then is stowed quietly away in the cellar of the undesirable. The small boy thinks wistfully of the cowboy life, with its feats in the saddle and its roaming of the plains. To the banker or business man that he becomes, these particular things are perhaps still mildly inviting, but if their price is the cowboy life as a whole, they would seem unendurable. Or consider the growth of taste. It has been said that no true poet admires Macaulay's *Lays*. I hope that is wrong. It must be admitted, however, that the *Lays* are the sort of verse that, bright with excitement for us at first, and pleasantly enough returned to at moments later on, do make a somewhat feeble show when their vivid little candles are surrounded by the illumination of great poetry. Again, the code of morals that appeals to the man or the race in adolescence, with its exaltation of the fighting spirit, is felt after a time to be hardly compatible with the greater goods of order and peaceful growth. And so on throughout. In feeling as well as in practice, as one becomes a man, one puts away childish things.

14. It will now be clear what are the virtue and weakness of those theories which, following Hobbes, would equate the good with what is in fact favoured, liked, or desired. Their virtue lies in the major insight that good is somehow connected with satisfaction. This insight is enough to eliminate the 'eternal goods' of Nicolai Hartmann and Dean Inge, existing in sublime indifference whether they will ever be wanted or not. On the other hand, there are two conspicuous weaknesses in these theories. First, they fail to take due account of the elastic and expansive character of desire, because they fail to connect it with the fundamental teleology of mind. Mind just *is*, in the view here taken, a set of activities directed to ends. It is these ends alone that are, or would be, good without qualification, for only they are fully satisfactory; that is, in them alone would the activities that constitute mind gain fulfilment and satisfaction. But at any given stage of our advance, these ends are indefinitely far ahead. Hence to take the objects in which our desires, cognitive, moral, or aesthetic, find satisfaction at the moment, and call them good without qualification, is to freeze into immobility what in its very nature is in motion and self-creative. It is true that what satisfies is so far, good. But if present satisfaction is looked at in the light of the history and prospects of mind, it is equally true to say that what satisfies is never good. There is no real paradox here. There is only the requirement that we see things in perspective, that we view the career of mind as the long pilgrimage that it actually is, in which the values of a given time offer us, not a continuing stay, but rather a halting-place for the night. Once we see this plainly, we cannot go on saying without qualification that whatever is liked or desired is thereby good.

The second error is to infer that because the good must satisfy, its goodness varies with satisfaction or pleasure alone. This is untrue because goodness depends also on fulfilment, and fulfilment is not the same as satisfaction. Fulfilment is achieving the end that our impulse is seeking; satisfaction is the feeling that attends this fulfilment. We see the difference clearly in Spinoza's account of the *conatus* toward 'adequate ideas'. What the *conatus* seeks is a comprehensive view of things, so ordered internally as to satisfy the logical sense. This comprehension or understanding is that which, when it comes, will fulfil the impulse or desire, but this fulfilment is not the same as the satisfaction felt in its coming.[1] If the goodness of knowledge is to be attained, both must be present, since it is a function of the two jointly. The error of the satisfaction theories is to suppose it to be the function of feeling alone. If it were, the only way in which

[1] *Ethics*, V. Prop. 27

good could be increased would be to alter the factor of feeling. That it can be thus increased we may agree. An insight achieved with delight is more worth having than the same insight without it. But good can also be augmented by enlarging the insight itself, even though the satisfaction remains the same. To solve the problem of free will would be far more worth achieving than to know the name of one's neighbour down the street, even though, at the moment, one had no more interest in one than in the other, and would get equal satisfaction from them. It would be more worth achieving because it would provide a more complete fulfilment of the desire to understand one's world. It is entirely possible that the ecstasy felt by some primitive beater of a tom-tom is a more intense satisfaction than that of an accomplished musician playing a masterpiece. But it is hard to see why for that reason we should have to call it better. In spite of the high authority of Sidgwick, we cannot reduce the good of an experience to the pleasure it gives us, nor can we even take this, with McTaggart, as an accurate index of the good. It is one of two variables in whose presence the good lies jointly, and which may vary independently of each other.

15. It is an argument of weight for this view that it clears up in straightforward manner the old difficulty of the hedonists about the quality and quantity of pleasure. Bentham, Mill and Sidgwick all maintained that what made an experience good and measured the amount of its goodness was the pleasure it contained. But when Mill worked out the implications of this view, he found it leading on to an absurdity from which any sensible person must recoil. It is entirely possible that if you took equal intervals in the life of Socrates and that of a moron, indeed even that of a pig, the amount of pleasure felt by the moron or the pig would be greater than that of Socrates. If pleasure were the sole component in goodness, their lives for that period should therefore be better than that of the Socratic life. Mill agreed with his critics that this was absurd. He therefore introduced a second component which he called *quality* of pleasure, and held that the higher quality of Socrates' pleasure outweighed the greater quantity of the porcine pleasure. Most later moralists have recognized that this would not do. A man is not really making pleasure the sole criterion of good if he admits that, of two experiences, the second may be more pleasant and yet less good. Mill thus ended in self-contradiction.

On the theory here proposed, the difficulty is dealt with as follows: the feeling of satisfaction or pleasure taken in an experience *is* a condition of its goodness; in this the insight of the hedonists was sound. But it is one condition only, and there is another. This other is the fulfilment of impulse-desire. Socrates' life was better than that of the pig or the moron because it involved a fulfilment of impulse-desire, a development and flowering of powers, beyond the reach of commonplace minds, and of course still further beyond the reach of the animal mind. Comparison in this respect is possible because the three levels of life are not simply discontinuous; the desires for knowledge and companionship, for example, that were fulfilled so remarkably in the life of Socrates are sturdily at work in the plainest citizen and are at least stirring in the form of impulse well down in the animal scale. It is therefore entirely intelligible to say that Socrates' life was the best, whether it was the most pleasant or not. The place taken in Mill's theory by quality of pleasure, is taken in ours by fulfilment of impulse-desire. This can no longer be confused with pleasure, since it is recognized as a different dimension; and while higher and lower rank among the qualities of pleasure has proved a most obscure notion, degrees of fulfilment of the same impulse-desire is a straightforward and indeed inevitable notion. An old puzzle of ethical theory thus receives a clear solution.

16. (8) *The good, in the sense of the ethical end, is the most comprehensive possible fulfilment and satisfaction of impulse-desire.* By a comprehensive fulfilment I mean one that takes account not only of this or that desire, but of our desires generally, and not only of this or that man's desires, but of all men's. That there is and must be such a good, supreme over all others, we can see by considering how conflicts are resolved. Two distinct and important trends of impulse-desire have been repeatedly mentioned, the cognitive and the aesthetic, each with its special type of good, measured by its own immanent standard. Suppose these two conflict. Suppose that a youth has interests and talents for philosophy on the one hand, and music on the other, and feels drawn in both directions, but that one or the other must be sacrificed, if proficiency is to be reached in either. In any concrete case he would no doubt need to take into account the importance of these two activities to his community, but by way of taking one difficulty at a time, let us exclude these considerations. The youth must then decide the conflict by considering his good as a whole. He will have to ask himself the question, How may I, as a person who can gain some measure of fulfilment through each of these channels, gain most of this on the whole—by making myself a philosopher, by making myself a musician, or by making myself some sort of hybrid between them? And if he is really free in the matter, the obvious way to settle it is to take stock of his interests and powers. If he has a very strong interest and bent for speculative analysis, and a feeble enjoyment and skill in music, then, as between these two, the choice will be easy; his good will be in philosophy, since he would find a completer fulfilment there. If the reverse holds, the choice will similarly go to music. But the case in fact may well be harder; he may discover an approximately equal bent for each. Then, if he must drop one or the other, he will consider which of the two would carry with it the larger range of subsidiary satisfactions. The two walks of life will involve different incomes, associates, surroundings, holidays, hours of work and freedom; the one activity may stimulate and support more fruitfully than the other all sorts of minor interests, scientific, political, and literary. In practice he will probably select one or the other as his principal business and try to keep the other alive in a secondary role.

If all this is very obvious—and I must admit that it seems so to me —it none the less shows how naturally our theory of the good explains what is involved in such major choices. I cannot think that other theories do so with equal naturalness. There are moralists who would say that philosophy as such is better or higher than music, whereas neither of them in the abstract has any value at all; where they do have value, it is only as an activity in somebody's mind. Hence, if one is to compare them, one must compare certain amounts of each, realized in individual lives and in particular circumstances. One may gain a far greater fulfilment and happiness through being a good farmer than through being a bad philosopher; indeed William James complained that our graduate schools were full of the bald-headed and the bald-hearted, who were the ruins of excellent farmers. Again, the emotivists would say that the decision about relative good was not a judgment at all, which is very much harder to believe than that it is a judgment, concerned with comparative fulfilments of capacity and desire. Professor Perry would say that the goodness resolves itself into the fact of awaking interest, and the hedonists that it resolves itself into the fact of being pleasant, whereas we hold that the content is as indispensable to the goodness as the interest or the pleasure. Dr Ewing holds that if in a given case the philosopher's experience is better than the musical, that means that it is more fitting to favour it. I agree that this is more fitting, but think it possible to go further and say why it is more fitting. Many moralists of weight, such as Rashdall, Moore, and Ross, would say that the goodness of either type of experience is a simple, unanalysable quality or attribute. I do not consider it un-analysable. There is always, I think, some content that fulfils impulse-desire, and a feeling of satisfaction attendant on this fulfilment. Goodness is neither the fulfilment apart from the satisfaction nor the satisfaction apart from the fulfilment; it is the two in union. If a synonym is wanted, perhaps the best is satisfactoriness.

17. Though this account of the good lays stress on desire, it is not so much on *de facto* desire, the want or wish of the moment, as on reflective desire, the desire that emerges after correction by thought and experience. The good is what brings fulfilment and its attendant pleasure to desire of this self-amending kind. These desires arise because we are the sort of beings we are, and wisdom lies in making them more accurately and fully expressive of human nature; 'our aims', said Emerson, 'should be mathematically adjusted to our powers.' There is nothing novel in such an account of the good; indeed it is as old as the Greeks. We shall not try to show this by chapter and verse. It will perhaps be enough to quote a passage in which A. E. Taylor sets out the drift of the ethical thought of Plato and Aristotle. In philosophy there are no authorities, but at least there is some comfort in having such august names on one's side. Taylor notes that

'εὐδαιμονία, for both of them, is not primarily getting something which I desire; it is living the kind of life which I have been constructed to live, doing the "work of man", and if we want to know what life rather than any other should be pronounced εὐδαίμων, we have to begin by asking what is the "work" which man, and only man, in virtue of his very constitution, can do. It is true, no doubt, that Plato holds that all of us also do desire εὐδαιμονία, if only most of us were not as unaware as we are of the real nature of our most deep-seated desires. But the very reason why we all have this insuperable *desiderium naturale* for a certain kind of life is that it is the life we have been constructed by God or by Nature to lead. We are unhappy, without clearly knowing why, so long as we are living any other kind of life, for the same reasons that a fish is unhappy out of water. The true way to discover what it is that we really want out of life is to know what kind of life we have been sent into the world to lead. We do not lead that life as a "means" to the "enjoyable results" of doing so, any more than the fish lives in the water, or the bird in the air as a means to the pleasure of such a life; we enjoy the pleasure (as the tenth book of the *Nicomachean Ethics* explains) because we are living the kind of life for which we were made.'[1]

[1] *Mind*, Vol. 48 (1939) 280

CHAPTER XII

'GOOD', 'RIGHT', 'OUGHT', 'BAD'

1. The attempt of analysts to find a meaning for 'good' which should be at once recognizable as its major meaning and also precise has led to such a variety of conflicting definitions that we were moved in the last chapter to try another approach. We would study how values arose in human experience and how they are connected with impulse and desire. Such a study might reveal features in goodness which were likely to elude direct analysis, but which analysis might confirm when once suggested. Has anything of the sort come to light?

It has. As was gradually disclosed in this study, 'good' is not the name of a simple abstraction, but is, on the contrary, a term with a complex meaning that has long roots in human nature and its history. It is a term like 'life' and 'mind', which are clear enough for practical purposes without examination, but whose definition, once it is attempted, takes us far. 'Good' has the meaning it does because we are the sort of beings we are. Human nature *is* essentially a set of activities directed toward ends, and human life is a striving toward these ends. As this striving, beginning in impulse, passes on into desire, it comes to have some awareness of its ends, but it never knows them wholly. Good is relative to this process of seeking. Only that would be good altogether which wholly satisfied by wholly fulfilling this end-seeking process. Anything else is good in the degree in which it thus fulfils and satisfies.

Before asking where this carries us by way of implications, let us see where it places us among the theories of the day. It requires us to take a middle course in controversies about the objectivity of goodness and its naturalness. As regards objectivity, it would agree with the emotivists that goodness does not belong to things in complete independence of attitudes and feelings about them; a thing is good because, and in so far as, it fulfils and satisfies. On the other hand, whether it does or would fulfil and satisfy is an objective fact about

it, and the stress we have laid on fulfilment makes this a fundamentally different fact from that of merely being liked. As regards
naturalism the theory again steers a middle course. The non-natural
quality of goodness, even fittingness as a non-natural character, both
of which have proved so hard for naturalists to detect, are no longer
required. Whether an object does in fact fulfil and satisfy is something that can be determined without going outside nature as we
conceive it. But then on the other hand we do not conceive human
nature as naturalists commonly do. It is so thoroughly teleological
that it cannot be understood apart from what it is seeking to become.
What is good, then, in the sense of what would wholly fulfil and
satisfy, is not to be determined by an empirical study of what men
actually like, desire, or approve. That is evidence, to be sure; whatever does in fact fulfil and satisfy is good so far; but human desires,
and therefore human good, run immeasurably beyond this. No such
good is ever final.

2. Neither the analytic nor the genetic path to goodness is sufficient
by itself. Any account of it that is to be acceptable, must be one
upon which the two paths converge. The ascetic, reflecting fastidi-
ously on the quality of his yearnings, may conclude that the good life
lies in the repression of all 'animal impulse', but human nature will
correct his theory by expunging him and his kind. He might say
that extinction is not refutation, which is true enough. But most men
would think, and rightly I suspect, that if a course of life is such as to
invite extinction, there must be something wrong with the intuition
that sponsors it. A proposal regarding the good which elicits a veto
from human nature is doomed. On the other hand, goods recommended as 'natural' are themselves many and conflicting. The
suggestion has been made, for example, that the ethical struggle is
simply a continuation of the biological struggle, and that whoever
is victor in that struggle, however 'red in tooth and claw', is best. It is
to the credit of Huxley that when called upon to endorse the suggestion, he replied that men's ordinary sense of what 'good' meant put
it out of court. Claimants to the role of natural must submit themselves, like others, to the judgment of this inner tribunal. Will our
own theory of goodness pass its scrutiny?

The only way to tell is to bring cases before it and see. Take any
case you will of experience regarded as intrinsically good, and ask
yourself whether its goodness does not turn on two facts about it—

first that it brings satisfaction in the form of some degree of pleasure, and second that it fulfils a want. Try it with any experience of love, of friendship, of intellectual insight, of sex, of beauty, of victory in contest, of success in skill or creation. Our suggestion is that both these characters, and only these, will be invariably there.

The most obvious objections to such an account are perhaps (1) that experience may be good when pleasure is absent, (2) that it may again be good when fulfilment is absent, and (3) that even when both are present, this does not give us what we *mean* by 'good'.

3. (1) We often call experiences valuable when they are not obviously pleasant. The bearing of suffering, a hard football game, the dangerous ascent of a mountain, the throes of examination, the vigil of the doctor with a patient critically ill, the personal or material loss that leaves one stronger, the mere cold bath of a cold morning—are not these good? But how could anyone call them pleasant?

It is true that all of these may plainly be goods, in the sense of instrumental goods. And no one who is not ready to take foul weather with fair in trying to reach ulterior ends is likely to reach them at all. But it is one thing to face pain and suffering hardily in the interest of such an end, and quite another thing to welcome them as goods in themselves. As for the experiences just mentioned: the examination and the doctor's vigil are cases of strain accepted as unavoidable means to a much desired result. The football game, the ascent of the mountain, and the cold bath are certainly not cases of unmixed pain; there are disagreeable elements in them, but also exhilaration, without which (or the consequences) the experiences would surely not be sought. As for the others, suffering and the shock of loss are not goods in themselves, however useful they may be in steeling one against the future. When people deliberately inflict pain on themselves, they generally do it as a means to an end perhaps imperfectly realized, such as the approval of a Deity or their own or others' admiration; to seek suffering for its own sake would be thought the sign of a morbid and disordered mind.

It may be said that experience may be good when, though not positively painful, its affective quality is merely neutral. But this is questionable. We saw long ago in considering the Stoics and Mill that with the loss of power to take satisfaction in the exercise of a faculty there goes also the sense that the exercise is worth maintaining. The total loss of this power is, to be sure, a rare affliction. Normally there is a mild satisfaction attending even the most prosaic activities of common life; and few people, however unhappy they call themselves, would prefer to be dead than alive. But if satisfaction does vanish completely from these activities, an apathy supervenes that, far from being the greatest of goods, as the Stoics hoped, is merely grey and insipid. 'All values are vain, unless we can feel, as well as see, their value. Knowledge without feeling is like an electric motor without current.'[1]

4. (2) Are there not valued experiences that, conversely, are pleasant without fulfilling any sort of want? Someone tells me a funny story, and I laugh; but I was not hungering for his funny story. Mozart hears the church bells at three, and takes an instant delight in them, but he could hardly have wanted them before first hearing them. I turn a corner on a mountain drive, and am confronted with a glorious sunset; but it is something I neither expected nor desired.

The objection is sound if it means that experiences found good are not always the object of preceding desires. Definite desire must draw its material from satisfied impulse, and impulse is at first exploratory and without definite guidance. But we are not straining language when we say that a want or need may exist without being in active and conscious exercise. Mozart may have a disposition to notice and respond to musical sounds before he hears them, and if he hears them with exceptional delight, we take that as evidence of the disposition. If he had been deaf, or tone-deaf, or as indisposed to respond to such things as the cow in the neighbouring field, he would have felt no interest in the bells and found no value in listening to them. It was because he did have a faculty and disposition, even though previously unawakened, that he responded as he did. So of our response to the humorous story and to the sunset at the turn of the road. If we lacked a sense of humour or a sense of beauty, such things would fall on deaf ears and blind eyes. These senses need not be in perpetual exercise. But unless they were there, the funniest of stories and the most gorgeous of sunsets would elicit nothing from us.

It may be said that at this rate every response will be the sign of a capacity and a disposition, and hence that no response will give more indication of their presence than another. But this latter conclusion does not follow. The sense of humour or of beauty is a matter of degree, so that one person's response to a given stimulus will be much

[1] F. L. Lucas, *Literature and Psychology*, 261

more complete than another's. If our theory is true, we should expect that the person who could respond more completely would find more value in his response than a person of feeble sensibility. This, so far as we can tell, is just what happens.[1]

5. (3) It may be objected, again, that satisfaction and fulfilment may both be present in an experience and yet not give what we *mean* by calling it good. The proof is (a) that if this is really what we mean, then, regarding anything that we do not believe to possess these characters, we should be contradicting ourselves in calling it good, whereas in fact we should not; and (b) that, regarding an experience which we do know to be satisfactory and fulfilling, we can still ask with meaning whether it is good, whereas this would be impossible if having these characters was all we meant by good.

(a) The word 'good' has many meanings; Dr Ewing has usefully distinguished ten of them.[2] And if a person says that there is nothing self-contradictory in calling the suffering of a serious illness a good thing, he may of course be right; such suffering may be far from fulfilling or satisfying, and may still be *instrumentally* good; to say this is no contradiction. But that does not show that our definition is wrong. All it shows is that there are other senses of the word. The goodness we are talking about is that which belongs to an experience thought worth having in itself. And if we are clear regarding such an experience as suffering that it neither fulfils any impulse or demand of our nature nor carries with it any feeling of satisfaction, *could* we consistently ascribe to it this kind of goodness? I do not think we could. In calling it so we *should* be contradicting our own belief. Of course we may use the word without realizing quite what we mean by it, so that when someone proposes this meaning, our first impulse is to reject it. But if when he goes on to ask whether we should really apply the word where these characters are seen to be absent, we have to say No; we could not, consistently with our meaning, say anything else. This objection to our definition turns into evidence in its favour.

(b) Our analysis of goodness would probably be called a naturalistic analysis. As such, is it not open to the famous objection by which G. E. Moore dismissed all naturalistic notions of goodness? Take any such definition you will, said Moore—length and breadth of life, being pleasant, being the object of desire, being what we desire to desire, or any other; could you not meaningfully ask regarding something known to have these qualities whether it is good? If the question is meaningful at all, your definition must be wrong. For if having the property in question is what 'good' *means*, and you know the object to have it, then you know the answer already, and to ask what it is would be pointless. If 'good' means pleasant, for example, you could not honestly ask if pleasure was good, for that would be asking whether pleasure is pleasant, which nobody in his senses would ask. The fact that we *can* meaningfully ask whether pleasure is good shows that 'good' cannot *mean* merely pleasant. Similarly the fact that we can meaningfully ask whether that which fulfils and satisfies is good shows that 'good' does not *mean* having of these properties. That is the objection.

Now I think Moore's argument does dispose of most naturalistic definitions of 'good'. But, as Mr Frankena has shown,[1] to say before examination that it disposes of all of them is to beg the question. The only way to tell whether a proposed definition will fit your meaning is to try it. And we are quite ready to face this test. Take any experience you wish that at once fulfils a drive of human nature and brings pleasure or happiness with it, ask about this experience whether it is intrinsically worth having, and we suggest that you have the answer already. The experiences you would naturally think of as meeting the requirements—the experiences of beauty, friendship, sex, play, creation, knowledge—are those about which it is least possible to have any genuine question as to their goodness. If these things are not good, what in the world is?

A reader may protest, however, that he does genuinely doubt whether they are good. This may show indeed that we have failed to catch the true meaning of the term as he uses it. But it may equally show something else. It may show simply that his meaning is so indefinite that any crystallization of it into words would strike him as failing to equate with what he had in mind. If this is the case, his rejection of our proposed meaning has no significance, for he would reject any other definite suggestion with equal promptitude. A definition of good is not to be dismissed merely because it fails to comport with a mental cloud. One may argue, to be sure, that good is indefinable not, as Moore believed, because it is simple and unanalysable, but because it is so amorphous and complex. The term may be used to focus upon an object a composite but nebulous mass of

[1] W. K. Frankena, 'The Naturalistic Fallacy', *Mind*, Vol. 48 (1939), 473

impulses, affects, emotions, and ideas of which no possible verbal formula would be admitted to give the equivalent. Press such reflections home, and one will soon be saying that no two people ever use the word with the same meaning, nor the same person twice. In a sense that is true. But unless we could go beyond this anarchy to some community of meaning, the business of dictionaries, of science, and indeed of ordinary intercourse would be at an end. No definition of 'good' will fit exactly the shifting wracks of meaning that float through our minds as we use it. All we claim for what we have proposed is that it gives the minimal common character that we assign to an experience in calling it worth while.

6. Without stopping to discuss the many less obvious difficulties, let us go on to ask what our theory commits us to regarding some other ethical terms. Granting for the moment, that an experience is good which satisfies and fulfils, what light does this throw on the meaning of 'right'? Our answer can be predicted readily enough. We have argued that there is no means for determining the right apart from the good. If one is to defend an action as right, one must do so by showing what it entails; and for us this means showing that it tends to bring into being as much good as any alternative. In the light of what we have seen about good, this means in turn that an action is right if, and only if, it tends to bring into being as much experience that is at once satisfying and fulfilling as any alternative action.

This somewhat awkward way of putting the case is required by certain facts of a technical kind. (a) Why not simply say that the right act is that which produces the *most* good? Because it is possible that the largest good should be attainable in several different ways. In that case to speak of *the* right act would be misleading, for any one of several acts would be right. We must therefore say that an act is right if it tends to produce *not less than* the greatest good attainable.

(b) But why 'tends' to produce? Why not say simply 'produces'? Because in some cases this would have consequences that no one would care to accept. A child becomes suddenly ill and the anxious mother goes to the medicine closet for a remedy she has found effective in such cases. But a pharmacist has confused the labels, and she inadvertently gives the child a medicine that causes its death. Should we appraise the rightness or wrongness of her action here by its actual consequences? That is certainly not what we actually do.

L

We appraise actions as right and wrong, not in virtue of their actual consequences, but in virtue of the consequences which we conceive that actions done in these circumstances and with this intention would normally produce. Hence the awkward phrase 'tends to produce'.

(c) Again, we have said, 'an action *is right if, and only if*, it tends', etc.; why not say 'rightness *means*' so-and-so? Because there has been a protracted and somewhat unprofitable controversy over whether productivity of good is what rightness actually means or whether it is merely a 'right-making characteristic'; and I should prefer at the moment not to get involved in the controversy. If a dogmatic answer to the question were called for, I should say that such productivity is not the meaning of right in the sense that it is the plain man's explicit meaning; but then I suspect that he has no sharply definite meaning in mind at all, and that this sense comports as well as any other with what he means.

Finally (d) we have spoken of our actions *bringing into being* certain goods or experiences; why not simply *producing* good consequences? There is generally no harm in saying this; but it has a danger that is perhaps worth averting. Not all the goods by which we appraise an action are necessarily results that follow it in time. Some of them may be states of mind, or relations between these, which are brought into being by the action but are simultaneous with it. The state of mind in which an act of justice, generosity, or loyalty to truth is done may itself be of value.

7. A right act, then, is one that tends to bring into being at least as much in the way of satisfying and fulfilling experience as would any available alternative. But experience for whom? For me, or you, or some third party? We can only answer that from the point of view of value, this query is irrelevant. We are often called upon, of course, to choose between producing goods for ourselves and goods for others, but the choice is in principle the same as in choosing between goods of our own. If what makes anything good is the fulfilment and satisfaction of impulse-desire, and a given experience of my neighbour's performs this office as well as one of my own, it is as good as my own, and in the reckoning of rights and duties must count as equal to it. Goodness is no respecter of persons, only of the potentialities of persons. If my neighbour's capacities are such as to carry him further than mine toward a rich and satisfying life, his life is more significant, more important, than mine. If the village fathers in Stratford had known what they had in a certain boy named William, outwardly very much like the Thomas, Richard, and Henry that sat on the benches beside him, and, knowing what they had, had been as ready to make of him a road-cleaner or a chimney-sweep as any of the others, they would have been acting neither in his interests, nor their own, nor the community's. Each of us is a quiverful of assorted arrows of desire. In general design these arrows are alike in all of us; we all undoubtedly have desires to know and love, to make things, to dominate, to be admired. But in some of us certain arrows are very long and others very short; in others these lengths are reversed; and the chances are that in no two of us is the combination of longs and shorts exactly the same. But such as they are, we always shoot them at infinity. Each man blunders along after the good that his powers make possible for him, not knowing quite what these are, or how far they will carry him. Nevertheless, it is his potentiality of good that is the ground of his rights. We owe him duties because he has wants that our action may frustrate or fulfil. We do not feel called upon to provide educational facilities for our cows and horses, because they could get no good from them if we did. But if, when we are providing such things, we ignore deliberately the possibilities of any youth, however obscure, we are plainly failing in our duty. We may not be able to provide for all; we may have to leave some out entirely; there are no rights independent of circumstances. But we must at least *consider* the claims of all. I am not clear what is meant by the sacredness of human life as such, and should think the maintenance of hopeless imbeciles at the expense of normal persons a dubious practice morally. But there can be no doubt of the immorality of allowing people to come into existence and then denying the facts of their possibility and desire, and the right to consideration based on these facts. The dignity of man rests as much on what he might be as on what he is.

There may be readers disposed to complain that we have talked too much of non-moral goods, to the neglect of specifically ethical ones. But all goods are ethical goods. Any value or disvalue which, by being thrown into the scale, could affect a decision on right or wrong is of ethical moment. The good whose production makes an act right may be of any kind. The question whether to award a scholarship to X or Y is a moral problem, even though the capacities considered are intellectual only. The question whether, in one's will, one should leave money toward an art gallery, a college, or a playing field, is as truly a moral problem as the question whether one should tell a lie or break a promise. A question becomes a moral question at the moment when competing values, of any kind whatever, enter upon the scene.

8. To this account of the rightness of actions, and to all accounts that derive the right from the good, there is a formidable objection, which may as well be faced now. The rule we have proposed is the simple and sweeping one: So act as to bring about the greatest good. This rule, if valid at all, should be valid without exceptions, for if here and there it guided us wrongly, how could we rely on it anywhere? Now the deontologists hold that it does have exceptions.[1] They hold that the rule of the greatest good sometimes requires of us actions that would by general agreement be wrong. The two types of case most commonly adduced are those of promises and punishment.

Suppose I have borrowed some money from A, who is a man of means, and promised to return it on the first of the month. On that day, with the money in my pocket, I start out for A's house to repay him. I meet on the way a friend B, who is badly in need of help. I have the money in my pocket that would give him the help he needs. Should I give it to him? I call to mind my principle of producing the greatest good. Is it not probable that a greater good would be produced by my giving the money to the man in need than to my creditor who would not miss it? And yet is it not perfectly clear that men generally would have no patience with me if in this case I were to act on that principle? They would say that if I promised to pay, my first obligation was to keep my promise, not to give the money away, even to someone who would get more good out of it than my creditor. My obligation is not to produce the greatest good but to honour my engagement.

Now of course we agree with the deontologists that in such a case one ought normally to keep the promise. We agree further that if an ethical theory is to be taken seriously, it must agree with ordinary responsible judgment about what is right and wrong, since what it is looking for is the ground on which that judgment is implicitly based. Where we cannot agree is in saying that keeping the promise in such cases would break the rule of the greatest good. We admit that it

[1] For a statement and initial criticism of the deontologists' view, see Chapter VI above.

seems to do so. But we should hold that even in cases like this the reason for keeping the promise is the greater good involved in it.

Let us note, to begin with, that the deontologists themselves do not hold that one should keep one's promise though the heavens fall. If one's child has fallen suddenly ill, and can be saved only by an expensive prescription, and for this prescription the only available money is what was meant for one's creditor, they would agree that one should break one's promise and save one's child. Why? Because the good achieved by this course would outweigh the obligation to keep the promise. Yet the curious thing is that what is outweighed by this good is declared itself not to be a good at all; the obligation to keep my promise is not based on any good whatever that is entailed by such action. In throwing the prospective courses into the scales, I have on one side a foreseen good, on the other the keeping of a promise in which there is declared to be no good, but which is obligatory none the less. There is something strange about such a situation. Must there not be some good about keeping the promise that can be compared with and in extreme cases outweighed by, the good of not keeping it?

9. Now for keeping an inconvenient promise there are many reasons which we do not commonly think of in the act of keeping it, but which come to light with a moment's thought. Most of them take the form of the evils we should bring about by not keeping it. In this case we should forfeit the confidence of our creditor; we should not only disappoint him, but leave ourselves deeper in difficulty; we should encourage in ourselves an insidious habit which makes the meeting of obligations harder; above all, perhaps, we should lower in some measure the general confidence in promises—a serious matter, since the commerce of men with each other would grind to a stop if such confidence were destroyed. We all know these arguments. And yet they leave us dissatisfied. It does not seem difficult to meet them one by one by inventing special cases in which the breaking of a promise would involve none of these evils, while we should insist nevertheless on its being kept. Suppose the debt were a secret one; then public confidence would not be lowered by our default. Suppose we knew that our creditor had quite forgotten both loan and promise; then he would not be disappointed. Suppose we broke the promise after explicit calculation of the goods involved on both sides; then we need not worry about bad habits, for any habit we have initiated is a good one. These arguments all seem relevant. Yet they leave us cold. We watch the evils involved in promise-breaking disappearing one by one from before our eyes, and if the greatest good theory is right, we ought to find ourselves ready at the end to acclaim the promise-breaker and go ourselves and do likewise. But the fact is that we do not. We feel that there is something sophistical about this whole line of argument, and that in spite of all the evidence it adduces that we could break the promise with no ill results, we ought to keep it just the same.

10. Why is this? It is because we feel that in the rule of promise-keeping as such there is something of value that would be compromised by light-hearted violations of it, and that it is somehow illegitimate to consider the advantages and disadvantages in the particular case apart from the practice of which it is an instance. A long succession of moralists have obviously been moved by this conviction. Plato held that we cannot pass upon the rightness of a particular act without taking into account the frame of life to which it belongs. Kant went so far as to hold that in considering whether to break a promise, the principle was all-important; to break a promise—any promise—was to subscribe to the view that promises could be broken at will, which was virtually to deny that there were such things at all. Joseph argues that in keeping a promise there is a good which deontologists fail to recognize, a good that lies in acting in accordance with the rule, and ultimately in the 'pattern of life' to which the rule itself belongs. These moralists are clinging tenaciously to an element in common thought that is clearly present and important. But the question is whether one can do justice to the importance of rules while still adhering to the principle of the greatest good.

I think one can. But to do so one must penetrate into the kind of choice which the plain man conceives himself as making in such a case. In deciding whether to keep a promise, he is not choosing between two particular acts whose particular effects provide the whole ground of choice between them. He is deciding whether a *kind* of conduct, a public practice, shall be maintained, and he feels that if he decided to break it, he would be voting against the practice itself, which he is most reluctant to do. He is reluctant because he feels that the practice is bound up in a vital way with his order of life, and that to undermine it would involve dimly-seen but far-reaching and disastrous consequences. In short, he refuses to consider the value of keeping this particular promise without considering the value of the practice of which it is an example. Is this mere confusion on his part?

11. That it is really not confusion has been ably argued by Mr Rawls.[1] He points out that rules may be conceived in two very different ways. On the one hand a rule may be a summary of what has been decided in cases of a certain kind. When the community has considered the matter of promises, it has generally found keeping them to have better results than breaking them, and the rule records this verdict. If we do conceive the rule in this way, we may approach our particular problem with a free mind, and consider the case on its merits. We may find that the advantages lie where the rules would lead us to expect, and then we shall conform to it; or we may find that they lie on the other side, and then there is no call to conform to it, for the case is evidently one of the exceptions to which the rule does not apply. Now when the utilitarian is charged with holding lightly the rule of keeping promises, it is this statistical conception of rules that is attributed to him. And if this is all there is to a rule, the charge is true.

But it has too seldom been noticed, says Professor Rawls, that there is at work in our minds a very different idea of what a rule is. A rule may *define a practice*. In some very important areas of conduct, we can see that if everyone were to act on independent calculation, it would be impossible for anyone to count on how others would act, and the result would be a general uncertainty amounting perhaps to chaos. 'As an alternative one realizes that what is required is the establishment of a practice, the specification of a new form of activity; and from this one sees that a practice necessarily involves the abdication of full liberty to act on utilitarian and prudential grounds.'[2] One cannot even conceive correctly what keeping a promise is unless one sees it as part of a wider convention. To make a promise is to accept this convention; it is to say that one will *not* decide whether to keep the promise by appeals to its special effects in this case, but will be bound by the over-riding commitment. To decide the particular case as if it stood alone is to break this commitment; and to break the commitment is to strike at one of the main strands that bind society together. For if I claim the privilege of deciding this case on its

[1] John Rawls, 'Two Concepts of Rules', *Philosophical Review*, Vol. 64 (1955), 3–32
[2] *Op. cit.*, 24

isolated merits, I must in mere consistency grant the same privilege to others, and their acceptance of that privilege would be disastrous. What is at stake is not merely the value of my act, but the value of the practice of which that act is a part.

12. One may illustrate this notion of a rule as a practice by analogy to a game.[1] Outside the game of baseball, a man may do something that looks very like sliding for a base, 'taking a called strike', or hitting a home run. But he is not really doing so. For these performances are by definition parts of a game and cannot occur except as the game is being played. And just as it is unreasonable for a man who hits a tennis ball a long way with a broomstick to claim that he has hit a home run, so it is unreasonable for a man who is playing the game to claim the freedom of the man who is not. By undertaking to play at all, he has given up that freedom and accepted the rules of the game. If after hitting a home run he decided that in this case it was best, all consequences considered, not to run the bases, his teammates would regard him not as a philosopher but as an idiot, and the umpire would quite rightly call him out. Now when we make a promise, we enter, so to speak, into a social game, of which promise-keeping is one of the rules. We cannot play that game and also choose whenever we wish *not* to play it, to pretend that we are as free to keep a promise or not as we are to take, or not to take, our umbrella. If we and others claimed that sort of freedom, the game would be at an end, which means that the sort of community we know would be at an end.

Of course we may decide not to play at all. If the player who has hit the home run sees that his small son in the stands is about to fall over the railing, he may decide to run to his aid rather than to run the bases. But that is not breaking a particular rule; it is temporarily forsaking the game itself in the interest of what seems more important. That is what we do when we break a promise in the interest of some great alternative good. If, having promised to repay a debt, I find that if I repay it I shall not have the wherewithal to save the life of my child, I act of course in the child's interest. But that is not to treat keeping my promise as I would the taking of my umbrella. I am ready to break with the whole convention so far as it stands in the way of my doing this, or if one prefers, I am interpreting the convention itself as containing these built-in exceptions, and am quite willing that everyone else should interpret it that way also.

[1] *Op. cit.*, 25

13. We said that when deontologists attacked the maxim of the greatest good, their most telling arguments were based on promises and punishment. We have considered promises. We shall delay over punishment only long enough to say that we should deal with it in the same way. The trump card is usually the judge who is tempted at a time of social strain to convict an innocent man for the sake of maintaining order in the community. It is argued that action in line with the greatest good would call for conviction of the innocent man, and that this is outrageous. Outrageous it certainly is. The judge is plainly not free to take this line, but the question is, Why not? Our answer is that the judgment of a court is not like taking an umbrella; it does not stand alone; by definition it is performed under rigid conditions. The court has been expressly appointed, and has given its pledge, to render judgment in accord with the evidence only, rejecting all appeals to expedience or advantage; to act otherwise in this case would betray the judicial system as a whole and indeed the wider official system of which this is a part. That was why the French people took the Dreyfus conviction so seriously, and why they were generally thought to be right in so doing. They felt by a sound instinct that what was at stake was more that the fate of a single officer, more even than the reputation of the high command; it was the integrity of France on its official side.

We hold, then, that the maxim of the greatest good still stands. The cases adduced to overthrow it are cases out of context, and usually cases whose very description serves to reveal the missing context. When this is taken into account, the calculation that seemed to make for an anarchic looseness is seen to support that loyalty to principle which common sense so plainly feels. This does not mean that we recognize two different and independent ways of justifying an action, one by bringing it under a rule, and another by appealing to the good involved. We recognize only one way, the latter. But if we are to do justice to actual thought, we must take some actions as embodying practices which go beyond them, and which must be accepted or rejected as wholes.

14. We have been discussing what makes an action right, and we have implied from time to time that if we see an action to be right, it is our *duty* to do it. We must now ask what is meant by calling an action our duty. In the light of what has been said we can exclude some common suggestions. Duty is not a divine command, at least

in essence, since it binds the atheist, who does not recognize a divine
being, in exactly the same way as it binds the devotee. It is not a
categorical imperative if that means that its commands have no
regard to consequences or desires. Is it then what Kant described as
a hypothetical imperative? To say so has often been supposed inconsistent with the rigour of duty. '*If* you want health, then have a
care for diet and exercise'; '*if* you want friends, be considerate of
others'. But then suppose you are the sort of eccentric who is indifferent to health and friendship; does not that mean that you are
absolved from such duties? And are we not making duty likewise
rest on the mere contingency of having certain impulse-desires?

We answer, and stress the answer, that this is *not* a contingency,
and that therefore with us too the command of duty is really categorical. A human nature that did not have these impulse-desires
would not be human nature. Mind itself is a set of activities directed
toward ends, and to halt or remove them would blot us out altogether.
Look again at the theoretical impulse. This is an impulse which,
as we have seen, is already at work in the most rudimentary perceptive
judgment and is still there, pushing for completion, in the most
complicated theories of physics or metaphysics. One could not carve
this impulse out of man without annihilating him as man. His whole
common-sense world may be regarded as a single complex judgment,
elaborated through millenniums of pressure on the part of this central
impulse. We could no more divest ourselves of this impulse and its
work than we could leap off our own shadows. Even in denying that
we have such an impulse, we are obviously exercising it. To cease to
exercise it would be to cease to remember or expect or infer or even
recognize; in short, it would be to resign from the world.

So of other central impulses, the aesthetic for example. The Gestaltists have shown us that we cannot really choose whether to be
interested or not in certain forms or shapes, since nature has settled
this for us; certain sounds carry emotional meaning from the start;
in the rhythm of the drumbeat or the dance there is an appeal as
ancient as the race. We can develop the interest or stunt it; we cannot
remove it, or sensibly deny it is there. Some people have tried to rid
themselves of the whole embarrassing problem of good by refusing to
admit that there is such a thing, of any type whatever; there are
things and happenings, but none of them is better or worse than any
other. But if a man chooses to make this point, it is presumably because he regards it as better to make it than not, and then he is back

with a grotesque suddenness in the world of values he is trying to escape.

Nature itself has thus determined that we should seek certain forms of self-fulfilment. It is only through the seeking of these ends that we have become what we are, only by continuing to seek them that we can become what we may be. The command to continue the search is thus addressed by human nature to itself: 'If you are to be what you want to be, and what you cannot help wanting to be, do this.' I am not, of course, suggesting that a person cannot help wanting to learn trigonometry or read Ruskin; I am suggesting that from his very constitution he does and must regard knowledge and beauty as goods to be pursued. He is so made as to desire them, and fulfilling and satisfying such desires is what 'good' means. And of course the fulfilment and satisfaction in which goodness consists are not mine alone, but those of anyone capable of them.

15. Now this gives the meaning of 'ought'. To say that I ought to do something is ultimately to say that if a set of ends is to be achieved, whose goodness I cannot deny without making nonsense of my own nature, then I must act in a certain way. There is of course no *compulsion* to act in this way. I am free to follow the lesser good if I choose. And if I do so choose, no outward penalty may overtake me. But 'the greatest penalty of wrongdoing', Plato said, 'is to grow into the likeness of the bad man', and that penalty is inescapable. The ethical ought is like the logical ought; indeed the logical ought is a special case of the ethical. The logical ought says, 'If you want to attain truth, think consistently'. It does not say that you cannot contradict yourself; we are all more or less experts in that ancient art. It only says that if you do contradict yourself, you will nullify the aim of your thinking because you cut yourself off from truth. The ethical ought is to desires generally what the logical ought is to the particular desire to know. It stands over them all; it is the voice not of this or that end, or of this or that possible good, but of *the* end, *the* good, to which all desire is directed, which all men alike are seeking. That is what gives it its authority. It concentrates, in a sense, the whole weight of human hope and desire. I do not mean, of course, that what our sense of duty says at any moment is infallible; for it remains true enough, as Leslie Stephen said, that conscience is the voice of racial experience speaking in the individual ear, and regarding the particular prescriptions of duty, the race itself may be mistaken. But that there is some greatest good purchasable by my present act cannot be denied without stultification; if error comes, it comes in construing what this is. Our account leaves the fact of duty palpable and its supremacy secure. Duty is the imperative laid upon us by a *summum bonum* which is prescribed by human nature itself. As Butler said of conscience, 'if it had power, as it has authority, it would absolutely govern human life'. It speaks with so great an urgency because it is dimly felt to be representative of the hope and will of mankind.

16. Here a serious difficulty crops up. Does not our account do away with any distinctively *moral* good altogether? It seems to make of moral goodness, that is, dutifulness or the good will, something that is good merely as instrumental to other and non-moral goods. If it really does this, it is sharply at variance with much weighty teaching on this matter. Kant began *The Metaphysic of Morals* by saying that the only thing in the world that was good without qualification was the good will, by which he meant loyalty to duty as such; and moralists who differ from each other as widely as Rashdall and the deontologists agree that dutifulness is not only an intrinsic good, but the greatest of all such goods. Is this teaching to be rejected?

There is at least a genuine paradox in it. Duty, as we have seen, is always a duty to produce good; the goodness, then, of dutifulness, or the disposition to do one's duty, would seem to lie in its being the condition and promise of this good. But to make dutifulness itself a good, in the sense of something to be sought in its own right and independently of other goods, seems unintelligent and hardly intelligible. If it is my duty to do my duty, it is because this latter duty is to produce some good, and unless it promised to do so, it would not be my duty at all. Thus the duty of being dutiful is not independent and self-justifying; it is derivative from the good that such regard for duty brings about. To make dutifulness, as Kant did, an end in itself, indeed the only end that ethics as such could recognize, is to leave the chain of duty hanging in the air, without any concrete good to which it can attach itself. Hence the curious emptiness of Kantian ethics. We are to go on cultivating and refining our sense of duty; we are to hold the moral law in awe above the starry heavens; we are to do our duty though those heavens fall; but if we venture to ask Kant *what* it is our duty to do, he can only repeat that we are to be dutiful; that is itself the good that morality is to aim at. Yet by itself it is a vacuous good. The very nature of duty is to aim beyond itself, and if it has nothing but itself to aim at, it can only stand despondently still. There can no more be a duty to act, if there is no good to attain by it, than to think, if there is no truth to be won by thinking.

Are we to say, then, that dutifulness, the disposition to seek and do one's duty, is an extrinsic, not an intrinsic, good? No, that will hardly do either. The truth would seem to be that it is a mixture of the two. That it is an extrinsic good, and a very great one, is undeniable. Indeed it is probably the most important single fact about a man, since without it, opportunity, position, and powers may be useless or used for evil, while with it, we have the warrant that he will at least try to play his part in the world. In a sense it is more important than any of the goods it may lead him to realize, for it stands as guarantor of all of them. But there is no reason to deny that, on our theory, it may be an intrinsic good also. Such a good is for us the fulfilment and satisfaction of impulse-desire. Now while impulse-desires are commonly aimed at the goods that duty might produce, they can also be aimed at the perfection of the moral mechanism, so to speak, by which goods are engendered and judged. Just as a musician may transfer part of his interest from the music that he is playing to his technique in playing it, or a philosopher some of his interest from the solution of his problem to the logical skill required for solving it, so the person interested in achieving good for himself or others may come to take an interest in his own sensitiveness of distinction among goods and firmness in following what appears the best; he may pursue these as a distinct end. And so far as he finds fulfilment and satisfaction in the pursuit, moral goodness becomes a good, in the sense that knowledge and the experience of beauty are goods.

Nevertheless, on our view its primary goodness is, and should remain, extrinsic. This is not to make it unimportant, any more than to regard health as only extrinsically good is to make it unimportant. And it serves to suggest a genuine danger in making dutifulness an end in itself. Rashdall somewhere remarks that the moral sense is a sense of the relative importance of ends. That, I think, is the right way to conceive it. A healthy moral interest should be fixed rather upon the goods to be achieved than upon the mechanisms or attitudes of our own mind in achieving them. Moral obligation *is*, we saw, the claim upon us of ends appointed by our own nature. As Kant recognized, a perfectly healthy moral will—what he called the holy will, that is, one in which desire and the sense of duty exactly corresponded—would have no worries about the state of its conscience; it would simply do its duty with delight. It is even possible that a pre-occupation with goodness should stand in the way of goods that would otherwise be achieved, just as an attempt at introspection when we have a certain desire will destroy the desire by diverting attention from its end. Moral goodness is one of those priceless things, of which culture is another, that tend to wither away when placed in too bright a light. I have been told, indeed, that an eminent woman contemporary, having concluded early in life, that she was neither good-looking nor socially gifted, decided that she would go in for goodness, and I must admit that the result has been excellent. But if one looks more closely, one sees that far more is at work than the interest in goodness, for there is an absorbing interest also in the goods that she is busy about.

Without such enthusiasms, the mere devotion to goodness has something artificial about it, and even a touch of morbidity. Arti-ficial, because of the unnaturalness of working laboriously to produce goods for which the worker has no heart. One likes to receive a gift from a friend when it is a testimony to his liking and his pleasure in one's own pleasure; one receives it gingerly when one knows that it springs from the sender's sense that he must do his duty, come what may; gifts without the giver are bare. In the preoccupation with moral goodness there is sometimes a touch of morbidity too. The man with sound health is more disposed to eat than to finger his pulse. It is probably the preacher, with his professional obligation to fix his eye upon goodness as such, and urge its claims, who feels the danger most acutely. A Greek of classic times would have been astonished and nonplussed at the Hebrew's concern over the state of his soul, and I suppose there is no parallel in other literatures to his passionate 'Create a clean heart within me', or to his passionate aversion to sin as 'the body of this death'. To deprecate this strain in our western culture or to depreciate its power to keep a refractory human nature in order would be absurd.

It is not absurd, however, to point out that without strong inde-pendent desires which it can stimulate and moderate, the pursuit of goodness as a state of the 'heart' may easily cross the line that separates health from morbidity. In Thomas à Kempis, in the *Theologia Germania*, in St Theresa, in George Fox, in Amiel, in Kierkegaard, there is, of course, much that is noble; there is also something of the hothouse and the sick-room. When the emphasis in preaching is very strongly on the 'inward parts', as it is in the admirable sermons of

James Martineau,[1] one gets, at times, the same sense of the need for opened windows; and in the continual stress on sin of some of the later Kierkegaardians—the insistence that the human will, even at its best, is one vast festering sore—we see the pursuit of goodness virtually turned against itself and eating out its own vitals. The prayer book confession that there is no health in us seems to me simply untrue, the relic of a theology committed to the doctrine of the fall, though perhaps if often enough repeated, it does tend to become true.

17. Besides the question of moral goodness, there is one other that our account of the good is sure to raise immediately, namely what is meant by evil. Like ‘good’, the term ‘evil’ is most ambiguous; it covers, if we may say so, a multitude of evils. When called upon to give examples, people would think of very different things. Some would mention Black Deaths and Great Fires and Lisbon earthquakes; others would name ignorance and ugliness; others, old age and death; others still, sin; some few, perhaps, would talk of the niggardliness of nature, and point out that most of the planet and indeed of the known universe is uninhabitable by man. Some of these evils fall outside our present interest, since they are clearly instrumental. Uninhabitable snowfields and deserts, epidemics, fires and earthquakes, are commonly called physical evils, but strictly speaking there are no such things. What are called so are instrumental only; they are not bad in themselves; they induce experiences that are bad. Disease as a mere state or process within the body has nothing evil in it; neither does a big fire or a big wave or a barren soil. Most of the universe, as far as we can see, is neither good nor evil. When certain events in it directly give rise to suffering or privation, we call them bad by metonymy, because they are the immediate causes of what is intrinsically bad, namely conscious states or their relations. It is only with intrinsic evil that we are here concerned.

Now if goodness consists in the fulfilment and satisfaction of impulse-desire, one would expect evil to consist in one or other of the following things: (a) the failure of impulse-desire to reach its goal, (b) its active defeat or frustration, (c) the coercive presence of that from which impulse-desire is seeking to escape. We find all these types of evil illustrated in fact, and they seem between them to exhaust the types of intrinsic evil.

[1] *Endeavours After the Christian Life*, and *Hours of Thought on Sacred Things*.

18. (a) Everyone has impulse-desires, strong or weak, for such things as knowledge, beauty, and easy relations with others. Suppose one conspicuously falls short of these; suppose, for example, that one is too stupid or too ignorant to enjoy any but the most elementary grasp of the world about him; we call such a state an evil. Why? Not because the man is actively suffering in any way or feels that he has anything to complain about; he may be extremely self-complacent. We call his state evil nevertheless, because it marks so evident a failure of the impulse-desire for knowledge to reach even a normal level of fulfilment; that it has not even gone far enough to become aware of its own failure does not better the situation. Again, we consider bad the sort of insensitivity that is content to live in a squalid litter, with no taste for order, no eye for beauty, no sense for the graces of speech or movement. Once more, when one hears of persons who feel at the end of their lives that they have nothing to repent of, meaning that they have never done anything that would land them in jail, we feel again a failure that we must call evil, even though the agent may be unaware of it. Our own theory of good and evil covers such cases fully, in the sense that, in the light of it, we can see plainly why we call them bad. If good means the fulfilment and satisfaction of impulse-desire, these are evil because in this respect they are failures.

Since, in our view, there are two factors in goodness, fulfilment and satisfaction, it is conceivable that a given experience should fall short on one account, but not on the other; it might fulfil without satisfying, or satisfy without fulfilling. I think that approximations to both these states occur, and that when they do, we recognize that we have at best a defective good. We saw in discussing the passionless sage of the Stoics that much light of an intellectual kind may be achieved with very little of the satisfaction that such achievement commonly brings. We saw too that while such a state could not be called an evil, its value or goodness had largely vanished. Fortunately such states are abnormal and rather rare. In ordinary life the achievement of a desired end is the most certain of all things to bring satisfaction. On the other hand the mere continued possession of the end is no guarantee that the satisfaction will remain. When T. H. Huxley was awarded the medal of the Royal Society, he was in raptures; a little later he wrote: 'The thing that a fortnight ago (before I got it) I thought so much of, I give you my word I do not care a pin for. I am sick of it and ashamed of having thought so much of it, and the congratulations I get give me a sort of internal sardonic grin.'[1] Even such a prodigy of success as Goethe said of his life when he was an old man: 'at bottom it has been nothing but pain and burden and I can affirm that during the whole of my 75 years, I have not had four weeks of genuine well-being. It is but the perpetual rolling of a rock that must be raised up again forever.'[2] Frank Chapman Sharp thinks that such cases, in which the good seems to have vanished because, though the fulfilment is still there, the satisfaction in it has gone, show that the goodness lies in the satisfaction alone, and he ends as a hedonist.[3] But the inference is illicit. What such cases show is that satisfaction is essential to goodness, not that it is exclusively essential. Indeed, attentively considered, they seem to show that satisfaction *cannot* be the only factor. Suppose that the satisfaction felt by Huxley or Goethe in his own level of achievement was small (that it was really zero or less I take leave to question), can we say that the goodness of such lives is really no greater than that of other men with similarly low satisfaction but a tithe of their attainment? That is certainly at odds with what we actually think. We should say that the goodness of an experience was greater if the achievement or fulfilment was greater, even though the satisfaction remained the same. If the satisfaction actually went down as the fulfilment went up, a situation that is conceivable, I think we should be genuinely puzzled as to whether the experience was better or not; we should begin to talk in terms of comparative amounts. In any case our present point is clear, namely that a fulfilment that is without normal satisfaction is to that extent a defective good.

19. The same holds where there is satisfaction but low fulfilment. There appear to be diseased minds who live in a state of perpetual euphoria, cackling and cooing with idiot's delight over the little nothings of their daily round. In sheer satisfaction with themselves and the world, they would make the Huxleys and the Goethes seem like melancholiacs. If the hedonists were right, such a state would be highly desirable. But we certainly do not so regard it. We think, rather, that for an experience to be genuinely good, there must be not only satisfaction, but something worth taking satisfaction in, and the worth of this object will be measured, not by the satisfaction itself, but by the immanent standard of the activity involved, cognitive

---

[1] *Life and Letters of T. H. Huxley*, I, 101
[2] Quoted by James, *Varieties of Religious Experience*, 137
[3] See his *Ethics*

if it is an activity of knowing, aesthetic if one of appreciating, ethical if it involves diverse activities and ends. It is no doubt better that the idiot's life should be a perpetual grin than a perpetual groan, even if his life is a 'poem in praise of practically nothing'; but it would be very much better still if, answering to the delight, there were the sort of object that would fill a normal mind or engage a normal sensibility. Satisfaction, even great satisfaction, without the corresponding fulfilment is at best a defective good.

Indeed, even when fulfilment and satisfaction are both present, there is a point of view from which every life may be regarded as evil, and our theory renders such judgments, otherwise perverse and peevish, at least intelligible. It was the cheerful and courageous R. L. Stevenson who wrote, 'failure is the fate allotted'; 'our business is to continue to fail in good spirits.' 'Take the happiest man', said James, 'the one most envied by the world, and in nine cases out of ten his inmost consciousness is one of failure. Either his ideals in the line of his achievements are pitched far higher than the achievements them-selves, or else he has secret ideals of which the world knows nothing, and in regard to which he invariably knows himself to be found wanting.'[1] The goodness of such achievements is clearly a matter of degree; and a climb that, regarded from below, is a triumph, may also, when seen from above, be a falling short. The two judgments are equally true. Goodness in its essence is relative to an endeavour, and any stage of that endeavour is called good or evil, depending on the point of the journey from which it is regarded. This is, or ought to be, an embarrassing reflection to a theory that holds goodness to be a simple quality like yellow, which, in a given experience, is either present or absent. On the theory here offered, such a reflection is natural and inevitable.

20. (b) Besides evils of failure there are evils of frustration. Failure and frustration are perhaps the same thing in the end; they are both defeats that spring from a disproportion between inner power and outer circumstance. But what specially distinguishes failure is some deficiency in one's self; what distinguishes frustration is some marked untowardness of circumstance. We say that the inadvertent burning by Mill's maid of Carlyle's manuscript of *The French Revolution* was an evil; that Milton's blindness and Beethoven's deafness and Wilson's paralysis and Maupassant's insanity were evils; that the

[1] *Varieties*, 137

cutting off of Schubert and Shelley at thirty was evil; that the removal of Lincoln from the scene at the height of his power and usefulness was an evil. Why are these things called evils? Partly, no doubt, because of the loss of what would have been very valuable, but surely also because of the frustration of promise and endeavour. Death, though the common lot, is the greatest of evils because it writes such an uncompromising *Finis* to all our efforts. These estimates are what one would expect on our theory of good. If good consists in fulfilment and satisfaction, their frustration will be regarded, naturally and universally, as evil.

21. (c) What about ugliness, a foul smell, a grating noise, and above all, pain? Many reflective persons have tried to take evil as the privation of good, but it is hard to hold this convenient theory in the face of evils like these. Intense pain is certainly more than the absence of something; it is positive, and positively horrible. In such phrases as 'pleasure and pain', there is the suggestion that it is the same sort of experience as pleasure, only opposite in quality, which is of course untrue, since pain is not an 'affection' like pleasure at all. It is a sensation, a sensation at times of appalling intensity, to which there is perhaps nothing corresponding among the experiences we call good. Again, the experience of a foul smell, or a jarring discord, or a finger-nail grating on a blackboard, is not a mere lack or absence, but something positive, something aggressively disagreeable. Such cases require us to hold, I think, that just as there are experiences marked out as natural ends by reason of their fulfilling impulse-desire, so there are others from which there is a natural averson and desire to escape. Pain is the type and chief of such evils. At every level of sentience, it is something to be fled from. Instead of feeling satisfaction as the experience of it increases, one feels satisfaction in the degree of one's relief from it. The claim has been made that there are exceptions, that some people take satisfaction and pleasure in pain as others do in heard harmonies. In the east I have often seen fakirs pushing themselves about on beds of upturned nails. But I am unconvinced by such cases. There is no reason to think these men prefer pain; it is precisely because they regard it as an evil difficult to be borne that they think to curry favour with God and man by the hardihood with which they bear it. Nor is it necessary, I should suppose, to say that the masochist finds satisfaction in pain itself as distinct from all that may attend it in an abnormal mind—the obscure stimulations of sex, the relief of feelings of guilt, the thought of oneself as suffering in some imagined cause. There are strange cases like that of Albert Jay Chapman, who permanently crippled one hand by plunging it into a fire as a symbolic atonement for a wrong done; there is the large company of martyrs who faced pain almost eagerly; there are the people who give thanks sincerely for the discipline of pain. But it is mere muddle to think that these things settle the question whether in any case whatever pain *is* good, as opposed to productive of good results. If there is any case on record of a person finding intense pain good in itself, I do not know of it. It may be said that the issue is pre-judged, since part of what we mean by pain in thus generalizing about it is that it is disliked. That may be true. But this is not all that we mean. Pain, as we have said, is not an affection primarily, but a sensation, with a content of its own.

It was argued in an earlier chapter that when we call a past pain evil, we do not mean to say merely that a pain occurred. But we found it hard to discriminate the pain from the badness or evil of it. I know of no satisfactory analysis of this distinction, and do not profess to have arrived at one. But it seems clear that when we say a painful experience is evil, we do not mean merely that what is painful is painful. We have seen that in describing an experience as intrinsically good we are saying that it satisfies and fulfils. In saying that it is evil, we say correspondingly that it flouts satisfaction or fulfilment or both. Pain flouts both, and it seems to have an added way of doing this that is peculiarly its own. (i) Pain, particularly if intense, makes a free and normal exercise of powers impossible; it tends to contract our being to one dreadful point. (ii) It carries with it dissatisfaction, that opposite of pleasure for which we have no convenient word, but which the Germans call *Unlust* as distinct from *Schmerz*. (iii) *Schmerz* or pain proper has a character of its own. Its evil is not exhausted by *Unlust* and frustration, though these are both there; and it is hence to be doubted whether an account of evil can precisely parallel an account of good. What makes an experience good is the satisfying fulfilment of faculty. What makes an experience bad is the flouting of such fulfilment with its attendant blight on satisfaction; but the blight may take more than one form. It may be the mere failure of satisfaction where this was normal or possible; it may be the presence of *Unlust*; or it may be the presence of pain.

22. (d) As for *moral* evil, the disposition to, or choice of, the worse rather than the better, it is to be understood in the same way as moral goodness. We condemn it primarily because it is the potentiality and the generator of all kinds of other ills. There is a distinction between vice and the vices, just as there is between goodness and the virtues. A vice is a disposition either to produce evil in a particular way— indolence and carelessness are examples—or to produce evil of a particular kind, as mendacity and cruelty do. The vice that is opposed to moral goodness is the disposition toward the bad because it is bad. It is plain enough why we should regard these as evils, and the latter as by far the greater evil. Malice is a seed-plot for every kind of evil that the human will can produce. Anger and hatred are not necessarily malicious, for they may be directed only against what is harmful in other men, and thus tend to good rather than evil, though unhappily they are not as a rule so economically used. But a man who was malicious generally would be a standing enemy to every kind of good of everyone around him.

Some writers have questioned whether pure malice, either of the special or the general form, exists. I have already questioned whether anyone takes satisfaction in pain as such, but unfortunately it is harder to doubt that some people take a genuine satisfaction in inflicting it on others. As one reads Macaulay's account of Jeffreys, for example, one can scarcely resist his conclusion that this hateful creature showed 'the most odious vice which is incident to human nature, a delight in misery merely as misery'.[1] On our own theory we should expect that most such cases would be explicable in other ways than as examples of mere 'motiveless malignity', for example, as instances of the love of power accompanied by relative lack of fellow-feeling and imagination; and we should regard a man who took delight in inflicting misery when there was nothing to gain by it as not merely morally bad but as abnormally or inhumanly constructed, a monster lacking natural perception and sympathy. That, I think, is how we do feel. Futhermore, we should regard pure moral badness, the attitude that took as its motto 'Evil, be thou my good', as not really possible. It is hard to see how anyone could consistently take what we regard as the great evils as goods, or the great goods as evils; those goods are appointed for him by his nature as human. Even Iago, in deceiving, betraying and murdering, did not elect evil simply for evil's sake; his creator seems to have felt that this would make him unreal. Granting that Iago was thoroughly selfish, completely unsympathetic, and

[1] *History of England*, Ch. IV

remarkably adroit, 'the most delightful thing to such a man would be something that gave an extreme satisfaction to his sense of power and superiority; and if it involved, secondly, the triumphant exertion of his abilities, and thirdly the excitement of danger, his delight would be consummated'.[1] Odious as Iago was, he was not a mere and pure devil.

23. Nor is anyone else. Our own theory of human nature is nearly the opposite of that which, founded on the myth of the fall, regards man as rotten at the core and utterly to be condemned except as divine grace, distributed on inscrutable principles, interposes to save him. He is, on the contrary, so made as to seek, inevitably and universally, a set of great goods; his whole life is a groping after them. Even the criminal, as Socrates saw, does not choose evil merely as evil; no one is such a complete fool and knave as to do that. When vicious and harmful acts spring, not from a rush of passion, as they often do, but from something that can be called a motive, the motive is never simply to work evil, conceived as such. Some twist of thought makes the worse appear the better reason; the act, looked at through the vapours of anger, fear, or jealousy, is seen in a false light; even sin, I have heard a theologian say, is 'an effort to be blessed in ways not approved by God'. If human nature is governed, as we hold it is, by certain powerful impulse-desires whose fulfilment and satisfaction provide the meaning of good, we should expect that there would be no such thing as moral badness, if that means a settled will toward the bad because of its badness, that choices of the bad as such would seldom or never occur, and that when they did seem to occur, they would generally turn out, on examination to be choices of evil *sub specie boni*. All these expectations, I think, are confirmed by fact.

[1] A. C. Bradley, *Shakespearean Tragedy*, 228

CHAPTER XIII

THOUGHT AND DESIRE

1. The duty of a given moment is to try to find the right act and do it. The right act is one that produces the greatest good (or, to cover the case of equal goods, not less than the greatest). What is good is what fulfils those impulses or strivings of which human nature essentially consists, and in fulfilling them brings satisfaction. The ends sought, and therefore the goods recognized, at any given time are provisional only; the fulfilment of present desire always leaves much to be desired; and hence our conception of the good is in course of constant revision. *The* good is nothing short of what would fulfil and satisfy wholly. These are the main positions we have so far taken. We now have to ask what the function of reason is in determining and moulding the good.

The exercise of reason is a matter of degree. The theoretic impulse has as its end a system whose parts are necessarily and intelligibly interconnected, but such a system is realized only very imperfectly even in the most advanced of the sciences, and still more imperfectly in the common-sense order. And if we ask as to the place of reason in the moral life, we find this to be analogous to its place in the theoretical life. Reason is in neither case a form imposed from without on a content alien to it. It is already working immanently in desire just as it is at work in perception. Its business in the moral life is to order and unify desires, just as in its theoretical career its business is to order into a coherent whole the world of the perceptually given. The analogy is so illuminating that we shall do well to remind ourselves of the function of reason in knowledge.

Experience begins for each of us in a state of awareness that clearly falls short of knowledge. It is true that in the first days of post-natal life we use our eyes and our ears, our mouths and noses, and thus no doubt we experience colour and sound, taste and smell, pain and pleasure, discomfort and fear. But it is an experience unimaginably different from our present experience. Nothing is discriminated from anything else, nothing is recognized for what it is, nothing is grasped as connected with anything else. There is a welter of sensations, affections, emotions, impulses, but as yet there are no ideas, no desires, no self as opposed to objects, and no objects as opposed to self.

In our maturity we live in a world of *things*. It takes some effort to realize that for the child at the beginning there are no things, and that it must work its way out of this primitive welter into the world of things by a long effort of discrimination and synthesis among the qualities that are presented to it. If the colour red is presented over and over again, first in a ball, then in a dress, then in a goldfish, and a name repeatedly attached to it, the child comes to single out and recognize red *as* red; if roundness is presented in a succession of balls, plates, and cups, he comes slowly to discriminate that too, and, after a further interval, to use concepts of these qualities, to think of red-ness and roundness as such. How are the various qualities linked with each other? That also takes much learning. Some are commonly presented together, move together, and are found to have a joint utility; these will probably be grouped as forming a single thing, a spoon, for example, or a table. Then when one of them is presented in future, a characteristic shape perhaps, the thought of the others will be aroused, not necessarily in explicit expectation, but at least in the form in which their presence is taken for granted. This is the type of experience that we call the perception of a thing.

But this mere togetherness is not the sort of relation in which the impulse to know can rest. Although to know is always to connect, some connections fulfil the demand of the cognitive impulse more completely than others. It is interesting to discover that the cat purrs, but the alert young mind is not content with that; it goes on to ask *why* the cat purrs, indeed why the ball should be red, perhaps in time why the ball should take up less room than a square block of the same width. And if the reflective impulse is insistent, it finds that it can gain more satisfying answers to some of these questions than to others. If it asks why the round thing should be also red, there seems to be no answer but chance; the two qualities sometimes go together, sometimes not, and from one to the other there is no straight path. But it is certainly not chance that cats purr, since their purring follows causally from something else about them; as a first venture, they purr because they are pleased, and of course there is a cause why they are pleased, and a cause for that, so that we can follow a speculative train as long as we care to think. But the connection between the volume of the ball and the volume of the cube with the same diameter is something else again. Of the various relations we have mentioned, it answers most completely the interest of the theoretic impulse, since it is a necessary relation; one can see that the first volume *must* be smaller than the second, and to go on asking Why? after one sees this clearly would be foolish, since no clearer answer is possible. Thus mathematics has always had a special fascination for rationalists, for the clearness and inevitability of its connections satisfied the desire to understand in a degree that no other science could approach. To be sure, we do not usually confine reason to the sphere of the mathematically necessary; we take it as an exercise of reason to find the cause of anything, or to study its likeness to other things, or its differences from them. But reason is generally thought to be most at home when it is moving along the lines of the logically necessary. Such necessity is not exhibited alone, however, in the entailment of one quality by another, for it may also be seen in the mutual exclusion of qualities. The same surface *cannot* be at once brown and green, the same line at once straight and curved, the same figure at once round and square. Incompatibility is as necessary a relation as entailment.

To sum up on the operation of reason among the qualities with which experience begins; the intellectual impulse is at work from the beginning, seeking to order the welter of impressions into accordance with its own pattern. It works in the following principal ways. (1) It recognizes in particular impressions examples of universals or *as suches*. (2) On the ground chiefly of association, it organizes groups of these universals into things, with the result that in perception it can take one of them as indicating the presence of the rest. (3) It grasps some of these characters as mutually exclusive. (4) Between the others it grasps a great variety of connections, some apparently accidental, some necessary, some—like the causal connection—that are neither wholly the one nor the other. But relations that fall short of necessity also fall short of full intelligibility, and hence it is perpetually trying to resolve them into the necessary relations with which it can rest content. (5) In like manner, it is perpetually trying to expand the field of knowledge. If it follows the lines of causality or logical entailment, or space, or time, it will be carried right off the map of its present little world. To put the whole matter more briefly still, the theoretic impulse is a persistent *nisus* to throw back the frontiers of knowledge on all sides, while organizing its conquests in such a way as to avoid inconsistency and render the interconnection of parts intelligible.

2. Now the function of reason among impulse-desires is very much like its function among sensory impressions. Consider the parallel between the way it turns sensation into perception and the way it turns impulse into desire. The child soon comes, on seeing the shape of the chair to expect certain other qualities to put in their appearance; it completes the given by the expectation of the non-given. In very similar fashion it completes impulse into desire. It has experienced hunger followed by food that allayed the hunger, and thirst followed by an allaying drink. When they first arise, the impulses of hunger and thirst are blind, just as, according to Kant, sensations are blind without conceptions; the child wants, without knowing what he wants. Desire removes the blindness by supplying impulse with the idea of its own completion, and from that point on, impulse no longer needs to grope in the dark, for, knowing now what it wants, it can go relatively straight to its goal.

If the implications of such facts were understood, the question whether thought enters into the determination of the good would be very quickly settled. It would be no more possible to deny that thought plays a part in determining what is good than that it has a part in determining what we shall accept as the order of nature. This order is not, of course, a web spun by pure reason out of its own vitals. If thought is to work at all, it must have something to work with, and this material, in the form of the given, must be supplied *to* it, not *by* it. But this material may be ordered in any number of ways—for example, as the ant presumably orders it, or the ape, or the savage, or the scientist, or as an intelligence might order it that was as far beyond the scientist's as his is beyond the ant's; and to say that the world of our common experience, as it stands, is mere presented fact, which reason contemplates from the outside is a superficial notion. The relations between impressions are no less real than the impressions themselves, and these relations are in course of a continual slow remoulding at the hands of intelligence. Whether this remoulding is essentially discovery or creation, a process of accommodating our thought more closely to relations that are independent of it, or of remaking the order of experience into conformity with the ideal, or both together, as I should hold, we need not further explore. In any

case, the world as we know it is largely the construct of reason—not
wholly, for the building must have its bricks, and reason finds these;
it does not make them. The house is not merely bricks, however, but
bricks in a design; and this design is supplied, or, if one prefers, disclosed at varying levels of completeness, by reason.

Substitute, now, for the welter of impressions the welter of impulses. These impulses are the raw material of the good life, just as
sensation is the raw material of knowledge. Without them there
would be no goods. Food and drink would not be good if there were
no hunger or thirst to satisfy, nor Maxwell's equations if no one cared
about knowing them. But the goods of actual life are not mere impulsive satisfactions. When thought supervenes upon impulse, it
transmutes it into desire by supplying it with conscious ends. Our
goods, from that point on, lie in the fulfilment not of bare impulses,
but of desires into whose nature thought has entered once for all,
with its own demands for consistency, integration, and expansion. It
is one of the merits of T. H. Green's great book on ethics to have
driven this truth home. Thought and desire are different, he agrees,
but so intimately bound up together that thought is impossible
without desire, and desire without thought. To think is to desire,
because it is to seek the answer to a question, and 'in every stage of
the process we are moved by a forecast, however vague, of the result'.
On the other hand, to desire is to go beyond impulse to the thought of
what would fulfil it, and normally farther still, to the thought of steps
to that fulfilment. Thought and desire are means to the same general
end, the removal of a maladjustment between idea and fact. Each
deals with the maladjustment in its own way. Thought is an attempt
to modify idea into greater conformity with fact. Desire, if given its
way, would modify fact into conformity with idea. The two, though
different, are inseparable; and 'our conclusion must be that there is
really a single subject or agent, which desires in all the desires of a
man, and thinks in all his thoughts, but that the action of this subject
as thinking . . . is involved in all its desires, and that its action as
desiring is involved in all its thoughts'.[1] It is thus absurd to say that
reason and goodness are extraneous to each other. So far as thought
enters into desire, it is the architect of the good.

3. If Green is right about this, we can see already that in the debate
about reason and feeling Hume and his succession were wrong. It is

[1] *Prolegomena to Ethics*, Sec. 136

not empirically true that 'reason is the slave of the passions'. The Humians were right, indeed, in holding feeling to be so linked with goodness that its presence was a condition of goodness; we have argued that satisfaction is necessary, and satisfaction is a feeling. But it is not this feeling that impulse-desire is seeking; it is a special kind of fulfilment which, when attained, brings the feeling with it. To lodge the goodness in the feeling alone, as many of Hume's successors have done, and as all hedonists do, is arbitrary. To say, as Hume himself did, that reason is merely a servant or instrument to ends independently set by feeling, is to misdescribe plain fact. What is good is the achievement of the end; in this end the fulfilling content is as important as the satisfaction; and in the determination of that fulfilling content, reason is absolutely essential.

Consider an example. A mathematician wants to solve a problem. This, Green would rightly point out, is a case of desire. There is a specific desire which gives the theoretic impulse its direction, a desire to round out the conditions of the problem with an answer following from those conditions with logical necessity. We have held that the achievement of such insight is a good which consists of fulfilment and satisfaction jointly. It is absurd to call reason the slave of passion here, and passion *the* source of the goodness. It would be at least equally true to say that passion is the slave of reason. For it is reason operating in and through desire that has specified the end to be achieved, and it is reason again, not feeling, that decides when the end has been attained. Dr Schiller used to argue that the test of logical validity was the feeling of satisfaction that arose at a certain point in the thinker's mind. Most logicians were unconvinced, for it was too obvious that if the satisfaction appeared at one point rather than another, it was because thought had achieved an end *other* than the satisfaction itself, in which satisfaction could be taken. That end was appointed by reason; it was the solution of a given problem in accordance with logic. The surge of satisfaction was merely the chorus off-stage applauding the denouement. To make reason the slave of feeling here is to get the cart conspicuously and awkwardly before the horse.

It may be thought that this is an exceptional instance, since the desire that is at work is so clearly in the service of the intellectual impulse. But the case is not essentially different if we take other impulses instead. Consider the aesthetic. A composer sits down to begin a sonata. Its completion is the good that he sets before him, and to achieve this good he must satisfy the requirements of the impulse that is at work in him. But *what* exactly will bring this satisfaction? Impulse alone cannot say. The composer discovers what he wants only when the end takes form as a composition in a certain time and key, and gets progressively specified with the addition of each bar. The kind of structure that will satisfy is plainly different here from what it was in the last example, for it is the aesthetic not the intellectual impulse that is seeking expression. But the work of reason or intelligence is no less essential. The consistency of time and key, the elaborate demands of harmony and counterpoint, could be dealt with only by an intelligence of a high order, though working within the boundaries of a specifically musical desire. The fulfilment of the impulse would be as decisively defeated by defect of intelligence as by lack of musical sense itself; indeed a musical sense without intelligence at its service would not be such a sense at all. Remove from the desire the intelligence that is at work in it, and it would collapse in an unrecognizable mass. So would the good achieved in the fulfilment of the desire. Reason is integral to aesthetic and to every other kind of good, just as it is to intellectual good.

4. We must now add that reason operates not only within desires, but between them. Consider first how it brings to light their occasional inconsistency. We have already seen how it performs this office in the sphere of qualities. Qualities, taken by themselves, are not inconsistent with each other; brown and green, straight and curved, are not incompatible as such, but merely different. Incompatibility appears only when they are asserted of the same subject—the same surface or the same line. (Their mutual exclusiveness when so considered belongs to the nature of things and is perceived by reason; current attempts to represent it as a linguistic convention have proved unconvincing.) Similarly, desires in the abstract do not conflict; the desire to be a saint and to be a thug, to be a free untrammeled spirit and the faithful knight of a particular fair lady, are merely different until they are proposed as a policy for a particular man, and then if he is endowed with normal intelligence, he will see that they are exclusive of each other. The conflict between desires may break out at various points. Sometimes it appears in the ends themselves, as when a man realizes that to be a free untrammeled spirit and also the knight of a particular lady are incompatible ends. Sometimes the conflict lies in the means to ends that would in themselves be consistent enough, as when a man sees that he cannot prepare himself at once to be a competent doctor and a competent lawyer. Sometimes it breaks out between the means that a given end requires and something else that one wants, as when the boy who would like to go to an engineering school perceives that if he is to master the mathematics required, he must 'scorn delights and live laborious days'. A man can, of course, merely surrender himself to impulses and desires as they come, without taking note of their bearings upon each other. But that is to live as the animals live.

Indeed the importance of intelligence in revealing and allowing for the incompatibility of desires could hardly be more prettily illustrated than in some of Köhler's experiments on the intelligence of apes. Once when a chimpanzee was on a chain, he put a banana a little outside the orbit of the chain. On a wall near by he hung a stick long enough, if used by the ape, to rake the banana within reach. The animal, in contemplating the situation, obviously got the idea of using the stick for this purpose, and repeatedly started toward it. Unfortunately, in order to reach the stick it had to pass the point at which the banana lay nearest to its orbit. Confronted with this temptation, its intelligence invariably broke down in vainly renewed attempts to get at the fruit directly. The notion that to indulge this impulse was to exclude the only means of getting what it wanted was too much for its struggling wit. A human intelligence, even of low order, would grasp this at once and save itself futile effort.

5. More important, perhaps, than what a desire excludes is what it implies, and the apprehension of this too is the work of intelligence. Hume would admit to the full the importance of intelligence as determining the means that must be adopted if the end is to be achieved, but he seems to have ignored its role in developing and elaborating the end itself. The desires of a mature man are not simple. There are usually many impulses in us that are pressing for satisfaction, and desire is a funnel through which we pour as many of them as we can. We have the hours from two to four free on a given afternoon, and we can spend them in reading a novel, in taking a walk, or in many other ways. We may solve the problem as an animal does, by surrendering to impulse or habit. Apparently the animal mind does not choose, for choice lies between represented alternatives, and it is doubtful whether that mind can rise to the level of such alternatives. When in our own minds we reach that level, we soon find that the competing desires represent, not the ends of single impulses, but complex ends that would satisfy many together. Suppose we choose the walk; why do we do so? As we give ourselves to the thought of it, we find the idea burgeoning; it is not simply the suggestion that we escape for a while from a stuffy room; it becomes in a moment the suggested fulfilment of half a dozen wants or interests all converging upon the same proposal. I shall work better for a swing along a country road; it is spring, and where the road winds through the woods there is a bank of blue-bells that will be at its best; I shall pass Smith's house, and I haven't seen him for weeks; perhaps he will come along, and if he does, I can get his views on whether Jones is the right man to add to our staff; further, I missed the newspaper this morning, and I can pick up a copy on my way home. What looks like a single projected course of action may thus fulfil many wants at once. The intelligence at work within desire, starting from the end of a single impulse, widens and modifies the prospect so that the final election is by the massed votes of many independent impulse-desires.

According to Hume and his followers, the office of reason in all this is simply to disclose means to ends determined by feeling. I cannot think this an inspired analysis. That reason does perform this means-end calculation is undeniable; it tells me that if I want the goods of refreshed work, of a sight of the blue-bell patch, of a talk with my friend, of the morning's news, I must go about it in a certain way. But surely that is not all it does. At least two further functions must be noted. (a) It enters into my thought of the nature and amount of each separate fulfilment. How much, if anything, shall I get from the newspaper? That is not a matter of feeling only. We have already considered this point and need not return to it. (b) Reason discloses the mutual implication of goods. As I think of the talk with Smith, it comes to me, not explicitly perhaps, but none the less effectively, that this exchange of ideas would at once keep the lines of friendship open, settle my doubts about Jones, and increase the exhilaration of the walk. Of course feeling is involved in this, but so also is intelligence. Thus when election time comes, the impulses vote in blocks. The ordering and contemplation of alternative goods *en bloc* is not itself carried out by impulse or feeling. This must be set down as the work of intelligence operating through desire.

6. We may now go further. In important ways, reason, instead of being the slave and tool of impulse, is its master. Thought can remould the ends of impulse without destroying the satisfaction proper to it. This power has taken the race some millions of years to achieve, and remains very imperfect, even in man. It will repay us to take a few moments to look back over the course of this extraordinary achievement.

In the lower orders of life, instinctive behaviour is so fixed that some biologists have regarded it merely as a chain of reflexes; a slight change in the situation to which it is called on to respond may defeat it utterly. Take an example or two from far down the scale. The insect Chalicodoma lives till its maturity in a small clay cell from which, when it is grown, it eats its way out. Fabre found that if he pasted a paper over the cell, the insect would eat its way through without difficulty, but if the paper was not pasted on the cell but was kept a hair's breadth away from it so as to form a separate encasing cell, it would die rather than make a second attempt. 'The Bembex carefully feeds her grubs, and never makes a mistake in finding her way to her cell, although it is covered with sand and is then undistinguishable to us from the surroundings, but when M. Fabre removed the earth and exposed the cell, the Bembex did not appear to recognize the young that she had so carefully tended.'[1] Here instinct is ready to deal, and deal expertly, with one situation, but it is almost as helpless as a machine would be to adjust itself to any other. The stupidity of these remote creatures is often astonishing. The wasp will seal up her hole as carefully when there is nothing in it as when her eggs have been laid there. Fabre redirected a line of pine processionary caterpillars in such a way that the leader was following the rear member, whereupon they went round and round on the top of a flowerpot for seven days before breaking the parade. Such creatures seem almost as truly mechanisms as toy electric trains.

Yet I believe Hobhouse is right in holding that not only in man, but also very far down in the biological scale, there is at least a rudimentary intelligence working within the domain of instinct. The very insects that appear so much like mechanisms reveal at times an unmistakable power to adjust themselves to the circumstances of the case and to fulfil in novel ways the impulse that apparently moves them. Instinctive action differs from reflex action in being, to all appearance, the expression of a felt need, and even at low points in the scale this need can fulfil itself variously. For example, the hermit crab, soon after hatching, 'goes in search' of a suitable shell to live in.

[1] Hobhouse, *Mind in Evolution*, 77

If it finds a vacant snail shell, it moves in. If it fails to find a vacant one, but does find one with a live snail in it, it stands guard till the snail, unable to come out and get food, dies, whereupon the crab pulls out the body, eats it, and triumphantly moves in. This looks very much as if it were using some sort of intelligence which enabled it, if one way of reaching its end proved a failure, to devise another. But of course such inferences are treacherous. It may be so constructed that if one stimulus is offered it will respond to it in a predetermined way, but that failing that, it will respond to another in an equally pre-determined way.

Still, the attempt to explain behaviour by instinct without intelligence is bound to break down sooner or later, and the evidence suggests that it breaks down early. The Peckhams, in their famous study of the solitary wasps, thought it had already broken down at this lowly level. When a wasp has laid her eggs and provisioned her nest so that her young will have food when they hatch, she seems to feel it necessary to close securely the hole where she has left these treasures. But not only do wasps vary greatly in their way of doing this; an individual wasp will suit its expedients to the material at hand, trying successively pebbles, pellets of clay, and leaves, and not stopping till the job is effectively done. When trying to drag a spider into her hole, the wasp may show an extraordinary persistence and ingenuity in doing it. She may try at first to pull the spider in while it is standing up; this will not do, because its legs then spread out, umbrella fashion; so she turns it over on its back; then when pulled from below its legs fold up on its thorax and, if it is not too big, down it goes. But sometimes it is too big, and something else must be tried. The Peckhams saw one of their wasps, who had got a spider part way down by this method, but could not pull it farther, drag it out again, and vigorously squeeze its legs together, after which, with much tugging, she succeeded in getting it in. These are cases of instinctive behaviour undoubtedly. But it is certainly not rigid or merely mechanical behaviour. It is as if the need or impulse were already directed to a generalized end; the wasp must get the prey into its hole *somehow*, or she must get *something* to roof the hole with; but any one of a variety of expedients will satisfy the impulse equally well, and if defeated in one, she will turn to another. As we go up the ladder of animal mind, the range of adjustment becomes far wider. The bird will vary the architecture of its nest to suit the facilities that are open to it. Anyone who has kept and observed various species of

M

mice, as I have, will have noted how prompt and ingenious they all are, when they build their nests, in utilizing in appropriate ways the material they are supplied with, such as paper and cotton batting, whether it is of the sort they would have found in nature or not. Their behaviour is the product of instinct, but with intelligence built in. Instinct, instead of giving an inflexible penny-in-the-slot response, takes the form of a need that can be variously satisfied.

7. This plasticity is at its highest in man. It is so high, indeed, that the notion of distinguishable and definite human instincts has been all but abandoned by present-day psychologists. They would agree that there are hereditary tendencies to behave without prevision in ways that benefit the agent, but the last half century has revealed so wide a divergence as to their number and classification that the notion has virtually been given up as hopeless. Hocking would group them all under one main drive, directed toward power; Freud recognized two, those of sexuality and destruction, or love and death; Thouless recognizes three types of instinctive drive, self-preservative, reproductive, and gregarious. McDougall in the earlier editions of his *Social Psychology* enumerated twelve instincts, which grew in later editions to eighteen; William James numbered about fifty; Thorndike preferred to have over two hundred. This looks more like anarchy than in fact it is. It represents the gradually made discovery that there is no right and single way of classifying drives or propensities. Once you abandon the notion of instinct as the fixed automatic response to a stimulus, and introduce the notion of end-seeking (and no psychology that fails to do this will throw much light on human nature), you find that instinctive activities are exceedingly hard to pin down. The same end may be secured by different sorts of behaviour and different ends by the same behaviour; and when you have specified both behaviour and end, you may perfectly well take the process as serving a more general end. Splinter sufficiently the ends that instinctive responses serve and you can get instincts by dozens or hundreds; group the responses under successively more general ends, and you get eighteen, or two, or one.

The rise and fall of instinct psychology has established an important conclusion. The wants that come welling up from lower evolutionary levels are increasingly indeterminate, and when they reach the human level, most of them may be satisfied in varying ways. Instinct loses its rigidity, and becomes plastic to intelligence. The centre of gravity, so to speak, shifts from mechanism to purpose, and purpose is thought. Even the drives that, biologically considered, are most fundamental are inhibited or redirected under the influence of ideas. Take hunger. 'There is no society in which the entire range of edible objects is included in the diet.'[1] The religious convictions of the orthodox Hindu lay an interdict on beef, those of the Mohammedan on pork; in some societies a given animal is conceived as related to the group, and to use it for food would be like cannibalism; in others, again, the ban is placed on fruits or certain plants. There have been many ascetics who conceived that there was something gross in eating and drinking at all, and have reduced them to a minimum; they would no doubt have abolished them wholly except that by an unco-operative arrangement of nature they would then also have abolished themselves.

Or take the maternal instinct. This was formerly supposed to prescribe a fairly definite pattern of behaviour for the mother toward the child. Anthropologists have left little of this prepossession standing. They insist that the matter must be discussed in terms of cases, not a priori'.[2] Margaret Mead has shown that among the Arapesh the child is kept close to its mother, fed when it cries, and constantly caressed. On the other hand, when one moves over to the Mundugumor, one finds that 'the infant is kept in a hard uncomfortable basket, is not suckled unless clearly in need of milk, is not fondled or caressed, is made early to fend for itself and in general is so harshly treated that only the strongest survive'.[2] In short, even the maternal instinct has no fixed pattern.

8. What is replacing the notion of instinct? My impression is that most psychologists, while retaining the notion of end-seeking drives, are discontented even with the degree of fixity that would be accepted by James, Freud, and McDougall; they are accounting for less and less by inborn factors, and more and more by experience. In the writings, to name but a few, of Stern in Germany, of Sprott and Thouless in Britain, and Woodworth and Gordon Allport in America, there is an increasing stress, under varying names, on the 'functional autonomy of motives'. This phrase, coined by Allport, means simply the independence of an interest, motive, or drive, from any innate structure or instinctive tendency. It implies that human nature is

---

[1] D. W. McKinnon, in Boring, Langfeld and Weld, *Foundations of Psychology*, 124.
[2] *Ibid.*, 125

plastic enough to acquire as a result or experience new ends of goals, which, though not marked out by instinct, have all the strength and organizing power that were once assigned to it. The sailor's love of the sea is not born in him; it is probably a gradual acquisition; but, for all that, it may be the dominant force in his life. 'Workmanship is not an instinct, but so firm is the hold it may acquire on a man that it is little wonder Veblen mistook it for one. A business man, long since secure economically, works himself into ill-health, and sometimes even back into poverty, for the sake of carrying on his plans. What was once an instrumental technique becomes a master motive.'[1]

Once this autonomy of acquired motives is recognized, the older explanation by instinct seems strained. Freud would no doubt explain the love of fine workmanship as an obscure expression of sexuality, perhaps of narcissism; McDougall would probably attribute it to the instincts of construction, submission, and others, operating jointly. There is, to be sure, some force in these explanations. No sensible person can deny that there are inborn tendencies to seek certain things, to satisfy the demand, for example, of hunger, thirst, and sex; and there is no reason why the list of such tendencies should not be long. Why, then, the general shrinking from them? Because they explain so little in detail. Even the fundamental drives just named never account for the particular form their fulfilment takes, and the less fundamental ones are far vaguer still. If they are invoked at all, it can be only as slight pressures or inclinations whose actual outworking must be explained by special experiences. Further use of them is likely to be mythology. To go behind the conscious motive and tell a man who takes an interest in fine watch-making that he is thereby fulfilling a sexual drive is, at best, to commit the 'psychologist's fallacy' of identifying a present process with what it sprang from, for even if the interest did spring from this source, which is improbable, it has now thoroughly emancipated itself and follows a line determined by its own subject-matter and by acquired associations. McDougall used to conceive of each of us as having a limited supply of psycho-physical energy which was entirely at the disposition of a dozen or two instincts, each with its own aim. If any project were to be carried through, it must therefore link itself up with one of these pipe-lines of energy; otherwise it would fall flat like a toy balloon when one's breath gives out in inflating it. I should not want to reject this theory wholly. The notion that there is a conative and purposive process

[1] G. W. Allport, *Personality*, 196

running through the entire evolutionary series, that each man is a branch from the same trunk, and that each of his activities is a twig growing from that branch and fed by it, is, I think, a better founded metaphor than that of nature as a machine. It is a conception which, since Aristotle's time, has proved irrepressible, in spite of the mechanistic trend of modern science. McDougall belonged to this Aristotelian tradition, and he wrote with an understanding of its philosophical force that not many psychologists have had. Still one cannot now accept the view that the energy placed at our disposal by the life force flows through the set of pipes he enumerated, or that a complex and reflective activity is to be explained by saying that a special set of taps has been turned on. We are less exclusively pushed from behind than this suggests, and freer to follow the lead of ideas. 'Human nature', as Margaret Mead has said, 'is almost unbelievably malleable'.

9. It is time to return from this little expedition into contemporary psychology. We come back fortified. We had suggested that the good is to be conceived as that which fulfils and satisfies impulse-desire. But what was the function of reason or intelligence in determining this good? We had gone some way with our answer. We had seen that thought enters into the very nature of desire; it formulates and sets before us the end that will satisfy impulse, and in so doing, introduces complexities into the end—as we saw in the case of the composer —which impulse alone could not have supplied. Furthermore, it reveals conflicts between goods, and mutual implications between them. Could it go further still? Could it actually remould impulse by transforming the ends in which it found satisfaction? This seemed to be denied both by classic writers like Hume and more recent writers like McDougall. The sole function of reason in morals, said Hume, was to reveal means to ends with whose position as ends reason had had nothing to do. McDougall agreed. An end was an end and was good simply because it satisfied feeling, and he added that it must satisfy feeling in one of the forms appointed by instinct. If this teaching were true, it was extremely important for our view of goodness. It would mean that the whole range of human goods was preappointed by a set of instinctive demands which were not only nonrational in nature and origin, but presumably unalterable by rational methods. This claim could not be left unnoticed. We therefore asked the psychologists whether it was corroborated by their more recent findings, and have learned that it was not. Though contemporary psychology can certainly not be accused of any weakness for theories that would make man rational, still, on the question whether our ends are inflexibly appointed by instincts, its voice is clear and decided: these instincts on the human level are so malleable and plastic, they demand so little in the way of definite ends or routines, that we can make almost anything of them. Instinct indeed provides the frame of the picture; it surrounds our life with certain confinements and pressures within which the portrait must be drawn; but it leaves human nature a very large freedom to fill in the features as it will.

10. Our question now is as to the office of reason in filling in these features. May we say that the good is a genuinely rational good? Is it in any important sense shaped by reason and defensible by it, or are we to say that ultimate ends are not matters to be argued about, but are fixed by *de facto* liking or preference? I am convinced that this latter view is wrong. And the best way to show it wrong is to go again to fact, to show that our actual goods are moulded and remoulded by reason. This moulding is a continuous process in which reason acts, not like a modeller working from without, but like a yeast within. As we look back over the course of this inward activity, we can see more clearly both the character of the process and the ultimate form toward which reason is exerting its pressure. Let us look more closely at this process of shaping our ends.

What fulfils and satisfies impulse, we have said, is, so far, good; let us start with that. It is better to indulge an impulse—any impulse —than to inhibit it, unless there are reasons to the contrary; the burden of proof is on any veto to such indulgence. This view is not likely to pass unchallenged. 'So you would call it good, would you, to indulge any impulse at all?' Very well; I have an impulse today to throw up my work, to go and lie on a sunny bank and listen to the birds. I have an impulse to tell Mr Z, who employs me, in richly descriptive terms exactly what I think of him. Is it quite obvious that it would be good to obey these impulses? And what about impulses that are brutal and sadistic? Boys have an impulse at times to pull the wings off flies. Judge Jeffreys took genuine satisfaction in inflicting misery and pain. These are people whose impulses would lead them, unless firmly checked, to every known variety of wickedness. Are you telling us that the fulfilment of such impulses is good?

This is a perfectly fair question. The answer is this: that if the in-dulgence of these impulses is wrong, as of course it is, this is not because impulse is being indulged, but because of some further circumstance attending the indulgence. There is nothing wrong in principle about lying on a bank and listening to the birds, or telling the naked truth to someone; what is wrong is to do these things under circumstances where they do more harm than good. In the more formidable case of cruelty, what is so repellent about the impulse is that, unlike those we have just considered, it is not sometimes happy in its results and sometimes not; its nature is such as inevitably to produce, and to go on producing, gratuitous misery. But abstract from it all harm-producing prospect and tendency, consider it simply as a want in whose fulfilment satisfaction can be taken, and its evil seems to vanish.

We cannot say, then, as Schopenhauer and Kierkegaard did, though for different reasons, that the natural man and normal human life are evil. If that has any meaning at all, it is the reverse of the truth. Just to be alive and to have one's animal wants fulfilled is good. To eat when one is hungry, to drink when thirsty, to sleep when tired, or—rising a little higher—to drive a nail or peel a potato well, to have someone that one cares for near at hand, to talk things over of an evening with a friend—these are goods; they are what most men rely on to make life worth living; and happily they are within most men's range. If life were as barren of good as some pessimists say it is, one would expect them to adopt the obvious and sovereign remedy for such a state of things which lies always ready to hand, but of course they seldom do; they find the satisfactions of the life they deride, including that of deriding it, too good to let go.

Sometimes what is complained of, however, is not that life is so lacking in intrinsic goods but that men are morally wicked by nature. Hobbes thought that in the natural state all men hated, feared, and made war upon, each other. But this also is untrue. The notion of original sin is a malignant myth, for which there is no sort of respectable evidence and whose retention in some quarters is a theological disgrace. Human impulse as such is neither good nor evil, and if it gets directed to evil ends, that is no necessity of human nature, but, in general, a matter of ignorance, of special defect, or of ill conditioning. 'On the whole', as Professor Sprott says, 'it would appear that we are prepared to like people who are like us and who live with us, and that hatred is a secondary development based on frustration.'[1] In biological

[1] *General Psychology*, 15

descent, and hence in instinctive complexion, we are connected far more closely with the most gregarious of animals than with the tiger or python. There is, to be sure, some truth in Dean Inge's remark that when the ape and tiger in us die, we are still left with the donkey, a very intractable animal. But some measure of intelligence too is given us by nature, and the inner pressure of intelligence is everywhere toward justice and the elimination of cruelty.

11. Now to look at the course taken by that pressure: it begins virtually at birth. The child is equipped at the outset with senses, feelings, and impulses, out of which he must fashion goods. How does he do it? To begin with, by restless experimentation. In early months he is a little monkey who will try anything once, and is only prevented from bringing his career of adventure speedily to an end by the careful watch of nurse or mother. As he becomes able to attend, some things fascinate him more than others—brightly coloured things, for example, noisy things, and, above all, things that move. He does not need to acquire an interest in these, for his tendency to respond to them is innate. So is his tendency to do something about them. If he can manage to get hold of them and push, pull, bounce, throw, smash, roll, or suck them, he may be depended upon to do so. He is like Lloyd Morgan's chick, which would peck at anything indiscriminately if it were about the right size—beads, bits of thread, cigarette-ash, its own toes, its neighbour's eyes, anything. But among these things it was quick to learn where its profit lay. It pecked at yolk of egg, and evidently liked it, for it went on pecking at similar bits. Then Morgan played his classic trick on it. He cut some orange peel into tiny bits that looked very like yolk of egg, and the chick seized on one of them. It dropped it at once, shaking its head. It tried another, dropped it again, scratched at its beak as if to wipe away the bad taste, and then swore off from orange peel once for all; indeed for a time thereafter was gingerly and distant even about yolk of egg. Before long it had the two permanently sorted out. The egg-yolk it would greet with avid peckings; the orange peel had acquired an aura for it of the distasteful and the forbidding. The fact is that without knowing it the chick had eaten the fruit of the tree of good and evil. This is a little paradigm of the entrance of valuation into the world. The child follows the same route. He dips his spoon in the sugar, revels in the tasty mouthful, and takes the earliest opportunity to do it again. Only, the next time, what he dips his spoon into happens to be salt, and then the iron enters his soul. He is forced to discriminate between two things that look alike, one of which is good and the other bad.

With this the process of valuing has begun, and intelligence is already at work in it. Of course neither chick nor child is at this stage making a *judgment* of good or bad in the full sense; to think these ideas or to use the words for them, is an achievement that still lies far ahead. Yet something very like judgment is going on. The child is carrying over and pertinently applying the results of past experience in the estimation of what is now before him. As a result of his experience with the sugar, he has formed an expectation from the salt. This expectation, if he could put it in words, would be that the salt would fulfil and satisfy his impulse in the way the sugar did. He finds that it does not. He has made a value judgment—or, if you prefer, the sort of response that on a somewhat higher level would become a judgment. Moore, Inge, and Hartmann would have it that at this point a non-natural element of goodness or value insinuates itself into the process. I see no necessity for this element. The expectation that the impulse will be fulfilled and satisfied *is* the belief—in incipient form—that the salt is good; with the experience of frustration begins the experience of evil; with the expectation, on the next appearance of salt, that this, if eaten, would frustrate again, we have the incipient judgment of badness.

It may be said that in this action of intelligence there is no remoulding of impulse, and none of that modification of our idea of good which we were going to show. This is true of two of the responses, but not of the third. When the child sees a second bowl of sugar, exactly like the first, and expects from it what he got from the earlier one, impulse is not being modified, except in the way of intensity; the expectation does arouse the impulse more strongly, but it does not attach it to any new object or break any former attachment. Similarly of the response to the salt, once this has become a habit; in the future avoidance of the salt as bad there is no modifying of impulse. But it is otherwise with the judgment passed when, upon expecting sugar, the child gets salt instead. Here there is a genuine modification of impulse and a genuine corrective of what was taken as good. What was taken as good turns out to be a fraud. To be sure, it is revealed as bad not by any rational process, but by the experience of frustration. The child saw something that he wanted; it turned out to be ashes, or worse than ashes, in his mouth; when next he saw it, he valued it differently because intelligence had come into play and interpreted the present in the light of the past.

12. This is the beginning of a course of correction and re-correction that goes on throughout his life. Let us carry the child down the years and complicate the picture slightly, while retaining, at the risk of boredom, the gastronomic emphasis. The young man has oysters for dinner. He has enjoyed oysters very much whenever he has had them, and they come to him clothed in vestigial delight. But unfortunately this is not the only meaning they carry for him. Every time without exception that he has eaten them, his pleasure has been followed the next day by headache and low spirits. What he is responding to in this case is therefore a relatively complicated prospect; his intelligence sees to that; he is accepting or rejecting, not simply the delight of a plate of oysters, but a causal sequence starting in delight and ending long after in the doldrums. Apparently no animal is ever faced with quite such a problem, for though an immediate ill effect will register itself and prevent a like response in the future, the animal mind cannot link with the present response an effect as distant as this, nor therefore respond to an extended sequence as a whole. Man can do just that. And because he can do it, the modification of impulse by intelligence in his history is far more profound. It is not that the young man with the oysters before him feels alternating surges, first of appetite at the thought of attacking them, then of revulsion at the thought of to-morrow; the complex prospect presented by his intelligence of today-followed-by-tomorrow calls out a response that is different from either of these, a response to the prospect as a whole. He may of course refuse to exercise his intelligence and fix his thought on one point of the sequence alone, for example the sating of hunger that is just ahead. But if he does exercise his intelligence, impulse is transformed by it. For the impulse that is now evoked is neither one that would have been appropriate to a part of the object, nor a chorus of impulses responding to all parts alike, but a new sort of impulse, adjusted to a new whole.

13. His notion of the goodness of indulging his impulse is similarly affected. It will not do to say that its good remains just what it was, but that now it must be offset by the prospective apathies of tomorrow. The thought of the consequences is not something tacked on to the present action while leaving it the same as before, as a trailer can be hitched to a motor-car. Intelligence enters into the character of the action and transforms it. The dinner is not simply the ingesting of something, boa-fashion, nor even the doing so with delight. Looked at from the inside, an action *is* what the agent takes it to be; for example, a man who shoots at someone he thinks is the president is essentially an assassin, whether he is mistaken or not, and whether he succeeds or not; choice is of appearance, not reality. The man who chooses or rejects the dinner is choosing a course of experience as it appears to him, and if it appears not in isolation but as an item in a sequence that is responded to as a whole, then its value will be modified, if only because his satisfaction in it will be altered, and satisfaction is a component of value. The proposed act has been set in a larger context where it no longer shines like a detached jewel; its attractiveness is diminished by its setting.

Here, then, we have intelligence modifying both the impulse and the good involved in its satisfaction through bringing remote but foreseen effects to bear on present activity. There is hardly any limit to such modification. It may proceed so far that the impulse is blotted out. Many a man who once enjoyed hunting or shooting has lost all taste for it after hearing the screaming of a mutilated hare. Persons who have been enthusiastic about driving a car may want nothing more to do with one after they have had a serious accident. To a man who has worked hard for the sake of a son on whom his hopes were focused, and has suddenly lost him, the whole of his work may now be pointless and spiritless; he is like Wordsworth's Michael who went out into his fields again, but 'never lifted up a single stone'. All this is familiar enough, and if we call attention to it, it is because, in a time when there is so much talk about the influence of impulse on thought, we may well note that thought or knowledge may not only influence impulse but even extirpate it. What has been added in recent times is the insight into how impulse may be affected by what Freud would describe as the *unconscious* operation of ideas. It has been shown that if, instead of the normal kindly feelings toward pets, a man displays dislike and fear of them, it is often because of retained but suppressed memories of frightening experiences in early days; and the proof consists in showing that when these memories are brought to light and seen to have no present bearing, the unnatural impulses tend to die away. Even so powerful an impulse as the sexual may be effectively killed, at least in its normal form, by some early disastrous adventure with it, whose effects are so retained as to overcast and blight it.

14. We have been considering how impulse, and therefore the goods
that satisfy impulse, may be modified by bringing to bear the
knowledge of effects. But the knowledge of many other relations
besides the causal may serve in the same way. I recently heard a well-
read novelist, Sir Compton Mackenzie, describing the books that had
aroused his enthusiasm as a boy. One of the authors that he devoured
with relish was G. A. Henty (I may add a parenthetical ditto to that).
After 'Winning His Spurs', 'By Sheer Pluck', 'Through Fire and
Storm', 'With Clive in India', 'With Wolfe in Canada', and 'With
Kitchener in the Sudan', and going on through some thousands of
pages of this, he had had an intermission of Henty for several years.
Then he tried him again. A few pages now and he was yawning. He
closed his Henty, and never opened him again. What had happened?
No analysis was offered, but one can surmise the line it might have
taken. When the boy read Henty first, he had no set of appraising
ideas to apply to him. The account of a youthful prodigy of valour, a
hairbreadth escape, or an East Indian scene complete with Nabobs
and elephants, was accepted gapingly at face value by a mind that could
surrender itself to the tale without doubts or criticism. Even in
maturity we could do that if a hypnotist got hold of us and put to sleep
all the areas of our mind except those concerned with his own
suggestions; we could then abandon ourselves to proposals that would
normally be surrounded and smothered by inhibitions. But in a
mind that is normal and mature, impulses are under the influence not
merely of what is immediately suggested, but of a great mass of
implied ideas which, through altering the object of impulse, alter the
impulse itself, and may change its value-sign from positive to negative.
When the man of letters or the man of the world reads the boyish
adventure book, it is likely to be with an impatient running comment:
'but no sixteen-year-old boy would talk that way'; 'but he could never
have made that escape if the guard was what it is said to be'; 'why all
the respect for such a stuffed shirt of an officer?', and so on indefinitely. That is, the implications of the tale clash continually with
what the reader has come to know of nature and human nature. The
values first put upon the book are frozen out by the new context of
ideas.

Happily the process that discredits some enjoyments confirms and
increases others. Sir Richard Livingstone has deplored the fact that
poetry is often read only in youth, whereas, as a rule, it means far
more to us in maturity. We have already quoted Newman on how

passages in Homer or Horace which, to the schoolboy are but
'rhetorical commonplaces', 'at length come home to him, when long
years have passed, and he has had experience of life, and pierce him,
as if he had never before known them, with their sad earnestness and
vivid exactness'. The good found in these passages is very different in
kind and amount at the earlier stage and at the later. Why the change?
Because the reader is now ready for the meaning the author charged
them with, because they come freighted with a significance brought
to bear on them from a wide experience of his own. Outwardly, the
reading or repeating of the lines is the same as before. In fact it is
profoundly different, because it is now infused with a hard-won
knowledge of life.

15. We are sure to be met here by an objection. When we suggest
that the value found in the dinner, the story, or the classic authors, is
changed by the entrance of *ideas*, and that these ideas are in part
constitutive of their goodness, we may expect the demurrer to arise
again that the office of intelligence is purely instrumental, that it
marshals before the contemplative eye the implications, associates,
and consequences of a certain kind of behaviour, but can only leave it
to impulse and feeling to assign the value. This protest must be
firmly rejected. It assumes that functions of the mind are divisible
from, and external to, each other in a way that the facts belie. It
imagines the mind that is considering what course to choose as a sort
of parade ground, with alternative actions and their consequences
trooping by, and impulse as the reviewing officer, standing apart and
contemplating with changing emotions, now of approval, now of enthusiasm, now of repulsion, the units that file before him. But this
officer does not exist. If one is going to use the metaphor, one must
say that as the contingents troop through the agent's consciousness,
some of them have bands playing and colours flying, while others are
dispirited and bedraggled. But it is safer to abandon metaphors. The
fact is that the impulse is not an entity that can exist, or be designated,
or intelligibly talked about apart from its content or filling. The
impulse to scratch one's nose and to read Shelley are equally impulses and perhaps equally strong, but is there not something a little
dubious in putting their fulfilment therefore on the same level? What
distinguishes them is far more important than any likeness between
them, and of course what distinguishes them is their object. They are
both wants; their fulfilment will in each case bring satisfaction; but

it is surely arbitrary to lodge the value exclusively in this one aspect of the experience. In any case such a view can hardly pretend to agreement with our actual valuations. No one does in fact put the fulfilment of these impulses on a level. The reason is that they take their character from their objects, and are unthinkable apart from these. No one announces 'I have an impulse', and stands ready to direct it at request upon scratching or *Adonais*, either of which, since it satisfies, is to be regarded as equally good. The impulse *is* an impulse to what would fulfil it; and if we recognize a difference in the value of the fulfilments, that is not on the ground that one satisfies and the other does not, for both do, but on the ground that the object, the content, the filling, of one impulse is more worth having than that of the other.

So we see again how myopic the theory is that would make value a matter of feeling alone. It is not merely that of two experiences whose value as satisfaction of impulse is the same, one may be, and often is, more highly valued than the other, though in point of mere logic that would be decisive; it is also that the very element in which, on the emotive theory, the goodness lies exclusively is itself largely at the mercy of the intellectual factor. We are not denying the importance of feeling; we have admitted that in the form of satisfaction it is indispensable to value. What we are pointing out is that there is another and independent variable—we have called it fulfilment— which is indispensable too, that this element is organic to the impulse, endowing it with its special character, and that this formative element is itself so plastic to intelligence, so shaped and reshaped by it, so susceptible to its excisions and corrections and enlargements, that one may almost say it is constituted by intelligence. Human good, in short, is a rational good.

16. But it is never rational wholly. Let us return to the path that must be followed by any advance in rationality. The course runs at the beginning, we suggested, through the discovery that some ways of fulfilling impulse—swallowing the salt, eating the oysters, reading the adolescent novel—carry with them implications that nullify their promise and force a revaluation downward, while others—the assimilation of great poetry, for example—have their value confirmed and intensified when their filaments with a wider experience have had time to take hold. We have no space to follow this development in detail. But it will throw much light on our particular topic, the rational character of moral advance, if we consider how close the parallel is between advance in knowledge and advance in the attainment of good generally. The two essential processes in the advance of knowledge may be called quantitative and qualitative, the addition of new facts to one's existing store, and the improved internal ordering of that store. Advance in the achievement of good follows the same pattern.

In the first place, just as it is good to know more rather than less, so, other things equal, the larger the range of impulses we can fulfil the better. If a boy wants to whistle or whittle, or a girl to sing or dance, if a man wants to play with his tool-chest in the cellar or a woman to re-decorate the dining-room, the burden of proof is on anyone who would say no to them; anyone who represses them arbitrarily is reducing human good.

It follows that Freud is right about repression being evil. What does not follow is the preposterous suggestion, sometimes confused with it, that it is good to indulge impulse regardless of circumstances. It does not even follow that we should allow the young to learn for themselves which indulgences are profitable and which not. The race has acquired an immense capital of experience as to what kinds of behaviour irritate, what kinds of risks are over-dangerous, what are the most useful rules about sleeping and eating and exercising, even what studies it is profitable or otherwise to pursue; and if we decline to discourage firmly a good many youthful impulses, we are exhibiting not so much liberalism as a gratuitous denial of aid. Age owes more to youth than a bare sustenance; it owes it also such of its wisdom as is transmissible. The remarkable American experiment with the free elective system, based on the assumption that the content of university education is best determined by student interest, is now presumably a closed chapter. Critics justly protested that there is something absurd in asking each generation to start its experimentation afresh, that there are some things, indeed many things, which may now be regarded as settled, that there is some knowledge and poetry and music that in virtue of having been found fulfilling and satisfying by actual ventures into it, repeated ten thousand times, may now be held without presumption to be really good, and enormously superior to some others. If experience can establish nothing, one wonders what education is for.

17. All this is true enough. But our present concern is with the other side of the picture. Though some of these activities have proved far more remunerative than others, still a second-rate activity pursued because capacity and impulse prompt one to it—and these almost always prompt in the same direction—may be more remunerative than a first-rate one pursued without such promptings. That is why impulse must be left as free to experiment as is consistent with its own safety and that of others. Hazlitt has some fine pages on a certain John Cavanagh,[1] who was distinguished by one thing only; he could play a rubber ball against a wall in the game of 'fives' better than anyone else in the world. Was this worth doing? Let us try to be clear about it. With those hedonists who would say that an activity of this kind, if it gave equal satisfaction in the way of pleasurable feeling, was as good an activity as that of a statesman or a great scholar, we cannot for one moment agree. Democracy in the realm of values, if that means that one activity is as good as another, or one man's vote as weighty as another's, or one man's life of as much worth as another's, is an impossible notion; it takes us in one more step to the conclusion that nothing is better than anything else, and then all values are abandoned together. One of the needs of our time, marked by so much half-fraudulent art and so much hesitation to talk of superior and inferior cultures, is a vigorous reassertion of the existence and all-importance of differences in value. The notion that equalitarianism in values is somehow scientific is mere confusion. Natural science places activities and cultures on the same level only in the sense that it does not consider their values at all. But once we have entered the sphere of value, as practical men must, our proper course is not to lump all activities together, but to discriminate between them as judicially as we can. If we are called on to do that in the case of John Cavanagh and his like, we shall say, not that fives-playing is as rewarding an activity as statesmanship or scholarship—that would be obtuse or invertedly snobbish—but that, being what he was, the good he derived from playing fives superbly was a greater good than he could have derived from being an incompetent statesman or scholar.

This suggests that each man's good is to be found in a different place. Probably no two living persons have quite the same set of bents and powers. And few if any persons who have ever lived can have enjoyed precisely that set of circumstances which gave those bents and powers their freest outlet. The pursuit of good is therefore a continually renewed experiment in inner discovery and outer adjust-

[1] In his essay on 'The Indian Jugglers'.

ment. We know that scholarship and carpentry and mending broken watches and broken bodies are admirable and satisfying employments, but this does not tell us where *our* good lies, and we shall never find out except by trying. Our case is far less hopeless than if our instincts, like those of the lower animals, inflexibly appointed our manner of life for us, to lose which was to lose all; we can find some measure of fulfilment along many different roads. Still, with our particular powers these roads are not all equally profitable; and hence the importance for human happiness and good of a society that is un-regimented, where youth—and, for that matter, maturity—can try its wings in various directions. Here modern society has made an enormous advance over the social stratification that marked even the democratic countries two or three generations ago. The pervading zest and hopefulness of American life are surely connected with the fact that the American boy and girl have so much freedom of motion in finding their individual place and that so many of them are allowed to try out their powers not only in schools but in colleges and universities. One cannot think it likely that in present-day America or Britain there are many 'mute inglorious Miltons' eating their hearts out in obscure frustration; free schools, scholarships, workers' education classes, cheap classics, radio and television, give countless suggestions as to what one might be and do, and opportunities for doing it, which were denied to earlier times.

18. If what we have been saying is true about the goodness of fulfilling impulses, it enables us to take the measure of a practice that has been adopted by surprisingly large numbers in both east and west, that of asceticism; and we may close with some remarks upon this practice. The ascetics have held that the good life is not stunted but furthered by the repression of at least a large range of our impulses. In Christianity itself there has been an ascetic strain from the beginning, though it was less marked in the founder himself than in his followers of later centuries. From the third century to the fifth it became a matter of rivalry among persons who tried to live the religious life exactingly which could treat the desires of the natural man with most contempt. 'If one man lived on top of a low pillar, his neighbour must mount a higher one; if one dragged about a weight of eighty pounds, a rival would tie himself to a hundred and fifty pounds. One would become famous by living at the bottom of a well, another by wallowing in a marsh infested with mosquitoes. Some rolled in thorn-bushes, a sovereign remedy, it was thought, for the lust of the flesh; others went about on all fours, and tried to eat grass, like cattle.'[1] The almost incredible details are given in a memorable chapter of Lecky.[2] In less violent forms asceticism still has its devotees in Christian society, particularly in Catholicism, where large numbers still lead a monastic life, and some cut themselves off even from those nearest to them by vows of Trappist silence. Nor is this voluntary renunciation of so large a part of life a peculiarly Christian development. It has been practised by Greeks and Jews, Buddhists, Muslims and Hindus; at the beginning of this century the number of ascetics in India was estimated at close to five millions,[3] and it must still be large. Hindu asceticism has frequently taken extreme forms, such as spending one's life on a bed of spikes, or keeping one's arm fixed above one's head till the cartilage sets and the arm atrophies. The views we have suggested as to how the good is to be achieved run so flatly counter to this curiously ancient and widespread trend that a brief comment seems desirable.

19. The assumptions on which asceticism has proceeded are, I think, all false, though in different degrees. (1) Behind most, if not all, ascetic practices there has been the conviction that they have religious merit. They are evidence of one's devotion, one's detachment from the natural life and dedication to the supernatural; and there is the conviction that in another world this loyalty will be rewarded and this suffering, even if self-inflicted, will receive its compensation. The conviction seems incoherent. If the Creator were really so pitiless toward his creatures, if his moral standards were so different from ours, that he could endow us with capacities and desires for happiness and then, to all appearance arbitrarily, decree that the path to his favour lay through flouting and crushing them, what reason should we have to suppose that he would be interested in what we call justice at all? In the face of protest from the Kierkegaardians, who are not bound by mere 'natural reason' when they discuss the Deity, we must insist that one cannot say of him that he takes toward us the attitudes *both* of the loving father *and* of the cat toward the mouse. To say both these things is to say nothing, since the two sides cancel each other out. And if one has no better warrant than in-

[1] W. R. Inge, *Christian Ethics and Modern Problems*, 109
[2] *History of European Morals*, II, 101–140
[3] Cf. Article 'Asceticism' in *Encycl. of Religion and Ethics*.

coherent dogmas of this kind for approving human frustration and misery, one has no warrant at all. The goods of health and society, however modest, are certain goods. The dogmas that would preclude them are, to say the least, uncertain.

20. Impulse is at times curbed and thwarted not in religious interests but for the sake of discipline. William James thought it was a useful practice to do something daily on the express ground that one did not want to do it, by way of keeping one's hand in at the very necessary business of doing the disagreeable. One would hardly have supposed that special contrivances of such tasks were needed, since ordinary duty is so liberal with them; but the spirit of such self-discipline is wholly admirable. Character means the habitual dominance of certain ends; this dominance implies the power to repress impulses at variance with these ends; and if a man's life is to have any architecture about it, he needs iron in his composition, a touch of that military quality that, having counted the cost of an enterprise in discomfort and difficulty, is ready to pay it unflinchingly. Asceticism draws its name from the Greek term $\overset{\prime}{\alpha}\sigma\kappa\eta\sigma\iota\varsigma$, which means a course of self-discipline, such as that undertaken by the athlete; and so far as it has revealed to us the power of the human will in 'bringing the body under', it has served a useful purpose. Of such self-training, limited by a clear perception of its end, we have only praise to offer. But this is not asceticism at all in the ordinary meaning of the term.

21. (2) Asceticism has commonly assumed that the impulses connected with the body are base and are to be treated accordingly. The appetites were to be overruled by periodic fasts; the love of bodily ease and comfort was to be countered by hair shirts, coarse garments, and hard beds; sex was, if possible, to be disregarded totally, and the celibate life set up as an ideal. It is true that the so-called bodily satisfactions have an intensity that make their solicitations dangerously powerful and may lead us to prefer them to the more difficult and complex goods of the cultivated mind. A warning of their poverty and transience as compared to some other satisfactions is therefore quite in order. (May I confess in passing that I find something singularly unattractive in the amount of time and care devoted by such a distinguished mind as A. E. Housman on his French holidays to running down the towns and hotels that had the most tasteful vintages of wine, just as I think Beau Brummel's pre-occupation with his shirts and buttons hardly worthy even of his own smaller spirit.) Still there is no reason to say that because food and drink and comfort and pleasing appointments are not the greatest of goods, they are not goods at all. Nor is there any reason for dismissing them on the ground that they are bodily goods. Strictly speaking there are no such things. All goods are equally bodily, in the sense that all the experiences that have value are equally dependent on bodily conditions. On the other hand, all goods are equally non-bodily if that means that they are dependent on minds. Some satisfactions, like those of eating and drinking, involve physical activities a little more obviously than others like composing music or metaphysics, but a smart blow on the head will end all of them equally. The attempt to discredit some goods as merely bodily rests on a half-thought-out dualism that has itself been long discredited. The impulses to such goods are wholly natural and innocent, and those who would place a ban on their fulfilment as somehow base or sordid do so with no rational ground.

22. (3) But Puritans and others of ascetic temper have often taken a different line. They have held that the satisfactions of the natural man were not so much evils as distracting baubles, frivolities that were better dispensed with because they got in the way of more serious concerns. Pictures and images in church diverted attention from higher things; the theatre, the dance, games, fictions, music, were vanities rather than evils, pleasing apples of Sodom with only ashes inside and no nutriment for the spirit; the man of serious mind would have none of them. This too was short-sighted. Puritanism, though a nobler ethic than hedonism, made a curiously similar mistake; it did not conceive of human good as a sufficiently organic whole, and by concentrating its interest unduly, impoverished that interest itself. Worship is not necessarily richer in the bare meeting-house than in the cathedral; and while pure meditation requires a higher flight of the spirit than the ministries of eye and ear, these are not really rivals and distractions; in most minds they are aids to it. The whole hierarchy of ideas in which the world and the flesh are associated with the devil, and the body is 'Brother Ass', an alien beast of burden, is the relic of a theology and metaphysic that in the west have largely disappeared for lack of any ground in experience, and will similarly fade out in the east as evidence makes its way.

For the evidence leaves no doubt that Brother Ass, far from being an enemy or an alien, is the appointed means by which if at all, the spirit must reach its destination, and that if one neglects to feed and water it, it will not only refuse to proceed, but will manage to breed strange humours in one's own brain. The mediaeval mystics were inclined to regard the feverish imaginings of self-imposed starvation and torment as signs and wonders from another realm, and sought them deliberately. They paid the price, first in illusion and later in disillusion. 'Attempts to force on artificially these very abnormal mental states inevitably lead to severe nervous reactions, in which the depression, wretchedness, and fear of being abandoned by God are quite as violent as the joys of the mystical state.'[1] It has been notorious since Freud that the sex impulse also, if repressed, will probably avenge itself by cropping up in perverse forms, of which a vaguely erotic mysticism has been identified as one.[2] I do not suggest that periods of retreat from 'the world' into silence and self-assessment are not on occasion most valuable, but these are not attempts to suppress or frustrate impulse, but rather to freshen it. Our principle is a simple one; when impulses do not actually get in each other's way, their fulfilments tend to support and enhance each other. Milton and Purcell were not less religious, but more, by reason of the poetry and music by which their religion was expressed, as is prettily intimated indeed in Purcell's epitaph in Westminster Abbey: 'he hath gone where alone his harmonies can be exceeded'. A George Fox brought up on Shakespeare as well as the Bible, a Mather mellowed by fiction as well as drilled in Exodus and Leviticus, would have been different men from what they were, and possibly less effective. But they would have been less fanatical, more understanding, and more sane.

In sum, our view that goodness lies in the fulfilment and satisfaction of impulse conflicts with the ascetic assumptions on which countless earnest persons of both east and west have conducted their lives. Should this give us pause? A brief review of these assumptions suggests, on the contrary, that they are profoundly mistaken. Why have they been so widely accepted? Not, certainly, because of any warrant provided by experience. The proximate cause has usually been a religious belief as to the merit acquired by suffering, but behind this belief is no process of rational argument; it springs, rather, from the desperate desire, in times when life is cheap, or when the material

---

[1] Inge, op. cit., 110
[2] Cf. J. H. Leuba, The Psychology of Religious Mysticism

conditions are grinding, or when coarseness and sensuality are widespread, to find some haven of dignity for the human spirit. The desire is natural and pathetic. Unfortunately neither fulfilment nor satisfaction is to be found along that road.

CHAPTER XIV

REASON AND POLITICS

1. Political science and political theory are very different kinds of inquiry. Political science, as we here use the term, is a study of fact. It describes the various forms of government; it explains the formation and function of the American Congress, the British Parliament, the French Chamber of Deputies; it studies the various methods of passing, amending, and enforcing laws. These are matters of fact, not of value. But political theory, or the philosophy of politics, is specially concerned with problems of value. What are the ends a government should serve? Where should the ultimate power in government reside? By what right does a government claim that we should obey its laws? What are the limitations, if any, to our right to freedom of speech and action? These are all questions of what *ought* to be. They are really questions of applied ethics.

Why, then, should there be a separate study of political theory? Why not absorb it into ethics and have done with it? The answer is that political and moral obligation seem to differ, and that the simple dependence of the one on the other that we have just suggested has been widely disputed. A legal or political obligation is one that is imposed by law; a moral obligation is commonly believed to hold independently of law. The two seem not only different, but at times even to conflict. Suppose a Fascist or Communist state passed a law that would send into concentration camps whole classes of citizens that one believed to be innocent. It would then be one's legal obligation to aid and abet the government in its work of running these people down and rounding them up. But many persons believe that it would be their moral obligation to break the law deliberately and help such hounded persons to escape. Again, a legal or political *right* seems quite a different thing from a moral right. If British women have a moral right to the suffrage on the same terms as men, they no doubt had it in Victorian times; but they did not get it as a political right till 1928. Political and moral rights thus seem to fall sharply asunder.

We shall see, I think, that they are much nearer together than they seem.

2. Suppose that the question is raised of the basis of a political right or obligation. *Why* ought I obey a given law? It will not do to say, Because it is on the statute books; for if that were a sufficient answer, it would follow that I should obey everything on the statute books, and in extreme cases that may be immoral. The question is not one that can be answered by pointing to any law or sovereign or governmental machinery, for it is a question as to the ultimate justification of any of these things. There must be some ground for the immense (and increasing) claims the state makes on us in the way of taxes, for example, and military service; and there must be some ground for the great privileges we demand from it in return in the way of freedom, equal treatment, and protection. Can these grounds be rationally set out and defended?

I think they can, and even that it may be done in fairly small compass. In the discussion that follows, I have two purposes in mind. The first is to deal independently with the political question by showing that among the more notable answers there is only one that has any high degree of plausibility. The second is to show that this one accords so well with the account of the ethical end supplied in the last three chapters that the two accounts corroborate and fortify each other.

The fundamental question of political theory is, Why should I obey the law? An adequate answer to that question would carry with it the answer to such questions as, Why should there be a government at all? What are the grounds of its rights against me and my rights against it?, and How in principle are these rights to be limited? In the history of political thought there have been six dfferent types of answer to the question, each advocated by philosophers of some substance.

These types of theory admit of modifications, but the choice must apparently be made from within their circuit, for it is difficult to think of any outside that circuit that has the least plausibility. Some may find in them a rough progression, fixed by the order in which they would occur to a questioning mind, and I have put in the last place the theory that seems to me best to survive such questioning. All have their difficulties, and if we are to see the strength of any of them, it must be against the background of the others. I shall sketch and comment on each of them. The theories are that our political rights and duties are based on (1) nothing, (2) force, (3) the will of God, (4) contract, (5) self-evidence, (6) a rational will.

3. (1) Some people have a short way with political rights and duties: they put them down as myths. The state, with its expensive machinery for the making and enforcement of law, is an excrescence that should be done away. This is the view of anarchism. The name has come to be associated with bombs and the black hand, though the creed does not necessarily include violence, and has been held by such gentle souls as Kropotkin and Tolstoy, as well as by avowed advocates of violence like Bakunin and Sorel. Anarchism at its best springs from a passionate belief in freedom on the one hand and human goodness on the other. It begins by asking you whether you really believe in freedom. You say 'Yes'. It then asks you whether laws that reach down into your pocket and take your money, and that place restrictions on your travel, on the way you conduct your business, even on what you shall read and write, are not interferences with freedom. You say, 'Yes, they are, but in a democracy these are restrictions imposed upon us by ourselves, and hence are not vicious or oppressive.' 'But *I* did not vote for them', replies the anarchist, 'so to tell *me* that they are self-imposed is false'. 'Well', you say, 'they are at least imposed by the majority, and majority rule is not tyranny'. 'But if a man's freedom is cut down', answers the anarchist, 'is it any the less truly cut down because this is done by a majority?' 'No', you say, 'I suppose not'. 'Very well, by what right, then, does the majority cut it down? Can you claim that the majority is necessarily right?' 'No, I could not say that.' 'Then majority rule means the coercion of people by a power that admits it may be wrong and the people it is coercing right?' 'Yes, I suppose so.' 'Well, that', says the anarchist; 'whatever nice names you may call it by, is as truly tyranny as rule by Czar or dictator'. 'What do you propose to substitute for it?' 'What I would substitute for it', he replies, 'is the most effective of all known forces in producing good citizens, and indeed the only force that is enough by itself to produce them, namely, the sense of decency and justice. If men have such a sense, there is no need of hounding them into decency by threats and the police; and if they do not have it, you will certainly never put it into them by coercion; in fact, you will prevent their acquiring it, since they will be bound to think of the state and its demands as hostile impositions. "You cannot make men moral by act of Parliament", but if you allow their moral sense to have its way, you can dispense with Parliament entirely'.

4. It sounds fairly plausible. And yet a moment's reflection will show that it is doctrinaire idealism of a pathetically irresponsible sort. What is wrong with it? (a) For one thing, it makes the quite ungrounded assumption that if there were no law or police, everybody would be animated by the spirit of *noblesse oblige*, and hence no one would need protection by government. It would be pleasant to think this, but surely it would be visionary. In every large community there are persons who, by will or nature, are moral defectives, just as there are defectives in sight and hearing. The multiple murderer Lacenaire said in a published confession that he had no more feeling when he killed a man than when he killed a fly. Why should anyone suppose that Al Capone and Lucky Luciano would walk the paths of righteousness if only there were no state and no police to provoke their pure spirits to just resentment? If the old doctrine of *homo homini lupus* is true of only one man in a thousand, none of the others is safe; one man running amuck will terrorize a whole community. Freedom without government would in all practical probability be the Utopia of a frontier mining community before vigilante squads were organized, in which the majority who had scruples were goudged and plundered by the minority who did not.

(b) But it is not merely to keep thugs in order that government is necessary; it is also to keep the rest of us in order. We saw long ago in considering St Francis that even universal love would not by itself provide a solution of the problems of actual life. My neighbour and I may have all respect and the best of intentions toward each other and still may differ as to where our properties join, whether I shall have the privilege of turning my house into a crematorium, and whether he shall be permitted to use his for a glue factory. There are endless communal conflicts that cannot be settled by good will, because within the limits of good will there remain very deep differences in interest and belief, even as to what it is that good will requires, and there must be some impartial agency to give judgment and, if need be, to enforce that judgment.

(c) There is certainly very little chance of convincing most men by argument that society would be better ungoverned, so it is natural enough that anarchists should have turned so commonly to violence;

that is virtually their only hope. But it is a vain hope, because self-contradictory. If the minority did succeed in overthrowing the government and imposing its will by force, that would not be a situation in which the monster, government, had been finally slain; it would be in effect the setting up of another government, more nakedly coercive than before. It might be said that violence, though a necessary means, could be dispensed with, once the end of overthrow had been achieved. But there is plenty of evidence in history, including very painful recent evidence, that that is not the way violence works. Successful resort to it breeds reliance on it; reliance on it breeds resistance to it; and before long the supporters of what they thought a programme for freeing the people find themselves bound more firmly by force than ever.

5. (2) The next step in political theory is a swing to the opposite extreme from anarchism. Once it becomes plain that government is necessary, and a government ready to employ force, it may seem that the exercise of force is the essential thing about it and that the possession of power is all the justification it needs. Carlyle somewhere says that the ultimate question between two men is 'Can I kill thee?' or 'Can'st thou kill me?' and many persons have seemed to see a great light when it occurred to them that human morals were artificial conventions, and that when the frippery was torn off, what one had left was the bare biological fact that one man was a better man than another in the sense that he was a more viable biological specimen. That bull in a herd is the leader which can gore the others into submission; that man is the natural leader who by his strength and cunning can compel others to do his will. He may seek to justify himself by their need of him, and they may agree; but that is a rationalization. What really justifies the dominance of man over men, class over class, governors over governed, is the power to make the dominance good; there is no ulterior or rational morality by which an Attila or a Napoleon can be condemned if he passes the supreme test of success. Hitler lost, so he was wrong; if he had won, would he not have been a hero?

This doctrine was defended by Thrasymachus in the *Republic*, and by Machiavelli in *The Prince;* in essentials it was accepted by Hobbes in the *Leviathan*, by Mandeville in the *Fable of the Bees*, by Treitschke in his *Politics*, by Nietzsche in *Beyond Good and Evil*, by Santayana in *Dominations and Powers*, and by the jurist Oliver Wendell Holmes in a curious panegyric of 'natural law'.[1] It was practised by the Borgia whom Machiavelli so much admired, and has been adopted by a host of predatory seekers after power. When one of these, of unhappy memory, wanted to send an appropriate birthday present from Berchtesgaden to Rome, he sent a magnificently bound set of Nietzsche's *Werke*. No genuine superman like either of this precious pair will allow his will to be blocked by what is called reason and justice. *L'état c'est moi;* power cannot corrupt, because what it does is right by definition; states have no morals. It would be an error in fact and in tactics to suppose that the history of this ancient doctrine has now come to an end. It needs to be examined continually anew. What is wrong with it?

6. (a) In the first place it can hardly mean what it says. If one man bullies another, or one state subdues another, and we ask how either would justify such behaviour, it hardly makes sense to reply that this was an exercise of force and therefore good as such. If men use force on others, it is because they have an end to be gained by it; they want to get what someone else has, or to avenge some fancied wrong, or to achieve the feeling of an enlarged ego. The mere exercise of force is never actually an end in itself, and when anyone tries to justify such exercise by making it out to be a great good, it is generally clear that he is confusing an end with a means. Take away the goods that the use of force was expected to bring, and the force itself has little or no attraction.

(b) The theory would justify actions, causes, and governments, that in all our ordinary thinking are held to be incompatible with each other. If Islam succeeded in imposing itself at the expense of Christianity in the Middle East, Islam was right and Christianity wrong; if, farther west, these results were reversed, Christianity was right and Islam wrong. Communism is right because it is in the saddle—in Russia and China; but a free economy is right because it too is dominant—in the Americas. It may be replied that the real test is applied when the two powers come directly into conflict with each other. Such conflicts have often resulted in the past in a seesaw movement, in which dominance passed from one side to the other and back again. Are we to say that the same cause is alternately right and wrong as its fortunes wax and wane? It is to be doubted whether anyone really thinks this way.

[1] *Harvard Law Review*, Vol. 32, pp. 40–44

(c) If a programme were justified by its success in imposing itself, the question whether any cause espoused in human history *deserved* to succeed would be a meaningless one. If we know that it did succeed, the question of its merit is already answered; if it did not, there would equally be no point in asking about its desert, for to say that it did not succeed is all we could mean by saying that it ought not to have succeeded. But this is simply to refuse to admit a distinction that everyone sees and makes unless arguing for a pre-conceived theory. It is very far from meaningless to ask whether if Hitler had succeeded in imposing himself he would have been right; it was a question actually asked by millions and actually answered by them, at a time when he seemed irresistible, in a way that would have had no sense if might *meant* right.

(d) To say that might makes right is to commit oneself to the further view that whatever is, is right. Whatever actually happens, whether a tidal wave or a human volition, happens because an event has power to exclude alternative events; it proves its power, and therefore its rightness by the fact that it happens at all. *Die Weltgeschichte ist das Weltgericht.* By such reasoning one could justify every crime in the statute books, and make a successful thug or border terrorist into a better man than the martyrs, who proved their wrongness by getting destroyed. People can talk this way, but one can hardly suppose that they believe what they say, or that they make any attempt to practise it. When they are browbeaten or robbed themselves, they do not as a rule acclaim their attacker as right; they will probably be heard protesting as loudly as anyone else. The more candid and clearheaded of them usually see where the doctrine is taking them and drop it before they reach overt absurdity. When Huxley was asked to give the Romanes lecture on 'Evolution and Ethics', he was expected to take the line that whatever proved itself by its power of survival was ethically best. He fluttered the Oxonian dovecots by advocating the opposite proposition. 'The practice of that which is ethically best—what we call goodness or virtue—involves a course of conduct which, in all respects, is opposed to that which leads to success in the cosmic struggle for existence. In place of ruthless self-assertion it demands self-restraint; in place of thrusting aside, or treading down, all competitors, it requires that the individual shall not merely respect, but shall help his fellows; its influence is directed, not so much to the survival of the fittest, as to the fitting of as many as possible to survive.' If nature dictated power politics, what that showed was not that power politics were legitimate but that the laws of biology could not settle ethical questions.

(e) To reduce right to might is not so much to adopt a new kind of ethics as to do away with ethics. If any sort of policy that a man or a state can impose by force is right, then the distinctively moral meaning of the term has vanished, and one is using it in a quite new sense, as if one said, 'by the word "sour" I will from now on mean a shade of red'. ' "Might makes right" means, in plain English, that there is no *right* at all . . . But by saying "might makes *right*", rather than "right is a fiction", a quality is imported from a rival system which gives the doctrine a moral aroma . . . the reader who understands will not be deceived by this delicate odour of sanctity. He will recognize it as the perfume of a floral offering placed upon the bier of deceased morality in memory of long association.'[1]

7. (3) Governments are not to be justified, then, by their power. They may use power wrongly, and therefore power is not sufficient reason for its own use; there must be some further authority by which its use it to be justified. Very well, what authority? The next step in many minds was to say *divine* authority. If governors did not rule by right of any position granted them by nature, it was presumably by a right coming from beyond nature and sanctioned by God himself. This view is not popular today, but it has had a vast vogue in the past. It was held by countless able mediaeval thinkers, was accepted and put into practice by the Geneva of John Calvin and the Boston of the Puritans, and is still orthodox theory in Spain and some of the states of South America. The strength of its appeal is not difficult to understand.

Suppose one starts, as early Christians did, with the view that in the recorded words of Christ one has unerring truth and guidance. What was his attitude toward politics? He said very little about it. We were to render unto Caesar the things that were Caesar's, but Caesar's, after all, was not the important kingdom, but another, the Kingdom of God, which was not of this world, and was soon to supplant all earthly kingdoms. His attitude was interpreted by St Paul as one of passive obedience to the temporal authorities. 'Let every soul be subject unto the higher powers. For there is no power but of God; the powers that be are ordained of God.'[2] The same teaching

[1] Max Otto, *Things and Ideals*, 85–86
[2] *Romans*, XIII, 1–7

was echoed by Peter, or the writer of the first epistle bearing his name:'Submit yourselves to every ordinance of man for the Lord's sake; whether it be to the king, as supreme; or unto governors, as unto them that are sent by him for the punishment of evil-doers and for the praise of them that do well.'[1]

But the years and centuries wore on, and the expected spiritual kingdom deferred its coming till the hope of it dimmed. By the time of Augustine in the fourth century, the Church itself had become a power that rivalled the empire. What was more, the two powers impinged upon each other at so many points that passive obedience in the expectation of an early release was no longer practical politics. And when there was conflict, which was to have precedence? The answer was given in a letter apparently written by Pope Gelasius to the Roman emperor in 494: 'There are two systems under which chiefly this world is governed, the sacred authority of the priests and the royal power. Of these the greater weight is with the priests in so far as they will answer to the Lord even for kings in the last judgment.'[2] When a difference of opinion arose between St Ambrose and an Arian rival for his see, and the Emperor Valentinian ordered that the matter be submitted to an imperial court, Ambrose answered that this was a matter of faith, and that 'in a matter of faith, bishops are wont to judge emperors, not emperors bishops.' The glory of princes was to the glory of bishops as the brightness of lead to the brightness of gold.[3] Not only questions of faith must be decided by the ecclesiastical hierarchy, but also the crucial issue what *was* a question of faith. By the time we reach Gregory VII in the eleventh century, we find the Pope maintaining that he is the ultimate court of appeal on all questions, civil or religious. 'It is for him to judge and punish Emperors and Kings, to receive complaints against them, to shield the nations from their tyranny, to depose rulers who are neglectful of their duties, and to discharge their subjects from the oath of fealty.'[4] After all, did not Scripture set the prophets above the kings, and record direct rebukes and castigations meted out by Samuel to Saul, and Nathan to David?

But then a curious thing happened. The very argument used by the Church was turned against it. As the states of modern Europe

[1] *I Peter*, II, 13–17
[2] Quoted in Dunning, *Political Theories, Ancient and Mediaeval*, 166
[3] *Ibid.*, 170
[4] Gierke, *Political Theories of the Middle Age* (tr. Maitland), 15. Indeed Gregory went even further: 'Nescitis quia angelos iudicabimus? quanto magis saecularia!'

began to develop and show a not unnatural restiveness under this doctrine, their scholars examined very carefully the ground of the claim to papal authority. This claim was supported from Scripture. The nationalist scholars found that they too could quote Scripture for their purpose, and show without much difficulty that heads of secular governments could also claim a divine right to obedience. 'The powers that be', said St Paul roundly, 'are ordained of God.' What could be plainer? The arguments for the independent authority of governors was not, indeed, in all states equally necessary. In states where the national church was subordinate to the state and the head of the state a loyal member of that church, as in mediaeval and modern Spain, the problem was not felt so acutely. It was otherwise in Protestant states. In England, Sir Robert Filmer felt it necessary to offer a separate proof that the king derived his right not from the church, but straight from Deity, as attested by Holy Writ.

8. One could hardly find a better instance than this controversy of how philosophic fashion changes. In democratic countries there are few persons left who would take this line of argument seriously. Critics would say that it not only proceeded from a questionable assumption but drew from that assumption a conclusion that was also questionable.

(a) The assumption has to do with the kind of authority to be ascribed to the Bible. To take this, as the Puritans did, and as Roman Catholics still do, as inspired throughout[1], is an impossible position for anyone who considers objectively the process by which the canon of scripture came to be adopted, or for anyone who has looked into the way primitive history and literature is written. The kind of argument, often dialectically acute, by which Roman Catholic apologists or Protestant 'fundamentalists' like Gresham Machen attempt to prove the plenary inspiration of the Bible, seems today singularly inconclusive because, as our knowledge of comparative religion, of the influence of will and feeling on belief, and of the processes generally of the pre-scientific mind has advanced, the notion that these writings can only be accounted for by an irruption from without the natural order has become less and less plausible.

(b) But even if the supernatural origin of these writings is accepted

---

[1] Cf. 'Providentissimus Deus' of Leo XIII: 'All the books which the Church receives as sacred and canonical are written wholly and entirely, with all their parts, at the dictation of the Holy Ghost . . . '

without question, what political inference are we to draw? The doctrine that prophets and priests outrank temporal rulers and may denounce them is clearly implied in some parts of the Bible; the doctrine that they should conform to the commands of such rulers is expressly taught in other parts; but these doctrines can hardly both be true. Roman Catholics have continued to cling to the doctrine that all parts of scripture are inspired, and have sought to save the consistency of the text by a system of exegesis so powerful that it can twist the straightest meanings into astonishingly convenient forms. Liberal Protestant thinkers, while disdaining such performances, have recognized that to insist on the revealed truth of both sides of a contradiction is not to exalt revelation, but to discredit it, and hence have gradually narrowed the scriptural channel through which it is conceived to have come. Having declined to accept the Old Testament books, with their stories of Samuel and Nathan, as revealed political theory, they went on to express doubts of the Pauline epistles, with their acquiescence in slavery.[1] There has been a tendency to narrow the channel of revelation still further to the authentic teaching of Christ. But this too has been self-defeating. For that authentic teaching contains, as we have seen, so little of definite bearing on political right or duty that the theory of government based on it can be hardly more than a set of cloud-castles.

(c) But the ultimate reason why politics cannot be based upon theology is not the difficulty of getting a definite or coherent teaching from scripture, serious as that is. It is rather that the notion of two standards of truth and right, one natural, the other supernatural, is not in the end intelligible. If there are these two standards, they may in theory clash; indeed there have been many cases in which revelation seemed to say one thing about people's rights or duties and natural reason something very different. Mediaeval judges read the order in Exodus that witches should not be allowed to live and, in spite of their human compunctions and sympathies, proceeded to burn thousands of miserable lonely old women; the Puritans read the order in I Samuel to destroy the Amalekites with all their wives and

---

[1] The use made of the Bible in the defence of slavery is a warning that should not be forgotten. Cf. the following from Alexander H. Stephens, Vice-President of the Confederacy: 'To maintain that slavery is *in itself sinful*, in the face of all that is said and written in the Bible upon the subject, with so many sanctions of the relation by the Deity himself, does seem to me to be little short of blasphemous! It is a direct imputation upon the wisdom and justice, as well as the declared ordinances of God . . .' Quoted in V. L. Parrington, *Main Currents in American Thought*, 92.

N

children, and thinking the American Indians limbs of Satan like the Amalekites, slaughtered them wholesale; Kierkegaard read the order to Abraham to drive a sword into the heart of his son, and indulged in a rhapsody on the duty of murder if divinely directed. What should be done in cases where natural and allegedly supernatural ethics thus come into conflict? There are three possibilities. The two imperatives may be taken as co-ordinate. But that means that they cancel each other out, and we are left without moral direction. Or the revealed imperative may be given the primacy, as it actually was in the cases just mentioned. That has meant in numberless cases a large correction and purification of ordinary insight. It has required in others that the plain dictates of reason and kindliness should be over-ridden, and hence it has in fact implied much more. It has suggested that since in such cases the clear dictates of reason and kindliness are mistaken, they may be so everywhere; the insights of our natural faculties are not to be relied on. But then morality generally is undermined, and such 'saints' as Kierkegaard can invoke divine sanction for the conduct of a cad. The third possibility is to recognize as the ultimate authority our own natural faculties in their self-critical exercise, which in the end means our reason. One may take the judgment of reason either as an independent verdict, or as the criterion of what revelation really is; these amount to the same thing, for in either case, the ultimate appeal is to rational insight. In my own estimation, this is the only course that will not involve our natural conscience and reason in hopeless discredit, and when that happens, we have lost our moorings utterly. A politics based on theology is either implicitly rationalist or else it is self-stultifying.

9. (4) With the failure to find a supernatural base for their political rights and duties, men began again to search for it on the human scene. Was there not some naturalistic way of accounting for how governments and laws and the mass of rights and obligations that go with them had come into existence? Unfortunately history fails us here. At the beginning of human records, men are already organized in communities with kings or chiefs. But there must have been some earlier state of things from which this organization emerged, now recoverable perhaps only by imagination and conjecture. A number of ingenious thinkers—Grotius, Hooker, Hobbes, Locke and Rousseau—tried to reconstruct this 'state of nature' and the probable route of escape from it. The pictures they formed of it varied greatly. Hobbes thought it must have been very like the state of things among the Indians of America, who were reported to be hunting each other's scalps in a *bellum omnium contra omnes*. Rousseau, who thought of civilized society as far gone in degeneracy, was inclined to picture the state of nature in the opposite way, as a sort of elysium where 'noble savages' lived in brotherly harmony. But though these writers could not agree on what the primitive state was like and had no means of settling their differences, they were in broad agreement on how men escaped from this state into orderly governed society.

They held that it was through an agreement or a contract. Hobbes' account of the matter was admirably clear. Suppose that no sort of government exists—no laws, no police, no ruler—and that there is no society either except a set of individuals or families scattered about in the primitive woods. Food is scarce; possessions are few; there is no protection for anybody against the envy and thievery of others; and since the strongest men can easily be done to death by the weakest if taken unawares, everybody is insecure. In a famous sentence Hobbes summed up the life in such a society as 'solitary, poor, nasty, brutish, and short'. The only way, he thought, in which government could have emerged from such anarchy was through the coming together of these human atoms and their reaching an understanding with each other. This would be to the manifest interest of all. If two of us are neighbours uncertain of each other's intentions, each of us will better his lot by getting the other to agree not to attack him on condition that the other foregoes the like privilege against him. Still, something more is necessary. For how does either know that the other will keep his promise? Hobbes thought that in a society, or rather non-society, in which all men were self-seeking, there was only one way of assuring that they would keep a covenant. That was to set up through the covenant itself a means of enforcing it, that is, an umpire and ruler whose word all parties would agree to accept as final and whose power would be absolute. No doubt at first this umpire was some particularly strong or able man. But in time he had to have helpers in the way of advisers, judges, captains, and tax-collectors; in short, he became a government. We must not let this increasing complexity deceive us, however, as to the simple facts about the origin and nature of government. Government is an authority set up by agreement among men who are insecure and who jointly surrender their rights to this authority for the sake of becoming secure. Hence, if I now have duties to the government or rights as against other men, it is in virtue of an implicit compact between us that we will obey the rules laid down by this umpire.

With all the anthropological knowledge that has accumulated since Hobbes' time at our disposal, it is easy to make game of this contract theory. Men have never at any time lived like scattered atoms in the woods; they have lived in families or groups of families from the beginning; of that we can now be virtually certain. There is no reason to think that they were ever so exclusively selfish as Hobbes supposed; there is no ground, indeed, for believing that the social compact was an historical occurrence at all. But then it is doubtful whether any of the political thinkers who talked about the social compact would have insisted on its having actually occurred, or have supposed their theory invalidated if this were disproved. It is perfectly possible, they would have said, to present a true theory of the state by means of a useful myth. If we have obligations to the government, if it has rights to put its long fingers down into our pockets and even to tell us how we shall or shall not behave, if we all claim rights against other persons to be let alone, and acknowledge duties to leave them alone, is it not really because of a tacit agreement among us, none the less binding because we have never sat down at a table and signed it, that for the sake of our common advantage we will recognize the state as authoritative and give obedience to its laws?

10. With this view, we have taken a long step beyond any of the theories so far considered. Unlike anarchism and power politics, it recognizes that there are such things as political duties; unlike theological politics, it looks for the grounds of those duties where there is a reasonable hope of finding them, in men's actual mind and history. Will it serve? Consider for a moment what it tries to explain. It tries to explain not merely how the state came into existence, but also how there came about the rights and duties toward each other possessed by citizens of the state. Before the contract was made there was no duty of keeping engagements, no duty of respecting others' lives and property, no right on my part to be left alone or on others' part that I should leave them alone. Once I have agreed with others to recognize these rights and duties, they are obligatory, but not before. They are instituted by the contract and valid only because of it. Now there is one great obvious fatal defect in this theory. It is that the apparently neat explanation is a complete begging of the question. I make a contract to the effect that in future I shall keep all contracts, including this one. Now before I make this contract, one or other of two things must hold: either I have an obligation to keep contracts or I have not. If I have not, then the contract that I should keep all future contracts is obviously without force, and hence they too will be without force. Clearly if I have no obligation in the first place to keep contracts, it is idle to suppose I can bring the obligation into existence by a contract, for I have just said that no such contract will place me under any sort of obligation. Suppose, then, that I do have an initial obligation to keep contracts. In that case, the very thing that the contract was invoked to explain is admitted to be present without it, and the theory becomes superfluous. So of all the other rights and obligations supposed to be explained by the contract. If, in the state of nature, I have the duty of helping a man in distress, of keeping a promise to go hunting with him, and of not pilfering his bow and arrow, then a contract is needless to explain such duties. On the other hand, if duty must wait for existence till a contract is made, I shall never acquire any duties at all.

11. (5) Rights and duties, then, have roots that run into a far deeper soil than can be provided by any contract, historical or implicit. They precede government and organized society; they do not spring from conventions or engagements; they are what makes these possible. They belong to us not as citizens but as men. It is absurd to suppose that if I meet a Frenchman in the tropics where there is no government, and reflect that we have never made a convenant to recognize each other's rights, I am therefore at liberty to cheat and rob him. No one but a barbarian would talk this way about individuals, yet there have been men of apparent sense and soberness who were ready to talk this pernicious nonsense about nations. They have held that in the absence of international government, no obligation and nothing that can be called a right is being broken by a war of conquest and annexation, at any rate if it is successful. This is Machiavelli without Machiavelli's excuse, and I have said all I propose to say about it. Our question is: if civilized man repudiates this way of talking and insists that men have rights and duties not granted by any government or engagement, what is their basis?

Here there enters the doctrine that underlay two of the three great modern revolutions, the American and the French, namely the doctrine of natural rights. On June 12, 1776, the representatives of the colony of Virginia adopted a declaration to the effect that 'all men are by nature equally free and independent, and have certain inherent rights, of which, when they enter into a state of society, they cannot by any compact deprive or divest their posterity'; and when the thirteen states, less than a month later, adopted the Declaration of Independence, they did so in similar language: 'We hold these truths to be self-evident, that all men are created equal, that they are endowed by their Creator with certain unalienable rights, that among these are life, liberty, and the pursuit of happiness.' In 1789 the French National Assembly adopted the following as articles I and II of the declaration of the rights of man: 'I. Men are born, and always continue, free and equal in respect to their rights. . . . II. The end of all political associations is the preservation of the natural and imprescriptible rights of man. . . .'[1]

One can see, as one looks back, that this doctrine was more than a passing outbreak of eighteenth-century rationalism, and that it was not merely extemporized for the occasion. The seeds of the doctrine were present in the Stoic teaching that all men partook of a common reason, in the Romans' practice of falling back on a natural equity transcending national boundaries when they had to deal with subjects of other states, in the Christian idea of the infinite value of each soul in the sight of God, and in Kant's teaching that every man should be treated as an end in himself. What exactly it was about a man that gave him these natural rights was not as a rule made clear. The doctrine was commonly used as a protest by those who felt they were being kept down; there was a strong sense that to use a man as a stick or stone or beast of burden was to do violence to his nature, and since what distinguished him most conspicuously from these other things was his reason, the rights to life, liberty, and the pursuit of happiness were ascribed to all rational men as such. Argument for this view was hardly thought necessary. 'We hold these truths to be self-evident', began the American founding fathers. Anyone who saw what a man was—a rational creature, capable of looking before and after, and choosing his own ends—could see that to take from such a creature his life, his freedom, or the work of his hands, was to act a lie; it was to treat him as if he were what he manifestly was not. And since he held these rights in virtue of his nature, they could never be taken away; they were 'unalienable' or 'imprescriptible'.

12. I think that here we are nearing the truth. That we do have

---

[1] These documents are given in the appendices to D. G. Ritchie's *Natural Rights*.

natural rights that rest on no government and no convention, and that these rights are to be made out by reason, will not here be denied. But has this doctrine hit on the true ground for them? We can see clearly, I think, that it has not. When we say that something has a certain property in virtue of being what it is, that from the nature of a circle, for example, it follows self-evidently that it has the shortest perimeter of any figure of equal area, we see that wherever the conditioning nature is present, the property must be present too. So also of rights. If they belong to the nature of man as rational, then rational men must possess them everywhere and always, as the revolutionists saw. But does it really make sense to say this? Take the right to life itself. Suppose a man wantonly attacks you in one of those desperate situations in which it is your life or his. If you take his life as the only possible means of saving your own, have you violated his 'imprescriptible' right to life? A Bluebeard commits a series of deliberate murders, is apprehended, and is judicially sentenced to the extreme penalty; is his right to life 'unalienable', so that the community is itself committing murder if it carries out the sentence? One's country, or perhaps the United Nations, is the victim of unprovoked aggression; are those who take up arms in defence of it, and do what soldiers in combat are called upon to do, violating a right to life on the part of their attackers which no circumstances can remove? If the right is possessed by everyone simply in virtue of their human nature, we should have to say Yes. But most of the defenders of natural rights would probably themselves say No in all these cases. They do not and cannot square their practice or actual judgment with the requirements of their theory.

If the right to life itself turns out to be so exceptional, one would expect the other rights to be so even more obviously; and this indeed is what we find. The American fathers named next after the right to life the right to liberty. Do we have any such right? Undoubtedly we do. But that the natural rights theory has failed to give the true account may be seen by considering that if the possession of a rational nature is all that is necessary to confer the right, then I am at liberty to do and speak what I personally think best, no matter what the circumstances, and this consequence is absurd. If the country is at war, and I think it best, during an air-raid, to leave my shades up and my lights on, I shall have to hold that it is an invasion of my inviolable freedom of action to make me put the shades down; if my house overlooks the harbour and I prefer to talk freely of the ships that move in and out, it is again a gross invasion of my freedom of speech to hush me up. If there are no circumstances that can 'alienate' my right to act and speak as I choose, then no law of any kind is justifiable, for it is the aim of law to set limits to individual freedom in the general interest. The 'unalienable' right to freedom must be set down as an illusion.

A person may possess a rational nature, then, without possessing the rights that this nature is supposed to guarantee. The converse also holds; he may have the rights without the nature on which they are supposed to depend, and hence they cannot really depend on it. When a man's rational faculties have failed, has he lost all the rights he formerly had to fairness and kindness of treatment? And what about the claims of dumb animals? They are a test case here. One's pet dog has no duties, for he is incapable of comparing better and worse and choosing the better; if he misbehaves, he is a nuisance, but it would be absurd to call him immoral. But has he no rights? Has he not the right, for example, to be treated without the infliction of needless pain? I think it clear that he has. But if he has, then the right to humane treatment does not follow from the possession of a rational nature only, for he has no rational nature. A theory that would base rights on the rationality of their subjects would justify a treatment of animals that is quite out of consonance with the thought and practice of humane men.

13. (6) Natural rights, then, break down. But with this, we come in full view of the position that, for us, is the end of the line. The rights to life and liberty do not depend on conventions because they exist before conventions and independently of them. They do not depend on the rational nature of their subjects (though duties do), for that nature may exist without them, and they without it. What is it, then, that *is* always present when rights are present, absent when they are absent, and variable as they vary? The answer is implicit in our criticism of all the previous positions. There is one circumstance that can over-ride any contrary claim, namely the general good. A man forfeits his right to life itself if he becomes sufficiently dangerous to the community; he forfeits his right to freedom if the exercise of that freedom would jeopardize the community. Now the suggestion is irresistible that if that which alone can modify or suspend a right is its relation to the general good, this must be what validates it also. If a man claims the right to do something that is clearly harmful to the community, we point to this consequence as full justification for refusing it to him. On the other hand, if he can show that what he is doing is of net value to those affected by it, we consider that he has made out his case and that to prevent his doing it would be an unjust restriction. Thus the variable element on which the justification of a right depends is prospective contributoriness to general good. The force of this conclusion is greatly strengthened when we note the connection of rights with duties. A right is the obverse side of a duty, a duty looked at from the other end. To say that I have a right to walk the streets unmolested is to say that it is your duty not to molest me. Now we have seen, at the cost of some effort, that the reason why an act is a duty is precisely that it promises the greatest good. If this is true of duties, and rights *are* duties, it must be true of rights as well.

14. In the end, then, every political right must be defended on moral grounds. But we cannot leave the matter there. For moral and political rights are not simply identical; there are many moral rights that no one would call political, for example, the right to be spoken to courteously and the right of parents to the consideration of their children. Political rights are rights that are, or appropriately may be, guaranteed by government, that is, by enforced law. Now it is clear that there are 'rights' thus enforced by law for which many who must heed them can find no moral justification at all. But now for the real difficulty. The state claims the right, for example, and enforces it by heavy penalties, to reach down into the pockets of its citizens and take a large part of their income for its own purposes. Many of these citizens are convinced not only that the particular purposes for which the state will use this money are bad, but also that an income tax as such is a policy opposed to the general good. To tell these people that what they regard as a wicked tax imposed for wicked purposes is a moral right, on all fours with the right to truthful speech and civil treatment, is not unlikely to provoke jeers. Clearly there is a missing link in the argument. These people are told that it is a moral obligation to do what produces the greatest good. They believe that a law passed by their government is inimical to the public good, and are told that they should obey it nevertheless. That may be a political obligation, but to call it a moral obligation looks very much like self-contradiction. How is one to make out that it is their moral duty to obey a law that they disapprove? This is probably the most searching question in political theory.

15. I believe that the true answer to this question has been given by philosophers over and over again, and that it is not the exclusive property of any school. But it has had a history so unfortunate as to rob it of much of its persuasiveness. It was suggested by Rousseau, but, as presented by him, was so embedded in mythology and bad argument that one can extract it only with difficulty from his incoherent text. It was stated again by Hegel, but was made an integral part of a system of logic and metaphysics which most philosophers have found it impossible to accept; besides, it came to be associated, partly by his own fault and partly not, with Prussian nationalism, which after precipitating two wars, earned general detestation. The doctrine was taken over from Hegel by the British idealists and given a more judicious statement by T. H. Green, whose *Principles of Political Obligation* remains, I think, the weightiest work in English on political theory. It was presented again by Bosanquet in *The Philosophical Theory of the State*, but with needless obscurity and with certain expressions that sounded suspiciously like endorsements of absolutism and nationalism. These were seized upon by L. T. Hobhouse in his *Metaphysical Theory of the State* and made the focal points of the most thorough-going attack that has been made on the theory.

Rousseau called his version a theory of the 'general will'; Hegel and Bosanquet talked, instead, of the 'real will'; if the version about to be presented is to have a name, I should prefer the 'rational will'. It may be of interest to say that my own conviction of the truth of the theory came through reading Hobhouse's attack on it. It had been so long out of favour and was mentioned with such general deprecation that, having made no careful study of it, I had come to think of it as pretty certainly indefensible. Its association with the name of Hegel, and the many attempts to link Hegelianism with Fascism did not help, though I follow Principal Knox in holding that the occasional outbursts of Prussianism in Hegel are excrescences on his system, and not organic to it. When I approached the doctrine of the real will, I began by reading the critics of the theory, expecting at least to find some amusement in watching the work of demolition, and thinking I should be more likely to find intelligibility among the critics than among the exponents. The first two or three broadsides I reviewed left me in mild surprise, for the target was still visibly standing when the roar had subsided and the smoke cleared away. But these were guns of low calibre. So I turned to Hobhouse, who had, I understood, destroyed the theory utterly; and as I warmly admire his work, I sat down to him expectantly. But as the arguments in the heralded parade limped slowly past, a conviction gradually formed itself in my mind. If this was really the best that could be said against the theory of the real will, I had been deceived about it. Wave after wave of argument broke against it only to leave it, so far as I could see, standing aggressively intact. By the time I was half way through the book, I had begun to think the case *for* it impregnable; at the end, my conversion was complete. I thought then, and have never wavered in thinking since, that this doctrine, if one penetrates through the sorry form in which it has so often been expressed, and gets rid of associations that cling to it like barnacles, offers the firmest available core for political theory.

16. The doctrine is quite simple. It is that men have a common moral end which is the object of their rational will, that the state is a contrivance that they have worked out to help them realize that end, and that its authority over them rests on its being necessary for that end. If it is politically obligatory at times to obey a law that one regards as bad, that is because the state could not be run at all if the citizens could pick and choose which laws they would obey. Ultimately, therefore, political obligation, even that of obeying a morally bad law, *is* a moral obligation; and when, as occasionally happens, it becomes a duty to disobey, the ground is still the same. I believe that this simple doctrine is what all the philosophers who have defended a 'real' or 'general' will, from Rousseau to Bosanquet and even Hobhouse himself, have in fact been arguing for. I shall not try to prove this by historical inquiry, for my prime concern is not whether the doctrine I seem to find in them is actually theirs, but whether it is true. The doctrine that does seem to me true may be expanded and made more explicit in four propositions: First, we can distinguish within our own minds between the end of our actual or immediate will, and the end of our rational will, which is what on reflection would commend itself as the greatest good. Secondly, this rational end is the same for all men. Thirdly, this end, because a common end, is the basis of our rights against each other. Fourthly, the justification of the state, and its true office, lie in furthering the realization of this end. Let us try to get these points clear.

17. (1) It is puzzling at first to hear of a real or rational will which can be set over against our actual will. Is not our actual will our only will, and whatever goes beyond this, myth? On the contrary, it is easy to see that what we have here is a distinction of the first importance.

A man goes to a dealer and buys a motor-car. There is no dispute about his actual will; it is simply to possess the car; that is what he immediately and unmistakably wants. Is there any sense in saying that he has a further and rational will that goes beyond this and might even veto it? Yes, undoubtedly; in fact, unless we concede such a will we shall never understand what really moves him. If possessing the car were an ultimate end, the question 'Why buy it?' would be meaningless. But the buyer would be the first to insist that it was anything but meaningless, and if he were like other eager buyers he would readily explain that the car was a means to all sorts of advantages, personal, professional, and social, and these, perhaps, means to still further advantages to a widening circle of beneficiaries. In short, he wills to buy the car, but he wills it subject to tacit conditions as to how it will contribute to an end beyond itself. The evidence that these conditions exist lies in what would dissuade him from the purchase. Convince him that through buying the car he will not advance his business, that his son and daughter being what they are, it will probably involve them in accidents, and that if he carries the purchase through, he cannot move into the larger house that is the family's most pressing need, and he will not improbably cut the whole business short. If his actual will were self-contained, if it were the end of the line rather than a link in a chain whose point of attachment lies far beyond it, all this would be irrelevant. It is only because his explicit will is *not* exhaustive, because its object is a means to a further end, or a piece in a larger picture which is more fervently wanted than itself, that his immediate will can admit such correction. He may hardly have known that he wanted these ulterior things; at the moment of buying he was probably not thinking of them; but if, the instant he sees how his will of the moment bears on them, he sets that will aside, is it not natural to say that in contrast to the objects of his actual will, they are the objects of his real or rational will?

This line of reasoning, we may be told, leads to an unplausible consequence. For if his present will is thus open to correction by ulterior considerations of advantage to himself and his family, these considerations themselves will in turn be open to correction by still further considerations, for example, his duty to his profession, his community, and his country. 'What you are saying, then, is that the

object of a man's real or rational will is that which an ideally competent reflection would show to be the greatest good attainable in the
circumstances. No doubt with ideal powers this is what he ought to
will. But you are saying that he does in fact will what he ideally ought
to will, and that is absurd.'

I do not think it is. To be sure, one may easily enough prove it
absurd if one takes the two wills on the same level of explicitness.
If to will something must mean to will it immediately and with full
awareness, then the suggestion that we always will what it would be
best to will *is* absurd. Very well then; out with the word 'will'; we are
not insisting on words; we are insisting on what we take to be a fact,
and one of the prime facts of the moral life. Writers describe it
variously. The theologian would say that at our best we remain miserable sinners; the moralist that we never do our whole duty; the poet
that 'what I sought to be, and was not, comforts me'. However
capricious or selfish or brutal a man may be in actual behaviour, if
we are right in calling him a moral being at all, what he is trying to be
and do is never exhausted in what he is. Whenever he makes a judgment of better or worse, whenever he does anything because he
thinks he ought to do it, even when he thinks this without doing it,
he is recognizing a claim as prior to the wants of the moment and
conceding it the right to overrule them. A man may flout this claim to
any extent in practice, and protest that he neither recognizes it nor
tries to fulfil it. Is his protest to be accepted? Surely not. We could
point, if we knew him well enough, to a thousand actions that belie
his own report. He continually defers present good to a later and
greater good, corrects impulsive choices by reflection, recognizes
the force of another's claim when at the moment he would prefer
not to. In doing so, he concedes the claim of a rational good upon
him, a claim which, if he is consistent, he must admit to have overwhelming force in confirmation or in veto of the will of the moment.
We agree that he does know in detail the object of this larger will.
We agree that it is not a will at all in the simple straightforward sense
in which the will of the moment is such. But it remains a will in the
extremely important sense of an ideal to which the man by implication
commits himself every day of his life and whose claims he cannot
repudiate without turning his back upon himself.

If this is true, the distinction must be accepted between a man's
actual will and his ulterior will, his real or rational will. That was
our first point. The others may be dealt with more briefly.

18. (2) The second was that the end or object of the rational will is the same in everyone. This looks questionable. But the fact is that we could not even argue with each other with any point unless it were true. Consider the matter first on the side of theory. When we argue, we both assume that there is a truth to be found, that its discovery is our common end, and that there is a standard way of gaining it. If we differ as to whether President Madison preceded or followed President Monroe, we have no doubt that one did precede the other, or that if the evidence is rightly assessed, it will point one way. If this were really in doubt, there would be no sense in arguing at all. What would be the use of your trying to convince me if what was proof to you was in the end mere fallacy to me? The very essence of your attempt to show me my mistake lies in appealing to our common end, namely to grasp what fact and logic require, and if you can show that in this respect or that I have fallen short of these requirements, you expect me to see and acknowledge my error. Unless our thinking is governed by the same ideal, unless what would ultimately satisfy you as cogent evidence or conclusive proof is assumed to be the same as what would satisfy me, argument is a waste of time. So long as we do make that assumption, there is hope. Argument is the joint appeal to a fundamental agreement in the hope of extending it to remove a relatively superficial disagreement.

The same holds on the practical side. Men expostulate with each other over wrongdoing just as they argue over fact. Now when another expostulates with me over an action that seems to him wrong, what sort of argument must he use if he is to convince me? He must show me that the action I am considering will not, as I suppose, subserve the sort of ends that we approve in common. Suppose he finds me set on buying the motorcar, and thinks it a mad-cap scheme; his argument will take essentially the following form: 'You think it of the first importance, don't you, that one's family should be comfortably and healthfully housed?' 'Yes.' 'Well, if you buy the car, you must sacrifice that end for occasional pleasures that you admit yourself to be less important.' That is, he appeals to an end about which he feels confident that I agree with him, and tries to show me that the action I am proposing would defeat it rather than promote it. If I were to betray to him that I had no interest whatever in the welfare of my family, he would be at a loss how to proceed, for his argument assumes that I attach the same value to this that other sane men do. Put in the abstract, what he is saying is: 'You agree with me that E is the important thing at stake; if you do M you will jeopardize it; if you do N you will get it; therefore you should do N.' Unless there is some broad agreement on the ends that are worth pursuing, neither of us would have any purchase on the thought of the other.

There is, to be sure, an element of paradox in this view. If the Russians get involved with the Americans in an argument over practical politics, does it really make sense to say that they are both driving at the same ultimate end? Yes, I think it does, and thinking so increases my hope in the work of an international forum where they may meet and canvass their differences. Indeed, considering the bitterness of their differences, their professed ends are surprisingly near to identity. The Russians insist that they believe as strongly as the 'democracies' in the dissemination of knowledge, in freedom for the masses of the people, in the cultivation of literature and the arts, and in the increase through applied knowledge of the comfort, health, and happiness of mankind. Their difference with the west is not in our accepting and their rejecting these goods, for both parties avow devotion to them; the difference is that whereas the communists think that capitalism is an atrociously bad means to these ends and communism an exceedingly good one, the west thinks that communism is a bungling and tyrannous means to them and a 'free economy' a more effective one. The United Nations has been treated to many strange scenes and strange arguments, but it has not yet, I think, been invited to listen to a plea for ignorance, misery, and slavery as the true ends of man. Since all alike accept certain ends, they can argue with some point about the means. If the Russians were seeking ends that really had nothing in common with ours, if they were aiming, for example, at unhappiness in widest commonalty spread, discussion with them would take a remarkable form; when we offered an argument to show that a Russian move was calculated to increase human misery, we should be greeted at the end with applause and the exclamation, 'Bravo; you put our case admirably.' It is happily to be doubted whether among sane and candid men this ultimate difference about ends ever occurs.

19. (3) The third proposition is that our rights against each other are based on our common ends. Smith borrows money from Jones, and when the debt falls due, Jones claims the right to repayment. On what ground? Not, surely, on the ground alone that it furthers his own interest, since that might not be Smith's, nor on the ground alone that it is Smith's interest; to say that would too often be hypo-critical and false. To get the key, we must ask another question, Is Jones's right to be repaid the same as Smith's duty to pay? We have seen that in substance it is, since a duty is the obverse side of a right. When Jones presses his claim against Smith, he is therefore insisting on Smith's duty to repay. Why is it Smith's duty to repay? Duty, as we have seen, is always based on the production of good. What is the good in this case? It is not merely Jones's satisfaction in getting his money back, though that will form part of the end for any considerate debtor. It is also the maintenance in society of a state of things in which promises are kept and debts repaid. When Jones presses his claim against Smith, he is saying in effect, 'You believe, do you not, as I do, that this state of things is better than one in which promises are broken and debts repudiated? Very well, if you do, your only consistent course is to pay.' That this common end is the basis on which Jones is urging his right may be clearly seen by his helpless-ness if Smith rejects it. Suppose Smith rejoins, 'I see no value whatever in a state of things in which promises may be relied on or debts re-paid; this may be an end or good for you; it is not for me.' What could Jones do? He could threaten him with the police, but that is not argument, and no argument he could offer would carry the least validity for Smith. To urge that Smith seek a good which for him was no good at all would be absurd. Jones's case in its entirety rests on the assumption that he and Smith are seeking a common end, and that when the repayment of the debt is seen to be required by that end, Smith will recognize it as his duty and do it. But that he should so recognize and do it is precisely what Jones is claiming as his right. To put it generally, your right against me and my duty to you rest on an identical ground, namely their necessity to our joint end.

20. (4) Now for the fourth proposition: it is because the state is the greatest of instruments to this common end that it has such rights as it possesses over its citizens. The state is more than a system of rights. If half a dozen hunters met by accident in the woods, such rights would hold among them, but this could not make them into a state. A state is a set of institutions—a legislature, courts, police, a chief executive—designed to give effect to these rights, to guarantee them in practice. The state is thus a means, not an end. It is a system of brakes and prods applied in the interest of reaching a goal beyond itself.

The simplest evidence for this lies in the answer we naturally give to two related questions, Why should I obey the law? and Why may I sometimes resist it? The answers to both are the same, and they amount to an admission that the state is an attempt at the embodiment of a common rational will, and is justified only as the instrument of that will. Why should I obey the law by doing anything so disagreeable as paying my income tax? Not because I have to, since with enough cleverness I might evade it, nor because I can point to any definite advantages to me or anyone else that would result from this particular act. I should obey it if at all because it belongs to a system of commands and restraints whose maintenance serves better than any available alternative as an instrument for the common good.

It is needless to work this out in detail. Everyone knows that a government is often a nuisance, whose rules about parking cars, stopping at street lights, paying taxes, keeping walks clear, and all the rest, are a source of endless major and minor frustrations. We all believe, nevertheless, that though government is a nuisance, it is a wholly indispensable nuisance. Why? Because without it the main goods of life, and for that matter life itself, would be insecure. If we can count on our house and its contents not being taken away from us, if the shops that supply our clothes and fuel and food are able to do their business, if there are roads on which we can get about, schools to send our children to, courts and police to deal with those who would take advantage of us, it is because behind these arrangements, protecting and guaranteeing them, is the power of the state. Without it we should be at the mercy of the worst elements in our society. We may concede to communists and anarchists that if the ends men are seeking in common could be realized without the complex and expensive machinery of government, it should be dispensed with. We cannot agree with them in supposing that, human nature being what it is, there is any prospect whatever of attaining these goods except with the aid of the state.

21. Does it follow that since the state is a necessary means to our major ends, we should in all circumstances obey it, that we never have the right to rebel? Not at all. Our view would not only justify disobedience in some cases; it would require it. If the state is regarded, not as sacrosanct or an end in itself, but as an instrument to certain great ends, then when it becomes so corrupt as to cut us off from those ends rather than further them, when it serves its purpose so badly that it is better to risk chaos for the sake of a better order than continue to suffer under the old, then resistance becomes a right and a duty. This will be an extreme and desperate case, since it will obviously be better as a rule to obey what we regard as a bad law and try by persuasion to get it amended than to seek the overthrow of the power which supports all laws alike. But there is no doubt that when government has ceased to serve its major ends, the people who have fashioned it to serve those ends have a right to replace it with something that serves these better. In doing so, they will appeal to the same ends that earlier led them to support it, and they will do so with full consistency and justification. Thus the theory of a rational will provides a natural and intelligible ground both for obedience in normal cases and for disobedience in abnormal cases. It is hard to conceive what better evidence could be offered for it.

22. Here then is a theory of political obligation. It holds that each of us is seeking an end that goes beyond the good of the moment, that besides his will of the moment for food, drink, and comfort, he has a rational will directed far beyond these to what would satisfy in the light of a fully critical reflection. The nature of that end we have explored in earlier chapters. At best it is conceived vaguely and pursued waveringly, but its presence nevertheless is both the magnet that draws us on and the monitor that reproves when we stray out of the way. This end, we have held, is the end of all men. Because it is, each can justly claim of another that he should be loyal to it; that is what we mean by a right. The state itself is an arrangement accepted as a necessary means to this ultimate end, and on this necessity rests its right to obedience.

This account of political obligation seems to me at once simple and compelling. There is probably nothing novel about it. Indeed I have suggested that it was what all the defenders of a real and general will, from Rousseau to Bosanquet, were in substance contending for. Rousseau maintained that in all men there is a will toward the same moral end, that government is a device set up by that will through a contract or agreement, that this will, as a striving for the good is, by definition, never wrong, though even the 'will of all' may mistake what it really requires, and that its requirements, even as to the structure of government, may vary greatly with circumstances. In these contentions I think Rousseau was right. Unfortunately this core of sound teaching was embedded in a mass of myths and mistakes that were as adventitious to it as moss to a stone. Rousseau dimmed and confused a remarkable insight when he held that men are animated by self-interest only, that the general will is aimed at a queer scarcely thinkable abstraction in which their selfish wills coincide, and that the government can impose no burden and confer no advantage except upon all alike. Indeed his doctrine as presented is so incoherent that all one can hope to derive from it is a general drift—a drift in the right direction nevertheless.

Something similar must be said of Hegel. His insistence that an identical and rational end was working itself out through individual minds, that every society showed in its laws and customs the working of this will, and embodied it in differing degrees, all this and much else that this astonishing intelligence had to say about politics is true. Unfortunately he put himself in the wrong with all manner of persons who would otherwise have been disposed to listen by talking gratuitous nonsense about the state as 'der Gang Gottes in der Welt', holding that the success of a state in dominating others was somehow evidence of its right to do so, arguing that the relations of states cannot be judged by moral standards, and suggesting that the state is not only an attempt to embody reason, but, in the case of the dominant state of the time, does embody it so fully that the citizen will achieve his highest morality by conforming to it and will have no case if he resists it. How far such doctrines belong to the essence of Hegel's political theory is a matter of dispute; I am myself inclined to think that they are extraneous to it.[1] But he cannot be aquitted of having said things that gave apparent benediction to totalitarian violence and oppression, and anyone holding a doctrine akin to his must be at pains to show that the charges heaped upon it do not apply to his own. That the inspiration common to the contract theories and to the Hegelians is really innocent of these charges can be shown easily enough. It will pay us to look briefly at the worst of the accusations.

23. (1) The theory, it is said, would not only justify but glorify wrong. If the state is the instrument of the general will, and the general will is a will to the moral end itself, what embodies this will must be right. Hence whatever the state does, however tyrannous and brutal, is to recieve our benediction. Each of us is supposed to realize, Hobhouse says,

[1] For a discussion of the rights and wrongs of this issue, see the papers by T. M. Knox, E. F. Carritt, and others in *Philosophy*, Vol. XV (1940), pp. 51–63, 190–6, 219–20, 313–7.

'That in society he is in the presence of a being infinitely higher than himself, contemplating a reason much more exalted than his own. His business is not to endeavour to remodel society, but to think how wonderfully good and rational is the social life he knows, with its Pharisees and publicans, its gin-palaces, its millions of young men led out to the slaughter, and he is to give thanks daily. . . .' Such a doctrine, 'instead of seeking to realize the ideal', 'idealizes the real'.[1]

Harold Laski wrote in similar vein: 'For him [Bosanquet] the good is always being realized. The subserving of our real will with the will of the state is taken to mean that the best that can happen to us is in fact happening at each moment.'[2]

Now if the doctrine of the rational will is examined, not in the light of occasional foolish phrases, but in the light of its essential drift, one can see that not only does the above inference fail to follow; the only legitimate inference is quite the opposite.

The real will goes beyond the actual will; it does so everywhere and always. That is the point of the contrast between them. The good that would completely satisfy me is never achieved in this act or that. To recognize the real will is to arouse discontent with what is, to indict the good I have actually achieved in the light of what might be. To say, in the *individual* case, that the recognition of the real will meant somehow glorifying the actual would be so patently contrary to the point of the distinction as to wear its falsity on its face. How is the case different when we turn to the will of a community? The recognition of a real will is the recognition that there is a greatest good for that community and that it is the business of the citizens to regulate their communal life so that this good may be as fully embodied as possible. The very insistence on the distinction implies that it is not so embodied now. To be sure, the doctrine implies that one is ordinarily to obey the law, but, as we have seen, one cannot so much as state the reason for that obedience without acknowledging an authority above the law, which we may invoke against the law itself if that should fail.

24. (2) The second charge against the theory is that it would give the state a power over the individual which is complete and beyond appeal. If he dares to call it in question, he is told that the maintenance

---

[1] *Metaphysical Theory of the State*, 87, 112.
[2] *Aristotelian Society Proc.*, 1928, 56. C. E. M. Joad took a similar line in his *Guide to the Philosophy of Morals and Politics*, 598.

of this state and its laws is what his real will desires, and that if he appeals from Philip drunk to Philip sober within himself, he will see that he has no case. To some critics of the general will, this is the least pardonable part of the doctrine. Mr Laski thinks it absurd to say that

> 'constraint is not the use of force by the state against the individual, but only its imposition upon him of the will which his real will desires. . . . Most of us, I think, would argue that the revolutionist is never conscious that the government which imprisons him is giving his true self freedom. What he experiences is constraint; and he regards that as a denial of his liberty. To tell him that he is made free when he is prevented from fulfilling the purpose he regards as the *raison d'etre* of his existence is, I would suggest, to deprive words of all their meaning.'[1]

The climax of absurdity is thought to be reached when the theory touches punishment. It is bad enough to say, when a law is passed which we tried to prevent, that the law is what we really wanted, and to compel us on this ground to obey it; but it is one degree worse to tell us, when we have been put in jail for resisting it, that we were really hungering and thirsting for incarceration at hard labour. To take this line is to cut from under our feet any ground to stand on in protest; it is to reduce us to the level of children who are to be told by persons wiser than they what is good for them and what is not. And it is to outlaw resistance to tyranny as the manifestation of wayward self-will.

Most of us would agree with the temper of this remonstrance; at least I should myself. For anyone, however high in authority to presume to tell others over their protests what is good for them is a repellent and dangerous business. But there are several things to be said about it.

25. First, the problem here involved is not peculiar to the theory advocated; it confronts every theory and form of government that is worth considering. It is the business of government as such to find and promote the good of its people. But there are nearly always persons, sincere and high-minded persons, who believe that what the government proposes is neither for their own good nor anyone else's, and who are prepared to resist its mandates. In such cases, what is the government to do? It has commonly put coercion upon

---

[1] *The State in Theory and Practice*, 59.

them in the interest of the many. It is not easy to see any alternative. If this leads to tragedy, it may be inevitable tragedy; indeed, as Hegel pointed out regarding Socrates, it is tragic because so inevitable.

Secondly, is such coercion necessarily tyranny? The theory of the general will regards government as an instrument to the common end of the greatest good. Can the citizens instruct their government in detail as to what this good consists in? Not if Burke's famous speech to the electors at Bristol is sound, and on this point it is hardly questionable. Government is not, or not merely, for the execution of mandates given; it is largely for the discovery of what mandates ought to be given. Now if a citizen wants a government, if he approves on the whole the method by which it gained power, if he has commissioned it to ascertain and promote as best it can the community's good, then in a quite intelligible sense its decisions are his decisions. He has willed that it should make them for him.

What if one of these decisions conflicts with a preference of his own? Can it reasonably be said that his real will is here conflicting with his actual or particular will, and that he himself is willing that this particular will should be set aside? Mr Laski thought this absurd. 'The Nonconformist who paid his education rate under the Act of 1902 did not do so because his real will approved of the Act. He did so because he took the view that, on balance, it was better to put up with one bad law than to challenge the authority from which all laws derive.'[1] This assents to our view in substance while rejecting it in words. The Nonconformist preferred, we are told, to keep the government in existence, even though it thwarted some of his desires, because he thought that better on balance. We accept this account and are proposing to call this preference his real will. Mr Laski thinks that so naming it is confusing. I do not see where the confusion lies. It is admitted on both sides that the Nonconformist wants the law not to be. It is admitted on both sides that he wants still more that the instrument which made the law should remain in being, in spite of its cost to himself. Where is the confusion in saying that what he admittedly wants most is his real will? We are not denying any facts or taking illicit advantage of him in saying this. We are not denying that he dislikes the law. We are proposing that theory should stay true to fact in noting that his desires are not of equal strength or importance. If he wills the machinery of government at the well-

[1] *The State in Theory and Practice,* 59–60.

known cost of occasional thwartings of his and others' wishes, there is, or need be, no confusion in saying that it is his real will that these thwartings should be imposed.

Even the ridicule about punishment does not stand up very well under scrutiny. It rests again upon putting all facts on the same level. When a motor policeman holds me up for careless driving, it *is* superficially absurd to say that I want to be held up and fined. But is this more than superficial? What citizen who takes his citizenship seriously has not in his heart, however colourful his actual language, given the policeman full marks for doing just what he did? Nobody wants to be held up when in a hurry; nobody wants to get a 'ticket'; but men have been known to 'go away thankful that an agency of theirs is so impartially on the alert in serving the interest of the community. In such cases, would the critics say that it is absurd and contrary to fact to be thankful that one's will has been frustrated? But the 'absurd' fact does occur.

Thirdly, while regarding government as the instrument of the general will is admittedly dangerous, it is less dangerous than its alternatives. Any conception of government will give grounds for injustice if used insincerely; but sincerity assumed, it is hard to conceive a criterion of governmental behaviour less likely to lead to oppression than reference to what the citizens genuinely want. It rules out *ab initio* all abuses based on power, and all government in the interest of a single man or class. The will which is to be expressed and to which government is responsible is conceived as working in every citizen and hence entitling him to be considered; and the content of that will can be ascertained only by remaining close to its source.

Fourthly, we repeat that if in the attempts to determine and achieve the common end a government blunders into cruelty, it is absurd to lay this cruelty at the door of the theory itself. As well interdict the aim to be rational, with the schools that subserve this aim, because if we pursue it we stumble at times into fallacy, as decry the pursuit through government of a common good because men at times misconstrue its demands. No other theory of government would bow to such criticism, and neither need this. Suffice it to say that in any state whose members take this high pursuit seriously there will be a constant pressure toward legal and social amendment. Men who believe in a common end and a common reason will naturally seek to make them prevail; and that such prevalence would transform society needs no arguing.

But the rational will must work, if it works at all, through individuals, and what its acceptance would mean for the temper and conduct of one's personal life is of more interest to most men than even its working on the ampler stage of the state. To this more intimate question, which is also our last, we must now turn.

CHAPTER XV

THE RATIONAL TEMPER

1. We have given a high place to reason in practice. Admitting that feeling and impulse are indispensable to any experience that is to be worth while, we have argued that if the good is that which fulfils and satisfies impulse-desire, reason enters, and enters increasingly as we advance, into the very nature of the good. It reveals to us how our desires are implicated with each other, how they conflict with each other, how, if at all, they may be harmonized with each other. As men's interests become more diversified, and the splintered and fragmented mind becomes harder to avoid, reason has more and more to do. It must select some interests as central, discard or modify others, and ruthlessly subordinate minor interests to major. Sometimes this is done for us by compelling outer circumstance, as it is for the explorer or for the mother of a large family. But to organize a life from within may prove a harder business. It calls for intelligence, for a willingness to reflect, and for firmness both in the pruning of irrelevant desires and the re-shaping of relevant ones for the sake of distant ends. It involves, in short, putting reason in the saddle and letting it apply both spur and bridle to the creature of impulse that every man so largely is.

All this implies a certain 'weather in the soul' that will distinguish the rational man from the man of impulse or feeling. We may well try to form some image of what this man would be like. He would be very different from our commonplace selves and from those around us. Rationality, as we conceive it, does not lie merely in letting reason appoint one's beliefs, hard as that is; it means carrying a rational spirit into the ramifications of practice, making it permeate one's feelings and pervade the decisions of one's will. It means to be a practising philosopher. This is a very much harder business than being a mere professor of philosophy. For it requires being what professors of philosophy so seldom are, reasonable men who live rational lives. Indeed if one's picture of the rational man had to be drawn from the flesh, one would search for a model in vain. He has never, in fact, existed, and can only be imagined. We do know, however, that he would fall somewhere between two extremes, and in trying to see what he is like, we may find it suggestive to begin with what he is certainly not.

2. At one extreme, then, stands the creature of impulse whose only principle is to have no principle, who surrenders to the mood of the hour, whatever that may be. He will do nothing unless at the moment his heart is in it; to be forced by himself or others into acting against his feelings seems to him slavery; freedom means following impulse. The classic picture of this sort of person, described by Plato as 'the democratic man' because all his impulses clamour for their rights as of equal importance with every other, is given in the eighth book of the *Republic:*

> 'he lives from day to day indulging the appetite of the hour; and some-
> times he is lapped in drink and strains of the flute; then he becomes a
> waterdrinker, and tries to get thin; then he takes a turn at gymnastics;
> sometimes idling and neglecting everything, then once more living the
> life of a philosopher; often he is busy with politics, and starts to his feet
> and says and does whatever comes into his head; and, if he is emulous
> of anyone who is a warrior, off he is in that direction, or of men of
> business, once more in that. His life has neither law nor order; and this
> distracted existence he terms joy and bliss and freedom; and so he goes
> on.'[1]

Happily, no such person exists in the fatuous perfection of the ideal. But we have all met with approximations to it in varying degrees; indeed as we look at our own face in the mirror we can see at moments a distressing resemblance. It is distressing because we know, without being told, the end of such people. Riding off, like the storied Irishman, in all directions at once, they never arrive; they scatter themselves over a broad landscape, making a perceptible difference nowhere except as nuisances, and disappear without a trace.

3. At the other extreme stands what Lord Russell was no doubt referring to when he spoke of 'that inhuman monster "the rational man" '. He is even less likely to be met in the flesh than 'the demo-

[1] *Republic*, VIII, 561 (Jowett).

cratic man', but here again there are adumbrations of him among persons we have met or read about. He tries to incarnate pure intelligence. The wheels of his intellect revolve in a vacuum, and if at a furious pace, so much the better. He acts always from calculation, never from impulse, affection, or even hatred. He sees a long way ahead, cunningly adjusts his means to his ends, is all things to all men while caring little for any, never forgets himself, and is never carried away by enthusiasm or sentimentality. While making no mistakes of his own, at least none that mere intelligence could avoid, he sees through everyone else, notes their stupidities, and uses them with superlative craft for his own purpose. He is icily competent, intimidatingly efficient, free from all romantic and humanitarian nonsense, knows what he wants, and moves toward it by the straightest line. He is Voltaire without his cackling laughter, Shaw without his Irish ebullience, Sir Stafford Cripps without his utopianism or piety. He is not necessarily diabolical, like Iago and Mephistopheles; he is a cool, thin-lipped, crafty observer like Shakespeare's Cassius, neutral between good and evil, but capable of astute service to either.

It is an unattractive picture. Most people would find it even less attractive than that of the unprincipled libertine. They would hate Iago, even before knowing what exactly he was about, while finding it as difficult as some eminent critics to imagine Falstaff in hell. Intellectual power is merely alarming when its moral allegiance is ambiguous.[1] But then our own notion of rationality is so far from all this that we should find the man we have just described a monster of *ir*rationality. The rational man as we conceive him differs from this monster in three ways, all of them fundamental.

In the first place, reasonableness is not exhausted in the exercise of reasoning. A rational man may well be an intellectual, but he will not be an intellectualist, if this means that he retreats into his own corner and contents himself with spinning webs. Indeed, to try to squeeze a normal man into the tiny bed of his own cognitive faculty, and then lop off whatever will not fit into it, is to stunt him and indeed to kill him; that came out clearly enough in our consideration of the Stoics.

Secondly, rationality has a far larger field than that of propositions and concepts. It is as truly at work in judgments of better and worse, of right and wrong, as in those judgments of analytic necessity to

---

[1] *Cf*. Goethe: Er nennt's Vernunft, und braucht's allein, Nur tierischer als jedes Tier zu sein.

which a narrow convention would confine the name of reason. It may exhibit itself, for example, in the sanity and good sense with which one appraises the types of human experience. The rational man, as we conceive him, would be incapable of summing up religion as 'the opiate of the people', patriotism as 'the last refuge of a scoundrel', or love as sex, still more of history as 'bunk'. He would presumably be clever in the manipulation of logico-mathematical symbols, for such cleverness is one expression of rationality, however thin and partial. But what is called good judgment is a far more massive and significant expression of it.

Thirdly, rationality extends to reasonableness in conduct. A man would not in our present sense deserve the name, no matter how clever he was, or how judicious in problems of value, who was incapable of translating his insights into action. How far the various forms of reasonableness can exist independently of each other is an intriguing question—how far logical acuteness and moral judgment, for example, can co-exist with imprudence and irresponsibility in practice. That these forms do not simply vary with each other is shown by such figures as Coleridge. 'The contrast between his grasp of philosophical principles and his total absence of ethical effectiveness is bewildering at first sight, but in the end it only shows how entirely disconnected reason and instinct can be. Coleridge could imagine wisdom, but he could not apply it.'[1] Without pursuing the many hares that here appear in our path, we must be content to follow tradition and withold the name of rational from the man who cannot establish connection between his insights and his practice. Our rational man will be reasonable in action as well as in thought because his action will issue from impulses that have been aligned and modified by thought.

He will be far, then, from the crafty monster, with ice-water in his veins, that romantics have sometimes pictured. Unless he were capable of feeling and impulse, there would be nothing that his intelligence could present to him as worth pursuing. He will have his enthusiasms and loves and hates like other men, and will translate them—not precipitately or rashly, indeed, but judiciously—into action.

4. But here the doubt arises that always crops up when one contemplates the portrait of the rational man. He is never to act 'precipitately', but always 'judiciously'. It is well enough for the philosopher to use

[1] A. C. Benson, *Rambles and Reflections*, 135

these words in his study, but they seem to be a mere counsel of perfection if applied to the rough-and-tumble life outside. Indeed it may be said that they are not even a counsel of perfection. The trouble is not only the practical one, tremendous as that is, of getting men of violent passions and prejudices to put a continual brake on them in the interests of some reflective good; it is the more fundamental difficulty that the ideal itself seems to be misconceived, that such a brake, habitually imposed, would kill all spontaneity. Rationality in practice implies acting in the light of consequences; so acting implies stopping to consider; stopping to consider means not only that the impulse to action will tend to vanish, but even that if it remains, it will be remoulded or inhibited; and such rationality, it may be held, would spread a killing frost over the life of impulse. Freshness, delight, *joie de vivre*, will have no play in this galling harness. If there is to be joy in life, there must be gusto, some freedom for feeling and impulse, some degree of abandon. Everybody knows that if one is angry and stops to count a hundred before expressing it, there is little or nothing left to express. The same holds of more constructive impulses. If we are to enjoy art to the full, we must surrender ourselves to it, not contemplate it dispassionately as a critic would; 'there are two ways of disliking art', said Oscar Wilde; 'one of them is to dislike it, the other is to like it rationally.' A lover who meted out his devotion in amounts determined strictly by rational appraisal of the worth of its object would not be particularly popular with that object. Even in religion a certain childlikeness has been held to be essential; we are urged to trust before our intelligence is satisfied; blessed are they who have *not* seen and yet have believed. Hence the absurdity felt in the supposed rationalist's prayer, 'O God, if there be a God, save my soul, if I have a soul.' Granting all that we have said about the difference between rationality and intellectualism, is it not still true that the man whose whole life is held under rational command is bound to be something of a monster?

If that means that such a mind would be an extreme rarity, it is true. If it means that the rational temper entails a life that is bleak, mechanical, and joyless, I do not think it is true. Let us take the less important point first, that reasonableness is a rarity.

5. That most men do not live rationally is hardly a thesis worth debating. It is only too obvious that they do not. Moralists and economists did once suppose that all men were bent on gaining their own greatest happiness, and that they chose invariably the course of action that presented itself as contributing most to this end. In this sense they were universally and automatically rational. From this starting point, James Mill elaborated a psychology and his son an ethics and economics. The pertinent comments are: first, that men who were moved by their own good only would, from our point of view, be *ir*rational; second, that even if they chose invariably what seemed to conduce to this, there would remain an infinite opportunity for going wrong in the choice; and third, that by John Mill's honest confession, men do not always choose even what *seems* to their greatest advantage; they face pain and death at times for the sake of others. And if men are not generally rational even in this low sense, still less are they rational in any higher sense.

Consider only one piece of very general evidence. What is called literature—particularly fiction, epic, and drama—is chiefly a study in human unreasonableness. Perhaps this is what makes it so interesting to us. One can hardly imagine a run on the circulating libraries for a novel all of whose characters were models of serene wisdom. When authors have introduced such persons, as Mrs Humphrey Ward introduced T. H. Green in the character of Grey in *Robert Ellesmere* or Lowes Dickinson did Sidgwick in the character of Martin in his *Modern Symposium*, the sages have not been very exciting. The characters that stand out in literature are, nearly all of them, variants on the theme of human irrationality: the adventurous and unscrupulous Odysseus, the David who would have his Bathsheba, the lovable, half-mad knight of La Mancha, Mr Micawber, Mrs Jellyby and the other extraordinary exhibits in the Dickens menagerie, Jane Austen's embodiments of pride and prejudice, the miser Silas Marner, Captain Ahab of *Moby Dick*, Mr Babbitt and Mrs Dodsworth, the brooding and murderous Raskolnikov. Some of these are out-size figures. But we feel that though they are all intensely unreasonable, they are the very stuff of life. Their annals are studies of what happens when human nature wanders from rationality in varying directions and distances.

To take a character that in intelligence and loyalty to it is well above rather than below the common level, to confront it with crucial trials and show how its very largenesss of stature may cause it to crack, is a rarer and greater achievement. Hamlet, for all his alleged madness, is a figure of this kind; so, in another way, is Othello, a mind not easily jealous, but being wrought, perplexed in the extreme.

Hegel thought that the material of the purest tragedy was found where all the chief protagonists were following the light of an objective reason as they saw it, and still involved themselves in fatal conflict; here was an antimony that went deep. Such a conflict was found in the case of Socrates, the most devoted follower of rational duty that had ever lived, put to death by his compatriots, not out of spite, but what they too conceived as rational duty. Even so, it is a kind of unreasonableness that makes the conflict possible, since one party or the other is clearly mistaking his duty. But it is not conflicts at this level of which literature is mostly made.[1]

6. We must admit, then, that the rational man *is* something of a monster, in the sense that he is a *rara avis in terris*. Is he also a monster in the other sense of being not only a departure, but a repulsive departure, from the norm? Swinburne attacked Christianity as a kill-joy faith:

> Thou hast conquered, O pale Galilean!
> The world is grown grey with thy breath.

The charge is surely unjust if lodged against a mind as warm and spontaneous as that of Jesus. But is it not valid to the full against the creature we have called the rational man, with his mind 'all sicklied o'er with the pale cast of thought'?

There is some point in the charge. Rationality is not bought without a price, and part of that price is a soberness of temper and deliberateness of decision that do put something of a damper on impulsive high spirits. As for the soberness of temper, it follows from mere reflectiveness on the human situation. Rationality in feeling and conduct will try to adjust itself to what rationality in thought reveals the world to be, and the man who is rational in his thinking cannot fail to note that it is a very checkered place. For

> Men at whiles are sober
> And think by fits and starts,
> And if they think, they fasten
> Their hands upon their hearts.

The person who sees things whole is not likely, indeed, to be cynical

[1] Cf. Renan, addressing Athena in his eloquent Prière sur l'Acropole: 'Une littérature qui, comme la tienne, serait saine de tout point n'exciterait plus maintenant que l'ennui.' *Souvenirs d'Enfance et de Jeunesse*, 67.

and despairing, as Housman was, but neither is he likely to be ecstatic, for among the facts he will take account of are these (to mention a few of many such): that no matter who we are or what we attempt, we are all beaten in the end by death; that man's inhumanity to man, past and present, runs up to a staggering total; that he hardly sits down to a dinner except at the cost of animal pain; that much of the suffering of the world falls on the wholly innocent; that civilization is producing the means of destruction far faster than it is producing temperate minds or the instruments of peace.[1] It was not a philosopher who sang 'God's in his heaven, all's right with the world', but an unthinking peasant girl of a natively sweet disposition.

Perhaps our temperament has more to do with our conclusions than our conclusions with our temperament, but the causation does not move in one direction only. There is clearly a sense in which increasing knowledge increaseth sorrow. The minds that have the most comprehensive picture of the human scene—minds like Dante or Goethe, or in our own day, Santayana—are not minds that one would think of describing as exuberantly or exultantly happy. There is more than quaintness in the remark of Dr Johnson's friend, Edwards, that he too had tried to be a philosopher, but that cheerfulness would keep breaking in.[2] When one meets a mind that is inveterately cheerful, like Emerson's in America, or that irresistible theologian Scott Holland's in England, one is too likely to find on closer inspection a certain colour-blindness; they habitually see the blues and golds of the world more vividly than the browns. The minds that do see things justly, that combine sweep with sensibility, like Leonardo's, Bacon's, Lotze's, or in a somewhat smaller compass, Butler's, are always sober minds.

Sometimes the brighter mood is induced not, as it was with Emerson, by a native bias for gold and azure, but by deliberate fixing of attention on these to the exclusion of the rest. There have been persons who achieved a kind of happiness by withdrawing from the scene where most men live into a cloister where they could dream undisturbed about 'Jerusalem the golden, with milk and honey

---

[1] 'Travaillons sans raisonner,' said Voltaire, 'c'est le seul moyen de rendre la vie supportable' (though it was certainly not his own method); and one recalls the world of Keats, 'where but to think is to be full of sorrow.' Both would sympathize with the Basuto tribesman described by Ribot, who started wondering about the winds and the stars, and ended by burying his face in his hands. *Psychology of the Emotions*, 371

[2] Boswell, Hill's ed., III, 305

blest'. It will not do. There is something defeatist and escapist about such happiness, with an unhealthy hectic spot on its cheek. The world seen soberly may be a sorry place, but it is all we have, and it will not be righted by dreaming up others that we know not of. I do not want to be cynical. I do not think we know enough about the relation of mind and body to offer a final negative of the fundamental human hope. I am saying that if such regions do exist we know nothing useful about them, that meanwhile life must be lived, and that it is irrational to sacrifice certain and attainable goods for what is only a hope. Carlyle summed up the situation admirably when Margaret Fuller came back from the country of visions and announced that she had decided to accept the universe: 'Gad, she'd better'.

7. We have suggested that if there is a certain sober colouring about the rational man's mind, it derives not only from what his fuller vision enables him to see, but also from a certain deliberateness of decision, a certain habit of inhibition. Reflectiveness looks before it leaps, and because it looks, it often does not leap at all. In extreme cases, therefore, it may become a blight upon action. When Napoleon made the great Laplace his minister of the interior, he had to remove him for incapacity in six weeks, remarking that 'he brought into the administration the spirit of the infinitesimals'. 'The cleverest man we ever had at the Admiralty,' said Lord Fisher, 'was Goschen, and he was the worst failure of all. He was always looking at all sides and we never got anything done.' Reflectiveness, like conscientiousness, may become a disease; sometimes they are the same disease. Rightness of conduct, in the objective sense, depends on goods and ills produced. Now the immediate goods and ills may be easy to see. But the remoter ones are equally relevant, and since there is no obvious point at which the attempt to catch the future in one's net should be abandoned, the man of ingrowing carefulness may find himself his own victim, like the man who is so anxious to cover all contingencies with insurance that he exhausts his income on it and has nothing left to live on. Even to reflect on consequences just ahead takes time. The possibilities of bemusing oneself over whether one shall have this or that for breakfast, whether one shall take excerise today or not, and if so, what it shall be, and so on, are nothing short of infinite.

8. Now all this is somewhat tiresome. There is no reason in the world why rationality should exclude common sense. Indeed it is part of the

O

reasonableness of the genuinely reasonable man to see when an insistence on reasoning is likely to defeat, rather than further, its own end. It is part of that reasonableness so to organize one's life that one will *not* have to waste oneself in incessant deliberating over what should be matters of mere habit. When it was objected to J. S. Mill that the man who tried to govern all his choices by consideration of consequences would be paralysed, he replied with justice that the race had not been experimenting with conduct for hundreds of milleniums for nothing, that most choices were already covered by well-tested rules, and that for a man to start from scratch and try to think them all out for himself would be the very reverse of reasonable. One may show wisdom by accepting the accumulated capital of the race on minor issues as well as by dissenting from and adding to it on major issues. According to James, the rational man, instead of perpetually questioning habit and so check-mating his will, like the unhappy centipede that began to consider how it ran, will make habit his ally, turning over to it the larger part of his life so that he may bring his intelligence to bear freely on the rest. In determining the strategy of his life, in putting first things first and a great many popular things nowhere, he can do what the unintelligent man, no matter how vigorous or devoted, is unable to do.

It is mere prejudice to assume that, seeing more clearly than other men what ought to be done, he will be less able to do it. Other things equal, he should be more able. Plato, it will be remembered, would have made philosophers kings. This is an experiment that has not often been tried. But there is no evidence that when it has been tried, it has generally ended as it did with Laplace and Goschen. Marcus Aurelius on the emperor's throne, Newton at the Mint, and Masaryk in a president's chair provided rather pleasant surprises. The disasters anticipated from the absent-minded scholar have often failed to materialize. The fact is that his absent-mindedness has been much misunderstood. It may be a work of extreme present mindedness in his own special work of theorizing, a mark of putting first things uncompromisingly first. And a capacity for losing oneself in the essential may at times be as important to a general or president as to a metaphysician. The rationality, then, that orders life reflectively is not at enmity with impulse in any crippling sense. It will assume direction of the larger strategy of life, but it will not come bustling in over matters of daily tactics; it will make itself felt rather as a gentle pressure toward ends reflectively determined.

9. But is it at enmity with joy? Will the habitually reflective man, the man who orders his action with reference to long-run consequences and sees himself against the background of a universe that dwarfs him, be able to surrender himself with any zest to those little activities of play, of family life, of walks in the countryside and talks of an evening, of looking at pictures—moving or not, of reading the newspaper and listening to the radio, that makes up so much of what renders life livable to most people, at least in the west? Here again, I think that he holds the advantage. To be sure, he must be a really rational man, and not a caricature of him. If he is perpetually trying to substitute the attitude of criticism for that of enjoyment, he will not get very far with either. And if his preoccupation with high things leads him, as it did the ascetics, to scorn food and drink, as it did the Roundheads to smash beautiful things, as it did the Puritans, to suppress the drama, or as it did George Fox to 'speak out against all forms of music', it will undoubtedly warp or stunt him. But this is not rationality; once more it is irrationality in masquerade.

The rational man does certainly feel distinctions, where others do not, between better and worse; his enthusiasm has a higher boiling point; and he may suffer foolishness less gladly. But the other side of this discrimination is that his enjoyments are richer enjoyments. If he considers one experience as better than another, it is, as we have seen, because it satisfies and fulfils more completely. The uncultivated man, looking at these enjoyments from the outside, may regard them as boring, or do mere lip-service to them; one of the sad things about a democracy is the number of people who try vainly to convince themselves that they like something because they think they ought to like it. To have been delivered from this self-deception is much. It is still more to be able to enter into 'the best that has been thought and said' with a response equated to its quality. The rationally better does not mean something that an esoteric and finical taste has set up as its special preserve, made the more attractive because it is beyond the reach of most men. The really good in art, for example, is what would give the fullest satisfaction to anyone who could enter into it, not necessarily what is at the moment under discussion in the cafés of the Boulevard St Germain. The really good in philosophy is the sort of understanding that we are all trying to reach when we think. 'The technique of the great artists in words is only a glorified form of a skill that we all seek, and in some humble degree learn to exercise.'[1]

[1] H. Sidgwick, *Miscellaneous Essays and Addresses*, 354

o*

The really good in anything is that which would give the appropriate powers of our nature their fullest and most satisfying play. Whoever finds his satisfaction in such things is getting the utmost possible out of his life. And, as Spinoza argued in his essay on the improvement of the understanding, it is only through rational reflection on the goods of life, and on our own powers and situation, that we can see where our happiness really lies.[1]

10. As for the charge that the rational man will live in too rarified an air to share the ordinary satisfactions, one might cite the vigorously dissenting testimony of Spinoza's barber. But we shall do better to point out that the charge rests on the old confusion between scholar and pedant, philosopher and doctrinaire. 'It is difficult for most of us', says E. M. Forster, 'to realize both the importance and the unimportance of reason. But it is a difficulty which the profounder humanists have managed to solve.'[2] In my youth a wise philosopher, proficient in mathematics, told me that I should master enough mathematics not to be taken in by it. It was sound advice. One is only too likely to be taken in by scholarship or mathematics or philosophy in the sense that, excited and almost intoxicated by the new ideas, one forgets how barren an abstract they are from the richness of actual life; one makes an idol out of 'the thin product of untutored fancy'. A little philosophy, Bacon thought, was a dangerous thing, but more of it brought one round to sense again. There are philosophers whose philosophy has become a sort of fanaticism, making them run to head like a bad onion, and unfitting them for participation or delight in the activities most men take pleasure in. 'Some eminent philosophers whom I have known', says A. C. Benson, 'never seemed to be really there. Their voices whispered drily of mortal things, but one felt that what they said was merely like rain dropping from clouds which sailed above the earth, and evacuated expressions rather than mingled with life.'[3] 'Nothing can be conceived,' said Burke, 'more hard than the heart of a thoroughbred metaphysician.'[4]

With such people in mind, William James once wrote to a critic who had taken him to task for his religious writing: 'Your bogey is superstition, my bogey is desiccation. . . . In my essay the evil shape

[1] Cf. Hume; 'We come to a philosopher to be instructed how we shall choose our ends, more than the means for attaining the ends.'
[2] *Life of G. Lowes Dickinson*, 120
[3] *Leaves of the Tree*, 64
[4] *Writings and Speeches*, V, 216

was a vision of "Science" in the form of abstraction, priggishness, and sawdust, lording it over all. Take the sterilest scientific prig and cad you know, compare him with the richest religious intellect you know, and you would not, any more than I would, give the former the exclusive right of way.'[1] It is this sort of thing that Professor Raleigh protests against when he says of William Godwin that he 'attempts to regulate all the most human feelings by the clockwork of the intellect, and seriously maintains that it is wrong to love your own father better than other men, unless you can prove that your father is better than other men'.[2] If reason is to appraise value rightly, it must know what it is talking about, and when it is dealing with art or poetry or play or religion, it cannot know what it is talking about if it deals with them in the abstract, as if they were so many counters that could be manipulated by rule, like the symbols of mathematics. Much of the positivism and behaviourism of recent times has been ludicrously philistine about these things, not even dealing with them as abstract counters, but substituting for them 'observables' in the way of behaviour that answer to the demands of a Moloch of their own manufacture called 'scientific method'. It is an idol from which James, who had the genuinely empirical temper of the scientist, would have prayed for deliverance.

11. Such theories really begin by putting out one of the eyes of science, blinding it to a large range of facts that are visible enough to all but the one-eyed. And the rational man cannot afford to be one-eyed. When he talks of values, he must have entered himself into the experiences of fulfilment and satisfaction that he is referring to; otherwise he will be talking about he knows not what. Anyone who attempted to write about the relations of triangles without having grasped the nature of a triangle would be thought absurd. Why should a writer who undertakes to discuss the value of poetry or baseball, the cubist phase of Picasso, or the discipline of Yoga, without entering into these things with imaginative sympathy, be thought any less absurd? 'One may enquire', said Aristotle, 'why a boy, though he may be a mathematician, cannot be a philosopher. Perhaps the answer is that mathematics deals with abstractions whereas the first principles of philosophy are derived from experience: the young can only repeat them without conviction of their truth, whereas the

[1] Perry, *The Thought and Character of William James*, II, 246–7
[2] W. Raleigh, *On Writing and Writers*, 190

definitions of mathematics are easily understood.'[1] There is truth behind the exaggeration of Dean Inge's remark that 'all the philosophers who are really alive have been poets'.[2] Since Raleigh held strong views on these matters, it will be well to listen to him again:

> 'It is possible to know only one fact, and yet to know that fact in such a way as to be entitled to the name of pedant. We talk of "furnishing the mind" with knowledge, but how rarely is it done. For the most part we store the second-hand furniture of knowledge in the bleak warehouse of the mind. It has no fitness or beauty there, it is put to no human use, there is a monstrous excess of it, and most of it is upside down. Now the opposite of a pedant I take to be a scholar. . . . The scholar sees all things in a vital relationship, and for him among dead authors there is no dead man . . . Judged by this standard, Lamb was one of the most superb scholars that ever handled literature.'[3]

Now the rational man will be the scholar in Raleigh's sense and Lamb's sense. Being more than an intellect, being a man of impulse and feeling, knowing that value can come only as these are brought into play, knowing finally that among the stablest satisfactions of life are the simple, universal, and primitive ones of food and drink, companionship and play, he would be failing in reasonableness itself if he despised or neglected the sources of so much good. There is a touching letter of John Richard Green, the historian, written near the close of his life, in which he says: 'what seems to grow fairer to me as life goes by is the love and peace and tenderness of it; not its wit and cleverness and grandeur of knowledge, grand as knowledge is, but just the laughter of little children and the friendship of friends and easy talk by the fireside and the sight of flowers and the sound of music.'[4] Green was no great philosopher, but he was a scholar in Raleigh's sense.

12. So far we have been on the defensive about the rationalist temper. We have been defending it against the charges of being over-inhibited and bleak. It is time to turn to the other side of the picture and ask what are the qualities that mark out this temper most distinc-

---

[1] *Ethics*, VI, 8, 6. (R. W. Livingstone's rendering).

[2] Cf. Lytton Strachey on Bacon: 'His intellect swayed him too completely . . . It is probably always disastrous not to be a poet.'

[3] Cf. Anatole France on the scholar: 'Qu'est-ce qu'un savant? C'est un être assomant qui étudie et publie par principe tout ce qui manque radicalement d'intérêt.'

[4] *Letters of J. R. Green*, ed. by Maitland and Stephen, 241

tively from that of other minds. They are chiefly three, I think. First, there is the delight in understanding for its own sake. Secondly, there is that virtue which is the reflection of such understanding in practice, namely justice in thinking and acting. Finally, there is the quality that forms its reflection in feeling, the quality best described, perhaps, as equanimity. Let us consider these.

13. We pointed out long ago that the impulse to know is a distinct trend in human nature, with its own special end or goal, though the interest most men take in this end is admittedly flickering and feeble. In spite of such lack of interest, the impulse on its lower levels is, in most men, kept alive. Why should this be? Because, unlike the aesthetic impulse, which has very little utility, the impulse to know has extremely useful results. Men prize knowledge for what they can do with it. They can see the point of study and thought if it makes a practical difference somewhere, if it enables one to pull a tooth, or conduct a case in court, or design an airplane, more expertly. But most men's theoretical interest is too limp to sustain itself beyond the point where this pragmatic trellis ceases to give support. If knowledge is not to be applied anywhere, what is the good of it, what is the use of it? It is significant that by so many men these last two questions are taken to mean precisely the same. To ask the good of a thing *is* to ask the use of it; the assumption is that if it has no use, it has no value, that value *is* usefulness. And this is untrue. The intrinsic value of things *never* lies in their usefulness; to say that something is useful is to say that it is valued as a means to something else which itself has intrinsic worth. But even after this distinction is pointed out, there are many who deny that knowledge is among the things possessing this terminal value. Most men apparently feel that to go on beating one's brains when there is no prospect of applying the result is a waste of time.

14. In many cases they would be right. There are two conditions under which continued effort of this kind is futile, one belonging to the knowing mind, the other to what it is trying to know. The first occurs when through lack of ability or lack of interest the further exploration of a field would produce nothing but inner dreariness. The remark was attributed to Dr Leete of Eton that any subject was educationally good so long as the boys hated it. It would be hard to devise a better recipe for killing all intellectual interest. Granting that

there is some discipline of character in doing what one does not
want to do, and that the early stages of a new study are likely to be
dull, still no activity can have value for us if we cannot feel satisfaction in it, and to persist in a study when there is no prospect either
of applying it in practice or of getting from it the satisfaction of some
degree of mastery is misguided virtue. 'You cannot think the truth',
says Royce, 'without loving it; and the dreariness which men often
impute to metaphysics is merely the dreariness of not understanding
the subject,—a sort of dreariness for which indeed there is no help
except learning to understand.'[1] The understanding and the love of it
usually advance together, and support each other. If through defect of
faculty the understanding does not come, the love dies out also; the
subject may be pursued, but there will be no heart in the pursuit;
concentration will be difficult; what is learned will not be retained;
the subject will suggest the shades of a prison-house, and the student
will be lucky if the shadows do not lengthen and spread themselves
over his studies generally. Knowledge so gained is hardly worth the
price.

The attitude of the genuine scholar is wholly different. The
reluctant student sometimes thinks of the scholar or scientist as
living permanently in the dusty barracks where he would live himself
if he tried to do their work. If he wants to understand their spirit,
let him think rather of the delight with which he does something
with his heart in it, say dismembering and reconstructing an auto-
mobile engine, and think of what it would mean to do this profession-
ally and at will. Only if some such delight can be transferred to
learning will talk of the intrinsic value of knowledge have any
meaning for its hearers.

15. There is a second condition under which such talk is idle. It
occurs when the knowledge sought is a mere miscellany, when it is
knowledge as opposed to understanding. Uneducated men often conceive the difference between the educated man and themselves as
lying in the fact that he *knows* much more than they do. So he ought
and probably does. The gaining of varied knowledge is part of an
education, and though it is less important than reflectiveness,
reflection cannot work in a vacuum, and the greater the knowledge or
experience at its disposal, the more significant are its results. But it is
not here that the essential difference lies. Mere multiplicity of known

[1] *The World and the Individual*, I, 9

facts is not a rational goal. Poincaré remarked that the universe is spawning billions of new facts every second; but what proportion of them, simply as items of information, would it be important to know? There are persons who already know far more of them than others without having the least title to be regarded as more enlightened or understanding than those others; 'a great memory . . . does not make a philosopher, any more than a dictionary can be called a grammar.'[1] Some people combine extraordinary gifts of rapid reading and firm retention, so that the amount of sheer information they accumulate in the course of the years is staggering. The stock example is Macaulay, a 'book in trousers', as Sydney Smith called him. He undertook to restore *Pilgrim's Progress* and *Paradise Lost* from memory if the need ever arose; he was the sort of mind that would always come out triumphant in any test about the major or minor prophets or the kings of Israel and Judah. But Emerson once remarked about him that no one ever knew so much that was not worth knowing. As regards Macaulay himself, the remark was less than just, for his immense erudition was admirably ordered and used; but it does serve to enforce our point. A man may in theory own the most prodigious mountain of learning that mortal man ever amassed and still be, in every fundamental sense, stupid, unenlightened, and irrational.

16. The point is one that acquires added importance with every passing year. Knowledge seems to be increasing rather by geometrical than arithmetical progression. As recently as the time of Bacon, one could take all knowledge for one's province without arousing any strong sense of the absurdity of the enterprise. Today the man who would take even the whole of chemistry, history, or medicine, as his province would be regarded as a sciolist; if he would know anything well he must 'specialize'. Yet the modern world presses upon us from every side its imperative and perfectly legitimate claims. There are thousands of things we could know with advantage, which, as specialists, we should never know. So the temptation is great, and is becoming greater, to acquaint ourselves hurriedly with as wide a diversity of subjects as we can. The art of popularization has been so widely developed that every field of knowledge has its own admirably readable digests and surveys.

That it would be well to be acquainted with all these fields seems to me undeniable. The danger is that such an acquaintance should be

[1] Newman, *Idea of a University*, 135

supposed to constitute an education. Newman was already protesting against the confusion a hundred years ago. 'The error of the last twenty years . . .', he said in his Dublin lectures, 'has been the error of distracting and enfeebling the mind by an unmeaning profusion of subjects; of implying that a smattering in a dozen branches of study is not shallowness, which it really is, but enlargement, which it is not. . . . What the steam engine does with matter, the printing press is to do with the mind; it is to act mechanically, and the population is to be passively, almost unconsciously enlightened, by the mere multiplication and dissemination of volumes.'[1] A half century or so later Paulsen in Germany was sounding the same note; 'the springs which scientific research has opened . . . flow and flow until historians and history itself are in danger of being swallowed up in the flood'. At the end of his long life, President Butler of Columbia was sounding the note again, with more ample reason now, and with greater urgency.

'These powerful agencies, the press and the radio, have substituted information for knowledge. The steady flow of that information which they give so absorbs the attention of tens of millions of human beings that they have no opportunity and little temptation to give to this mass of information that critical interpretation and reflective understanding which might transform it into knowledge. We are, therefore, in very large measure, living on the surface of the world's happenings.'[2]

17. When human knowledge is thus growing at a rate far faster than the power to absorb it, the obvious expedient is to limit attention, to give up the effort at general mastery and confine oneself to the important. But how judge of importance? Most of the proposals that are currently made wear their defects on their face. Thinkers of a pragmatic turn suggest that we should concentrate on utilitarian studies, pitching out great quantities of antiquated lumber that has been supposed to have 'cultural' value. They would part without a pang with much of history and literature, and all of speculative philosophy. The trouble with this view is plain. The rational mind wants to know the truth about the world, and much of the most illuminating truth has very little utility. Where would the theories of Newton, Darwin, or Einstein rank if measured solely by their importance in practice? Then there is the somewhat similar criterion

[1] *The Idea of a University*, 142
[2] *Address at Southampton*, L.I., September 1, 1940.

of the Communists who would appraise knowledge by its contributoriness to one kind of economic order; one type of biology will be preferred to another because it is more favourable to the prospects of this order. But what if this order should not, after all, be the ideal one? Then not only has a calamitous mistake been made; the possibility of correcting it has been destroyed by corrupting the only agency, namely the free play of reason, which could hope to achieve the correction. Then again there is the Catholic programme, which would take a set of beliefs revealed to an ancient people who were without science, art, philosophy, or critical ethics, place the most important of these beliefs beyond the reach of rational criticism, and make them touchstones for the thought and practice of the twentieth century. All these proposals fail in the same way: they are authoritarian, in the sense that they dictate to reason from the outside where it should place its emphasis. They are the doctrines of sceptics and unbelievers, who distrust the power of human nature at its best to give true and objective answers to the questions that most need answering.

Perhaps there is no ark that will float men to safety on this rising tide of knowledge. Some prophets think men will drown in their knowledge for sheer lack of wisdon, sheer helplessness to manage the flood their own energy has released. It may be so. We will not be tempted into prophesy. We are concerned with the question what *in principle* is a way of escape, not whether men can be induced to take it. We hold that in principle there *is* such a way, and one only. It is not an easy way; for some men it is not available at all, and then recourse to the likeliest authority they can find will be natural enough. The only safety lies in the philosophic mind. The problem is an inner one, beyond solving by any outward arrangements, a problem of the adjustment of mind and spirit to an overcomplicated world. The only solution, therefore, is an inward one. It lies in the selection and ordering that can be done, and done alone, by reflective intelligence.

18. We say *selection*. The other theories say that too, as all theories must. Where, then, do we differ from them? In this: whereas they say that selection must be made with an eye to utility, or to a classless society, or to conformity with faith, or what not, we say that the selection must be made with an eye to understanding what the world is like. Such understanding is the goal that the impulse to know is seeking from its inception. It is the only end that leaves the mind free; it is therefore the natural end of what we call 'liberal' education.

Now it is clear that for the understanding of the world, some things are more important than others. Some bits of knowledge provide keys that will unlock a hundred times as much as others will. If a detective is trying to solve a crime, there are a great many facts about the victim and the situation that he will probably ignore, and a few others that he will concentrate on as providing essential clues. We must do likewise if we are to have any success in the larger business of understanding nature and human nature. We must realize that some knowledge is irrelevant, in the sense that it unlocks virtually nothing beyond itself, while other knowledge is fundamental in the sense that with its aid we can unlock a hundred further doors.

Consider the natural sciences, such as physics, chemistry, zoology, human physiology. In point of complexity, you are going forward as you move along this series; in point of generality, and therefore of explanatory power, you are going backward. All the natural sciences are based on physics. All events studied by any of them are physical events governed by physical laws, and a knowledge of such laws would therefore aid in understanding these events, while the special laws of physiology, for example, cannot be carried backward to explain physical events generally. In the understanding of any natural science, physics is thus in a privileged position. A mastery of the laws of motion and gravitation, of heat, sound, magnetism, and light, will throw a long illumination down every corridor of natural science.

Or take what are sometimes called the human sciences, such as psychology, economics, sociology, history. Here the case is somewhat less clear, for reasons we need not at the moment explore. Yet is it not plain enough that all economic, sociological, and historical behaviour is also psychological, that the later and more concrete studies are all dealing with psychological behaviour as it appears under special complicating conditions? Since they are sciences of human nature as it acts in special circumstances, the laws governing human nature are at the root of them all. A mistaken view of human nature will spread its misapprehension through their whole range; as a matter of fact, it produced the classical economics, Tarde's sociology of imitation, and the Marxian interpretation of history. On the other hand, a sound psychology will correspondingly illumimate all these fields. (It is perhaps needless to add that by psychology I do not mean the timid parochialism that never lifts its eyes beyond overt bodily responses; I mean the study of a human nature that thinks, imagines, desires, and seeks; and until these activities can be shown to be physical events in the sense that patellar reflexes are, psychology will not be, in the same sense as physics, a natural science at all.)

Once more, consider the value disciplines, such as the general theory of value, ethics, aesthetics, perhaps the philosophy of religion. Fundamental to all these disciplines is the question what sort of being value has, whether, for example, it is a character of things or an attitude of mind. This question can be discussed without raising any problems about the special forms of value, yet its answer has the most important repercussions in every other value discipline. Among these disciplines, the theory of value is basic.

19. These illustrations may serve to make clear what is meant by selection in the interest of understanding. The notion of democracy among subjects of study, which lay at the base of the old elective system in American colleges, the notion that from the point of view of education one subject was about as good as another, is radically vicious. Some subjects, of which we have taken by way of example physics, psychology, and value theory, are profoundly illuminating about the world we live in; others, such as (we will play safe here) conchology, numismatics, and philately, however fascinating in themselves, are very much less illuminating. Some, like languages, drawing and dentistry, are not in the same sense fields of study at all, but techniques or skills. Since the end of a liberal education is the enlightened or understanding mind, it will be studies of the first kind on which it will lay its principal stress, not those of the second or third. One who has in any considerable measure achieved this end need not be overwhelmed by the modern world. Ninety-nine hundredths of the matter that is pressed with such profusion on his notice he may safely neglect. Much of it is included in better form in the limited set of studies he undertakes to master; some of it indeed is relevant, but must be regretfully and firmly forgone; a very great deal of it is unworthy of notice at all. The tests of knowledge, occasionally conducted through journals, radios and television, so formulated as to imply that one is not abreast of the times if one cannot identify some Hollywood 'star' or recent jazz recording, suggest the level to which confusion of values may sink.

20. In what we have called the philosophic mind, selectiveness is the first essential. We mentioned another, namely order, system, or interconnection. Indeed this is implied in selectiveness. To explain the moisture on a glass of cold water, or the Pythagorean theorem, or the American civil war, is to show that it follows from certain conditions which provide the key to it. To explain anything—and to understand it is merely to explain it to oneself—is always to grasp it in its relations, to see it as conditioned or necessitated by something else, to take it out of its fragmentariness and detachment and bring it into connection with the body of our knowledge. This process of integration may take various forms. Sometimes the thing to be explained is seen as an instance of a familiar law. When it is noticed that the cold glass cools the air around it, the presence of the moisture is seen as an instance of the rule that warm air will hold more moisture than cold, and hence must precipitate this as it cools. Sometimes what is to be explained is seen, not as an instance of some known principle, but as the logical consequent of it, as the Pythagorean theorem is seen to follow from earlier propositions in Euclid. Sometimes a complex event is seen as the joint result of a number of causes, each acting in accordance with its own law; thus the American civil war is explained as due to economic rivalries inflamed by passionate convictions about slavery and states' rights. The relations appealed to in explanation are thus various. But relations there always are. For to understand a point *is* to see its relations with something else in such a way that it finds a place and becomes domesticated within the system of our knowledge.

Now in the rational mind these threads of connections run through the whole fabric. Facts are not so many items of information lying like fallen timber about its estate; if they are included at all among its possessions, they are regarded as worth incorporating into the design of the whole. So incorporated, each of them has an interest and significance far greater than if it stood alone. We all view with a little envy the prodigious Sherlock Holmes who, picking up a stray hat, remarks that its owner, once a man of means, had recently come down in the world and was much grieved for his wife, whom he had lately lost. We could not have made the deduction ourselves, but we own the validity of it when made. We know that a fall in stock-market prices means much about the health of industry, though we are not clear what, that a red sky at evening presages a fair day, though we are not clear why, that liberalism in religion is in difficulties, though we do not know whether they are adventitious or spring from some essential antagonism between religion and liberal thought. A mind that really saw the connections here, and in the thousand parallel cases that could be mentioned equally well, would live in a different world from the mind that began and ended with particular facts. It would be a world crisscrossed with roads on which its master could move about freely from part to part. There would be no islands any more. There would be none of the arbitrary boundaries that now separate department from department in our university catalogues. The citizen of such a world would grow restive when he heard the theologian talk philosophic nonsense; he would note when anthropologists were urging conclusions fatal to all ethics, including their own; he would recognize some truth in the communist insistence that religion and poetry are economically determined, and not a little blindness and sophistry also.

21. The intellectual ideal is a system of knowledge in which there are no loose ends, no bare inexplicable facts. Nothing less will satisfy the theoretic impulse. So long as any loose end remains, so long as any theorem in geometry or algebra, any fact or event noted by any of the sciences, can still press on us the question why?, intelligence has not reached its final satisfaction. The critic may object that we are assuming every event to have a cause and every true belief to be connected intelligibly with others. So we are. So is the critic himself, if he will examine his intellectual practice. Whether reality is an intelligible system or not, reflection is continually trying to discern such a system within it, and nothing so far discovered, not even the emergence of quantum mechanics, has imposed a conclusive veto on the endeavour. In any case, the larger part of our experience falls within the network of system. If we accept the law of gravitation, we cannot doubt that every movement of matter on our planet, however minute, has consequences among the fixed stars. We should think it absurd for anyone to doubt that cancer and leukemia have causes and cures, whether as yet we have any idea of either. Though we have no notion of how changes in the cortex effect changes in sensation and emotion, we cannot doubt that they somehow do. Nor can we doubt that the winds of doctrine in politics, fashion, religion, and art, that seem so entirely capricious, would be explicable to the last detail if we knew enough. The perfect understanding of which rationalist thinkers have dreamed is not an achievement that may be expected in any predictable future. Yet these thinkers, I suspect, had a clearer glimpse of what the theoretic impulse is trying to achieve, than the lynx-eyed analysts of our present Alexandrian period.

Granting that a knowledge at once complete and perfectly ordered lies at the rainbow's end, still it is the business of the rational mind, so they held, to approximate it as nearly as might be. Brute facts were to be taken up in a web in which their 'bruteness' vanished. Prejudices and mere opinions were to be shamed into hiding their heads. Only those beliefs would be safe that could continue to be held when their grounds and consequences were made explicit. The known world is a larger place and fuller of intellectual pitfalls than was suspected when this ideal was first formulated. But if a better statement of the theoretic ideal has been offered than by this rationalist tradition, I do not know of it.

When we think of this ideal as in some measure embodied in a rational mind, there is a misconception we may well guard against. Though the world in which such a mind lives is an extended one, systematically ordered, it is a mistake to suppose that the owner somehow sits at the centre of it and contemplates it all at once. Plato, indeed, talked about the ideal philosopher as a 'spectator of all time and all existence', and Royce played with the notion of a protracted time-span that might make this possible. The 'specious present' of a normal man lasts a second or so. The specious present of a chameleon, whose tongue can retrieve a fly faster than the human eye can follow, seems to include minuter distinctions than our own, and may be considerably shorter; that of some insects may be shorter still. As mind goes up the scale, its time-span may well be increasing, so that more of the immediate past is included along with the present as an object of direct awareness. Suppose this span to be increased indefinitely, increased if you will to infinity. Then we might indeed be spectators of all time, at least of all past time, in one comprehensive vision. It is an intriguing idea. But it is mentioned here only to point the contrast with the pathetic actuality. For in fact we are condemned to live, even those of widest vision, in a miserably contracted focus of attention. No matter how wide our knowledge, attention must operate with a spot-light which it can shift about freely enough, but which it can never make to illuminate more than a tiny circle of objects at a given time. Roughly speaking, we can think of only one thing at once. And if this is true, what is the point of all this effort to get sweep and system into our knowledge? Are we not condemned to think in fragments anyhow?

22. The answer lies in a curious fact about the structure of consciousness. What at any given moment is at the focus of attention is affected in the most important way by such of one's knowledge as lies outside this focus in the shadow. The experienced judge does not have to recall explicitly all the laws and precedents that bear upon a particular case in order to form an opinion, and a weighty one, upon it. The experienced physician may be able to diagnose a case instantly, the experienced critic of art to appraise a painting at a glance. Very probably these persons could give a full and explicit justification of their opinion if challenged. But the competence of their opinion does not depend on this setting forth of their reasons. Those reasons, hidden away in the wings, have really been directing what has gone on upon the stage, whether they appear in person or not. The judge who has once thought through the principles involved in a particular type of case, and got clear as to their relations with those of other cognate decisions, does not need to rehearse them all over again for every subsequent case. Even if he cites no single precedent, nor so much as thinks of one, his judgment will have a weight incomparably greater than that of the layman, for it will be informed and moulded by his special experience and reflection. The upshot of this experience and reflection he carries about with him always, not consciously to be sure, but nevertheless in such form that he can call upon it at need. In many cases, as we have seen, it virtually gives the decision for him on the instant. And even where it does not, it does something almost equally useful; it enables him to detect quickly the precise point in the present case not covered by his experience, and to isolate it for further reflection. The fact, then, that even the expert must work through a small spotlight of attention, does not prevent his ordered knowledge from casting its own wider though gentler illumination; and thus his casual impression may be more valuable than the laborious conclusion of anyone else.

As a rule, such expertness of judgment is confined to one field. The professional man usually lives in a certain universe of discourse—medicine, law, mining, engineering or what not—within which his competence is high, and outside which it may fall to childish levels. It is notorious that Darwin, who was so much a master in biology, was helpless in music, and latterly almost nauseated by Shakespeare, while, Lamb, whose perceptions were so sensitive in literature, was not only similarly helpless in music, but out of his element in science or any kind of abstract thinking; 'nothing puzzles me more than time and space', he wrote, 'and yet nothing puzzles me less, for I never

think about them.'[1] In the field of each other's competence, Darwin
and Lamb would cut very sorry figures.

23. Does this mean that there is no such thing as good judgment
generally? If so, some very important undertakings must be pronounced visionary. Every year the Guggenheim Foundation attempts
to select from among a large number of projects submitted to it by
young American scientists, artists, philosophers, and scholars, those
that are most worth encouragement and subsidy. Its committee of
selection must manage to decide whether a set of strange new poems
is or is not of greater promise in its kind than someone else's theorizing about the foundations of ethics in its own very different kind.
That the decision is difficult goes without saying. But to hold that it
is impossible is in effect to deny that what we have called the rational
mind is even a valid ideal.

There we draw back. We hold that for any intelligent person who
would be in the full sense a citizen of the modern world, it is both
necessary and practicable so to enter into the main enterprises of the
human spirit, such as science, morality, and art, that he can understand their ends, form some idea of the success of a given venture in
attaining its end, and at least in a rough way compare the respective
attainments on a common scale of value. Only a mind that can move
freely about in its possessions and mobilize its resources at any
point on call can properly use this scale. None of the enterprises of
the human spirit is carried on in a vacuum. There is no such thing
as pure art which owes nothing to scholarship, or pure scholarship
which owes nothing to art. If one cannot enter into the ideas of the
Inferno or *The Wasteland*, one cannot properly respond to it even as a
work of art. But equally all expression is art, even scholarly or
scientific expression. The statement of an intellectual case will
normally be better, just as argument, if the artistic ideal of economy
of means to ends exerts its pressure on the writer's pen. Human
beings never merely think, and never merely feel; all the main sides
of their nature are at work in everything they do. Adequate criticism,
therefore, cannot be offered from a single point of view. It must
surround and enfold the work with a comprehensive knowledge and a
generous understanding of comparative values. It must be able to say
of a play, for example, that its wit is refreshing, its plot original, its
dialogue clever, its construction weak, its morals confused, its

[1] *Letters of Charles and Mary Lamb*, II, 90.

characterization sound, its theme important, its sense of dramatic development feeble. A wholly adequate criticism could be offered only by a mind to which nothing human was alien.

24. It follows from all this that the rational mind is the sanest mind. Sanity is a relative matter. A mind is less than fully sane if any of its ideas have formed cysts within the whole and become knots of cancerous tissue closed to free circulation from the rest of the mental organism. There is many a man in hospital for the mentally ill who will discuss things with you quietly and rationally until you mention his name, and then he will make it clear to you that you are mistaken about this, that he is really the king of Majorca, held in captivity by a conspiracy of these retainers who are around him; press him into a corner on this belief and he grows dangerous. He is insane because this idea is a 'complex' insulated from the influence of his other ideas. You can point out to him a hundred inconsistencies between his belief and the facts of his situation; he will only cling to it the more fanatically. Now we all have our complexes about which we are fanatics more or less, in the sense that we resist and resent rational criticism of them. I have known a scholar of international repute who was so rabid an anti-Semite that his unkinder colleagues would bait him for the sake of a little secret laughter; I know a thinker and writer of repute who held throughout the last war that all Germans should be exterminated. These men seemed to me, on these topics, not quite sane.

But who of us is quite sane? Brown cannot discuss money matters without getting anxious or furious; Smith is in such a state about communism that he regards Thomas Jefferson as a red; Jones passes as a reasonable man, though his family could give you a different story about his attitude toward playing the horses or the stock exchange. There is no one of us without his own reason-resistant quirks. These are not always harmful; indeed we may be grateful that Palissy and Robert Fulton and Henry Ford had a touch of the fanatic in their composition. Particularly in our hobbies this disproportion of interest to importance shows itself; but provided we can look over our own shoulder, so to speak, with that sense of humour which is one of the marks of sanity, they add innocently to the delights of life. The danger comes when the power of self-criticism and hence the sense of proportion are absent, when some agitator in a black, brown, or red shirt provides proof that molehills are mountains, or some fanatic of the faith, sure of a revelation beyond reach of reason, tries to throttle the thought that would imperil it. A man who is not quite sane is all the more dangerous if he is a genius. It is the duty of those who believe in that sanity which is also rationality to oppose and expose these people by every legitimate means.

25. We have been insisting that the only security against being distracted and swamped in the rising tide of knowledge is the philosophic or rational mind, and that this mind proceeds by discriminating essentials and tracing their interconnections. The only safe protection against that breadth without depth which is superficiality or that depth without breadth which is fanaticism is an inner one, a state of mind and spirit. We must point out now, however, that this state will never be achieved if it is sought simply as an insurance policy against apprehended evils. Understanding is useful, enormously useful, but this is largely because those who own it have kept their eye on truth rather than on usefulness. If they have succeeded in understanding and in seeing things as they are, that is because seeing things as they are has itself been a passion with them. Whitehead has pointed out that many of the discoveries that have proved most useful to the race were made with no thought of their possible utility and would hardly have been made at all if the discoverers had had nothing but the promise of such utility to move them; the Galileos, Newtons, Harveys, and Clerk-Maxwells have transformed the world of practice because they were sufficiently detached from it to pursue truth disinterestedly.

To be sure, it is easy to talk priggish nonsense about the love of truth. Much that passes for this is only too probably a feeble self-importance that seeks to compensate for its ineffectiveness by a name for profundity or scholarship, or else the rationalization of some passionate eccentricity in the way of research. And in view of the devotion of many young minds today to pedantic minutiae and wire-drawn subtleties, Whitehead's warning—and he had earned the right to give it—is worth heeding: 'if men cannot live on bread alone, still less can they do so on disinfectants.'[1] All who have engaged in University teaching have contemplated ruefully at times the young doctor of philosophy who is all spectacles and waspish argumentativeness, and whose trail can be followed by the withering of the spiritual

[1] *Science and the Modern World*, 84

landscape. These aborted and twisted intellectuals are among the liabilities of modern education.

But they ought not to make us forget what the true intellectual is like, the person who has a genuine interest in seeing things steadily and whole. 'The man capable of greatness of soul', says Russell, 'will open wider the windows of his mind, letting the winds blow freely upon it from every portion of the universe. . . . And he will see that the man whose mind mirrors the world becomes in a sense as great as the world.'[1] In everyone, perhaps, there are wistful impulses to lift the eyes to these wider outlooks. In most minds they are occasional and transient. But in some they are apparently continual, and a main source of satisfaction. One would expect to find this in the genuine philosophers, for 'what is philosophy in practice but wondering what it is all about, with a passion for trying to discover?'[2] In Plato this passion bursts out repeatedly. When Socrates asks a young Athenian whether they shall pursue a certain inquiry together, the young man answers: 'Should we, do you say? Are there any pleasures worth living for like these?'[3] 'To know, to discover truth', says a modern writer, '. . . is a desire whose fulfilment does not lead to disappointment and boredom, as does the fulfilment of almost every other human longing. For there is no end to truth; each part of it reveals, when found, yet other parts to be discovered. The man who desires knowledge knows no satiety, for the knowable is perpetually new. He might live innumerable lives and never grow weary.'[4]

26. In describing the interest in knowledge for its own sake, we have taken reflectiveness and breadth of interest together. In the rational mind as we conceive it, they do go together. But they are not the same. There are people with a voracious and indiscriminate appetite for knowledge who could not by any legitimate stretch of meaning be called thoughtful persons, and there are profoundly thoughtful persons whose knowledge is very limited; Spinoza's library, it was said, could be placed on a single shelf. The emphasis in education may be put on one of these sides to the neglect of the other. Mill wrote: 'The characteristic of Germany is knowledge without thought; of

[1] *The Conquest of Happiness*, 226
[2] H. S. Canby, *Alma Mater*, 123
[3] Noted by R. W. Livingstone, *Education for a World Adrift*, 121, who cites this, too from the *Phaedrus*: 'The intelligence of every soul rejoices at beholding Reality and, once more gazing on Truth, is replenished and made glad.'
[4] Aldous Huxley in *A Night at Pietramala*.

France, thought without knowledge; of England, neither knowledge nor thought.' We shall not debate whether, if a 'both-and' were substituted for a 'neither-nor' in that last clause, the statement would be closer to fact, but there is no doubt that it would be closer to the ideal. Indeed except for persons of great native retentiveness, the habit of reflection is the only way in which extended knowledge can be kept, and kept ready for use. Herbert Spencer is an interesting illustration of how a man of very imperfect health, of limited range of reading. and, by his own profession at least, somewhat feeble memory, gained command of an extraordinary range of knowledge through organizing it all reflectively about a single great idea, the idea of evolution. For a half-century or so, the main interest of his life was in studying and reflecting upon every manner of fact bearing upon this central idea, with the result that great masses of data, which he would never have retained for their own intrinsic interest, were organized in orderly ranks as evidence in the case, and could be poured out in floods of dictation when the time arrived for the next volume of the *Synthetic Philosophy*.

Because the reflective man does not stop with facts but is concerned with their grounds and bearings, he is likely to seem carping, cavilling and negative. His persistent questioning, though done not for the sake of being perverse or singular, but for the sake of understanding, does imply that many a religious conviction, many a political prejudice, many a popular slogan, as they pass his sentry-box, will get a sharp challenge instead of a salute. He will be, to the complacent, '*der Geist der stets verneint*'. People will feel somewhat insecure when he is about, for they will never know what pillar of their common-sense world is to be shaken next. Sometimes their irritation will be excusable. For in the questioner of established ways, ability and the interest in truth are at times so combined with showmanship and a desire to *épater les bourgeois*, as for example in Mencken and Nathan in America and Wilde and Shaw in Britain, that one is not quite sure whether it is the philosopher who is speaking or the harlequin. Still, the impersonally questioning temper is a boon to any community; and the more widespread it is, the better, since the aim of its questioning is not to tear down, but to build more securely. The ideal community for the man of intellectual interests is one in which each person is pursuing his own line, each throws his special knowledge into the common pool, and each does for the rest the kindly service of impartial criticism and supplementation. In such a community the revision of habits of thought may become itself a habit, and growth in self-civilization the order of the day. Any approximation to it in fact is at best a very imperfect one. But there were at least strong suggestions of it in the streets of Periclean Athens and in some of the French salons of the eighteenth century, as there are I think, today in some of the common rooms of Oxford and Cambridge.

27. Enough has been said, perhaps, of the first characteristic of the rational mind, its thirst to know and make sense of the world it lives in. We said that its second characteristic was justice. Justice is an affair partly of thought and partly of act. It is a very difficult virtue, because it requires giving full and exact credit to all the claims that may be presented to us, but like other intellectual virtues, it is almost bound to seem in practice cold and negative. The first step in justice, whether in thought or act, lies in keeping oneself in check. For where one's own claims, either in argument or in practice, come in conflict with another, the two tendencies most likely to defeat justice are the tendency to over-rate one's own claim and the tendency to under-rate the other person's. These are deep-seated biasses in all of us, and to curb them firmly is not pleasant. Still, it is an essential part of what reasonableness means.

28. Consider only how we over-rate our own claims in thought. The tendency to do so is far more difficult to guard against because of its unconsciousness. Men are as reluctant to admit that they are not fair-minded as that they have no sense of humour, and it is those who lack these qualities most conspicuously who will be most indignant at the charge. We shall hardly convince a man that he lacks fair-mindedness by telling him so in general terms, and to tell him so in the midst of an argument with him is about the least hopeful of ways to induce the conviction of sin. But there are two quite impersonal considerations that will prove to us, I think, that we are probably less rational than we seem, at least to ourselves.

The first is that on different sides of any religious or political frontier we find a virtual unanimity of belief in propositions that are the contradictions of each other. None of the people involved feel constrained to think as they do; to themselves it seems as if they had arrived at their views merely by a sensible use of the evidence. But it is of course incredible that the first ten thousand people one might meet in Britain should have arrived by an independent exercise of thought at Christian principles, and the first ten thousand one met in India should, by a like independent reflection, have arrived at Hindu principles. I knew a charming old lady who, when a speculation was once started whether, if she had been born and brought up in India she would have held the Christian views to which she was devoted, maintained stoutly that she would, that even in the midst of darkness she would have been lighted by the true light. Can there be any doubt that if she had carried with her into the changed circumstances this innocence of the causes constraining her belief, she would have been a peculiarly conservative Hindu?

It is easy for us to see that despite the feeling of freedom possessed by each one of the ten million Hindus, their unity can only be accounted for by supposing that they were *not* thinking freely and objectively, that there were overwhelming psychological pressures that swept them all one way. But if we believe that about them, are they not similarly justified in believing it about us? And if they are, is the conclusion not irresistible that the vast majority of us on both sides of the line have arrived at the beliefs we so confidently hold by no process that would logically justify them?

I do not want to suggest that religious beliefs are alone in this position, for the point could be made equally well about beliefs in politics. When I was a young student, enjoying the long-gone privilege of travelling anywhere in Europe without a passport, I was caught in Germany by the outbreak of the first world war, and was unable to get out for several weeks. The experience of moving across the channel from the midst of 'a people all convinced of one set of propositions about the war to the midst of another all equally convinced of the opposite was an experience calculated to make one think. At the lowest reckoning, many millions of intelligent people, confident that they were right, must have been wrong. That is a fact that might well give pause to dogmatism.

29. A second way of making clear to ourselves how often we over-rate the claims of our own beliefs is to consider how many of them we should find it hard to make out if called upon to do so. Take a few beliefs at random from various fields. In biology we all believe in the theory of evolution, but could we offer the sort of defence of it that would seem at all effective to a competent sceptic about it? In law we probably believe in trial by jury; but on the face of it, trial by judges would seem far more likely to achieve justice; have we any good case for preferring juries? Most of us in the United Nations believe that the best road to security is to arm and unite against possible aggression. We may well be right. But there are certainly many of us who, if confronted by a thoughtful Quaker with a New Testament in one hand and statistics of the cost of armaments in the other, would not cut a wholly convincing figure. If we are churchmen, we recite in the Apostles Creed our belief in the resurrection of the body; if we are Americans we declare that 'all men are created free and equal'; if we are women, we probably believe in equal pay for equal work; if we are Englishmen we probably believe in inheritance by primogeniture, and if Frenchmen, in equal division of property among children. Is it not clear that in these and hundreds of other beliefs, there is no relation at all between the certainty with which they are held and the sort of case that could be offered for them? And if great numbers of our most important beliefs are thus held with confidence on a basis which, if produced, would be inadequate, does not this suggest that the appropriate attitude toward any of our beliefs that may be called in question is one, not of dogmatic assertiveness, not of feeble self-distrust, not of touchiness at correction, but of impersonal readiness to amend, withdraw, or reiterate as the evidence requires.

It is perhaps too much to ask that we raise for criticism beliefs that we have always held, even when no one challenges them. The true test of our disinterestedness is what we do when they are challenged. I once heard that wise man Dean Woodbridge of Columbia say that he had almost given up hope for the League of Nations as a result of his experience in faculty meetings; if scholars and scientists themselves found it so hard to view with detachment the concerns of a department, what could be expected of diplomats, with the interests of their nations at stake? Of all living peoples, the French are supposed to take the greatest delight in the play of reason; yet we read in a newspaper not long ago that the austere French Assembly suddenly became 'a heaving mass of bodies, with tail-coated Assembly attendants struggling to separate the opposing forces'; six deputies had to be treated in the Assembly infirmary for cuts and bruises.

It is surprising how many persons of real light and leading have been mere spoiled children where their own beliefs or achievements were concerned. Pope, when admonished by Addison, and Swinburne when mildly chided by Emerson, are unhappy cases in point. One is told that it has not been uncommon among professors in Germany to feel that their personal honour was being impeached if their theories were questioned; if this is true, they would have profited, as a British philosopher has said, if they had been heckled and learned how to respond with good humour. British and American ideals of sportsmanship, which is essentially justice in play, have had a happy influence on intellectual controversy, and made scholars reluctant to claim advantages not clearly earned. One thinks with pleasure of that gallant pair, Wallace and Darwin, Wallace instantly resigning his claims when he saw that Darwin's book, published at the same time as his own, put their common case more completely, and Darwin achieving that statement because he had kept a special notebook over the years for all the weaknesses and difficulties of his theory. It is pleasant, again, to think of McTaggart, who met criticism, if it was sound, with a hearty 'I am a worm, and no man', and G. E. Moore's Olympian warnings against some of his own writings as peculiarly confused and unreliable. Though such objectivity about one's own work has no thought of ulterior ends, it usually has its reward in a prompt increase in the reader's confidence.

30. The third special characteristic of the rational mind is its equanimity. The word comes from *aequanimitas*, evenness of spirit, stability in the face of what fortune may bring, a word, by the way, in which the Stoic emperor Antonius Pius at the end of his life summed up his philosophy. Sir William Osler in his farewell address at the University of Pennsylvania, took this same word as his title. His comment, as a great physician, that 'imperturbability is largely a bodily endowment' and that 'natural temperament has much to do with its development', is one that we should heed. It would not be hard to name men of great gifts of mind who, because nature had mixed the elements carelessly in their nervous composition, were anything but equable in their personal lives. Sweep of mind may be cheated of its proper consequences by defects of body and temper. But even here its gravitational pull upon the spirit is at work, just as the sun is pulling the ball that nevertheless falls to the earth. And the direction of the pull is clear. It is upward, to a point from which our confining garden walls are just visible enough to allow us to see their place, their strangely contracted place, in the wider scene.

It seems to have been the Stoic thinkers who first perceived with full clearness the practical importance of the philosophic temper. Marcus Aurelius, Epictetus, and Seneca, were not great philosophers, but living in the intensely practical Roman world, they had a keener sense than many more distinguished thinkers of what the philosophic mind might mean to the world of practice. The life of reason did not end for them in knowing; its ampler vision was supposed to be reflected in the temper with which life was lived, in the moderation and justice of one's dealings with others, in the firm control with which the details of practice were ordered. They succeeded in impressing on the western mind an expectation that a philosopher would be more than an ingenious and subtle reasoner; his philosophy would bring him also an equable and serene spirit; he would not be above the battle if that meant that he would evade the burden and heat of the day, but he would be enabled by the quality of his spirit to bear that burden and heat better than others. He would be like Emerson's just man, who would retain in the midst of the crowd the serenity of solitude. Plain men have continued to think of the philosopher thus, despite the appearance of individual philosophers and conceptions of philosophy which gave them small encouragement to do so. Have they been right or not? Is the old Stoic view that there is some special connection between rationality of thought and serenity of temper a bit of professional egotism or is it true? If it is true, there must be some sort of path from one to the other of these characters that is not evident at first sight.

I believe that the teaching is true and that there is such a path. The connection is this: the two factors that chiefly destroy equanimity are irritation and fear, and rational understanding acts in verifiable ways to allay them both.

31. Take only irritation or anger. Many things arouse it in us. We may be vexed about national policy, irritated at the behaviour of a colleague, angry about some wanton cruelty reported in the newspaper. For a time these destroy our equanimity. But such bursts of more or less righteous indignation seldom last. They tend to blow over quickly like spring storms. It is a different matter if the injury done is not to the public, or to a neighbour, but to ourselves. Each of us knows in his heart that he is an honest, sensible, kindly, unselfish, intelligent, public-spirited, co-operative, fair-minded person; we have nailed our self-respect to that somewhat giddy mast; if it were to go over, our happiness would promptly founder. A blow to our self-respect is a blow directly at the heart, and that we cannot take lightly.

Nothing rankles like an insult. We wake up in the night and think about it, and get so angry that sleep is banished, for resentment holds a fiendish power over peace of mind. 'To think that Jones should say that about me, about *me* of all people; the thing is outrageous'; and we start enacting little scenes in which he is properly, icily, and un-answerably humbled, though of course with an impressive dignity. Strangely enough our anger is not lessened by the truth of the remarks; it is positively increased; for so far as they are felt to be true, the threat to our self-respect becomes real and serious. It is the man who is inefficient and knows it that resents most hotly the suggestion that he is open to improvement; and it is notorious how often the man who has made a mess of his life is sure that he has been hounded by malice from the beginning.

Now the only adequate physic for such resentment and rancour is one that passes into the body from the intelligence. There is not much use in trying directly to love our enemies. Our affections will merely mutiny if commanded to lavish themselves on objects which we are still convinced are hateful. If the emotions are to be altered their objects must be reconceived. A man has said something derogatory about me, and it is a despicable thing to have done. Yes, despicable undoubtedly. Well, almost undoubtedly at any rate. I start thinking about it. If I am to call it that, I must be sure of myself. What makes it so is that it is maliciously and wilfully false.

Here are three counts; am I quite sure of them? What of the falsity? People do not commonly prefer charges against others if there is no colour for them at all. Perhaps when X said that my speech was too long or that I am never on time, he was saying the bald unhappy truth, and my anger is my resistance to avowing it. If so, the road back to equanimity is straight and short; it is to face the truth without evasion, to recognize the root of my anger, and to see the silliness of hating someone for saying what was true! Indeed, without this prod, I might have gone on spreading offence without knowing it. On the other hand, what he said may be false. In that case our self-respect remains untouched. To be sure it is not easy to take the high line of the old motto: 'They say. What do they say? Let them say'; for the esteem of others, as well as self-esteem, is important to us, and the filching of our good name hurts. Even so, anger with the other would seem to be justified only if the second count in the indictment holds, and the untruth is a wilful one; for it is absurd to be hot with another about a mere mistake. Of course if a man has put about a deliberate falsehood, anger is justified if it ever is. But how often is this done? I should suspect that wilful and conscious libel was rather rare.

When it occurs, it carries us to the third count, that of malice. Malice in others, particularly if they pose as our friends, is of course deplorable. Still as a rule it is far more damaging to the malicious person than to his victims; and as a reflective man contemplates it steadily, he sees that most of his resentment against it is a waste of his own substance. Malice is the symptom of moral disease, the sign of a maimed and disfigured spirit. It always has its causes in frustration, inadequacy, self-misjudgment, and the like. To the master of serenity, like Marcus Aurelius, it has seemed a more appropriate object of compassion than of anger, in line with the old French proverb, *tout comprendre c'est tout pardonner*. The habit of meeting malice with a return of malice tends to die out with increasing largeness of mind; equanimity is a by-product of magnanimity. In such magnanimity philosophy always plays a part, whether it is the philosophy of the schools or not. If one wants an example, one can hardly do better than to look at Harold Begbie's description of a friend who, in his treatment by others, had more grounds for resentment than most men, Lord Haldane.

His 'tranquillity of spirit owed nothing to an unimpressionable mind or a thick skin. One came to see that it was actually that miracle of psychology, a philosophic temperament in action. . . . He has not only studied philosophy, he has become a philosopher, and not merely a philosopher in theory but a philosopher in soul—a practising philosopher. He might stagger for a moment under the shock of a tremendous sorrow to one whom he loved, but not all the shavings of all the half-penny editors of our commercialized journalism, not even the most contemptible desertion of his friends, could move his equilibrium by a hair's breadth.'[1]

32. But it is not the Haldanes of the world who are most admired. This chapter may be taken as a suggestion that our admirations be revised, and that our private gallery of heroes be hung with a different sort of portrait. Present-day tastes, more perhaps in America than in Britain, are for the dramatic, the colourful, the exciting, the people who live dangerously, whether they need to or not; Americans have been called the Latin branch of the Anglo-Saxon race. To such persons the voice of the rationalist is likely to be inaudible, but if it is heard at all, it will be heard to recommend that the popular heroes

[1] *The Mirrors of Downing Street*, 117

should be those of adults living in a complicated and precarious world, not those of adolescents, or of frontiersmen, or of Hollywood, which is a compound of the two. The really great man is not usually a flamboyant figure. Mommsen has noted that the greatest man of action the ancient world produced seems to have had no particular character or temperament at all; the genius of Julius Caesar lay in a quiet universal adequacy; confront him with any sort of crisis and that serene intelligence would come through like a force of nature.

In the gallery here proposed there will be a new arrangement of portraits. Among statesmen we shall find Asquith placed above Lloyd George; we shall find the pictures of Turgot, Jefferson and probably Wilson enlarged, that of Andrew Jackson put in a smaller frame, and that of Hitler thrown out with the rubbish. Among men of faith we shall find Luther and Knox occupying less space, and Emerson and Schweitzer rather more. Among literary folk we shall find ourselves in the tradition of Sophocles and Goethe and Arnold and Eliot rather than that of Baudelaire and Swinburne and Verlaine; and we shall give George Eliot a re-reading before dismissing her for George Sand. Among philosophers we shall not choose rationalists only; for some rationalists, like Tom Paine, have lacked the rational temper, while some empiricists, like Hume, have had it. Plato will be there, and St Thomas, and Spinoza, and Butler, and that most perfect exemplar of the reasonable temper, Henry Sidgwick. There will be open spaces where Rousseau, Schopenhauer, and Nietzsche once hung, and Kierkegaard will be packed and crated for permanent storage.

All this means many fresh valuations, of which my own are no doubt more capricious than to me they seem. But of two things one can hardly doubt. One is that the rational temper—that is, clearness of vision, justice in thought and act, and the peace which is the harvest of the quiet eye—is an end that men desire too waveringly. The other is that to achieve it would transform life.

INDEX

GEORGE ALLEN & UNWIN LTD

London: 40 Museum Street, W.C.1

Auckland: P.O. Box 36013, Northcote Central, Auckland N.4
Bombay: 15 Graham Road, Ballard Estate, Bombay 1
Barbados: P.O. Box 222, Bridgetown
Buenos Aires: Escritorio 454-459, Florida 165
Calcutta: 17 Chittaranjan Avenue, Calcutta 14
Cape Town: 68 Shortmarket Street
Hong Kong: 44 Mody Road, Kowloon
Ibadan: P.O. Box 62
Karachi: Karachi Chambers, McLeod Road
Madras: Mohan Mansions, 38c Mount Road, Madras 6
Mexico: Villalongin 32-10, Piso, Mexico 5, D.F.
Nairobi: P.O. Box 4536
New Delhi: 13-14 Asaf Ali Road, New Delhi 1
Ontario: 81 Curlew Drive, Don Mills
São Paulo: Caixa Postal 8675
Singapore: 36c Prinsep Street, Singapore 7
Sydney, N.S.W.: Bradbury House, 55 York Street
Tokyo: 10 Kanda-Ogawamachi, 3-Chome, Chiyoda-Ku